ABRAHAM'S HEIRS

ABRAHAM'S
HEIRS

JEWS AND CHRISTIANS
IN MEDIEVAL EUROPE

◆   ◆   ◆

Leonard B. Glick

Syracuse University Press

Permission to reprint from the following sources is gratefully acknowledged: *New English Bible* ©
Oxford University Press and Cambridge University Press 1961, 1970; *The History of the Franks* by
Gregory of Tours, translated by Lewis Thorpe (Penguin Classics, 1974) copyright © Lewis Thorpe,
1974. Reproduced by permission of Penguin Books Ltd.; *The Popes and the Jews in the Middle Ages* by
Edward A. Synan. Copyright © 1965 by Edward A. Synan. Reprinted with the permission of
Simon & Schuster.

The paper used in this publication meets the minimum requirements of American National
Standard for Information Sciences—Permanence of Paper for Printed Library Materials, ANSI
Z39.48-1984. ⊗

Library of Congress Cataloging-in-Publication Data

Glick, Leonard B.
    Abraham's heirs : Jews and Christians in medieval Europe / Leonard B. Glick. — 1st ed.
      p. cm.
    Includes bibliographic references and index.
    ISBN 0-8156-2778-5 (alk. paper). — ISBN 0-8156-2779-3 (pbk. : alk. paper)
      1. Jews—History—70–1789. 2. Judaism—History—Medieval and early modern period,
425–1789. 3. Church history—Middle Ages, 600–1500. 4. Judaism—Relations—
Christianity. 5. Christianity and other religions—Judaism. 6. Jews—Legal status, laws, etc.—
Europe. I. Title.
DS124.G575 1998
909'.04924'00902—DC21 98-16045

For Nansi

Leonard B. Glick is professor of anthropology at Hampshire College, Amherst, Massachusetts, where he teaches cultural anthropology and European Jewish history. Previously, he held teaching positions at Bryn Mawr College and the University of Wisconsin, Madison. A featured lecturer at the annual summer programs of the National Yiddish Book Center, Amherst, he is author of numerous articles on the anthropological study of religion and ethnicity.

CONTENTS

Maps

PREFACE

This book is called *Abraham's Heirs* to emphasize one of its central themes: the radical difference between how Jews and Christians in medieval Europe perceived themselves and each other. Jews considered themselves the true heirs to God's promises to Abraham, the people chosen to receive his commandments at Mount Sinai; Christians insisted that because Jews had rejected the Messiah, God had rejected them, instituted a new dispensation based on faith alone, and appointed a new people (the "Gentiles") to inherit all the biblical promises. Of course, each group viewed the other as grossly in error. Christians believed that Jews were eternally damned unless and until they repented their grievous sin, hence that Jewish suffering was proof of divine rejection; Jews believed that Christians were utterly deluded and that nothing whatever had happened to sever the sacred connection between God, Torah, and the Jewish people.

As will be evident, I focus on Jews in the Franco-German region, leaving aside not only the Jews of Italy but also the larger, and certainly equally noteworthy, population of Sephardic Jews in Spain. I do so because Ashkenazic Jewish society and culture in northwestern Europe merit consideration as unique historical developments—rooted, to be sure, in Mediterranean antecedents but representing a distinctive form of adaptation to a new set of environmental, social, and political challenges. The territory that was originally the Roman province of Gaul, particularly that part constituting modern northern France and western Germany, was the original heartland of Ashkenazic Jewish life and culture. This same region constituted most of the Frankish Empire created by Charlemagne in the early ninth century. The core of the empire was the country between the Loire and Rhine rivers, the region cited by F. L. Ganshof as "the original home of feudalism."[1] Studying medieval European Jewish society in relation to the emergence and decline of feudal society reveals connections, I shall suggest, that are crucial to understanding why Jews were first accepted, even welcomed, but later exploited, tormented, and ultimately expelled. In short, even though this is a history of only a segment of medieval European Jewry, that segment underwent the cardinal Jewish experience in Europe.

It was in northwestern Europe that Yiddish originated, probably in the ninth and tenth centuries, as the linguistic expression of the emerging Ashkenazic cultural tradition; and it was from there, some six hundred years later, that large numbers of Jews migrated into Eastern Europe, where they formed yet another distinctive variant of Jewish society and culture, but one that was still clearly Ashkenazic in style and manner.

Far from being just one of many groups in a "multicultural" society, Jews were the one group who stood wholly and obviously outside the mainstream: they were not *an* other people; they were *the* other people. Of course, there were any number of European ethnic groups—Franks, Burgundians, Saxons, and the rest—and later, as national identities evolved, there were Frenchmen, Englishmen, and so on. But from the earliest medieval centuries, Europeans had one thing in common: they were Christians. True, for a time many must have been only nominally within the Christian fold, still attached to the folk religious beliefs and practices of their "heathen" ancestors. And there were heretics, such as the Arians (not to be confused with Aryans), who argued, not illogically, that since Jesus was the son of God, he had to be a lesser form of divine being. But from the fourth century on, Roman Catholic Christianity gained steady ground in western Europe, and by the sixth century the battle had been largely won. When the pope crowned Charlemagne as the new western emperor in the year 800, he was confirming an accomplished fact: the Carolingian empire was now the heartland of Roman Christianity.

In such a world, where being Christian and being a member of society were one and the same thing, there could be no place for Jews other than as provisionally tolerated outsiders. Unconverted peoples

on the margins of the empire were destined for conversion and incorporation. But Jews—eternally scarred by the crime of their ancestors,
and themselves notoriously resistant to conversion—were acceptable
only to the extent that they were economically useful to the powerful,
and only so long as they recognized their role as exemplars of what
it meant to be not-Christian. That role, in relatively good times as in
bad, inevitably shaped Jewish experience and molded the Jewish
consciousness.

Jews and Christians shared a social system predicated on their ir-
reducible opposition to each other. As Christians saw it, Jews lived
among them as visible evidence of the truth of Christianity—as outcasts punished by the Lord for an unforgivable crime. The social
apartness of Jews, their vulnerability, their peculiar and disreputable
social and economic status were all perceived as the logical corollary
to their role in the Gospels as the enemies and persecutors of Jesus.

In the earliest period of Jewish settlement in Gaul, however, before
the Church had achieved the dominant status it enjoyed in the late
medieval centuries, Jews were relatively well accepted, and Jewish
men appear to have intermarried frequently enough with local non-
Jewish women (probably all of whom converted) to create a Jewish
population of decidedly mixed genetic origins. Modern physical anthropological studies of European Jews have demonstrated conclu-
sively that the term "Semitic" masks the large European component in
the Jewish genetic pool. Nevertheless, Ashkenazic Jewish *society* and
culture derived from Mediterranean foundations and are therefore best
understood as products of a specific historical process following migration and resettlement. What must be recognized is that an entirely
new way of life evolved in northwestern Europe—the adaptation of
an erstwhile Mediterranean people to the strikingly different demands
of a radically new (because overwhelmingly Christian) homeland. It
was life in what was originally Gaul, and the encounter with its mainly
Frankish and other Germanic inhabitants, that created the distinctive
variant of Jewish life called Ashkenazic.

Since my perspective is that of a social historian and anthropologist, my foremost subject is the social experience of Jews living among
Christians, not the internal development of Judaism as a religious tradition. The book touches only lightly, therefore, on the more explicitly

religious dimensions of Jewish life, instead emphasizing interactive aspects of the encounter with the Christian world. It is generally agreed that what we now call ethnicity is largely (although not entirely) a function of group affiliation in situations of social and political competition or conflict. With this in mind, I refer at times to Ashkenazic Jews as an ethnic group, employing the contemporary term that best expresses what I want to say about their identity—an identity rooted not in "racial" considerations, or even in religion in the narrow sense of that word, but in everything that constituted Jewishness: kinship, community life, occupational linkages, internal languages, and cultural style, as well as shared religious beliefs and practices.

But all other questions aside, why focus on medieval Jewish history at all?

Since the simplest answer—that the search for historical knowledge requires no justification—may not convince everyone, here is an additional (and perhaps more controversial) answer. I suggest that Jews in the Western world exhibit a "cultural psychology," a patterned set of behavioral dispositions and values, reflecting the historical experience and adaptive strategies of medieval Ashkenazic Jewry. To put it simply, contemporary Jews still think and behave in ways that derive partly from the experience of their medieval ancestors. That is not to maintain that contemporary Jews are somehow unable to "liberate" themselves from "medieval" ways of thinking and acting, which is plainly not so. Rather, I propose that medieval Jewish experience gave rise to a cultural style that is still recognizable (albeit transformed into a modern idiom) in contemporary Jewish life. This would include predilection for commerce and for professional occupations, particularly law, medicine, academic pursuits, and social services; financial aptitude; intellectualism and respect for education; firm community orientation and liberal donation to charitable causes; concern for the underprivileged and the oppressed; a strong sense of ethnic identity and resistance to complete assimilation; and critical perspectives on society, politics, and culture, leading to political sensitivity and at times to above-average interest in radical political movements. Finally, I might point to a state of mind, difficult to define but recognizable in many Jews, consisting of a vague sense of unease, feelings of not being quite at home, and acute sensitivity to hostility or aggression directed individually or categorically toward Jews. Obviously all this cannot be documented with a sentence or two, but I trust that the history to follow will provide some support for the argument.

A few additional words on style and emphasis: The book is not about Jews alone; it is about ways in which European Jewish culture, identity, and experience were molded in the crucible of western Christendom. Hence, the beliefs and actions of Christians come in for considerable attention, and I have tried to present enough general historical background to make their situation and attitudes intelligible. Christian-Jewish encounters, often but not always hostile, receive frequent attention, and my goal is to keep both groups on the historical stage as much as possible.

Although I deal with religious matters where appropriate, particularly in the first chapter, the emphasis, as I have indicated, is on social, political, economic, and cultural history: a portrait of Jews and Christians as communities in interaction. For this reason I pay about as much attention to the inner world of Christianity as to that of Jewry, perhaps even more. I examine a number of instructive Christian texts in some detail, trying to bring out the peculiar flavor of medieval Christian discourse on Jews and Judaism, in order to provide more immediate contact with such sources than one usually finds in histories focusing on Jews alone. In contrast, the internal history of the Jewish community—its indigenously derived legal and religious structures, as well as its spiritual life—come in for rather less mention than might be expected. Our foremost purpose will be to watch Jews struggling to find their place in a profoundly Christian, and therefore sometimes profoundly hostile, world and to try to understand how they were shaped by that experience.

Thus I write not about European Jewish history but about Jews in European history; not about Jews as an independent social entity, but about an encounter between two peoples who were fated to live together in a deeply problematic and wholly unequal relationship.

Although it is customary at this point to thank everyone who has assisted and supported the author, my list is short because for the most part I have worked alone. Being a cultural anthropologist, not a professional scholar in Jewish studies, and teaching in a small college, I had only limited contacts in the field of medieval Jewish studies. I do want to thank several individuals who read my work and encouraged me to persevere: Jim Wald and Aaron Berman, trusted friends and colleagues at Hampshire College; and Aaron Lansky, former student, now colleague and close friend, founder and president of the National Yiddish Book Center. I am especially grateful to the Yiddish Book Center for providing me with opportunities to deliver public lectures that led to my decision to write this book.

I want to express gratitude to all those scholars, some no longer among the living, whose work provided indispensable foundations for my own. I am deeply indebted to everyone on whose research and understanding I have drawn, and I hope that my efforts at interpretation do justice to theirs.

I want also to express my appreciation to John Fruehwirth, of Syracuse University Press, for his patience, good humor, and generous assistance; to Bettie McDavid Mason for her dedicated editorial work; and to Kate Blackmer for her fine maps.

I owe more than can be adequately expressed to my parents, Bessie S. Glick and Dr. Samuel S. Glick, who provided me with a loving home and an education that established foundations for what eventually became an abiding interest in European Jewish history and literature; and to the memory of my grandparents, Lena and Julius Stein, and Sarah and Morris Glick, who endowed me with an enduring understanding of the meaning of Yiddishkeit.

Finally, Nansi S. Glick has contributed so much editorial skill and loving support to the making of this book that her name should appear not just on the dedication page but on the title page.

ABRAHAM'S HEIRS

⋄ 1 ⋄

ABRAHAM'S HEIRS

Early in the fourth century, Eusebius, bishop of Caesarea and one of the church fathers, composed a treatise entitled *Demonstratio Evangelica*, "Proof of the Gospel," arguing that Christianity was not a young religion at all but was in fact "a renewal of the ancient pre-Mosaic religion, in which Abraham, the friend of God, and his forefathers are shown to have lived." Moreover, he continued, "if you cared to compare the life of Christians and the worship introduced among all nations by Christ with the lives of the men who with Abraham are witnessed to by Scripture as holy and righteous, you would find one and the same ideal." The religion of the Jews, Eusebius explained, was linked to this ancient tradition only in a degenerated version; the laws delivered to Moses at Sinai, which were of course unknown to Abraham and the other patriarchs, were not intended for posterity but were rather the Lord's provisions for retrieving a people who had declined into wickedness and idolatry: "like a nurse and governess of childish and imperfect souls."[1] But with the coming of Jesus Christ, the old laws had been completely transcended, and those who still clung to them had been left behind, abandoned to their fate by a God whose love was now bestowed on the more deserving people of his new covenant.[2]

Eusebius was restating a familiar argument, namely, that Christianity had not just separated from Judaism but had replaced it. In fact, as Christians saw it, the separation of Christianity from its rejecting and rejected parent—that immense hyphen in what is now called the "Judeo-Christian tradition"—had necessarily meant replacement. The Jews, descendants (in part) of the biblical Hebrews, were understood to be Abraham's "heirs in the flesh," the original inheritors of the glorious

1

blessings bestowed by the Lord on Abraham and his posterity. But they had committed the most abominable of crimes; they had rejected their own Messiah, God's only begotten Son, who had come to redeem them from their narrow lives in the Mosaic Law and to reveal to them a new life in the Spirit. And so they themselves had been rejected and replaced, while the Lord's blessings were now bestowed on his new heirs: the diverse peoples ("Gentiles"—in Hebrew, *go-im,* "nations") who constituted the population of the Roman Empire. They were a new Israel: an Israel of the spirit rather than of the flesh; an Israel justified not by obedience to the Law but by faith in the redemptive power of the life, death and resurrection of Jesus of Nazareth.

These convictions, particularly those centering on the doctrine of replacement, were not held in quite such finished form at the beginning; they emerged gradually during the century or so after the death of Jesus, and it was not until the middle of the second century that Christian theologians began to express more or less systematically the conviction that one people had been rejected and another had been appointed. By then the principle had become fundamental to Christian self-definition; but, in fact, it had been inescapable ever since it first became evident that the new religion was going to meet with far more acceptance among Gentiles than among Jews. For surely it was essential to convince one's own congregation that their new status was divinely willed—that they were not usurpers but proper successors, and that the Christian community was the newly constituted recipient of all God's promises to the Hebrew patriarchs: that they, the converted Gentiles, and not the Jews, were Abraham's rightful heirs.

Thus, although the meaning of the life and death of Jesus—the question of whether he was or was not the Messiah whom the Jews had long awaited—lay at the heart of the controversy between the first Jewish converts and their unconvinced contemporaries, the ultimate conflict had to do with the more immediately disturbing questions that the former were raising: Who belonged to the Jewish community and who did not? Was it not understood that the Covenant was eternal and unalterable? Was God's Law, as revealed at Sinai, still operative or not? Could it be that this was the time of a "new dispensation," and that everyone was now living under a new covenant and in a new age? Or had nothing whatever changed, and was the Law as much in effect as ever? In short, had something truly revolutionary transpired in what we now (accepting the Christian answer) call the first century; or were the earliest Christians (called Nazarenes then) deluded and their preaching a product of wishful thinking?

The foremost task, then, of the first Christians was self-definition and self-justification. They had to explain and identify themselves, not only to other Jews whom they hoped to convert but perhaps equally to one another; for their new religion—more accurately, their new Jewish reform movement—had at first little to support it other than their supreme certainty that the Messiah had appeared at last, and that although he had withdrawn for a time, he would soon return to reign over a reconstituted and renewed social order. For some two decades after the death of Jesus, from about 30 to 50 C.E., they tried to persuade their fellow Jews that a transformative event had indeed taken place, and that every Jew's prospects for salvation had gained immeasurably, provided that one accept the reality of the Messiah's arrival. That was their original "gospel," their "good tidings," and in the earliest years it was directed almost exclusively to their own Jewish communities.[3]

Not suprisingly, most Jews found the claim completely unacceptable—not because they did not believe in a Messiah, but because Jesus of Nazareth met none of their expectations for the kind of man the Messiah would be and what he would accomplish. The Messiah idea, a rather vague one in the Jewish tradition, had evolved gradually as a political expectation in religious garb. He had long been expected, but ever since the middle of the first century B.C.E., when the Romans had conquered Palestine and converted it from a Jewish kingdom into a Roman province under puppet rulers, the Jews had awaited a liberator whose deeds would make his identity unmistakable. He would be divinely sent and heroic in stature, but he would be a fully human being: a warrior of royal lineage, a descendant of the great king David, who would appear at precisely the right moment to lead his people in a mighty rebellion against their Roman overlords. The Romans along with their sycophants would be expelled, and in their place would arise a new Jewish kingdom, ruled by David's legitimate descendants; the exiles (already far more numerous than the Jews of Palestine) would be gathered back into the homeland; a day of judgment would come, when all the righteous dead would be resurrected to live again with their kinfolk; and a millennial era of universal harmony, prosperity, and contentment would ensue. Other people—the Gentiles—would have their share of happiness in this ineffably glorious world, but they would have to acknowledge the supremacy of the one God of the Jews and the centrality of his city, Jerusalem.[4]

Given such expectations, it is no cause for wonder that most Jews were skeptical at best when confronted with a putative Messiah who had died a miserable death and was nowhere to be seen; or that the first Christian missionaries, the apostles, had to contend with a great deal of ridicule, rancor, and even violence. The Book of Acts, a record of their experiences, is in large part the story of how they met with so much scorn and rejection that they soon came to see themselves as a people apart, a remnant of Israel destined to receive the blessings that would be withdrawn from all who were rejecting the new dispensation.

What they had initially hoped to demonstrate, of course, was that their new religious movement was not a departure from Judaism but its continuation, not its negation but its "fulfillment." The words of the prophets and of David's psalms, they insisted, if read with understanding could be seen to have foretold the life and death of Jesus Christ; it was all there, but in hidden form, in allusive metaphorical language. Thus there was no reason for conflict if only their fellow Jews would recognize the urgency of the hour and be reconciled to the Messiah before the time of final judgment.

But although such arguments gained a few converts here and there, most Jews were unimpressed, and the apostles were frustrated at every turn. For some fifteen or twenty years they struggled with little success; they remained a distinct minority, a splinter sect, despised and shunned by Jews who saw no reason to believe that the Messiah had appeared in such an unlikely and unsatisfactory manner.

Thus, by the middle of the first century, some twenty years after the death of Jesus, and already well beyond the time when one might have expected his return, the Nazarenes were still a small, beleaguered congregation, searching for a means to survive. One path, until then explored only tentatively, lay open: toward the much larger and, as it turned out, much more receptive world of the Gentiles, some of whom were finding very attractive a religion that spoke of a coming kingdom in such glowing terms. They were asking to be admitted into the new fellowships as converts of a lesser order—"God fearers" was the term used for a time—who were promised a place in the kingdom even though they had not accepted the full burden of circumcision and ritual observance. The decision to begin accepting these people in larger numbers led ultimately to another even more momentous: to acknowledge them as fully constituted converts. And this was to have consequences infinitely greater than anyone at the time could have imagined: it was the crucial step in the creation of a new religion.

The decision to grant Gentiles complete equivalence in the New Covenant was initiated largely by one man, the apostle Paul. He was a Jew, of course, known before his conversion as Saul, and it appears that for a number of years he shared wholeheartedly in the Jewish consensus about Christian claims; we are told in the early chapters of Acts that he even participated in some of the most malevolent attacks on the earliest apostles, including the one in which the apostle Stephen was murdered. But not long afterward, probably as early as 35 C.E., he experienced a revelation, a dazzling vision that left him blinded for several days, in which Jesus appeared and asked, "Saul, Saul, why do you persecute me?" When a faithful apostle laid hands on him, urging that he be "filled with the Holy Spirit," the "scales fell from his eyes," and he was baptized into the new faith.[5]

For a few years or so thereafter, he probably missionized much in the style of his fellow apostles, appealing to other Jews with the same lack of success. But in time he seems to have realized that, unexpectedly, it was Gentiles to whom the new message was appealing most compellingly. What was one to do, though, about such major obstacles as circumcision and ritual regulations regarding food? Early Christian congregational life centered on a shared feast of fellowship—but how could one share a ritual meal with Gentiles who were so clearly outside the fold? In some communities distant from Jerusalem, where Gentile affiliates were beginning to outnumber the Jewish core membership, the Nazarenes were bending to circumstances: sharing food with Gentiles, accepting them into the new fellowship as spiritual brothers and sisters. From there it was a relatively easy step to admitting Gentiles into unqualified membership, accepting everyone solely on the basis of a declaration of faith in the redemptive powers of the risen Messiah.

Paul seems to have sensed with particular acumen the magnitude of this action and the significance of what might be called "the Gentile question." By the year 50, possibly somewhat earlier, he had decided that he had been called to reveal the new dispensation to everyone, of whatever ethnic type, who would accept it—to become, in his words, "a missionary to the Gentiles." Addressing himself to the Christian congregation at Rome, most of whom were probably of non-Jewish origins, he reassured them in words that have echoed through time: "Do you suppose God is the God of the Jews alone? Is he not the God of Gentiles also? Certainly, of Gentiles also, if it be true that God is one. And he will therefore justify both the circumcised in virtue of their faith, and the uncircumcised through their faith."[6]

As this passage indicates, Paul was reluctant to reject his fellow Jews entirely, hoping that at least some of them would yet enter the New Covenant. But since this lay in the indefinite future, the immediate task at hand was to bring the tidings of redemption to the Gentiles. When his letters to emergent Christian congregations are followed in chronological order (not as arranged in the New Testament), one sees him beginning with moderate optimism about prospects for converting at least some Jews but soon shifting to a strategy of all-out appeals to Gentiles. In the most revealing of his earlier letters, the one addressed to the Galatian congregation, probably written about 52 C.E., he takes the stand that was to become his hallmark, declaring unequivocally that "no one is ever justified before God in terms of law." Abraham's blessings, he continues, have now been "extended to the Gentiles, so that we might receive the promised Spirit through faith."[7]

In his letter to the congregation at Rome, probably written about 57 C.E., he develops the argument into its final form, particularly with regard to the question of obedience to the Law as a prerequisite for entry into the New Covenant. His answer is that not only is the Law no longer the path to salvation, but it may even be a hindrance to Jewish converts who remain so attached to familiar rituals that they fail to achieve complete spiritual renewal. Yet he is still not categorically dismissing Jews—his "natural kinsfolk"—for God has not yet abandoned them, only turned away from them in disappointment. In due time, he is confident, they will see the light and be welcomed into the new Israel: "For if their rejection has meant the reconciliation of the world, what will their acceptance mean? Nothing less than life from the dead!"[8]

Paul and the apostles thus realized that it was, above all, their rejection of the Law that underlay the breach with Judaism. But now even more was required: not just to separate from Judaism but to convince themselves and their converts that it was precisely by virtue of their recognition of the new dispensation from the Law that Christians were replacing Jews as God's anointed people. The Law, Paul declared, had never been intended for permanent observance; it was only a temporary expedient, a necessary yoke for a rebellious people who were slipping away from the path of righteousness. Neither Abraham nor any of his immediate descendants had required it. In fact, the time when the Law was in effect—the interval between Moses and Jesus—had really been only an interlude. Abraham had lived according to divinely willed "natural" moral law, the very same one that his successor, Jesus Christ, had preached; and the true Israelites, now as then, were those who did likewise. Now it was those who had accepted the New Covenant, Israelites of the Spirit, who were Abraham's true heirs:

> For it was not through law that Abraham, or his posterity, was given the promise that the world should be his inheritance, but through the righteousness that came from faith. For if those who hold by the law, and they alone, are heirs, then faith is empty and the promise goes for nothing, because law can bring only retribution; but where there is no law there can be no breach of law. The promise was made on the ground of faith, in order that it might be a matter of sheer grace, and that it might be valid for all Abraham's posterity, not only for those who hold by the law, but for those also who have the faith of Abraham. For he is the father of us all.[9]

The break with Judaism, until this time an obvious prospect but by no means a certainty, now became a conclusive reality, as each of the two religious communities turned to meet threats to its own survival and to redefine its own identity. The Jewish wars of rebellion

against the Romans, beginning in 66 C.E. and culminating in the destruction of the Temple in 70, seemed at the time far more determinative for Jewish history than anything Christians were saying or doing.
But Temple worship, centered on priests and sacrifices, had already
been relegated to a secondary role in the religious lives of most Jews,
particularly the very large number who were already living far from
Jerusalem. For these people it was synagogue worship, and the laws
of Torah as interpreted by learned rabbis, that constituted the core of
Judaism and the normative mode of everyday life. On the latter especially there could be no compromise: to reject the Law, to declare that
it had been rendered obsolete, would be to reject the bedrock on which
everything else stood. Spiritual fulfillment was not an inconsiderable
goal for Jews, but it was achieved through observance of the Law, not
despite it, and loyalty to Torah remained absolutely inseparable from
acceptance into the Creator's Covenant.

The two religions—for that is what they now were—thus emerged
in the final years of the first century as two distinct systems of belief
and self-identification. Jews remained firmly attached to what had always been their most profound conviction: that the one God had singled them out for his particular blessings and his Covenant, but that
in return he expected uncompromising loyalty to his Law as revealed
at Sinai. Indisputably theirs was, as Christians would often charge, a
particularistic religion that linked Covenant and observance with na-
tionality or peoplehood: closely akin in this crucial respect to the religions of so-called tribal peoples for whom belief and ritual are
inseparable from cultural identity and local community; distinct from
them, however, in its uncompromising monotheism and in its possession of a corpus of immensely fascinating sacred writings. Those
writings—the Hebrew Scriptures, or as Christians now called them,
the "Old Testament"—embodied a history and a behavioral code that
not only sustained the Jews as a people but also appealed irresistibly to
their Christian successors. For although Christianity had now taken
form as the very antithesis of Judaism, Christians were able only in part
to put the past behind them, as it were, and to move on. The dispute with
Judaism had to continue if one were to maintain self-justification and to
refute the intensely disturbing insistence by the Jews that nothing what-

ever had changed. Intrinsic to the struggle was the need to come to terms with the Lord's promises to the people of Israel—to explain how and why these promises had been transferred to new heirs.

Of the newness and distinctiveness of Christianity there could be no question. In contrast to the particularism and nationalism that were intrinsic to Judaism, Christianity was a transcultural, or universalist, creed, open to everyone, not connected to any one national or ethnic identity. In contrast to the rigorous demands of the Law of Torah, Christianity called for a spiritual rebirth that would be manifest in one's overall social and moral demeanor. To be sure, it was a religion stressing fellowship and community, but the door was open to all who chose to enter. The one God of the Jews was still in place, although his singularity was now compromised by a Son—a theological problem that would not be resolved for several centuries. As for the Hebrew Scriptures, they were now to be "completed" by a New Testament describing the ministries of Jesus and the apostles and laying out the basic arguments of life in the Spirit, abrogation of the Law, and replacement of the Jews. But the books of the Jews had not been—could not be—abandoned; for in order to maintain that Christianity was the divinely intended continuation of Judaism, and that Christians were therefore the rightful successors to Jews, it was essential to demonstrate that the Old Testament pointed unmistakably (albeit in veiled language) to the New; that if read perceptively, with Christian enlightenment, it could be seen to speak repeatedly of Jesus Christ and the call to the Gentiles.[10]

Demonstrating linkages between Old Testament and New thus became a compelling task for Christian writers, and it was not long before Jews were being characterized as a people of singular blindness and obtuseness in their inability (or was it their refusal?) to acknowledge those linkages. For the Christian-Jewish debate, as it had formed by the end of the first century, and as it has continued to our own time, returned always to the meaning of the original Covenant and thus to the questions on which the two were destined never to agree: Did the Hebrew Scriptures truly foretell the coming of Jesus as Messiah? Had the Jews committed a terrible crime by denying him? And had God, in response to that crime, called a new people to be Abraham's heirs?

Replacement and Fulfillment in the Gospels

The New Testament begins with four Gospels, attributed to Matthew, Mark, Luke, and John, telling the story of the life, death, and resurrection of Jesus. Composed at various times between about 65 and 100, they represent the Christian self-image as it was forming immediately after Paul's time and as the congregation was becoming predominantly Gentile. The Gospel of John, composed last, differs from the others in style and perspective: although each Gospel includes material antagonistic to Jews and Judaism, John stands out in this respect quite remarkably. In the first three Gospels such terms as "Pharisees" (meaning Jews committed to rabbinic Judaism) and "priests" suggest that the Jewish community was diverse and that not all Jews persecuted Jesus, but in John the categorical term "Jews" appears much more often and nearly always in a decidedly negative context.[11]

Matthew's account of the life of Jesus, composed about 80 or 85 but drawing on earlier sources, opens the New Testament and is probably the one most often read and cited. With regard to Judaism, its most pervasive theme can be summed up in the term "fulfillment." Matthew was intent on demonstrating that in Jesus the Law of Torah and the sermons of the Hebrew prophets were fulfilled, meaning that they found their ultimate realization and revelation. The Law had been fulfilled (ironically, one might say) through transcendence: not abandoned but elevated to a new moral plane, rendered inoperative in its literal sense so that it could be realized spiritually. The prophets had also been fulfilled, in that their various declarations about the future, often couched in ambiguous language, now turned out to have been pointing clearly to the ministry of Jesus Christ.

To illustrate with just one example: In Matthew's account of Jesus' infancy, an angel tells Joseph to take Mary and Jesus to Egypt to escape Herod's plan to kill the child; they flee and remain away until Herod dies. "This," explains Matthew, "was to fulfill what the Lord had declared through the prophet: 'I called my son out of Egypt.'" The original prophetic passage is found in the Book of Hosea as part of an admonition to the Israelites of his time (eighth century B.C.E.). The Lord, speaking through the prophet, reminds the people of their backsliding after the Exodus: "When Israel was a boy, I loved him; I called my son out of Egypt; but the more I called, the further they went from me."[12]

But if fulfillment of the Hebrew past is integral to the message of this Gospel, rejection of the world of living Jewry is certainly there as well. To be sure, some Jews are presented as acknowledging the healing powers of Jesus and the appeal of his ministry. But not the Jewish elite, the priests and scholars: they interrogate him, challenge him, insult him. At times he responds with less than Christian forbearance, calling them "hypocrites," "blind fools," "snakes," "vipers' brood," and "sons of the men who killed the prophets." "You are like tombs covered with whitewash," he tells them; "they look well from outside, but inside they are full of dead men's bones and all kinds of filth. So it is with you: outside you look like honest men, but inside you are brimfull of hypocrisy and crime." Finally, when the crucial moment arrives and, in the most dramatic passage in the New Testament, Pilate asks, "Then what am I to do with Jesus called Messiah?" the Jewish mob, egged on by the chief priests and elders, responds in unison: "Crucify him. . . . His blood be on us, and on our children."[13]

Already, then, in the very first book of the New Testament, we perceive that the ambivalence toward Jews first manifested in Paul's ministry was becoming a definitive feature of Christianity. It was deemed necessary to establish connection with the Hebrew past, to show that God's word was being fulfilled and that the Church was the legitimate successor to the Synagogue. But, of course, the corollary was that the Synagogue had forfeited its legacy, and that the Jews who remained bound to the Old Covenant were to be left behind in God's plan of salvation. The hope never waned that some day they would acknowledge their egregious error and be restored. But that day was seeming ever more distant. For the time being it was axiomatic that even while Christians insisted on an unbroken link with the Jewish past, they were separating from their Jewish contemporaries once and for all.

In the Gospel of John, composed in the closing years of the first century, the theme of replacement finds especially striking expression in vivid metaphors representing the contrast between Jesus and the Jews who reject him. The narrative of the struggle between Jesus and his antagonists is interlaced with sermons or declarations in which

Jesus poetically contrasts his new dispensation with the one he is about to replace, always to the consternation of the Jews, who are so confined to the language of literal interpretation that they are unable to understand him. The three most explicit contrasts, all resonating with one another, are between light and darkness (also represented as vision and blindness), between life and death, and between fruitfulness and dessication. Jesus and his disciples are of course the people of light, life, and fruitfulness, while the Jews are associated with darkness, death, and dessication. The narrative climaxes when Jesus triumphs over his own death (attributed categorically to "the Jews") and is reborn into eternal life.

The scene that epitomizes the entire argument comes in the eighth chapter, when Jesus engages in a bitter confrontation with his Jewish opponents over the meaning of yet another pair of contrasting images, slavery and freedom. Jesus declares that because the Jews have rejected him they have no share whatever in divine grace: they are not "God's children." He opens with a commentary on the meaning of freedom: "If you dwell within the revelation I have brought, you are indeed my disciples; you shall know the truth, and the truth will set you free."[14] But the Jews, as always, are puzzled and resistant; whereupon Jesus loses patience completely and accuses them of being children not of Abraham but of the devil:

> They replied, "We are Abraham's descendants; we have never been in slavery to any man. What do you mean by saying, 'You will become free men'?" "In very truth I tell you," said Jesus, "that everyone who commits sin is a slave. . . . I know that you are descended from Abraham, but you are bent on killing me because my teaching makes no headway with you. I am revealing in words what I saw in my Father's presence; and you are revealing in action what you learned from your father." They retorted, "Abraham is our father." "If you were Abraham's children," Jesus replied, "you would do as Abraham did. As it is, you are bent on killing me, a man who told you the truth, as I heard it from God. That is not how Abraham acted. You are doing your own father's work. . . . Why do you not understand my language? It is because my revelation is beyond your grasp. Your father is the devil and you choose to carry out your father's desires. . . . He who has God for his father listens to the

words of God. You are not God's children; that is why you do not listen."[15]

The Jews declare that anyone who speaks this way must be "possessed." And why has he been claiming to bring a gift of eternal life? "Are you greater than our father Abraham, who is dead? The prophets are dead too. What do you claim to be?" Jesus replies that his powers come from the God of the Jews, though they know nothing about him: "Your father Abraham was overjoyed to see my day; he saw it and was glad." "You are not yet fifty years old," the Jews reply. "How can you have seen Abraham?" Jesus responds with an elliptical reference to his own divine nature: "In very truth I tell you, before Abraham was born, I am." But, as usual, the Jews remain unconvinced, and the encounter ends on a note of finality: "They picked up stones to throw at him, but Jesus was not to be seen; and he left the temple."[16]

The departure from the temple and its hostile denizens symbolizes what had become an irreversible parting of the ways. The scenes in which the Jews apprehend Jesus and demand that he be crucified are in a sense anticlimactic, for by that point in the narrative they have been portrayed as the enemies of light, life, and revelation—a people immersed in sin and ignorance, fettered by their inability to understand anything other than the most literal statements, severed from the Lord's fruitful vine and condemned to wither away: a people who, having scorned their own redeemer and his promise of eternal life, were now fated to suffer the consequences.

The Jewish Response

We may be inclined to think of the early centuries of our era (this itself being a Christian conception, of course) as a time when Christianity was emerging as a world religion while Judaism remained essentially unchanged. But the truth is that between the first and fifth centuries both religions were evolving—and not altogether independently, moreover, but partly in response to each other. By the fifth century, when Christianity had become established as the official religion of the Roman Empire, the confrontation between parent and offspring had progressed to the point where the latter was overwhelmingly dominant. But to people of earlier times—the second and third centuries especially, but even well into the fourth—the very question of whether Christianity would survive was far from settled. Christians who suffered and died in the brutal persecutions of the second and third centuries knew nothing, of course, about how near their faith stood to vindication and triumph, and it was inevitable that persecution and threat of extinction went into the shaping of the early Christian mentality. The persecutors were Roman authorities, who were demanding that Christians either sacrifice to the gods or suffer execution, often in abominably cruel forms, and the many who chose to die rather than submit were sustained by a psychological climate in which martyrdom had become the highest form of religious affirmation. It was pagan Romans, not Jews, who posed the most severe and immediate threat to Christian communities everywhere.

It is all the more remarkable, therefore, to realize that there appeared during these centuries a substantial Christian literature expressing hostility toward Jews and Judaism—a hostility of a magnitude that could have derived only from a pervasive sense that the people and their religion posed an inescapable challenge to Christianity. Perhaps we can epitomize the matter by saying that while Romans persecuted and tormented the faithful, thereby strengthening their faith, Jews by their very existence called into question the foundations of that faith and thus constituted what was perceived as the more profound threat.

That Christianity posed an equally immense challenge to Judaism goes without saying. But for adequate perspective on how Judaism was itself responding to changing historical circumstances, we must recognize that Christianity was not the only, and probably not the most influential, challenge that Jews were facing. By the first century C.E., Jews were already widely dispersed throughout the Hellenized world of the Mediterranean, and in such cities as Antioch and Alexandria there were flourishing Jewish communities easily rivaling that of Jerusalem in numbers and importance. These people still made annual contributions to maintenance of the Temple, and some even journeyed there for seasonal celebrations. But for the majority religious life had to be shaped along new lines, with a new focus: the synagogue, the principal locus of communal life, headed by rabbinic authorities whose piety and learning qualified them to be both interpreters of Torah and communal leaders. The synagogue became the institution to which ordinary people gravitated as the center of their Jewish social lives, and prayer in the local synagogue under the guidance of one's own rabbi became the accepted substitute for Temple rituals that were no longer part of ordinary experience. This in effect was what came to be called "Pharisaic" Judaism; the "Pharisees" who appear as villains in the New Testament were in fact those Jews who had come to recognize synagogue worship and rabbinic authority as core elements in the newly emerging form of their religion. For modern historical purposes the terms *Rabbinic Judaism* or *Synagogue Judaism* are more informative.[17]

As a consequence of this radical reorientation, the destruction of the Temple in 70 C.E., despite all the attention it has received from Jews and Christians alike, was not nearly as devastating a blow as it might have been, for the simple reason that by then the Temple had already become more a symbol of the Jewish past than the focus of ongoing Jewish life. By the second century rabbinic interpretations of the Law that had been accumulating for several hundred years were codified in the Mishnah, a compendium of laws and commentaries regarding worship, ritual observance, and many aspects of everyday life, thereby providing commonality to Jewish life throughout the Diaspora. Over the next three centuries, the commentaries that continued to accumulate were assembled as Gemara, and together the Mishnah and Gemara constituted the definitive document of postbiblical Judaism, the Talmud.

The new Judaism, then, was still a religion centered on Torah, but with a decided twist. What had once been a localized people with a religion centering on temple rituals and sacrifices was now a widely dispersed people whose Jewish identity was rooted in synagogue worship and, as time went on, in study of the Talmud, a text essentially equivalent to the Torah in authority. It was this form of Judaism— "legalistic" certainly, but for good reason and to an urgent purpose— that confronted emergent Christianity and provided the foil, as it were, for Christian self-definition, even while it was sustaining Jewish life under circumstances that might otherwise have led to dissolution.[18]

For reasons that will now be evident, the emergence of Christianity may well have constituted more of a challenge to Judaism than the destruction of the Temple, for it called into question most of what Jews accepted as beyond question; and it was soon apparent that both religions could not be equally valid—not, at any rate, without a more generously "liberal" perspective than would have been possible at the time. Arrival of the Messiah in a completely unexpected manner and with an upsetting message; abrogation of the Law; a new Covenant; radically new interpretations of what the prophets said; new heirs for the promises to Abraham and his descendants: all of these were utterly inconsistent, of course, with everything that Jews held to be sacred, immutable truth. Their response was essentially what one would expect: ignore if possible; if not, deny and resist. Thus we find that rabbinic writings pay little attention to Christianity, mentioning it only occasionally in passing, for in the minds of these scholars the entire matter was beside the point—an apostasy of such magnitude as to merit only dismissal.

The Jewish response to Christianity can be characterized, therefore, as passive resistance: Jews simply refused to acknowledge that anything significant had happened. The Messiah had not yet appeared; when he did, he would be a wholly Jewish Messiah. The original and only Covenant was still firmly in place, and Jews were still the people appointed by God to obey his commandments and to worship him as their deliverer from bondage. Abraham, Isaac, and Jacob were still the ancestors of the Jewish people, and all of the Lord's matchless promises to them were still in effect. The prophets still belonged to the Jewish people, and their words, whether of praise or condemnation, meant precisely what they said—no more, no less—and therefore had nothing whatever to do with Jesus or Christianity. One lived according to the Law, as an upright and observant Jew, and that would wholly suffice to ensure personal salvation and a share in the messianic world to come.

What this meant in effect was that Christians had to take notice of Judaism for reasons that were bound to be associated with hostility, suspicion, and resentment. The older religion could present at least a surface posture of indifference, but for Christianity that was quite impossible. We have seen that Christians could not escape the task of self-definition: demonstration, to themselves no less than to the world at large, that the Jews had truly been replaced and that a New Covenant had been inaugurated. But if this was so, why had Judaism not passed quietly from the scene? Why had the Jews not faded away with their lost Temple? Why did they seem not only to survive but to flourish? Why were they still so much in evidence, praying in their synagogues, performing their rituals, and, worst of all, threatening to seduce innocent pagans and even Christians from the path of salvation?

Hence, the simple presence of Jews—visible evidence that the great majority of them were not going to convert, not going to accept what was supposed to be their destiny—must have been enough in itself to irritate Christian clergy. But at times the problem was even more immediate. It is somewhat surprising to learn from early Christian sermons and discourses that significant numbers of less sophisticated Christian folk found Jewish rituals attractive—so much so that they not only attended synagogue services but observed ritual celebrations and fasts, to the point that some seemed to be paying more attention to the Jewish calendar than to the one that was supposedly their own. Even the most committed and well-informed Christians were likely to endow Jewish rituals and scriptures with the ineffable power and magical qualities that come only with great age. Many believed that Jewish amulets and incantations had special medical efficacy, and they went trustingly to Jewish curers, who were probably convinced themselves that ritual phrases and symbolic objects associated with the ancient religion had the power to heal.

Such intercourse obviously implied that Judaism was at least equal in validity to Christianity, if not superior, and the Christian clergy, engaged as they were in a struggle for recognition and even survival, were understandably outraged when they saw members of their own congregations expressing interest in Jews or their religion. The term for such backsliding was "Judaizing," which encompassed not only such obvious misbehavior as attendance at a synagogue service but also the kind of confused thinking that might lead a Christian to suppose that one should try to follow the Law in its original form: observe sabbath regulations, abstain from forbidden foods, and so on. Behavior of this sort called into question the principle that the Law had been transcended—and, of course, on that principle everything else rested.[19]

The ultimate threat was Jewish proselytism, which was not brought to an end by the appearance of Christianity. For centuries Judaism had been attracting converts from paganism with rather surprising success (considering its demands), and many people in the Gentile world continued to find it attractive. The "burden of the Law" was indeed heavy, and only converts who agreed to shoulder the burden in its entirety were acceptable. But there were rewards: entrance into a well-integrated community, certain of its own place in God's plan, possessed of scriptures to which even Christians paid homage. In the battle for new converts, even in the struggle to hold on to the recently converted, Judaism presented a vigorous challenge. Whatever one might want to believe about the older religion, one could hardly maintain that it was defunct.

"We Are Not a Contemptible People": The *Dialogue with Trypho*

As a single example of how Christian writers were trying to come to terms with Judaism, I shall describe in some detail a second century "dialogue," probably fictional and entirely one-sided, between a Jew named Trypho and the author, Justin, later St. Justin Martyr, one of the early Fathers of the Church. Born about 100 into a non-Christian family in Samaria, Justin studied philosophy in Ephesus and converted there to Christianity—"the only sure and useful philosophy."[20] He moved to Rome, where he devoted the remainder of his life to defending the faith, and died as a martyr about 165. His *Dialogue with Trypho*, composed about 160, is a book-length discourse, divided into 142 short chapters, in which the two essential themes, fulfillment and replacement, are defended by copious citations from the Hebrew Scriptures. Trypho is portrayed as a moderately civil but unyielding antagonist who finds Justin's arguments impossibly fanciful. He is supposedly accompanied by other Jews who are even more difficult to reach; early in the discourse, when Justin has promised to explain his position, they break into "such loud, rude, and raucous laughter" that he almost gives up at the start.[21]

Justin's purpose is to demonstrate and defend tenets of Christianity that were still open to challenge: that Jesus was truly the Jewish messiah; that he had brought an entirely new dispensation; that there was no longer any reason, therefore, for literal obedience to the Law, specifically its ritual regulations; and that the Jews had been legitimately and irrevocably replaced by a newly appointed people. The significance of the *Dialogue* lies in its emphasis on Old Testament citations—evidence, it would seem, of an urgently felt need to support the new faith by reference to the old scriptures, but also part of the logical strategy for confronting Jews. The putative justification for the effort is straightforward: to convert Jews, one must first teach them how to read their own scriptures and show them that the coming of Christ's kingdom is evident everywhere to those who can penetrate beneath the surface of the text. Penetrating somewhat more deeply ourselves, we can see Justin's work as an early manifestation of a Christian perspective on Jews that would persist into medieval times and beyond—what might be characterized as a "younger brother syndrome": edginess about the simple presence of Jews; the feeling that by their very existence they constitute a threat; a nagging sense of uncertainty about one's own status in relation to them; and a compelling need to have them concede that the divine blessings have indeed passed unequivocally to their successors. Reaching back for self-justification into the Hebrew Scriptures, quoting them with overwhelming thoroughness, Justin seems to acknowledge their primacy even while he insists that they are prefigurations of something better to follow. Be that as it may, the *Dialogue* is an exemplary product of imaginative scholarship, and its strategy set the pattern for an entire tradition of *adversus Judaeos* literature, discourses "in opposition to the Jews."[22]

We have then a method of argument in which a people's own literature is employed to persuade them that its essential thesis—their particular relationship with God—is no longer tenable. This use of Old Testament texts as *testimonia*, "testimonies," or what are now called "proof-texts," became an essential feature in the mode of Christian writing called *demonstratio evangelica*, explanation, or proof, of the Gospel message: one demonstrated that events and statements were fulfilled, much in the sense already noted in the Gospel of Matthew. But in Justin's work fulfillment was developed for the first time as the basic rhetorical device.[23]

Justin presents two kinds of fulfillment. First, persons, events, and statements in the Old Testament are shown to be "types"—that is, prefigurations or advance representations—of New Testament counterparts. They are recognizable, of course, only to those with eyes to see beyond the obvious. Justin finds types everywhere, more than he can mention, even in a book containing little else. He could enumerate all the Mosaic laws, he assures Trypho, and show in every case that they are "types, symbols, and prophecies" of what would happen to Christ and his disciples; but, he adds, "I believe that I have already mentioned a sufficient number of examples," a statement that no one could have disputed.[24] The second form of fulfillment was also noted in the Gospel of Matthew: prophecy, divinely inspired utterances that seem to refer to events at the time or earlier (the literal meaning) but that in fact foretell events in the time of Christ and his Church (the figurative meaning).

Here is a single example of Justin's version of fulfillment. Chapter 17 of Exodus describes the victory of Moses and Joshua over the Amalekites in the battle at Rephidim. Moses watches the battle from a hilltop while Joshua leads the Hebrew troops, but it is Moses whose actions control the outcome: "Whenever Moses raised his hands Israel had the advantage, and when he lowered his hands Amalek had the advantage. But when his arms grew heavy they took a stone and put it under him and, as he sat, Aaron and Hur held up his hands, one on each side, so that his hands remained steady until sunset. Thus Joshua defeated Amalek and put its people to the sword."

As Justin reads the story, the Hebrews defeated their enemies because the name of Jesus (Jeshua, a variant of Joshua) and the sign of the cross were present at the battlefield. Moses performed "symbolic acts," he explains, prefiguring the Crucifixion. "What acts do you mean?" asks Trypho.

"When your people," I answered, "waged war with Amalec, and Jesus (Josue), the son of Nun, was the leader of the battle, Moses himself, stretching out both hands, prayed to God for help. Now, Hur and Aaron held up his hands all day long, lest he should become tired and let them drop to his sides. For, if Moses relaxed from that figure [of outstretched hands], which was a figure of the cross, the people were defeated (as Moses himself testifies), but as long as he remained in that position Amalec was defeated, and the strong derived their strength from the cross. In truth, it was not because Moses prayed that his people were victorious, but because, while the name of Jesus was at the battlefront, Moses formed the sign of the cross."[25]

The overarching theme of the *Dialogue,* the one to which all arguments for types and fulfillment ultimately point, is replacement: Justin is intent on demonstrating that the Jews are unworthy of God's love and that Christians have been appointed in their stead. Jews, he declares, are a "ruthless, stupid, blind, and lame people": ruthless because they persecute Christians; stupid and blind because they cannot understand their own Scriptures and could not recognize their own Messiah; lame because they have been punished by exile from their land, destruction of their Temple, and loss of the love and protection of their own God.

As if that were not enough, he informs Trypho that Jews are ultimately to blame for whatever antagonism and persecution Christians suffer anywhere: Having "crucified the only sinless and just Man," he declares, the Jews "not only failed to feel remorse" but even sent emissaries in every direction "to spread those ugly rumors against us which are repeated by those who do not know us." Thus, he concludes, "you are to blame not only for your own wickedness, but also for that of all others."[26]

The essential Jewish deficiency is their inability to understand their own sacred texts—"or rather not yours, but ours. For we believe and obey them, whereas you, though you read them, do not grasp their spirit."[27] Jews cannot understand the real meaning of even their most fundamental rituals; they take circumcision, for example, to be a mark of their appointed status, when in fact it is precisely the opposite: a badge of suffering for a people who cannot see that what they need is to circumcise (that is, to soften) their hearts. "You Jews," he exclaims (not without logic), "who have the circumcision of the flesh, are in great need of our circumcision, whereas we, since we have our circumcision, do not need yours. For if, as you claim, circumcision had been necessary for salvation, God would not have created Adam uncircumcised."[28]

Trypho is portrayed as a resourceful opponent, sensible and straightforward (at times he is surely expressing Justin's own doubts and uncertainties), but of course he is no match for his creator. Justin has argued that the Sabbath no longer need be observed in the traditional way. "Why," asks Trypho, "do you quote only those passages from the Prophets which prove your point, and omit those quotations which clearly command the observance of the Sabbath?" The Law is indeed as you read it, responds Justin, but it was instituted by God "only on account of your hardness of heart and ingratitude toward Him." Hence it is still appropriate for Jews, as a crutch of sorts, but for no one else.[29]

Having documented the unworthiness of the Jews, Justin must also prove the obverse: that the Gentiles have been called, and that they and the emerging Church are the New Israel. As always, the Jews must be made to understand that their own texts speak to them of their own replacement. "Do I understand you to say," asks a puzzled Trypho, "that none of us Jews will inherit anything on the holy mountain of God?" "I didn't say that," replies Justin, "but I do say that those who have persecuted Christ in the past and still do, and do not repent, shall not inherit anything on the holy mountain, unless they repent. Whereas the Gentiles, who believe in Christ and are sorry for their sins, shall receive the inheritance, along with the Patriarchs, the Prophets, and every just descendant of Jacob, even though they neither practise circumcision nor observe the sabbaths and feasts."[30]

Later he develops this argument: "[W]e are not a contemptible people, nor a tribe of barbarians . . . but the chosen people of God who appeared to those who did not seek Him. . . . For this is really the nation promised to Abraham by God, when He told him that He would make him a father of many nations. . . . And we shall inherit the Holy Land together with Abraham, receiving our inheritance for all eternity, because by our similar faith we have become children of Abraham."[31]

The *Dialogue with Trypho* merits this much attention on several counts. First, it was the foremost presentation of Christian doctrine on Jews and Judaism in the second century and a model for *adversus Judaeos* literature that followed for centuries thereafter. Second, it established citation of types and prophecies in the Old Testament as a basic rhetorical device in anti-Jewish polemics. Finally, it promoted more explicitly than ever before the doctrine that the Church was, and was always intended to be, the True Israel; and that the Jews—a people with a disreputable past and no future—had been dismissed, as it were, from the very course of human history.

Saint Augustine on the Purpose of the Diaspora

The most distinguished of all early Christian theologians was Augustine, the fifth-century North African bishop whose writings provided foundations for the Christian interpretation of history. Among his many treatises is an *Adversus Judaeos,* composed about 424, shortly before his death. His central theme is change and the distinction between old and new: the arrival of Christ ushered in a new covenant, a new kind of law, new expectations. But of course the Jews understand none of this; they have "remained stationary in useless antiquity," unable to see that their time has passed and that those "who hold fast to the new promises" are their successors.[32] If, in their deplorable obtuseness, they continue to insist that everything in the Hebrew Scriptures applies to themselves alone, let them take note of the many passages that address their deficiencies:

> If you truly want to say: "We are the house of Jacob," then say it when you hear: "Blind the heart of this people, and make their ears heavy, and shut their eyes." Then say, "We are they," when you hear: "I have spread forth my hands all the day to an unbelieving and contradicting people." Say: "We are they," when you hear: "Let their eyes be darkened that they see not; and their back bend down always." In these and other prophetic words of this kind say: "We are they." Without any doubt you are, but you are so blind that you say you are what you are not, and do not recognize yourselves for what you really are.

There is still time for repentance, if only the Jews will acknowledge their sins and atone in the only acceptable manner: "You, in the person of your parents, have killed Christ. For a long time you have not believed in Him and you have opposed Him, but you are not yet lost, because you are still alive; you have time now for repentance; only come now. You should have come long ago, of course, but come now; your days are not yet ended; the last day is still to come."[33]

But Augustine knew that the Jews were not coming, that in fact they were flourishing in their own manner throughout the Roman world. Though relatively brief, his attempt to explain their survival in diaspora was his most original contribution to Christian thought regarding Jews; its impact on European Jewish history was immeasurable, in that it shaped papal policy into modern times. The statement appears in his monumental composition, the *City of God*, a Christian interpretation of world history in the context of a defense against pagan critics. Augustine declares that the Jews were dispersed not only to punish them but so that they might fulfill a destined role as "testimony," or witness, to Christian truth: "They were dispersed all over the world—for indeed there is no part of the earth where they are not to be found—and thus by the evidence of their own Scriptures they bear witness for us that we have not fabricated the prophecies about Christ." Everyone except them understands that their own Scriptures, which they preserve even though they cannot read them rightly, testify time and again to the coming of Christ and his kingdom; and it is in order that people everywhere may learn about Christ that the Jews have been widely dispersed, and preserved, despite their manifest unworthiness:

> [F]or we recognize that it is in order to give this testimony, which, in spite of themselves, they supply for our benefit by their possession and preservation of those books, that they themselves are dispersed among all nations, in whatever direction the Christian Church spreads. . . . For if they lived with that testimony of the Scriptures only in their own land, and not everywhere, the obvious result would be that the Church, which is everywhere, would not have them available among all nations as witnesses to the prophecies which were given beforehand concerning Christ.[34]

From these statements popes and bishops drew the logical conclusion that Jews should be made to behave with appropriate humility but ought not be physically abused or tormented. As we shall see, one consequence was that Jews learned to depend on the higher clergy for protection when threatened by Christians who were not familiar with Augustine's writings.

Although Augustine could not have known it, by his time the struggle to achieve dominance over Judaism was all but won. The final decades of the fourth century and the first few decades of the fifth appear in retrospect as a transitional time from the ancient to the medieval period—a time when Roman civilization was already feeling the impact of the barbarian incursions that would transform it entirely. By then, too, Christianity had achieved the status of imperial religion. Although several more centuries would pass before its absolute triumph was beyond question, already in the early fifth century the Roman world had become largely Christian; and thus began the medieval period, the thousand or so years during which there emerged a new civilization, the product of the Greco-Roman heritage as shaped, interpreted, and transformed by Christianity.

For the Jews who were to become an integral but distinctively peculiar element in that civilization, the commanding reality was that they were now living in a Christian world. Ideas and images that had found expression during the formative Christian centuries—most particularly the doctrine of replacement and all that this entailed—were to play a determinative role in European Jewish history, shaping relations between Jews and Christians right up to our own time.

2

THE FIRST EUROPEAN JEWS

In the year 313, Constantine, emperor of the Romans in the West, and his eastern counterpart, Licinius, issued an edict declaring that thenceforth in the Roman Empire there was to be freedom of religious expression—even for Christians.[1] One year earlier, Constantine had won the imperial crown by defeating a rival in a great battle not far from Rome, and his biographers later claimed that he attributed his victory to newly awakened faith in the Christian God. Whatever the case, he continued to look with favor on the new religion, and it appears that just before his death in 337 he converted. By the close of the century, Christianity had been formally adopted as the imperial religion, and emperors had begun issuing edicts to combat the insidious influences of heretics and Jews.

Already by then the Roman Empire was well into its renowned decline, but it was still the undisputed center of civilization in its own part of the world. It included all the lands bordering on the Mediterranean and much more, including Spain, the part of Britain that is now England, and the great territory of Gaul all the way to the Rhine. Much of this land was sparsely settled, though, and in some areas epidemics had depleted the population even more. It was becoming especially difficult to maintain control over frontier regions, where for many years military garrisons had been staffed mainly by men recruited from local tribal groups.

During the final decades of the fourth century, "barbarian" peoples living in what is now eastern Europe began moving westward in large numbers, soon constituting a threat to the empire that would in time prove literally overwhelming. Most were ethnically and linguistically

Germanic, but they did not identify themselves by a single name; they were divided into any number of semiautonomous kin groups, loosely linked into tribal assemblages. Some were nomadic pastoralists who centuries earlier had made their way southward from homelands in Scandinavia and settled in territories north of the Danube. They included such peoples as the Visigoths, Ostrogoths, Burgundians, Lombards, and Vandals. Others, most notably the Franks, were relatively peaceful farmers who moved gradually westward, seeking better farmlands and more secure lives. Pressing relentlessly behind these groups, compelling them to move ever westward, were the most fearsome barbarians of all: the Huns, nomadic predators ready to ravage anyone who stood in their path.

Waves of nomads—Visigoths, Burgundians, Vandals—fought their way into Gaul during this tumultuous time; but the people who would ultimately replace them all were the Franks, whose arrival in the region was less spectacular but far more momentous. Long in contact with Romans in the frontier regions bordering on the Rhine, relatively familiar with civilized ways and inclined to accommodate, the Franks wanted to settle in warmer lands where they could farm without disturbance. Some received land when they retired from military garrisons, but most simply made their way unobtrusively into sparsely populated regions. By the late fourth century, they had become a substantial component of the population of northern Gaul.

At Tournai, a town in what is now southern Belgium, a Frankish tribal leader named Childeric established himself and gained renown by warring successfully against competitors. He claimed descent from a chiefly ancestor named Merovech, and his successors were for that reason known as Merovingians. When he died in 482, his sixteen-year-old son Clovis inherited the mantle of leadership. It would be stretching a point to call the teenaged Clovis a king, but less than thirty years later he was to die as such—the first and greatest of the Merovingian kings of Gaul. For by then most of that great territory, the heartland of what we now know as western Europe, was in Frankish hands, and he was its acknowledged ruler.[2]

Sometime around the year 500, Clovis, by then already a powerful and ambitious headman, made a historically momentous journey from Tournai to the nearby town of Rheims, where, along with a legion of his barbarian warriors, he underwent conversion to Christianity— most significantly, to the orthodox Christianity of the Roman Church. He thereby became the only Germanic ruler to have accepted the Catholic faith; all the others—Goths, Burgundians, Lombards, and the rest—having by that time accepted Arian Christianity, the heretical doctrine that the supernatural humanity of Jesus the Son was entirely distinct from, and of a lesser order than, the divine nature of God the Father. Whether or not Clovis had personally pondered this question, his conversion to Catholic Christianity endowed him with immense political prestige as the foremost supporter of the Catholic clergy, who now viewed him as an acceptable successor to Roman rule, a powerful ally against the Arian invaders who still occupied much of Gaul. Their confidence was well placed. During the early years of the sixth century, Clovis and his successors, illiterate and only semicivilized, overran virtually all remaining outposts of Arian Christianity in Gaul and created a united Frankish kingdom, politically independent but firmly allied to the Roman Catholic Church.

Gaul in the sixth century was a sparsely populated territory, much of it still woodlands, occupied by subsistence farmers and a few wealthy estate owners. Gallo-Romans, over whom the Franks now ruled and with whom they were soon intermarrying, were themselves products of an amalgamation of Romans and the native Celtic peoples whom they had conquered when they moved into Gaul during the first century B.C.E. They were already Christians, for until just a few decades before the time of Clovis they had been subjects of the western Roman Empire, which had been Christian for more than a century. Thus by the sixth century there was emerging in what was to be the heartland of Europe a population of mixed ancestry and culture but nonetheless increasingly united by a common language (a Romance form of Latin) and, above all, by adherence to a common religion, Christianity as professed by the Roman Catholic Church.

The Pearl in the Oyster

Living among this nascent European population, interacting with others on a daily basis, on occasion even intermarrying, were another people, small in numbers but undoubtedly recognizable as a distinctive group. For although possessing nearly all qualifications for acceptance into the social order, they lacked the one that was becoming definitive: they were not, and would not become, Christians. We know essentially nothing about a Jewish presence in Gaul before the Roman era, but it is certain that Jews were already living in Rome by the first century B.C.E., possibly earlier, and soon thereafter in other parts of Italy and Greece.[3] Thus, as the Romans moved northward there may well have been Jews traveling with them, probably as merchants and traders prepared to accept the rigors of a frontier existence for the potential rewards of commercial activity in an expanding society.[4]

As to where they may have settled, and in what numbers, we can only surmise on the basis of very limited evidence. By the fifth century one of the liveliest regions of this imperial outpost was along the eastern frontier, in the Rhineland and its immediate vicinity, particularly the towns along the Rhine and Moselle rivers. There the Romans had established major garrisons that attracted more than an average number of merchants and artisans.[5] It seems likely that among them were Jewish merchants, men who traveled much of the time but may have begun to establish homes and families in the region. One clear bit of evidence in this regard: As far back as the year 321, the Roman emperor Constantine the Great had issued an edict in response to a request of the town councillors of Cologne, a prominent Rhineland settlement, granting them the right to nominate Jews to the council. As a concession to the Jews ("in order to leave them something of the ancient custom as a solace"), two or three men were to be permanently excused from duty, presumably to be free to attend to specifically Jewish community concerns.[6] It would appear, then, that Jews were present in sufficient numbers to have formed a community and that they were reasonably well accepted. Moreover, if there were Jews in Cologne, it seems more than likely that others had settled in such neighboring commercial centers as Mainz and Trier.

They were probably also living in a number of locations in central Gaul. As we have noted, most of the population everywhere was rural, and many towns of the time were hardly worthy of the name, having been battered by warfare and ruined by neglect: "mere dilapidated fortresses," one historian calls them.[7] Some—Paris, Orléans, Lyons, and a few others—endured, however, and even prospered in a modest way, having survived probably because they were surrounded by sturdy, virtually indestructible masonry walls,[8] and merchants naturally gravitated to such sheltered locations. But these were not fullfledged commercial centers; a more accurate term would be episcopal centers, for they were communities that grew up around cathedrals and were occupied mainly by clerical personnel.

Adjacent to the cathedral there was usually a marketplace to which local merchants would bring their modest wares. But in the more prominent and relatively prosperous towns there might also be seen other merchants of a more exotic type, most dealing in goods of higher value, buying and selling items that had traveled long distances and passed through the hands of several middlemen like themselves. Some were "Syrians" (i.e., eastern Mediterranean peoples) or Greeks, long accustomed to traveling far from their homelands. Others were Jews, probably more inclined to look upon Gaul as a new homeland, establishing residences along the Mediterranean coast and along rivers from Provence northward.

How much did Jewish commercial activity matter to the Merovingian economy? Were Jews a prominent element in an active economy, or were they marginal actors of no great importance? Despite arguments about causes and timing, historians agree that Merovingian Gaul was a society in economic decline well before the seventh-century Arab conquest of the Mediterranean, and that although commerce of sorts persisted throughout the period between the fifth and eighth centuries, it consisted mainly of transport of a limited number of items— spices, silks, and the like—from the Orient westward and movement of slaves in the opposite direction. They agree also that whatever may have been the relative vitality of commerce during the period, it was dominated by "Syrians" and Jews, but that after the Muslim conquests of the seventh century the former faded from the picture. Until the seventh century the homelands of "Syrian" merchants had been within the eastern Roman Empire, but Arab conquests brought them into the Islamic orbit, rendering them no longer welcome in Christian Gaul.

In contrast, most Jewish merchants, whatever their origins, had by then settled permanently in Gaul; it seems unlikely that significant numbers had arrived very recently from the eastern Mediterranean. Though they were surely in contact with Jewish merchants to the east, that was no longer their homeland; they were already what might be called "proto-European" Jews. Arab conquest of the Mediterranean in effect left Jews as the sole international merchants in Gaul, uniquely able to travel between the Christian and Muslim worlds for the simple reason that they were neither.

The answer to our question, then, seems to be that Jews were moderately important in economic life during Merovingian times and, as we shall see, more so from the late eighth to the tenth century. But relative to what preceded and followed, European economic life during the entire period from the fifth to the tenth century was dormant. That Jews and other peripheral peoples appear to have dominated commercial activity during these centuries only further emphasizes the point that this was a long economic hiatus.[9] It might be argued that Jews were instrumental in maintaining European commerce when no one else could or would. Certainly there were Frankish and other merchants, particularly in the north, but they were few in number. In short, although Jews undoubtedly contributed notably to the maintenance of commerce during these centuries, they were able to do so partly because the indigenous economy was so weakly developed that they were faced with little serious competition.

Although Jews were, as one historian puts it, "industrious, adaptable, orderly and intelligent," and although they spoke the language of the region and were not especially distinctive in appearance, they remained an alien element: "a society within a society, a pearl forever irritating the oyster."[10] The single characteristic that set them apart, of course, was their religion, but that made all the difference. It is ironic that as people whose habits and occupations drew them to towns, Jews came into regular contact with the one small segment of the population for whom they bore an altogether special significance. As we have noted, most towns were above all ecclesiastical centers, some being hardly more than a cathedral along with other buildings belonging to the clergy. Jews, living "within walls that stood under the protection of saints whom they would by no means propitiate,"[11] found themselves not only situated in uncomfortable proximity to bishops, abbots, and priests, but obliged to deal with clerical officials as the principal or sole sources of local authority. The significance of these circumstances for Jewish life can hardly be overestimated. For no matter how respectable, orderly, and useful they may have been, Jews were looked upon by their clerical neighbors as people whose very presence constituted a threat to Christian society. In one sense they were what might be called a symbolic threat, in that to bishops and priests they recalled the Christian struggle for self-definition through unequivocal separation from Judaism. But they were also a more immediate threat, for in a world where there were still countless souls to be won, they were still active proselytizers who sometimes competed successfully with Christian clergy. Largely dependent on semiliterate priests thinly distributed through an almost completely illiterate population, the Church was uncertain of its ability to hold the line against Jewish influences. The historian Bernhard Blumenkranz in particular has argued that Jews were vigorously seeking converts as late as the tenth century, and that much anti-Jewish legislation should be understood as a feature of the struggle for converts.[12] Another historian even states that most Jews in Merovingian Gaul "were almost certainly descendants of converts," but he provides no documentation.[13]

Both religious groups were competing for pagans, whether slaves or freemen, but the struggle extended even into the ranks of the Christian faithful. The later Roman emperors, driven by Christian zeal, issued a number of edicts designed to restrain Jews from activities that might threaten Christian dominance. Anxiety of this sort is even more apparent from the fifth century onward, when, as we shall see, most anti-Jewish legislation originated in ecclesiastical councils. The ultimate goal of the Church was of course to bring Jews, along with everyone else, into the Christian fold. But at times the immediate challenge was confronting Jews in the battle for converts.

In short, the picture is one of Jews holding their own astonishingly well in the struggle with Christianity—utterly overwhelmed, to be sure, in numbers and power, but remarkably tenacious, already demonstrating the familiar Jewish talent for survival. They must have represented a much deeper threat to Christian clergy than might be supposed for such a small number of people. As Jews they were coming to occupy the very role that had been the lot of Christians a few centuries earlier: that of the most obviously unassimilable element in society. At that early date the struggle between Christianity and Judaism did not appear as definitively decided as it does now, and to a rather beleaguered Christian clergy the ever-present Jews may well have epitomized their deepest anxieties.[14]

Laws and Legal Status

Even while the Franks were establishing themselves as the new rulers of Gaul, they were adopting much of the Roman legacy, including Roman law. Although they had their own legal code, they recognized the right of others, including Jews, to live according to the traditional imperial code. Until the end of the fourth century, while there was still an undivided Roman Empire, Jews residing in Gaul and neighboring regions had been Roman subjects, treated with reasonable equity and justice, even after the empire became officially Christian. But there can be no question that Christianization transformed their status forever. Prior to the fourth century, when Rome was still "pagan," Jews had been looked upon as a rather peculiar and potentially troublesome people, but little more. What the Romans found most annoying was the refusal of Jews to perform routine rituals of homage to the gods, rooted in their stubborn insistence that there was only one God and that he could not be represented in visual images. But the empire was, after all, an amalgam of diverse cultural types, and Romans would not benefit from persecuting Jews as long as they were well-behaved citizens.[15]

By the close of the fourth century, however, the situation had changed dramatically—one might say crucially. For by then Christianity had been adopted as the official religion, and imperial legislation now took note of Jews as one group that, along with various heretical Christian sects, required special provisions. The concerns expressed in the legislation reduce to five main categories: conversion in both directions, Jewish ownership of Christian slaves, intermarriage, sources of possible Jewish influences on Christian belief and practice, and the rights of Jews to live unmolested so long as they did not intrude into Christian domains. Violent assaults by Jews on Jewish converts to Christianity evoked perhaps the most passionate legal response. An early fourth-century law set the tone: "It is Our will that Jews and their elders and patriarchs shall be informed that if, after the issuance of this law, any of them should dare to attempt to assail with stones or with any other kind of madness—a thing which We have learned is now being done—any person who has fled their feral sect and has resorted to the worship of God, such assailant shall be immediately delivered to the flames and burned, with all his accomplices."[16] The phrase "worship of God" refers of course to Christianity.

Legislation relating to Jewish ownership of Christian slaves, obviously a source of anxiety and contention, appeared repeatedly from the fourth to the seventh century. A complete section of the Roman legal code is devoted to this matter alone.[17] The five laws in the section progress chronologically from careful circumscription of Jewish privileges to complete rejection of any Jewish ownership of Christian slaves. The fifth and final, issued in 423, declared: "No Jew shall dare to purchase Christian slaves. For We consider it abominable that very religious slaves should be defiled by the ownership of very impious purchasers."[18]

That these and other regulations were not being strictly enforced in sixth-century Gaul is evident from canons issued by several ecclesiastical councils (assemblies of bishops and other clergy) of the time. Their legislation regarding slave ownership and conversion exhibits the same progression from grudging and limited acceptance to complete prohibition. By 583 they were no longer willing to accept Jewish ownership of Christian slaves under any circumstances—even though they accepted enslavement of Christians by other Christians. "No Christian," they declared,

> must henceforth be slave to a Jew; and if a Jew has a Christian slave, any Christian can purchase him for twelve soldi, either in order to set him free, or to employ him as his own slave. If the Jew is not contented, and hesitates to accept the sum defined, the Christian slave may live with Christians where he will. If, however, a Jew is convicted of having wanted to persuade the Christian slave to apostasy, he loses the slave and the right to make a will.[19]

Twelve soldi would have been roughly a half-pound of silver, a modest payment.

Already by 388 a Roman law prohibited intermarriage between Jews and Christians: "No Jew shall receive a Christian woman in marriage, nor shall a Christian man contract a marriage with a Jewish woman." The subtle distinction suggested here is made explicit in the "interpretation" (explanatory detail) that follows: "By the severity of this law it is prohibited that a Jew should enjoy marriage with a Christian woman or that a Christian man should receive a Jewish woman as his wife."[20] Two sixth-century ecclesiastical councils in Gaul issued the same prohibition. In 533 they declared that there was to be no intermarriage, and that if any had already taken place, "it must be dissolved on pain of excommunication." Five years later, as an addendum to legislation concerning Christian slaves owned by Jews, and almost as though it were an afterthought, they stated: "Christians must not marry with Jews, nor even eat with them."[21]

An obvious conclusion that might be drawn from this legislation is that Christians and Jews were not only eating together at times but were even intermarrying. Even the most hostile legislation against a category of persons may reflect resentment of their social and economic status. Bernard Bachrach, author of a study of early medieval policies toward Jews, believes that much of the anti-Jewish legislation of the period can be read in this light: that in fact Jews in Gaul grew "in power and prestige" during the sixth century; and despite expectable hostility from the clergy, they were generally well accepted by most of the population.[22]

The upper ranks of the clergy, those who issued legislation, were recruited at this time largely from the Gallo-Roman elite, literate men steeped in the Gospels, who may have been trying to impose their own views on a Frankish population of less committed Christians. The clergy seem to have been wary of any contact with Jews. In 465 they declared at one of their earliest councils that members of the clergy should not eat with Jews (since the latter rejected Christian food), and later, as we noted, no one was to eat with them.[23] An edict of 583 declared that "Jews are not to enter the convents of nuns for any reason or any kind of business, or to have any conversations with nuns, or to be familar with them, whether secretly or otherwise."[24] The same council warned Jews not to appear in public during the Easter period and to be appropriately deferential to clergy: "From Thursday in Holy Week to the Easter festival . . . Jews may not show themselves on streets and public places, because they have done so to insult Christians.

Moreover, they must testify respect to all clerics, and must not sit down before priests, unless they are invited to do so."[25]

To balance this negative picture, it should be emphasized that many Roman laws relating to Jews, still operative in the Merovingian period, were intended to ensure their basic rights. There were, for example, regulations exempting synagogue officials from public service, affirming the right of Jews to assemble without hindrance, prohibiting attacks on Jews or desecration of synagogues, providing for repair when synagogues were damaged by hostile mobs (indication, of course, that at times this occurred), and releasing Jews from summons for public or private business on Saturday.[26] In short, as we have already had occasion to note, the general inclination during the entire period of the fifth to the seventh century was to grant Jews all ordinary civil rights, even while they were being regularly reminded of their pariah status (at least in the minds of the clergy) and warned that they must do nothing to obstruct the practice, propagation, and absolute domination of Christianity.

"O Faithless and Perverse Generation": Christian Proselytizing

If Jews had occasional success as proselytizers, the Christian clergy were by far the more determined warriors. For a time the Jews of a town might be subjected to more or less benign urging by the local clergy, but eventually they might insist that everyone either accept conversion or be expelled from town. Our best source for information here is the *History of the Franks*, by Gregory, bishop of Tours, who wrote with remarkable flair about his own times and personal observations and experiences. Jews appear surprisingly often in Gregory's history. He provides several accounts of conversion efforts, the most memorable being a description of his own "disputation" (religious debate) with a remarkable Jewish merchant.

In the year 581, Gregory reports, he traveled to a nearby village to greet the visiting king, Chilperic, grandson of Clovis. He must have visited Chilperic only as a matter of duty, since he considered the king irreverent and boorish. But Chilperic thought himself a proper Christian and may have wanted to impress the bishop with his piety. Just as

Gregory was about to depart, "there came in a Jew called Priscus, who was on familiar terms with the king, having acted as his agent for some of the purchases which he had made."

This was not to be a good day for Priscus. "The king put his hand on the Jew's head in a kindly way and said to me: 'Come along, Bishop, put your hand on him too.' The man drew back. 'O faithless and perverse generation,' said the king, 'why can you not comprehend what has been promised to you by the words of the prophets?'" Chilperic seems to have known how to proselytize Jews: by citing their own scriptures to prove that the Hebrew prophets foretold the appearance of Jesus. But either Priscus was a brave man or he understood that Chilperic valued his services highly, for he responded with astonishing boldness: "'God has no need of a Son, He has not provided Himself with a son and He does not brook any consort in His kingdom.'" Chilperic now pressed the point with a few lame quotations from Psalms and Isaiah, but Priscus stood his ground: "How should God be made man," he asked, "or be born of woman, or submit to stripes [lashes], or be condemned to death?"

This silenced the king, says Gregory, whereupon he himself joined the debate, showering Priscus with even more citations, including several from the New Testament. But to no avail: "Despite all my arguments, this wretched Jew felt no remorse and showed no sign of believing me. Instead, he just stood there in silence." Realizing that Priscus "could not be moved to compunction," Gregory and Chilperic let the matter drop; the bishop gave the king his blessing, Chilperic departed for Paris, and Priscus remained a Jew.[27]

Sadly, Priscus died a year or so after his encounter with Gregory— victim of a murder. In 582, Chilperic ordered that all Jews in his kingdom be baptized, and served as personal godfather to some of the converts. But Priscus, says Gregory, "could not by any persuasion be induced to accept the truth." He gained a respite with bribes, promising to reconsider after his daughter's forthcoming marriage—"although he had no intention of giving in." Meanwhile, he quarreled with one of the converts, a man named Phatyr; and one Saturday, while Priscus was walking with friends to the synagogue, his head wrapped in a prayer shawl, "and carrying no weapon in his hand, for he was about to pray according to the Mosaic law," Phatyr suddenly appeared, drew his sword, and killed Priscus and the others. Phatyr was permitted by Chilperic to flee the kingdom, but a few days later he too was killed—by kinsmen of Priscus.[28]

A grim tale, but with much to say about Jewish life. For one thing, both men had Latin names, suggesting that their parents (or perhaps they themselves) were inclined to at least some degree of acculturation. We learn that there was a synagogue in the town (not identified), meaning that there were at least ten Jewish men there, hence probably forty or more Jews altogether. We learn that Jews of the time owned weapons, knew how to use them, and were prepared to exact vengeance. Finally, of course, we learn that whatever their degree of acculturation, and whatever high status a few may have attained, all Jews were subject to conversion campaigns.

Gregory gives a detailed account of what happened in 576, when Avitus, bishop of Clermont, managed to gain one convert. On Easter Sunday the man walked in a procession of newly baptized Christians, all in white gowns. As they passed through the town gate, a Jew (perhaps standing on the wall above the gate) stepped from the crowd and, "no doubt put up to this by the Devil, tipped some rancid oil on the head of this new convert." People wanted to stone the offender, but the bishop, responsible for maintaining law and order, rescued him. Later that day, however, the infuriated mob destroyed the local synagogue, and soon thereafter the bishop sent a message to the Jews, which Gregory reports as follows: "I do not use force nor do I compel you to confess the Son of God. I merely preach to you and I offer to your hearts the salt of knowledge. I am the shepherd set to watch over the sheep of the Lord. It was of you that the true Shepherd, who suffered for us, said that He had other sheep, which are not of His fold, but which He must bring, so that there might be one flock and one shepherd." (This statement, which refers to a parable of Jesus recounted in the Gospel of John,[29] in fact applied originally not to Jews but to Gentiles, who were of course the sheep outside the Jewish fold being invited to join the new religious community.) "If you are prepared to believe what I believe," Avitus continued, "then become one flock, with me as your shepherd. If not, then leave this place." The Jews resisted for several days, but eventually, says Gregory, they were persuaded and sent this answer to Avitus: "We believe that Jesus Christ is the son of the living God, promised to us by the pronouncements of the prophets."

It goes without saying that however this beleaguered band replied to Avitus, it was surely not in those words. But it does appear that some converted, or at least went through the motions of conversion to avoid expulsion. The bishop was overjoyed, says Gregory, when "the whole company of Jews lay prostrate before him, begging for baptism." And when they had all been brought "into the bosom of the Mother Church," there was pure exaltation: "Candles flamed, lamps burned, and the whole city shone bright with the white-robed flock. The joy felt in Clermont was no whit less than that experienced long ago in Jerusalem when the Holy Spirit descended on the Apostles. More than five hundred were baptized."[30]

Aside from the hyperbole, the final sentence is open to question. Gregory was either misinformed or intentionally exaggerating, or else we have a miscopied text, for it seems impossible that a sixth-century town, with at most a few thousand inhabitants, had a population of five hundred Jews; fifty is a much more likely number. More significantly, some Jews resisted to the end: those who were not baptized, reports Gregory, moved to Marseilles, where presumably other Jews were prepared to take them in.

The most influential pope of the early medieval period, Gregory the Great, issued a statement in 591 that would be remembered by his successors, to the incalculable benefit of generations of European Jews. Writing to the bishops of Arles and Marseilles, Gregory said that he had learned from local Jewish merchants in Rome that many Jews in southern Gaul had been brought to baptism "more by force than by preaching," a practice that might have effects opposite to those intended: "the loss of the very souls which we wish to save." His advice to the bishops: "Let, therefore, your Fraternity stir up such men by frequent preaching, to the end that through the sweetness of their teacher they may desire the more to change their old life. For so our purpose is rightly accomplished, and the mind of the convert returns not again to his former vomit."[31]

As we saw in the actions of Chilperic, kings as well as bishops sometimes initiated conversion campaigns. One of the last of the Merovingians, Dagobert, is said to have ordered in 629 that all Jews in his realm either convert or be expelled—possibly because they were supporting a hostile political faction—but the evidence is thin.[32] Some historians have concluded that Dagobert thereby eliminated the Jewish community from Gaul, but it seems more likely that most Jews remained, doing what they could to survive in difficult circumstances.

The seventh and early eighth centuries were times of political chaos in Gaul; relatively few records remain, for Jewish or any other history, so that for a time the curtain falls on our story. By the mid-eighth century, though, Jews were clearly present in the region, and, as we shall see, were about to enter a period of growth and prosperity that would establish foundations for centuries of Jewish life thereafter.

· 3 ·

"THEY DISPLAY DOCUMENTS"

Jewish Life in the Carolingian Empire

Dagobert was the last of the Merovingians to reign with authority over the Frankish kingdom. After his death in 639, a number of territories broke away under local rulers, and for nearly a century thereafter the political map was in disorder: weak kings, few living beyond young adulthood, ruling over unstable realms. The historical record is sketchy, but there is at least one fragment of evidence for Jewish continuity during this period: a dedicatory funeral plaque from a synagogue wall, dated at about 700, was found in the town of Auch, in southwestern France; much of the text is in Latin, but it ends with the word *shalom* in Hebrew letters, and it is decorated with a picture of a ram's horn (shofar) and other Jewish ritual objects.[1] Jews probably did disappear from some locations. Judging largely from the absence of references to communities in surviving records, it appears that Jews in the Rhineland towns along the eastern frontier—Cologne, Mainz, and others—where some of the worst devastation occurred during the barbarian invasions of earlier centuries, were either killed or else abandoned their homes and fled westward into interior regions of Gaul where conditions were more favorable. In any event, it is certain that by the later decades of the eighth century there was again a flourishing Jewish community in what had been Merovingian Gaul. This may be attributable, of course, to fresh immigration, but it is equally likely that at least part of the community was descended from earlier settlers. Linguistic evidence points to the same conclusion.[2]

The real power during this century of political chaos shifted from kings to so-called mayors of the palace, administrators whose accumulation of power eventually relegated the nominal rulers to puppet status. In 687 one of these palace mayors consolidated much of Gaul under his personal control; and upon his death in 714, his bastard son, Charles Martel, rapidly established authority, moving into remaining territories and reigning over a united Gaul. He was succeeded by his son, known as Pepin the Short. In 747, Pepin deposed the last Merovingian puppet king, and in 751, with the pope's approval, declared himself king of the Franks. As a token of gratitude for the pope's support (and a well-aimed political tactic) he defeated the Lombards in Italy and delivered some of the conquered territory to the pope—the "Donation of Pepin," affirming the alliance between Frankish kings and the Catholic Church that had been initiated by Clovis.

Pepin died in 768, leaving two sons, one of whom soon died. The survivor, Charles (Carolus), instituted a long and remarkable reign during which the western Roman Empire was "reborn" as the Carolingian Empire, and Charles earned the name by which he is remembered: Charles the Great, or Charlemagne. He conquered territory all along his borders, and by the end of the century nearly all of what is now western Europe was under his hegemony. In the course of a visit to Rome at Christmas in the year 800, the pope crowned him emperor and declared the Western Empire once again in existence.

Charlemagne's foremost purpose was to unite the disparate peoples of his kingdom and to create a stable society with a sense of common destiny. The source of their potential unification was of course to be the Christian faith, consistent in ritual practice, properly managed by a well-regulated clergy. Theology as such was hardly his concern, but what he did understand was the capacity of a compelling and widely accepted religious faith to provide the necessary foundations for a stable social order. Since the poorly educated clergy of Gaul were not up to the task he had in mind, he invited to his court scholars from other lands and encouraged them to establish a center of Christian learning. The essential task of these men was not to create original materials but to copy texts accurately and to transmit a well-ordered Christian orthodoxy.

Considering Charlemagne's commitment to creating a thoroughly Christian society, it is remarkable that at no time in their entire European history did Jews experience better living conditions than they enjoyed during his reign and that of his son, Louis the Pious. Jews were encouraged to settle in imperial towns, where they were granted communal autonomy and protection. They were welcomed at the imperial court, on occasion serving as emissaries. They were encouraged to engage in commerce and were even employed as soldiers and trusted as frontier settlers in newly conquered Spanish territories.[3] They were permitted to testify in public courts, in cases involving Christians as well as Jews, and to take appropriate oaths on a Hebrew Torah. They were not only granted ordinary civil rights but were protected and encouraged to prosper. Aside from a few minor and not unreasonable restrictions, they were granted as much freedom as almost anyone enjoyed. The picture is indeed so favorable that the period encompassing the reigns of Charlemagne and Louis (768–840) appears as the high point of medieval Jewish history: a "springtime" after which their circumstances were never again as favorable. To understand this seemingly paradoxical situation—a world in which Jews thrived while everyone else was expected to be an observant Christian—we need to look more closely at this society and to think about how and why Jews played their particular role.

Protected Aliens

Carolingian society was organized hierarchically, and everyone of consequence, including the emperor, had obligations corresponding to his position in the hierarchy: those above received loyalty, and especially military service, from their social inferiors; in return, those beneath received favors and protection. Charlemagne's position at the top was symbolized by the requirement that every male inhabitant of his realm should swear an oath of lifelong loyalty and obedience. As in all such cases, this was a Christian oath, sworn on relics of saints.[4] How and where could Jews fit into such a social system?

By the year 800 there were at most some six to eight thousand Jews in the Carolingian Empire—only a small percentage of the world

Jewish population at the time[5]—but they were concentrated in towns where they could establish the social and commercial ties that were intrinsic to their way of life. Occasionally a Jew may have been a land-holder, and a few may have derived most of their income from vine-yards or even agriculture. But to understand Jewish life we must focus on urban communities. Jewish life was so completely dominated by commercial considerations that the locations of markets and of Jewish communities closely corresponded.[6] Nearly everyone thought of Jews in this connection, and such phrases as "Jews and other merchants" or "merchants including Jews" were commonplace in documents.[7] The most prominent Jewish communites were situated along rivers—the Rhone, Rhine, Loire, and others—that provided access to and from the Mediterranean, and in major seaport towns at the mouths of rivers. For example, from the Mediterranean ports of Narbonne and Mar-seilles goods could be transported via Arles up the Rhone to Lyons and beyond, then westward along the Loire to Orléans, Tours, and the Atlantic coast; or via the Moselle and Rhine to such commercial centers as Mainz and Cologne. In all of these towns large-scale, long-distance commerce was heavily in Jewish hands. There were equally important communities in towns functioning as crossroads centers for major trade routes combining overland with river transport and linking the empire, Spain, and the Mediterranean to eastern territories. Two such communities were at Verdun and Rheims; trade routes connecting Strasbourg, Mainz, Cologne, and other towns led toward Verdun and Rheims, whence there were connections to Lyons and down to the Mediterranean. Obviously goods moved along these routes in both directions.

The heart of the Carolingian Empire was the Rhineland, the center of urban life and commerce. Here were such towns as Cologne, Mainz, Worms, Speyer, and Trier—all major loci of Jewish settlement—and Aachen, where Charlemagne held court. At the same time other Jews were venturing into more distant regions and establishing settlements of almost equal importance. Along and beyond the eastern frontier there were developing trade networks extending outward toward Rus-sia and ultimately to the Orient. A major settlement appeared at Mag-deburg, for example, on the Elbe River in Saxony, at the frontier between the empire and Slavic territory. Others were in Prague and Regensburg, the latter providing access to commerce via the Danube to and from Hungary.

Clearly then, although some Jewish merchants may have confined their activities to their own or nearby towns, many were engaged in long-distance ventures requiring regular contact with (and dependence on) fellow Jews throughout the commercial network. So we can envision Jewish merchants as a circulating population in this largely static society: first, in the sense that they literally moved about far more than most people; and second, in the sense that they were responsible for transporting not only goods but probably information about other people, places, and events.

A few cautionary words are in order here. It is one thing to note the scope of Jewish commercial activitiy; it would be another to maintain that Jewish merchants dominated economic life during those centuries. The fact is that they did not—rather, we have a picture of a small number of resourceful individuals who found a rewarding niche for themselves. For it appears that the largest proportion of ordinary trade, particularly in such basic foodstuffs as grains, cheese, and fish, was in the hands of Christian merchants. Moreover, a great deal of petty trade in food and other everyday items took place among ordinary folk who had no need of professional intermediaries. In contrast, Jewish merchants specialized in ventures involving long-distance travel across political boundaries. For obvious reasons their principal commodities were exotic, expensive, and marginal to the ordinary economy. From the Mediterranean and the Orient they transported such items as silk, spices, dyed textiles, and papyrus—all obviously scarce and destined for sale to a wealthy elite.[8] Others dealt in furs, salt, weapons, and expensive wines.[9]

Finally, unfortunate to relate, some Jews were also transporting slaves, people captured mostly beyond the eastern boundaries of the empire, primarily for sale in Spain and the Middle East but also available to local purchasers. The slave trade probably peaked at about the time of the reign of Charlemagne's son, Louis, and although it would be too much to argue a direct connection, this was precisely the time when Jewish merchants were being teated with extraordinary favor.

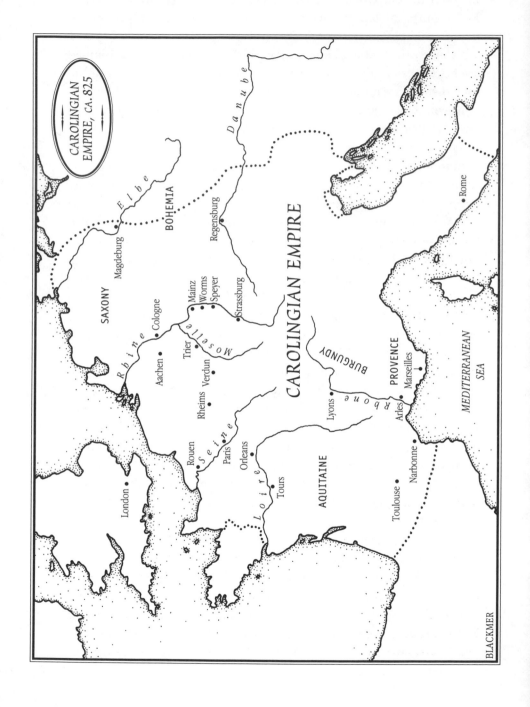

CAROLINGIAN EMPIRE, CA. 825

CAROLINGIAN EMPIRE

Danube

Elbe

BOHEMIA

Magdeburg

Regensburg

SAXONY

Cologne
Rhine

Mainz
Worms
Speyer

Strassburg

Moselle

Trier
Aachen

Verdun

Rheims

BURGUNDY

PROVENCE

Marseilles

MEDITERRANEAN
SEA

Rome

Seine

Rouen

Paris

Orleans

Lyons
Rhone

Arles

London

Tours

Loire

AQUITAINE

Narbonne

Toulouse

BLACKMER

Not surprisingly, slave trading has received rather little attention from Jewish historians, but it says something fundamental about the Jewish situation in medieval Europe. Slave caravans usually originated at the eastern frontier or beyond, forming at such major market centers as Prague and Regensburg, traveling to the two main slave trading centers of Mainz and Verdun, then southward to Lyons and Arles, and on to Narbonne, the point of departure for Spain and the Middle East.[10] Some slaves converted to Christianity, but even the enslavement of Christians was accepted, and "heathens" who converted were not freed on that account.[11] The clergy did try to ransom Christian slaves en route to Moslem lands, though, lest such people be permanently lost to the Christian fold. What the clergy most wanted to prevent was ownership of Christian slaves by Jews and especially conversion of any slave to Judaism. But they were particularly disturbed by Jewish slave merchants who were as willing to traffic in Christian slaves as in any other. Although battles were fought over ownership, the real conflict centered on whether Jewish merchants should be permitted to transport Christian converts, or even potential converts, to Islamic territories. In short, every slave in Jewish hands was a soul potentially lost to Christian salvation.

The obverse of the concentration of Jews in commerce was their virtual disappearance from agriculture and crafts. A few Jews who engaged in agriculture employed Christian laborers and sold their crops at markets. But most Jewish landowners were engaged in viticulture: grape growing for wine production. There were strong motivations for owning vineyards and producing wine. Jewish consumers required kosher wine—that is, wine produced and handled exclusively by Jews, for according to Talmudic law, wine handled or even poured by non-Jews was unfit for use. Prices for kosher wine were high, and Jewish producers stood to gain substantial profit from sales to other Jews. Moreover, the Christian nobility and higher clergy soon learned to appreciate the excellent quality of much of the non-kosher wine produced by Jews, and they too were willing to pay high prices. Care was taken to ensure that wines for Christian and Jewish buyers were kept separate.

Jewish involvement with land-based enterprise, such as it was, was thus clearly distinct from that of the Christian population. Whereas land ownership meant high status for Christians, Jews viewed land simply as another source of commercial enterprise. As the historian Irving Agus notes, Jews achieved social and political status "solely and completely in, and as members of, the Jewish community."[12] He mentions one Jew who avoided the road tolls imposed on merchants by presenting himself as "lord of a manor," but the fact was that the so-called lord was traveling like any other merchant.[13]

During earlier centuries some Jews were engaged in crafts—as tailors, glass makers, tanners, dyers, and so on. But by the ninth century this had become almost entirely a thing of the past. What evidence we have is negative: Jews employing Christians as laborers, builders, smiths, house servants, and even tailors.[14] Did they choose this situation, or was it unavoidable? The answer probably lies somewhere in between. In the final analysis, Jews, no matter how well treated, were looked upon as an alien people: alien in geographical origins and to some extent in physical type, alien in culture and social organization, and, most important, alien because they were descended from those whom the Gospels portrayed explicitly as slayers of the Redeemer. It was appropriate that if Jews were to live among Christians, it should be in a well-demarcated role; they should not, indeed could not, participate in the social order as full-fledged members. Given that premise— which, we should remember, the Jews themselves accepted in the sense that they not only acknowledged but insisted on their own exclusive identity[15]—it was "natural" that they would find a niche of their own. Moreover, as an occupation for people with uncertain prospects, commerce offered decided advantages. First, the Jewish community had already accumulated collective capital in the form of commercial knowledge and far-reaching commercial contacts; hence, virtually no one else was able to perform with Jewish efficiency, particularly in the realm of international trade. Second, commerce was lucrative in a society where very few individuals became wealthy, and tax payments had to flow steadily outward if communities were to be properly protected. Finally, because they were engaged in activity that served the interests of the high and mighty, Jews could count on protection and even favored treatment that would have been most unlikely otherwise.

"That the Earth May Not Swallow Me Up":
Legal and Political Status

The Carolingian Empire included people of diverse ethnic origins, many living at least in part under their own legal codes dating back several centuries. Jews were part of the group known as *cives Romani*, whose status as citizens was based on presumed residence in Gaul as "Romans" since the time before the Frankish occupation, and to whom traditional Roman law applied. But now there were new considerations. First, distinctions between "Romans" and other peoples—Franks, Saxons, Bavarians, and the like—were dissolving as all became citizens of Charlemagne's Christian empire. Second, Jews obviously had their own legal and social codes, which had been granted validity for their internal affairs. A final point was the need for an oath to be pronounced by Jewish witnesses and litigants in public courts. For all these reasons some Carolingian legislation applied specifically to Jews. But although a few laws might be interpreted as hostile, the most remarkable feature of Charlemagne's administration—and even more so of that of his son Louis—was the protection, patronage, and even favoritism granted to Jews, particularly with regard to their commercial enterprises.

Charlemagne's father, Pepin the Short, had established policy precedents in the mid-eighth century, following his conquest of portions of Aquitaine (southwestern France) that had been for several decades under Moslem rule. The newly acquired territory included the western Mediterranean coastal region called Septimania (modern Languedoc), a region where Jews were well-established merchants and also landowners. Several of his edicts granted Jewish landowners rights to retain hereditary properties and to employ Christian laborers—the latter a contradiction of Roman and canon law.[16] Predictably, this legislation elicited a response from the clergy. Aribert, archbishop of Narbonne (the principal city of Septimania and a center of Jewish life in the region), expressed his disapproval to the pope, Stephen III, who replied with emphatic agreement. "We have been distressed to the point of death," he informed Aribert, to learn that "these unbelievers" were granted privileges that had been "rightly abrogated as punishment for the crucifixion of the Savior."[17]

But the papacy was too dependent on Carolingian goodwill to offer more than token resistance to pro-Jewish policies, and neither popes nor archbishops were to resist successfully the decision of these monarchs to encourage Jewish settlement and enterprise. Charlemagne saw to it that Jewish merchants were restricted only when necessary and with legislation that cannot be called unfair. For instance, an edict issued in 806 and repeated in 814 with stronger sanctions (presumably because it was being violated) stated that neither Jews nor other merchants could purchase church treasures or accept them in pawn from the clergy. They are boasting, the edict declares, that they can obtain whatever they like. Aside from the obvious justification here, it is noteworthy that the edict was not addressed to Jews alone. In any event, after 814 punishment for such purchases was so severe— confiscation of all property and amputation of the right hand—that the practice must have ceased. Another edict of 814 stated that Jews were not to accept Christians as human pledges for debts (presumably to be sold into slavery if the debtor defaulted). Finally, in the same year it was decreed that Jews were not to mint coins or to sell wine and staples privately at their homes but were to conduct business only in public markets—probably to promote stable coinage, proper taxation, and open access to wares.[18]

A new oath for Jews, also instituted in this final year of Charlemagne's reign, recognizes Jewish religious requirements. When appearing as a litigant or witness in court, a Jew was to wrap himself from head to foot in his prayer shawl, hold a Hebrew Torah in his right hand, and declare as follows: "So help me God, the God who gave the Law to Moses on Mount Sinai, and that the leprosy of Naaman the Syrian may not come upon me as it did upon him, and that the earth may not swallow me up as it swallowed Dathan and Abiron, in this case I have committed no evil against you."[19]

Some indication of how far Jews might be trusted in matters of state is provided by an account of the experiences of a Jew known only as Isaac, who in 797 traveled as a member of Charlemagne's embassy to Baghdad to establish political relations with the caliph, Harun al Rashid. After two Christian noblemen, probably the principal emissaries, died during the journey, Isaac assumed leadership. With their mission completed, the survivors returned some five years after their departure (accompanied by an elephant as a gift from the caliph). Isaac may have been included primarily for his abilities as an interpreter, but it also likely that there were advantages to traveling with someone who could expect hospitality and assistance from Jewish communities along a route extending far beyond the imperial boundaries.[20]

Although Charlemagne clearly did all he could to encourage Jewish merchants, he appears not to have questioned the accepted principle that Jews should not occupy official positions or otherwise exercise power over Christians. Above all, they were not to seek converts among Christians or anyone else. They could not own Christian slaves, although others were acceptable. A Christian who converted to Judaism in order to marry a Jew was considered an adulterer, and any Christian who converted could not will property to heirs.[21] The overall strategy seems clear: Jews were to be encouraged to play their customary role but not to step out of it. On balance, however, these regulations and restrictions seem modest enough when ranged against the substantial protection and privileges that were accorded to Jews.

With that much said, it seems self-evident that despite their extraordinarily favorable situation, Jews were looked upon as a marginal people, uncommonly resistant to conversion and hence to full incorporation into Christian society—but, paradoxically, valuable for that very reason. Carolingians, if they pondered the matter at all, must have had to file Jews in a separate mental compartment and to accept their presence in Christian society as a puzzling feature of an imperfect world: if Jewish apartness was proof of the truth of Christianity, Jewish persistence was a source of uncertainty about that very truth.

Halcyon Years:
Life under Louis the Pious (814–840)

Although conditions of life for Jews were good under Charlemagne, during the reign of his son, known as Louis the Pious, they reached a high plateau possibly unique in Jewish history. The situation seems to have been precisely right for them: a mild and well-disposed emperor; an imperial court and landed elite who wanted slaves and other appurtenances of wealth and high status; and a society still overwhelmingly rural, in which very few Christians were equipped to compete in import-export commerce. In any event, Louis moved well beyond his father in granting Jews not only encouragement for their commercial pursuits but also extraordinary freedom in matters relating to the ongoing antagonism between Christianity and Judaism. His own court at Aachen, already a center for Jewish settlement in his father's time, was now even more welcoming. It appears that in turn Jews faithfully supported Louis in the bitter political struggles that plagued the final decade of his reign.

Jewish merchants were protected even at the risk of antagonizing others, including government officials and clergymen. Imperial documents issued to individual Jewish merchants were based on a model (called a formulary) which guaranteed their receiving substantial privileges. They were exempted from tolls levied at roads or town gates, rivers, bridges, and ports. They could not be required to provide food, lodging, or horses for government officials. They were exempted from labor on public service projects. They were even declared exempt from responsibility for damage to fields in the course of their travels. Everyone was enjoined against harming or coercing them, and they were to be permitted to conduct their business affairs without obstruction.[22] An imperial administrator called *magister Judaeorum* was assigned to regulation of matters pertaining to Jews, his primary role being not to restrain them but to protect them against mistreatment.[23]

But the most radical of Louis's policies were those relating to the question of how much influence and control Jews were to exercise among Christians. In effect, he reversed legislation that had been operative for some five hundred years, appointing Jews to positions as government officials and tax collectors. Even more remarkable, though, was his legislation concerning employment of labor, particularly slaves. Jews were still not permitted to purchase Christian slaves for their own use, but that was just about the only restriction remaining. They were now permitted to employ free Christian laborers. Moreover, not only could they purchase pagan slaves but they could refuse to have them baptized—and, if they chose, could even circumcise them and convert them to Judaism. Since Jewish law required that a slave be either converted within a year or released, this was a concession with major consequences; in addition to the obvious implications, it meant that Jews might undertake large-scale agricultural enterprises. Anyone who tried to interfere with the rights of Jewish slaveholders was to be punished.

As if this were not enough to infuriate the clergy, Louis also declared that markets should not be held on Saturday but were to be permitted on Sunday. In addition, Jews were granted startling latitude in their role as potential challengers to Christianity: they were permitted to preach in public, to dispute publicly with Christians, and even to distribute literature promoting their own religious views.[24] Whether any Jews actually ventured into such risky undertakings is another question.

Louis also instituted a revised court oath for Jews that, as Bernard Bachrach observes, "was even more thoroughly Jewish in spirit than the one instituted by his father." It ran as follows: "I swear to you by the living and true God and by the holy law that the Lord has given to the blessed Moses on Mount Sinai, and by the good Lord, and by the pact of Abraham that God gave to the children of Israel, and so that the leprosy of Naaman the Syrian may not cover my body, and so that the land may not swallow me up alive as it did Dathan and Abiron, and through the arc of the alliance that appears in the heavens to the children of man, and the holy place where holy Moses stood and where the blessed Moses received the holy law, I am not guilty in this case."[25]

"A Disgusting Insolence":
Bishop Agobard and the Jews of Lyons

During the middle years of Louis's reign, a conflict developed between one of the most prominent clergymen of the century, Agobard, archbishop of Lyons, and the Jews of his diocese. In the course of events, Agobard wrote a set of letters defending his own actions and attacking the Jews, memorable now because they are among the most informative surviving sources on Jewish life in Carolingian times. The conflict began when Agobard tried to convert Jewish children and servants and slaves belonging to Jews, but the entire affair was connected with his outspoken opposition to Louis's policies relating to political unification and the status of the Church. Agobard insisted that Christianity must be the foundation of civic unity and that conversion campaigns and suppression of heresies should be accepted as essential public policies.

He viewed Louis as well intentioned but weak and politically inept, too inclined to accept loose moral standards in his court, too well disposed toward Jewish merchants who supplied the court with luxuries.

The affair began in 820, apparently after the Jews of Lyons had complained to the imperial court that Agobard was trying to convert their children. Agobard responded with a letter entitled "Epistle on the Baptism of Hebrews," arguing that he was acting appropriately, ministering only to children who expressed willingness to accept baptism. Several parents sent their children away to the Jewish community at Arles, but he was having some success nonetheless and was planning a baptism ceremony for Easter.[26]

Agobard also began soliciting slaves belonging to Jews, both pagans and converts to Judaism. A slave converted to Judaism could not be sold out of the Jewish community; the fine for this, imposable by a Jewish court, was ten times the selling price. So the lines were clearly drawn: Agobard wanted to convert slaves to Christianity; the Jews were required to convert their slaves to Judaism and to retain them.[27]

The Jews appealed to the emperor, who dispatched his *magister Judaeorum,* a man named Evrardus, to reprimand Agobard, which he did, making it clear that there was to be no interference in Jewish affairs. Frustrated and confused, Agobard traveled to Aachen to argue his case in person. Two abbots and a count heard his presentation, then reported to the emperor while he waited. Eventually he was summoned to the imperial presence, only to hear the original reprimand repeated and to be curtly dismissed. He returned to Lyons, "weighed down with embarrassment and shame," and wrote another letter, "A Solemn Deliberation and Entreaty Regarding Baptism of Slaves of the Jews," dated at 822 or 823.[28] What are we to do, he asked, when faced with people who want to be Christians even though they are owned by Jews? They have learned our language, they know about our religion and are impressed with its solemn services; they are drawn to the Church and are asking for baptism. Are the Jews to be permitted to possess the souls of these individuals as well as their bodies, just because they have paid a few coins for them? He would even ransom them, but the Jews refused. What then was he to do? If he granted baptism, he would be defying the imperial emissaries and, he hinted, might even be placing himself in personal danger; if he refused, he risked eternal damnation for himself as well as for the unfortunate slaves.

The struggle simmered along for several years. Local priests, supported by Agobard, tried to convert slaves over the protests of their Jewish owners. Soon afterward, imperial emissaries arrived, forcibly returned slaves to their owners, and threatened the priests. Agobard wrote another letter of protest, arguing now that he was not even trying to convert Jews, only their slaves, but that he was being prohibited from achieving his essential mission of rescuing souls for salvation. Louis replied with additional edicts reaffirming Jewish privileges and threatening punishment for anyone who resisted. Agobard now responded with yet another letter, "On the Insolence of the Jews," discoursing bitterly not just on the Jews of Lyons but on Jews in general.[29] Why, he wanted to know, was he being publicly humiliated when his only offense was trying to rescue Christian souls? He had warned against allowing Christian slaves or servants to come under Jewish influence. He knew for a fact that Christian women serving in Jewish households were observing the Jewish sabbath and working on Sunday; not only that, they were eating meat during Lent. He had warned also that Jewish butchers were selling inferior meat that Jews themselves had rejected. Likewise, he had exposed the Jewish practice of maintaining separate barrels of obviously poor wine for sale to Christians.

The Jews, he continued, are behaving with outrageous arrogance. They maintain that the emperor esteems them because they are descended from the biblical patriarchs. They claim that some of the most eminent members of the imperial court attend synagogues because they find the services so attractive. They are presumptuous and ostentatious: their women parade about in gowns said to have been gifts from ladies at the court, and they themselves boast that they can build as many synagogues as they like, despite legislation to the contrary. They persuaded the imperial emissaries to change market day from Saturday to Sunday, pretending that this would be more convenient for Christians, but of course it has meant interference with the usual peasant practice of coming to town for a full market day on Saturday, attending church on Sunday, then returning home.

As a final note Agobard added a postscript remarking that he had spoken with a young man, an escapee from slavery in Spain, who said that he had been kidnapped as a child by Jews. The local people said that Jews were still engaging in the practice and that captured boys suffered injuries too terrible for words.[30]

The ultimate outcome of this conflict is unknown, but it seems unlikely that Agobard ever gained satisfaction. Whatever the immediate motives of the Christian actors on both sides, Agobard's most cherished goals—unification and stablization of the empire and establishment of Christianity as the unquestionable foundation of civic identity—no doubt transcended his dealings with Jews. But in a sense the Jews with whom he came into such bitter conflict must have represented all that he found distasteful in the court of Louis the Pious: what he perceived as its moral laxity and weak discipline, its love of material splendor, its lack of understanding that eternal life was granted only to those who sought and deserved it. He would have been dismayed, no doubt, to know that we now read his letters as witness to how well Jews were accepted in his society.

Once again, though, we should not be misled into assuming that Jews were favored for any reason other than their usefulness. Agobard, for whom politics and religious orthodoxy were inseparable, rightly understood Christian faith and ritual to be the foundations of empire, and he must have viewed Jews as pernicious obstacles in his path. Louis too knew how essential it was that he rule over a Christian domain, but apparently he saw no conflict between appropriate piety and a life enhanced by the kinds of material comforts that Jewish merchants could best provide.

Crossing Over: Bodo-Eleazar

One of the most notable conversions to Judaism in European history involved a young deacon named Bodo, a chaplain at Louis's imperial court. Bodo was an educated man of noble birth, well favored at court, with prospects for high office in the Church. In 838, when he was in his mid-twenties, he departed for Rome, supposedly on a religious pilgrimage, accompanied by a nephew and a retinue of servants. The accounts of what happened thereafter differ, but at some point in the journey Bodo announced his intention to convert to Judaism. Why he reached this decision is uncertain; he may have concluded that he could no longer accept Christian doctrine, but it is equally likely that, having entered clerical training as a boy, he realized later that he did not want to live as a celibate. He later admitted that, despite vows of celibacy, during his years at court he had engaged in many love affairs.[31]

In any event, he journeyed not to Rome but to Saragossa, a town in northern Spain (under Muslim rule) where there was a prominent Jewish community, and there he underwent conversion to Judaism, including circumcision and adoption of the name Eleazar. His nephew was persuaded to convert as well, but the hapless servants were sold into slavery. Bodo-Eleazar soon married a Jewish woman of Saragossa and settled into his new identity. When Louis the Pious learned the story he was profoundly distressed but could do nothing.

Plunging with fervor into his new identity, Eleazar engaged two years later in a formal disputation with a Spanish Christian theologian named Paulus Alvarus (ironically, a descendant of converts from Judaism) on the question of whether Jesus fulfilled biblical prophecies regarding the Messiah. He also issued anti-Christian polemical tracts for a number of years thereafter, causing such a stir that Spanish Christians, fearing that a conversion campaign was being mounted against them, appealed to Frankish secular and religious authorities for assistance. Nothing seems to have come of all this, other than that the story of Bodo-Eleazar was often retold to show what could happen when an emperor treated Jews too leniently.[32]

CULTURAL COUNTERPOINT

Later Ninth and Tenth Centuries

Charlemagne had left only one living son when he died, but Louis left three, and that spelled doom for the empire. Louis's widow, Judith, was determined that her son Charles should inherit a territory of his own, and of course the other two surviving sons, Louis's offspring by his first wife, were equally intent on receiving their shares. After several years of struggle, the matter was settled for a time by a compromise that in effect ended the life of the empire. According to the Treaty of Verdun in 843, the eldest son, Lothar, was to be "emperor," but he would rule over only the central region of what had been his father's empire: the territory bounded roughly by the Rhine to the east and the Rhone to the west (Lorraine and Burgundy), and extending southward to include much of the Mediterranean coastal region (Provence) and parts of northern Italy. This "Middle Kingdom" included many cities with influential Jewish communities: Mainz, Rheims, Troyes, Lyons, Arles, and others. (It became known as Lotharingia, a name that would enter Yiddish as Loter.) Lothar's brother, called Louis the German, ruled over an East Frankish Kingdom extending from the Rhine into Saxony and Bavaria. Their young half-brother, later called Charles the Bald, ruled over a West Frankish Kingdom, embracing much of what is now France and extending southward into Carolingian territory in northern Spain. But further deaths and divisions over the next few decades led to the disappearance of Lothar's inheritance, and by the tenth century there were only two territories: in effect what would become France and Germany.

Adding immensely to political instability were fierce assaults from three sides: North African Muslim pirates raiding the Mediterranean region; mounted Magyar warriors invading from what is now Hungary; and, worst by far, the Norsemen, or Vikings, who from the mid-ninth century onward descended from Scandinavia, overwhelming everyone in their path and creating unimaginable havoc.

Nothing specific is known about the effects of these events on the Jewish population, but surely merchants must have suffered heavy losses of commercial goods and property. To add to their troubles, they found themselves sometimes accused of traitorously assisting Vikings or Muslims in their assaults on Christian towns. That Jews were secretly allied with Muslims was a commonly held belief that would gain strength as time went on. There may have been some truth to these accusations, since the struggle to survive at times may have led Jews to cooperate with invaders.[1]

France: A Fragmented Land

Faced with endless battering by ferocious enemies, late ninth- and early tenth-century West Frankish kings steadily lost control over most of their land, and with it their royal authority. What we now call France became a cluster of more than fifty loosely associated territories, each dominated by a duke or count whose absolute local authority was legitimated by his ability to defend himself and those who served him. Powerful lords of this kind owed nominal allegiance to the king, who remained in a formal sense the lord at the summit of a hierarchy. But the king fully controlled only his own limited domain, a rather small territory in the region around Paris; and his actual power, such as it was, now depended on the willingness of his noble vassals, some of whom ruled over more territory than he did, to provide military assistance when called upon.

When the last Carolingian king died childless in 987, he was succeeded by a duke named Hugh Capet, first of the so-called Capetian dynasty that would rule France for some four centuries. But Hugh and his successors were hardly more powerful than their predecessors; they too were confined to a modest royal domain, and they too depended on the goodwill of other lords for whatever authority they could exercise.

For the Jews of France recourse to authority no longer applied beyond the local level; they had to stay in the good graces of the local lord or suffer the consequences. In troubled times his personal whims and prejudices might determine the fate of a community. At best the situation was precarious: amicable lords died and were replaced by brothers or sons with new plans for how best to extract wealth from Jews; relationships between lords shifted and with them loci of power; today's dependable arrangement might not work nearly as well tomorrow. As always, Jewish security was best served by a strong central administration committed to preserving civil order—the situation under the most capable Carolingians. But that had become a thing of the past, and Jews in France now had to function in a much less favorable political climate.

Germany: A New Holy Roman Empire

Germany by this time was a politically distinct region, better integrated than France and more stable, particularly because it was out of the path of Viking raids. German monarchs (who were still members of the Carolingian line) remained relatively strong, although the throne was no longer occupied by anyone of the stature of Charlemagne or Louis.

In 911 the last Carolingian king died, at age seventeen, and German barons began choosing kings from among their number. The second of these was the duke of Saxony, who ruled as Henry I, a capable man who repelled Magyar invasions, consolidated his rule over Lorraine (the region that had once been Lotharingia), and established a new dynasty. He was succeeded by his son, Otto I, known as Otto the Great, whose reign marked a turning point in German history. Otto saw to it that local barons and bishops retained their authority only as his representatives. In 955 he defeated the Magyars at a major battle in Bavaria, thereby effectively ending this last great threat to his kingdom. Soon afterward he moved into Italy to rescue the pope from a local enemy and as a reward was crowned emperor of a reconstituted Holy Roman Empire—no longer quite as extensive as Charlemagne's domain but large enough, embracing Germany, Lorraine, more than half of Italy, and tributary states in Burgundy, Denmark, and Bohemia, as well as other territories on the eastern frontier.

Otto's empire was relatively stable and peaceful, free from the threat of barbarian invasions, and favorable to progress in agriculture, commerce, and industry. For the Jewish population this social and economic environment provided more security and prosperity than were probably available anywhere else in Europe. Like their counterparts in France, German Jewish settlements were small, but they flourished on the same foundations of mutual dependence and mercantile talent. The largest communities may have attained a size of nearly a thousand by the end of the tenth century.

Although subject as in France to the authority of local lords and bishops, the Jews of Germany could depend on the presence of a powerful monarch who maintained a policy of general toleration. As in France, they were prominent as town merchants wealthy enough to attract the cupidity of the authorities. In 965, Otto I granted the archbishop of Magdeburg full jurisdiction and taxation privileges over "Jews and others locating there as merchants," and his son, Otto II, granted a similarly worded concession to the same town in 973.[2] Jewish physicians enjoyed excellent reputations here as elsewhere, and the nobility and higher clergy often sought them out for personal care.[3] Jews thus continued to be accepted as useful, even though culturally alien and socially distinct.

Occasionally, as might be expected, a clergyman placed conversion of Jews above all other considerations. In 936, for example, the archbishop of Mainz asked the pope for permission to offer the Jews of his town a choice between baptism and expulsion. The fact that he saw fit to address the question to the pope suggests in itself that such ultimata were exceptional for this time and place, but the pope seems to have found the prospect of expulsion quite plausible. He responded that the archbishop's duty was "to preach without ceasing, with sagacity, with the prudent counsel of God, and with reverence, faith in the Holy Trinity and faith in the mystery of the Lord's putting on flesh." If that most unpromising tactic proved successful, everyone should thank the Lord "with praises beyond counting." If not, then expulsion might be in order.[4] Apparently the archbishop decided that the more prudent course was to go on preaching indefinitely, and for the time being the Jews of Mainz were permitted to remain unconverted.

It was in the Rhineland region, in northwestern Germany not far from France, that Jews first began speaking their own dialect of German, the ancestor of what we now know as Yiddish. A natural outgrowth of the fact that Jews were in effect a society within a society, Yiddish emerged as a complex blend of several languages, a new form of native speech for Ashkenazic Jews. The very fact that they now spoke their own language tells us that whatever their level of everyday interaction with Christians, Jews had a social and cultural existence of their own, and that their primary reference group was undoubtedly the Jewish community. Yiddish was a Jewish variant of tenth-century German, but from its beginnings it was a unique creation, with elements reflecting the entirety of Jewish history and experience. With words from Hebrew, Aramaic, French, and Italian as part of the vocabulary, Yiddish became the international language of an international people, and it soon departed clearly from its German origins, developing a style and cadence all its own.[5]

Jews in the Feudal World

By the late tenth century, particularly in France, the elite population of western Europe was developing the form of social and political organization that we call feudalism. As a way of life it contrasted remarkably with just about everything that was coming to characterize Jewish society. The two coexisted in a kind of symbiotic relationship, in which the weaker served the needs of the stronger; but, as we shall see, the equilibrium, such as it was, could not last indefinitely.

The key differences between Jewish and feudal societies can be summarized in a few words: Feudal society was land-centered, each baron and his followers being attached to their own particular region and concerned with rather little beyond. It was rigidly stratified, hierarchical, firmly authoritarian, and geared toward military efficiency. Each baron looked to his own knights for military support and defense; in return he granted them land of their own and a modest share of his wealth and prestige. Theirs was strictly a men's world in which military efficiency and bravery counted above all else.

Jews lived in a world of urban communities, in itself enough to distinguish them clearly. But they were oriented not merely to their own immediate communities. Their society was radial, in the sense that they maintained intimate ties and steady correspondence with neighboring Jewish communities. They were at least nominally egalitarian, with everyone (or at least every man) having some say in public affairs. They recognized only scholarship, commercial ability, and skill in negotiation as sources of prestige and authority. Above all, they were geared toward techniques of survival in a social environment where Jews were heavily dependent on the good graces of Christian lords who never granted more than qualified toleration.

To understand more fully how distinctive—and alien—Jews were in the feudal world, we have to examine both societies more closely. We begin with feudal society, then turn to what I call its cultural counterpoint.

An early form of feudal society, headed by the Carolingian emperor, had already appeared in the ninth century; but, as we noted, it was only by the late tenth century, when the most powerful barons became almost entirely independent, that feudalism became the definitive form of social organization in much of western Europe—particularly the region between the Loire and Rhine rivers, which was also the heartland of Ashkenazic Jewry.[6] Feudalism was rooted in a reciprocal relationship: a wealthy and powerful lord received homage and pledges of loyalty (fealty) from knights who swore to defend him and his lands from all enemies; in return, he might endow them with a portion of his land, but at the very least they shared in the bounty that he extracted from the multitude of peasants who worked the land for him. The social structure was hierarchical; powerful landowners with many knights might themselves owe fealty to even greater lords. Relationships were intrinsically authoritarian: lords commanded their knights, and everyone who possessed arms (*bellatores*, warriors) held complete power and authority over those who labored in the fields (*servi*), who depended on lords and knights for whatever security life offered. The peasants were of course vulnerable to every form of exploitation and had to endure oppression from those who were supposedly protecting them. Paralleling these two social orders, but ranking with those who fought, were those who prayed (*oratores*), the bishops, abbots, and lower clergy. At its upper reaches this order included men who were themselves lords, possessors of land, laborers, and knights, participants in the worldly struggles for power that they had explicitly renounced. At times some of them even rode to war.

Knights were, above all, warriors. Although hunting, tournaments, and life's familiar physical pleasures were their recreations, their true calling—the focus of their lives and the source of their sense of personal worth—was warfare: face-to-face combat by mounted men in armor for whom the supreme experience was to confront and perhaps kill one another in personal encounters. For such men there could be only one ultimate virtue: fearlessness. They were Christians, of course, but that meant little in their everyday lives, for surely they had no interest in theology, and piety of the routine sort was for priests, monks, and women. They took their oaths as Christians, swore homage over relics of saints, and accepted Christianity as part of the order of things, but they could not have taken seriously the dictum that the meek would or should inherit anything worth having. Men like themselves were honorable and free—masters of their own fate, not bound to labor on the land—precisely because they could inflict violence and could defend themselves against it.

In clear contrast to the feudal way of life, the main pursuits of townspeople were religious affairs, administration, and commerce. Tenth-century towns were not only too small to be called cities but lacked the diverse social and occupational roles associated with that term. Rather, they were religious and administrative centers, occupied principally by clergymen and monks, occasionally noblemen with their families and employees, and a few merchants, artisans, and laborers. Most power and authority in a town was wielded by the local count or viscount, a feudal lord who was likely to live elsewhere on his own estate, and by the resident bishop, who (ironically enough) was usually the individual with whom the Jewish community had to deal on an everyday basis.

By the late tenth century there were probably some twenty or twenty-five thousand Jews living in the region they called Ashkenaz, roughly what is now northwestern Europe. They were still only a small percentage of the world Jewish population, for most Jews were to be found in Spain and in lands bordering on the eastern Mediterranean. Though they were an even smaller percentage of the European population, they were located and concentrated so as to be influential well beyond their numbers. At a time when important urban centers were no larger than our small towns, European Jews were already true urbanites, prominent everywhere as merchants, a role for which few local Christians were adequately prepared. Only in towns, of course, could Jews establish the social and commercial ties that were intrinsic to their way of life. Occasionally a Jew might be a landholder, and, as we have noted, a few may have derived most of their income from vineyards. But this meant nothing in the world of feudal relationships; for although a Jew might be required to declare dutiful submission to a lord, obviously he did not pledge military support, and certainly he could not receive homage under any circumstances. Thus, whatever role land played in the experience of a few Jews, it is to urban centers and to the world of commerce that we look for an understanding of Jewish life.

Paralleling the obvious differences between Jews and Christians in residence and occupations were cultural differences that reached to the core of their life experiences and shaped their mental attitudes in remarkably different directions. For in striking contrast to the land-centered, hierarchically conceived structure of feudal society, Jewish society can be envisioned as a radially organized network of essentially autonomous but intimately connected urban communities, by necessity egalitarian in social philosophy, that accorded highest social status only to men who combined religious learning and piety with commercial talent and political wisdom. Each community was concretely linked to all others by social, economic, and cultural bonds extending in every direction within and beyond Europe. In this sense, even Jews who had been settled for generations in France or Germany were an international people.

Living in the midst of a feudal social order that assigned all men to the categories of lords, knights, priests, or serfs, Jews were in fact creating a social order of their own that contrasted definitively with that of the larger society. With the possible exception of rabbinic authorities, Jews had no comparable social categories: being Jewish was the sum and substance of their identity. Life centered almost entirely in the Jewish community, and security for the individual Jew was for all practical purposes unattainable without membership in such a community.

First and foremost, each Jewish community had to maintain satisfactory relationships with the local count and bishop, for it was to such men that they had to turn when anything went seriously wrong—accusations by Christians, threats, physical assault, and the like. In return they provided dependable revenue as well as desirable trade commodities that might not otherwise be obtainable. And since merchants were often the only source of money in a largely barter economy, they could be solicited for loans. (Contrary to the popular image, however, Jews did not engage in moneylending on a large scale until late in the eleventh century—and then, as we shall see, mainly because this occupation was in effect forced upon them.) Since taxes were assessed on the community as a corporate entity, it was the responsibility of community leaders to collect the required amounts and to pay in lump sums. Obviously it mattered not at all to the assessors how the money was obtained, so long as it appeared on demand. But from the perspective of community leaders it was clearly essential that everyone perceive assessments to be equitable, and that they pay promptly and willingly in the interests of collective welfare.

Management of taxation, perhaps the most stressful responsibility of the community and its leadership, can be taken as a model for how all affairs were conducted. What mattered most was that everything be managed in an orderly, cooperative manner that would ensure communal harmony and integrity. Although every Jewish community included recognized leaders, men who were both learned and prosperous, their role was that of facilitators and mediators. The ultimate recourse in every disputed or uncertain matter was rabbinic law, and people turned naturally to learned men in their own communities or beyond for rulings. There were no professional rabbis, however, and no one could lay claim to unchallengeable authority. Rather, a number of men, perhaps the majority in some communities, were sufficiently learned to have a voice in public policy and conflict resolution, a right accorded to them by common consent. But no one, no matter how learned and respected, could rule arbitrarily, without being subject to challenge and debate. Ultimately every communal policy—whether having to do with taxation, commerce, marital contracts, relations with transient Jewish visitors, or disputes with outsiders—had to be established by consensus. Aside from disputes in which Christians were directly involved, outsiders were unlikely to participate in Jewish affairs. Each community was an autonomous social unit, self-regulating and collectively managed.

The ultimate sanction against those who seriously violated norms of the community or defied its regulations was *kherem*, exclusion or excommunication. Survival as an individual Jew apart from a community was all but inconceivable; a person subjected to any form of *shamta*, shunning, was in serious trouble, for excommunication might be the next step. Another form of *kherem* was known as *kherem ha-yishuv*, exclusion from the community until one had been granted formal acceptance by vote. The insistence on controlling entry into the community may have been grounded in fear of competition for limited commercial opportunities, or it may simply have been a way of preventing the entry of people known to be troublesome or untrustworthy. Decisions of this kind were vested in the community; there were no external authorities.

Irving Agus, a historian of European Jewish life in the tenth and eleventh centuries, emphasizes the commanding presence of rabbinic law in every aspect of medieval Jewish life—"probably far greater," he suggests, "than that of any other Jewry in historical times." It regulated just about everything in their social world:

> The organization of communal agencies; the establishment of political contact with the secular authorities; the raising of funds, through taxation, to cover all expenses and financial obligations; . . . the enforcement of individual cooperation; the regulation of business practices; the maintenance of a high level of security for life and property; the enforcement of law, peace and orderliness; the development and administration of communal, charitable, educational, and religious institutions; the legal authority to carry out these necessary functions of organized life; and the proper techniques for efficient administration—all these were grounded, probably for the first time in history, exclusively on Jewish law.

Rabbinic scholarship, he concludes, "was not a peripheral interest, not a mere luxury," for the Jews of northern Europe, "but the mainspring of their being, the essence of life itself."[7]

Thus there emerged, first in the Rhineland, later in northern France, men of extraordinary intellectual stature. The most eminent scholar of the late tenth and early eleventh centuries was Gershom ben Judah of Mainz (ca. 960–1040), known as "Light of the Exile" *(Meor ha-Golah)*, under whose guidance numerous ordinances were enacted governing every phase of Jewish social and economic life. But Gershom had immediate predecessors and contemporaries of nearly equal stature. He and his colleagues, referred to collectively by their successors as "the learned men of Lotharingia" *(khokhme Loter)*, accomplished as much as they did because they were part of a virtual renaissance of Jewish scholarship.

Before the eleventh century most rabbinic commentary was conveyed orally from teacher to student as text to be memorized word for word. Precise wording was of paramount importance, and scholars took great pains to teach without alterations. "A young student," says Agus, "learned from his teacher to read the text of the Talmud phrase by phrase and to interpolate between each phrase a few exact words— words that had once been carefully and painstakingly chosen, and then traditionally transmitted—that accurately elucidated that phrase in its particular context. . . . The young students would faithfully repeat the text together with the interpolated oral explanations until the exact wording of the whole was well fixed in memory."[8] During the eleventh century it became the practice to compose written commentaries based on the orally transmitted models. These commentaries concerned themselves with questions extending well beyond what we would call religious matters; their subject, in fact, was the entire social and economic life of the community. But distinctions between the religious and secular domains were hardly to the point for people whose lives were conducted in a pervasively Jewish cultural environment; they pondered questions about property, commerce, legal damages, and divorce with literally religious dedication.

It is apparent, then, that although Jews were in a limited sense part of feudal society, they were also living in a world of their own construction, internally constituted and regulated, rooted in premises entirely distinct from those underlying the general social order. Feudal society created exclusive and intrinsically unequal relationships between individuals; Jewish society was communal, cooperative, and, at least in principle, egalitarian. Social status (for men) was a function of scholarly achievement and wealth (often found together, for merchants were scholars)—the one, because this was a society dependent on rabbinic law for order and stability, the other, because it was also dependent on regularly accumulated wealth for providing tax revenue to Christian authorities who protected it from assault and plunder. Since each community paid taxes collectively as a corporate unit, wealthy individuals could seldom gain special privileges for themselves alone but had to remain, as it were, beneath the communal canopy. And just as each individual recognized ties to everyone else in the local community, so did each community recognize others, near and distant, as part of the European Jewish social order. All were bound together, not only by material necessity, but by kinship, culture, religious tradition, and sense of historical destiny.

Moreover, as can be readily imagined, in a world in which violence was an accepted part of life, Jews were dependent on one another in the interminable effort to avoid it. Combat, the central preoccupation of the nobility—their foremost source of personal identity and self-fulfillment—was for Jews anathema, the very antithesis of the kind of environment they required for survival. We have already noted that Jewish communities had to deal in particular with either barons or bishops, the two classes with power and authority in each region. Obviously, neither the military preoccupations of the nobility nor the concerns of the Christian clergy met with responsive chords in Jewish culture. So the social distance between Jews and those persons with whom they were in most frequent contact was rooted in profound psychological differences.

Jews throughout Europe were linked not only by their culture but also as participants in a network of trading relationships extending almost halfway around the world. They were the principal, and until the end of the tenth century virtually the only, people engaged in an export-import trade that linked France and the Rhineland with England, Italy, Spain, North Africa, Byzantium, Hungary, Poland, Russia, and other distant locations extending into the Orient. Some merchants traveled immense distances, transporting commodities back and forth between their home regions and foreign lands, and goods themselves often passed through a number of hands (many Jewish) before reaching their ultimate destinations. Associated with the vigorous trade in commodities was a flow of capital, because every merchant needed access to money for investment when opportunities presented themselves. At market towns all over Europe, merchants gathered to buy and sell, to form partnerships, and to plan new enterprises. It was a way of life that required mobility, adaptability, readiness to explore new places and fresh prospects.

A remarkable feature of this period was the fact that because many prosperous merchants were also recognized rabbinic scholars, large gatherings of merchants presented opportunities for legal and political discussions among men who were responsible for rabbinic legislation. Markets were thus not just major economic events but an intrinsic feature of Jewish social life. Wealthy merchants arranged to have prominent visitors quartered in their own homes, which functioned in effect as trading stations, sometimes to the exclusion of the marketplace proper. At times the scene must have been one of feverish activity, with visitors coming and going, arranging transactions with local merchants and negotiating future undertakings.

Merchants also engaged in local commercial ventures. Some required journeys of a few days' duration that took them to nearby estates, where they purchased horses, cattle, pelts, and the like, and sold luxury goods purchased elsewhere. Even there, however, they may not have dealt directly with non-Jews, for some estates had Jewish managers who were responsible for commercial transactions. Since the average lord had neither the knowledge nor the inclination for such dealings, some preferred to employ Jewish managers whose commercial experience and, most importantly, personal relationships and cultural style, made ideal intermediaries. Even the clergy occasionally employed Jewish financial managers and depended on them for purchases of such items as tapestries and precious metal objects for their churches, fine wines, and other luxury commodities.

Some Jewish merchants became very wealthy, capable of producing sums equivalent in buying power to tens of thousands of dollars today. Large sums of money as well as valuable commodities moved back and forth among them as a matter of course. In this environment unreserved trust was essential, and there emerged a code of honor, based on personal reputation and private oaths, that governed business relationships. Merchants relied on their personal reputations, and anyone who made the mistake of cheating, deceiving, or violating an oath condemned himself to permanent exclusion from the indispensable cooperative network—for all practical purposes another form of excommunication. So in this sense, too, Jews were bound to one another as members of a larger community in which their common welfare was vested.[9]

To be sure, not all Jews were merchants. A few were more or less completely engaged as teachers and scribes, and a few others were employed in goldsmithing or other crafts, or in production of kosher wines and cheeses. Wine production in particular continued to be a fairly important enterprise. Kosher wines had to be meticulously prepared, without the intervention of non-Jewish labor in the final and more complex stages of production. For this reason, and because they were often among the finest wines produced in their regions, kosher wines were likely to be expensive. Wealthy noblemen and clergymen often patronized Jewish vintners, who kept some wine separate for Jewish patrons and sold the remainder to Christians. Perhaps because it was a mark of affluence, the drinking of fine wine reinforced the image of Jews as people associated with wealth and the wealthy.

Status of Women

It is not surprising that in communities dependent on maintaining a cooperative and egalitarian spirit, women were accorded relatively high status. Our best sources of information on this matter are rabbinic commentaries and correspondences.[10] Rabbinic statements indicate that women were recognized as social and economically active persons with substantial rights and responsibilities. Of course they were not accorded the right to become scholars, which was the essential prerequisite for community leadership, and in that sense they were clearly not on a par with men. But Jewish women received substantial respect in their communities, and participated in public life more than their Christian counterparts.

The definitive event in a woman's life was her marriage, the indispensable step toward entry into the community as an adult. Not only did young women not decide on this crucial matter, but in fact most were betrothed by about age eight or nine and married by eleven or twelve, their husbands being perhaps two or three years older. In these tightly knit, deeply conservative communities, intent on maintaining order and stability, marriage was necessarily an arrangement between families, and the negotiations were deemed far too weighty and complex for mere children. Typically, a girl would be betrothed to a boy in her own or a neighboring community with only the most perfunctory notification to either child; and at just about the time when both were reaching puberty (but presumably well before youthful attractions and whims could introduce obstacles) they would be married and channeled into a life of adult responsibilities. Because betrothal was a profoundly serious matter involving family property, dignity, and social status, rabbinic ordinances were enacted "to protect the daughters of Israel from possible humiliation"[11]—that is, to ensure that contracts once made would not be broken. Property in proportion to the wealth of the participants, often quite substantial in value, was transferred to the newly married couple by both families. A girl's dowry in particular was a major consideration, not only to provide for the new couple but to establish or confirm the social status of her entire family. Thus, although boys also received not inconsiderable dowries, a girl's brothers understood that it was she who was entitled to the major share of whatever wealth their parents could muster. A woman's dowry remained her property and was recognized as part of what she might hand down to her own daughters. Moreover, it was understood that acceptance of a girl's dowry entailed agreement on the part of her husband and his family that she would be treated as a person in her own right, granted dignity and respect, and recognized as a partner in the family's economic pursuits.

Most new couples settled into a home near that of the groom's parents. While some girls still lived near their own parents as well, others had to adjust at a very young age to adult life in an unfamiliar community. But although the transition may have been painful, young women soon became mothers of their own families, accepted by their husbands as partners in nearly every aspect of life. Often this included business affairs; after a man's death his widow might maintain the business on her own.

The one activity women seldom engaged in was commercial travel, a risky and dangerous business at best. In any event, someone had to be responsible for home management and child care, and in this society there was no question who that should be. Accordingly, a woman might be left alone at home for weeks or even months at a stretch, and during such times it was she who dealt with visiting merchants and managed business transactions. In this sense many families were organized in a truly cooperative manner, women often functioning as their husbands' trusted partners.

Some women operated more or less independently in various kinds of entrepreneurial ventures: for example, personal management of purchases and sales or depositing money with a merchant for investment and shared profits. A few appear to have gained reputations as successful commercial agents. In this context, it should be noted that women were entitled to full rights in Jewish courts, appearing on occasion as plaintiffs or defendants, and generally receiving recognition as independent litigants.

Except for the exclusion from formal scholarly pursuits, perhaps the only other situation to be counterposed to this positive description of the status of women was that of the woman without children. A man whose wife remained "barren" after ten years was expected to divorce and marry another; blame for the failure fell on her alone. Ultimately, then, despite a social environment that provided women with prospects for dignity, responsibility, and independence, everything still hinged on their ability to function acceptably in the traditionally defined roles of wife and mother.

Relations with Christians

In the course of everyday life, it was inevitable that most Jews—men and women—would come into frequent contact with Christians of every kind, from lords and bishops to town laborers and peasants. Jewish merchants maintained cordial relationships with favored Christian clients, and Jewish estate managers, stewards, and financial advisers also dealt regularly with noblemen on a personal basis. Jewish homeowners employed Christians as manual laborers and artisans for all kinds of work, and many Jewish households employed Christian servants and maids. Surely relationships must have been colored by mutual prejudices, but day-to-day interaction probably proceeded on a basis of mutual trust and at times even affection.

On the other side of the ledger, the prospect of perilous misunderstandings, malicious rumors, and the like were a source of constant uneasiness.[12] Moreover, at times Jews were harassed and humiliated as a matter of course. For example, in at least three French towns—Chalon-sur-Saône, Béziers, and Toulouse—annual assaults on Jews were a traditional practice, probably dating from at least the ninth century and persisting until the twelfth or thirteenth.[13] In Chalon, in northern Burgundy, it was the custom on Palm Sunday to throw stones at Jews, because, as the Gospels report, they had stoned Jesus. Apparently the local clergy not only encouraged but participated in this ritual. In Béziers, a southern town near Narbonne, the bishop preached an annual Palm Sunday sermon against Jews and urged the congregation to attack Jewish residences during Easter week—but only with stones, nothing more, probably so as not to frighten the victims into leaving town. Each year at Toulouse a Jew was forced to stand in the town square before the church and receive a public slap in the face. It is said that one man was struck so viciously that he died of a fractured skull.[14] Ritualized persecution of this sort kept Jews under pressure without exceeding accepted limits: one could harass Jews, but not to the extent that they might decide to go elsewhere.

Occasionally the situation became very dangerous. In 992 a convert from Judaism placed a waxen image, supposedly representing the local count, in the ark of the synagogue at Le Mans, a town southwest of Paris, then informed the count that the Jews were trying to kill him by stabbing the image. Since the count held ultimate authority in the region, there was no one to whom the Jews might have appealed. They insisted on their innocence, of course, but the count demanded that they engage in combat with their accuser, a standard procedure at the time. No record of the combat exists, but the community did survive the incident, probably by bribing the count.[15] We might note, incidentally, that Jews were still being accorded the right of free men to fight with weapons.

Although oppression of this kind was certainly a problem for Jewish communities, the matter was not entirely one-sided, for Jews themselves were intentionally exclusive and self-segregating in ways that could be perceived as mean and burdensome. Jewish practices with regard to meat and wine—both items available in quantity and quality only to the prosperous—were a continual annoyance to Christians and a source of much conflict. Jews would eat only ritually slaughtered animals of the proper kind, and then only the parts defined as kosher. Moreover, animals found to have even minor blemishes in lungs or other organs might be deemed totally unfit for Jewish consumption. Understandably, Jewish butchers tried to sell rejected meat to Christians, and some certainly bought it on the correct assumption that it was quite edible. But, as we already saw in Bishop Agobard's complaints, such practices were bound to generate suspicion and resentment, and at this distance one can empathize with Christians who viewed the entire business as additional evidence that Jews were not to be trusted.[16]

The situation with wine was much the same. Jewish law prohibited the use of wine that had been handled or even touched by a non-Jew. Thus wine for sale to Christians was kept strictly apart from that designated for Jewish use, and it is no wonder that Christian buyers (ordinarily the most prestigious individuals: bishops, barons, wealthy townspeople) suspected the worst. As for the possibility of sharing a friendly glass of wine with a Christian neighbor or client, the prospects were ludicrous: "the situation thus created would often cause the host to flutter over his guest in nervousness and agitation. Usually the Jew would watch his guest's movements with some anxiety, and as soon as the latter finished his drink, the cup would be taken away from him, the remaining wine would be poured out, and the cup rinsed."[17]

The compulsive avoidance of Christian lips was carried to such extremes that if acceptable wine was accidentally poured from a cask into a cup still moist with wine drunk by a Christian, all the wine in the cask was rendered unfit for Jewish use—vivid illustration of what one historian has identified as a definitive characteristic of medieval European Jewish behavior: "a method of personal conduct enabling the individual to preserve his inward sense of aloofness from those with whom he came into everyday social contact."[18] It goes without saying that such practices were bound to undermine whatever slim possibilities there may have been for cordial relationships with Christians.

A Deceptive Zenith

By the end of the tenth century, Jewish communities were flourishing throughout the territory that had once been the Carolingian Empire. If Jews were still looked upon as alien sojourners, they were nonetheless enjoying not just toleration but for the most part acceptance. But therein lay the irony of the situation: they had reached their zenith just when Christian Europe was about to begin the ascent to its own; and, as we shall see, the very conditions that enabled Christian civilization to reach new heights led inexorably to disaster and decline for Jews. Why this was so, and what it signifies for a broader perspective on European Jewish history, will be our next subject.

· 5 ·

"TO MAKE A CITY OF MY VILLAGE"

The Pivotal Eleventh Century

Historians often point to 1096, the year when Jews in the Rhineland were massacred by crusaders, as a pivotal year, after which Jews in Christian Europe began a slide downward from which they would never recover.[1] The fact is, though, that the entire eleventh century was pivotal—a time when everything about European society was changing dramatically, including the situation of Jews. But for Christians the changes were in the form of remarkable social and economic advancement, while for Jews precisely the opposite was true. In other words, just as life began to improve for Christians, it began to worsen for Jews. The key to everything was engagement in large-scale commerce: this was the century in which, for the first time, Christians achieved a level of commercial acumen that led them to challenge, and ultimately to replace, Jews as merchants on a national and international scale. The result was that Jews were relegated to the role of moneylenders: a misfortune greater than they could have foreseen.

France

By this time France and Germany were separate regions with quite different political situations. France was still an assemblage of loosely affiliated feudal domains, ruled by dukes and counts who exercised the only real authority in their own territories. Kings continued to rule, but only as the nominal heads of a feudal hierarchy, dependent on the willingness of powerful barons to accept their obligations as the king's vassals—which they did when it suited their purposes. During the course of the century there were usually some eight or ten men who controlled more territory and exercised more power than the king— and who fought endlessly with one another, of course, for the usual reasons. Then there were the lesser barons, many of whom had equally absolute authority in their own smaller domains. Men of this kind were vassals to the great lords, but for the most part they ruled alone, managing and judging as they saw fit.

Though Jews were to be found throughout France, they were concentrated in Paris, in the towns of Champagne in northeastern France, and in Provence to the south. They were still mostly merchants, dependent for protection on the rulers of their particular regions—sometimes a duke or count, sometimes a lesser lord who was no less powerful as far as they were concerned. Protection required, however, that a Jewish community be ready and able to pay taxes—as much as the lord demanded, on time and without complaint. It might also mean supplying him with commercial goods and, in some cases, assisting in estate management. Finally, as time went on, Jews found themselves being asked more and more often to supplement tax payments with loans. Later we shall see why this was so. The relationship, fragile at best, was sometimes further complicated because more than one lord might exercise authority in a region, in which cases the local Jews had to balance obligations and favors, being careful to keep everyone satisfied. For example, by the late eleventh century at least nine lords, from the count of Champagne downward, claimed some authority in the town of Troyes, site of a thriving Jewish community.[2] All were potentially in business relationships with Jewish merchants who had to be careful not to be caught up in their disputes or accused of favoring one lord over another. Every Jew had to recognize that long-term security depended on cooperating with other Jews in maintaining carefully balanced relationships. Trying to curry individual favor with a particular lord could be dangerous not only for oneself but for the entire community.

Like their modern counterparts, the Jews of medieval France were most likely to thrive when political conditions were stable and life moved on an even keel. But despite the inherent instability in this decentralized political system, eleventh-century Ashkenazic Jews had reason to be more optimistic than not. Jewish merchants, backed by centuries of accumulated experience, were still active participants in an economy that was expanding rapidly, and most Jews were still finding a fairly secure place in the society. Jewish communities were carefully managed to ensure that everyone cooperated and everyone received a fair share of support and protection. All in all, the high point achieved during the tenth century was still mostly in evidence, and in fact it was in the eleventh century that Jewish cultural achievement in the form of Talmudic scholarship matured and flourished throughout the Ashkenazic world.

In France the most eminent of all medieval Ashkenazic rabbis, Solomon ben Isaac of Troyes, better known now as Rashi (*Rabbi Shlomo ben Isaac*), achieved fame for Talmudic commentary that was universally admired for its clarity and precision. Born in Troyes in 1040, he studied at yeshivas in Worms and Mainz, then returned to Troyes to manage his family's vineyards. In 1070, by which time he was already a widely recognized scholar, he established a small yeshiva at Troyes. After 1096, when the great yeshivas of the Rhineland had been destroyed, Troyes became by default the center of European rabbinic scholarship, although never of a magnitude comparable to its predecessors. Rashi died in 1105, survived by several grandsons who were to become the outstanding rabbis of twelfth-century Europe.[3]

Germany

Even though Rashi lived in France and the Rhineland yeshivas were in Germany, his traveling there to study was not at all unusual for the time. Ashkenazic Jews living in France and Germany still thought of themselves as a single people, and they were in constant contact with one another—intermarrying, studying at one another's yeshivas, exchanging rabbinic questions and commentaries, cooperating in commercial ventures. But the German political situation was decidedly different. Ever since the tenth century, when Otto I and his successors had established a firm hold on the monarchy, German political power had been much more centralized than in France. German kings ruled also as emperors of the Holy Roman Empire, a huge territory that extended well beyond what later became Germany. They too had to contend with powerful barons who exercised a great deal of authority in their own territories, but never to the point of being more powerful than the king-emperor. This political situation was relatively more favorable for Jews: they could usually depend on being protected by monarchs who recognized their economic usefulness and saw to it that they were not mistreated.

The Commercial Revolution

By the beginning of the eleventh century, western Europe was on the verge of an economic transformation so profound that it has been called a revolution—a commercial revolution, because its definitive feature was the entry of large numbers of Christian merchants into commerce on a scale that had previously been associated mostly with Jews.[4] The foundation for all that followed was a surge in population that began in the tenth century and accelerated in the eleventh. Why this happened is uncertain, but there are several possible explanations. First, Europe was recovering from the death and destruction inflicted by the Vikings and other invaders during the ninth and tenth centuries, and there were no major internal wars. In addition, since about the mid-tenth century there had been no serious epidemics of plague or other massively fatal diseases. Finally, Europeans were becoming more efficient farmers. Everywhere they cleared large tracts of what had been forested land and began constructing better roads. They were learning to use iron ploughs and other equipment, with horses instead of oxen, and developing improved techniques for land management. Human labor was still the one indispensable resource, but farmers were getting better returns for their hard work.

More efficient agricultural output meant surplus products that could be sold elsewhere. In northern France some farmers began raising sheep, probably stimulated by the success of the developing wool industry in England, and the towns of the region became centers for production and marketing of woolen textiles. Christian merchants, until this time relatively few in number, began to achieve such prominence that we can call them a new social class. These men dealt not only in woolen goods but also in more traditional products of the region, such as timber, grain, wine, and metal weaponry. Naturally, this kind of activity attracted people who had never before been part of town life: young men without land of their own; peasants anxious to escape lives of dull labor; people for whom the prospect of life in town, no matter how risky, seemed preferable to life at home. Such men might begin at the bottom of the social ladder, but in time some of them joined the newly emerging class of local Christian merchants pursuing careers that set them apart from feudal society and its privileged nobility. Aware of themselves as having new kinds of economic interests, these men wanted independence—not just individual but collective, so that they could pursue their commercial goals without interference from barons and bishops.

Christian merchants differed from their Jewish counterparts in much more than religion. They were truly local people, connected with producers with whom they had personal ties of kinship or friendship. They dealt in goods designed for export to foreign markets, but the goods themselves were local products, whether harvested or manufactured. Their wares appealed to almost everyone, not just a wealthy elite. They formed connections with Mediterranean merchants—but not Jewish merchants. The Mediterranean trade was now controlled by northern Italians—merchants from Venice, Genoa, Pisa, and other cities—who had ousted North African Muslims from the region and spearheaded the growth of their cities into the largest and wealthiest in Europe. The result was that a much larger volume of goods was now moving across Europe in both directions: woolens, timber, and other products moving southward; and a variety of Mediterranean products such as spices, oranges, figs, and rugs moving northward in exchange. Champagne, the region around Rheims and Troyes in northeastern France, became a major marketing center, and by the twelfth century the towns of the region would be hosting annual fairs attracting merchants from great distances.

The rise of these merchants to prominence meant inevitable changes in local politics: they demanded and received rights to govern their towns themselves. The bishops were relegated to control only over their own ecclesiastical districts, while the larger and more dynamic commercial districts became self-governing municipalities, with the social and occupational complexity of true cities. Soon there appeared organizations of merchants, called guilds, which enabled members to buy, sell, and negotiate collectively; to defend their mutual interests against outsiders; and to provide for the general advancement of commercial interests in their regions. Although these merchants traveled on occasion, they moved in well-defended caravans, and as time went on they were more likely to transport their goods by common carriers while they remained at home to conduct their businesses in proper bourgeois fashion. Partnerships and contracts became common as the merchant class expanded in numbers and wealth. Credit became commonplace. Most importantly, profit making—supposedly anathema to the pious Christian—was now accepted as the obvious purpose of the day's work.

The legitimization of profit was no small challenge to the traditional social and religious order. Until this time, most goods moved about as "gifts"—not to be paid for, but with the understanding that friendships were created and maintained by regular exchanges of this kind.[5] But now an entirely new element had entered the picture: transactions based on money, that wickedly seductive invention of the devil himself, coldly impersonal, certainly not what one friend would present to another as a gift. The notion that money is dirty, the "root of evil," is familiar, but it requires a leap of the imagination to understand what this meant to people in the eleventh century. They looked upon money as filth in the most literal sense. By the later eleventh century it was being spoken of as feces, vomit, garbage, and even worse: it was the devil's own substance, the essence of his being, and anyone who dealt with it was bound to be devilishly contaminated.

Everyone, even the clergy, had to come to terms somehow with the new economic facts of life, but it was a slow process. Although merchants were looked down upon and ostracized at first, it was inevitable that before long they would be accepted as people deserving respect. Perhaps love of money was the root of evil, and perhaps the commercial districts of towns were the devil's own lair, but merchants were nevertheless part of the Christian community. The early response to this paradox was to deny it: people who came into such intimate contact with money, especially those involved with interest-bearing loans and credit, called themselves Christians but were behaving like Jews— because only Jews were so "carnal," so impersonal, so blind to Christian values that they could handle money with indifference. And only

Jews, linked as they were to the devil in enmity to Christ, could be expected to find the devil's own substance congenial. Somewhat later, in the mid-twelfth century, the most influential clergyman of the time, Bernard of Clairvaux, stated the matter unforgettably: "We are pained to observe," he said, "that where there are no Jews, Christian money-lenders 'Jew', or 'Judaize', worse than the Jews, if indeed these men may be called Christians, and not rather baptized Jews." With that, "Judaize," which previously had referred to religious practices considered too close to Judaism, came to denote dealings involving money.[6]

Christian merchants seem to have been inclined for a time to interact with Jews on a reasonably friendly basis (perhaps because they stood to benefit from Jewish knowledge and experience) but soon came to look upon them as potential competitors whom they wished out of the way entirely. One of the purposes of guilds was to eliminate just such competition.

Thus it was that by the latter half of the century Jews began to experience the first stage of a profoundly unhealthy narrowing of their role in the economy—and, probably connected with this, an ominous worsening of their image in the popular imagination. What was happening in effect was that people wanted Jewish money but not Jewish participation in commerce. And so Jews found themselves steadily squeezed out, relegated to the margins of economic life, converted from dealers in goods to dealers in money. The process was gradual, slower in some places than in others; in Germany they were still relatively active in commerce when their counterparts in France were already being forced into moneylending. But it was a steady process, and within a century or so Jews throughout Europe had become a truly marginalized population living largely on the proceeds of money lent at interest.

Their rates were high—exorbitantly high, sometimes above 40 percent. This was equally true for Christian moneylenders, of whom there were many, and who sometimes charged even higher rates than Jews. But there was a crucial difference: a few Christians loaned money; almost all Jews did so. Thus moneylending became identified as the Jewish occupation, and high rates of interest became known as a specifically Jewish version of wickedness. Peasants burdened with heavy debts, perhaps incurred when crops failed; noblemen who borrowed recklessly to finance a style of life they could no longer afford; ordinary men and women who needed loans to sustain them over hard times but resented the harsh terms on which they had to borrow: Just about everyone came to know Jews as their despised and detested creditors. Since Jews were already known as the eternal enemies of Christ, it requires no imaginative gift to understand subsequent Jewish history in medieval Europe.

The Religious Revolution

Even in the religious domain it would seem that events were conspiring against Jews—to sharpen their negative image, to bring it more into the open, to make it matter more in everyday life. Considering that western Europe had been almost entirely Christian since at least the time of Charlemagne, one might think that nothing that happened thereafter on the religious side could have affected Jews very much one way or the other. But the fact is that during the eleventh century the Roman Catholic Church achieved a supremacy greater by far than anything in the past. The European world had become what Pope Gregory VII called *Christianitas,* Christendom, the kingdom of Christ; and he and his successors were to be its supreme rulers. Emperors, kings, and lesser lords still reigned, of course, but now they had to contend with popes who claimed power and authority transcending those of all earthly kingdoms.[7]

The century's most bitter conflict pitted German emperors against Roman popes, and when it was over, the popes had won. The story begins with Pope Leo IX. He held office for only five years, from 1049 to 1054, but he was an exceptionally good administrator who recognized problems and knew how to deal with them. A central concern for the Church at that time was simony: high offices going to men whose only qualification was that they had paid a good price for them. But soon after becoming pope, Leo made his own intentions clear. While on a tour to preach reform, he stopped at Rheims to consecrate a new church dedicated to St. Remigius, the bishop who had baptized Clovis. With some twenty bishops and forty abbots in attendance at the convocation, and with the saint's bones on display as witness, Leo asked each of these dignitaries to rise and declare whether he had given any payment or gifts to obtain his office. The holy men were petrified, and one simply fled from the church. Several were censured or demoted, and no doubt the word went out that times were changing.[8]

An even larger problem was lay investiture—that is, appointments of bishops and other clergy by secular authorities. This had become routine practice for the German emperors in particular; as they understood matters, bishops and abbots were local authorities who administered towns, monasteries, and rural lands as agents of the crown. A similar situation prevailed in France, where the higher clergy functioned as feudal lords administering territory in cooperation with the dukes and counts in their regions. But now popes began to insist that clerical appointments were strictly for the purposes of the Church, and to demand that therefore they, and they alone, should make such appointments. The clergy were the Church's army in the field, and no outsiders, not even kings, should appoint or control them. For although the Church and its clergy were part of this world, ultimately they were only the material manifestation of a spiritual kingdom that utterly surpassed everything on earth. Each and every Christian, no matter how humble, was part of that kingdom, destined to live out his or her brief life in an assigned role, then to live in eternity as spirit. The entire civilized European world itself was only an earthly reflection of the sublime reality embodied in the Church.

It was in this mental climate that the so-called Investiture Conflict erupted, some twenty years after Leo's time, as a confrontation between a pope who insisted on absolute papal primacy and an emperor who was determined to maintain his own hegemony. The contenders were the formidable Pope Gregory VII and the no less assertive Emperor Henry IV. Henry was appointing his own bishops, who served him as local administrators. Considering this absolutely unacceptable, Gregory responded with a "Papal Declaration," a set of propositions presented to the European world not for its consideration but for its instruction. The pope's authority was universal and absolute. He alone could appoint, transfer, or depose bishops, and no secular authority had any say in the matter whatsoever. Indeed, emperors and kings ruled only with his assent, and he could depose them too if he so desired. As one historian has remarked, the two men represented incompatible conceptions of the relation between papacy and monarchy: Gregory standing for "a centralized papacy, which saw itself as carrying the ultimate responsibility for the salvation of mankind, for which it was answerable only to God"; Henry, for "a kingship which saw itself as holding a lordship founded by God which presupposed a harmony between church and Empire."[9]

The fortunes of battle between these two men, which shifted back and forth, need not concern us here. Gregory himself was a temporary loser and died in exile, but in the long run it was his papal declaration that spelled out the future course of medieval European civilization. By the close of the century, the Christianization of Europe, in the fullest sense of the term, was an accomplished fact. Europe had become a single society, united by an identity that quite surpassed what we ordinarily understand by the term "religion." To be European was to be part of Christendom—to possess a Christian soul and a Christian destiny. "Christian" became another word for "person."

A great deal changed. Warfare among feudal barons was now religiously regulated. Under provisions of the so-called Peace of God, no one was to attack or rob clergy or common folk, and there was to be no fighting near churches. A new Truce of God prohibited warfare on sacred days and from Thursday through Sunday of every week.[10] But the enemies of God were another matter entirely. First came the Muslims. The Christian reconquest of Spain was already under way by this time, the Mediterranean was again under Christian control, and talk of crusades was already in the air. But the Lord had other enemies, the equally despicable Jews, much nearer to hand. In fact, since they were suspected of being in league with the Muslims, it was all one struggle, although there was reason enough to despise Jews on their own account.[11]

Until this time, although Jews were certainly not universally liked, they had been generally accepted; they were real persons—spiritually blinded, to be sure, but with their own place in the social order. Now, however, there was almost no place for them at all. Aside from their dangerously declining situation in the economy, they now had to contend with an even more profound problem, impossible to overcome. To participate in the social order and to be Christian had become one and the same. Jesus Christ had suffered and died to redeem the world, but the descendants of those who had demanded his crucifixion had never repented. They remained, living and even thriving among Christian folk, unpunished for the most colossal crime in history. What injustice could be plainer than that?

"To Make a City of My Village": The Speyer Charter

In 1084 a fire broke out in the Jewish neighborhood of Mainz, probably the result of arson by a local mob. The Jewish chronicler who reported the event somewhat later said that the Jews "stood in great fear of the burghers." A Jewish visitor from Worms was killed by townspeople who thought he was carrying gold or silver. The experience was so upsetting that some Mainz Jews decided to move elsewhere—"wherever we might find a fortified city."[12]

They did not have to travel far. When the bishop of Speyer learned of their situation, he invited the Jews to settle in his town, because, as he explained, "I wished to make a city of my village" and "thought that it would add greatly to its honor if I should establish some Jews in it." He located them in their own residential quarter, on the edge of town; and to ensure that they would be "protected from the attacks and violence of the mob," he had the entire area surrounded by a wall. The Jews, with assistance from their servants, were expected to provide for the guarding and defense of their own walls—which is to say that they were considered an essentially autonomous community. The bishop granted them generous commercial and financial privileges. He permitted them to employ Christian servants and nurses, and to sell nonkosher meat to local people. They were to enjoy all possible judicial autonomy: the Jewish authorities were empowered to judge all cases "which arise among them or against them." They were to receive their own burial ground—a plot of church-owned land—which they would "hold forever." In return for all this they had only to contribute a modest annual sum for upkeep of the local monastery and, of course, to help promote the commercial growth of Speyer.[13]

It is easy to understand why this charter is among the most often cited documents in European Jewish history. For one thing, it appears to have been the first, or certainly among the first, of its kind. Distinct

Jewish residential districts were appearing at this time in a number of German towns as voluntarily semisegregated neighborhoods. For obvious reasons—proximity to a synagogue, availability of kosher food, personal and business relationships, security—Jews wanted to live together. But with the Speyer charter we have something new and noteworthy: an intentionally created and explicitly segregated district. Was it a ghetto? Not quite. Jews were still free to move about town, and the purpose of the districting was not to confine but to protect them. We have to assume that they themselves wanted to live just this way, perhaps even requested it as a condition for settling there. But clearly this charter signaled the onset of a new phase in medieval Jewish history; and despite its friendly language, it indicated that many townspeople did not want Jews in their midst.

The provisions of the charter say much about the situation of German Jews at this time. We note that it was issued by a bishop, not a local baron. German bishops still controlled their towns, granted authority by the emperor as his representatives; they were the men with whom Jews had to come to terms. For the most part, they seem to have treated Jews well, encouraging their commercial activities and, with occasional exceptions, not harassing them with conversion efforts. But we can see that although bishops may have wanted Jews in town, many townspeople obviously did not: the Jews were not only enclosed by a wall but were expected to defend it—perhaps against their "fellow citizens" of Speyer. Local Christian merchants were not the problem; they were very unlikely to join riots. The potential troublemakers, the "mob," were ordinary working people or unemployed hangers-on at the bottom of the social ladder. It is worth noting that the Jews were expected to defend themselves, which means that they had weapons and knew how to use them (a situation we recognized as far back as the sixth century), but that would soon change. The fact that the community was granted so much judicial authority confirms that German Jewish communities had essentially the same social and political organization as those in France. In fact, some of the people in Speyer and other Rhineland towns may have originally come from France.[14]

It seems remarkable that the bishop consigned church-owned land to this community for a Jewish cemetery; this alone says that he was going out of his way to be friendly and receptive. As we know, medieval Jewish history is filled with accounts of hostile clergymen and frightful conversion campaigns. But the other side of the story is that, ironically enough, bishops were often the only individuals to whom Jews could turn for defense against mob attacks. Bishops had a heavy stake in preserving "law and order" in their towns and ensuring that they prospered economically. Since riots against Jews obviously might damage a town's economic prospects, Jews knew that they could depend on bishops for protection—or at least for attempted protection. Later we shall see how such expectations shaped Jewish behavior during the crusader riots.

In 1090, just six years after the charter was issued, the Jews of Speyer requested and received a second charter, this time from Emperor Henry IV himself. They may have wanted this because it includes provisions extending their rights to commercial pursuits beyond the town; or perhaps they were especially sensitive to hostility from townspeople and hoped that a charter from the emperor would better ensure their safety. The wording suggests that they had already experienced trouble: "Henceforth no one . . . shall presume to attack or assail them on any illicit ground." But Henry also extended their commercial privileges, granting them the right "to exchange their goods in just trading with all men and to travel freely and peacefully within the bounds of our kingdom in order to carry on their business and trade, to buy, and to sell." Along with this he granted them exemption from tolls and from special taxes. He also explicitly warned against forced baptisms, particularly of children, and against abduction and conversion of Jewish-owned slaves. (The last provision may have been a customary addition rather than a reflection of actual conditions, since slavery had virtually ended by this time.) There were also injunctions against harsh judicial treatment: Jews were not to be subjected to "judgment" procedures involving hot irons, or boiling or freezing water; they were not to be lashed, and they were not to be imprisoned. They were entitled to adjudicate for themselves unless they requested outside assistance.[15]

Whether Henry's charter was issued because the Jews of Speyer wanted their privileges extended or because they felt threatened, or both, he went to considerable lengths to ensure their safety and general welfare. The charter was issued only for Speyer, however, not for the

Jews of Germany as a whole, indicating that each Jewish community was viewed as a separate social unit. This is confirmed when we learn that Henry granted an almost identical charter to the Jews of Worms.[16] We see, then, that by this time Jews were expected to function independently—that is, to establish themselves as a semienclosed community within a town, to attend to their own legal and administrative needs, and to operate for most intents and purposes as a society within society. To most townspeople, Jews (if they thought about them at all) must have been an enigma of sorts: real people, living in one's own town, but eternal aliens with a mysterious way of life and a reputation based mainly on their role in the Gospels. That Jews should live alone—and wanted to do so—was self-evident. But being segregated, even if by choice, made them readily identifiable, and thus prime candidates for focused violence. That became all too evident when, some twelve years after the bishop had invited Jews into Speyer, six after the emperor himself confirmed and extended their rights and privileges, those same Jews were among the very first to die in the massacres associated with the First Crusade.

· 6 ·

"IN WITNESS TO THE ONENESS"

The First Crusade and the
Jews of the Rhineland

Toward the end of the eleventh century, word reached Europe that Christians could no longer go on pilgrimages to Jerusalem without facing serious danger and that the sacred journey might soon become altogether impossible. Until 1071, Jerusalem had been under the relatively benign rule of Shiite Muslims whose capital was at Cairo. But in that year a band of Seljuk Turks had overrun Jerusalem and much of Palestine, and they were another matter. The Seljuks were a people on the move. Having first overcome neighbors in their home region between the Aral and Caspian Seas, they had spread westward into Persia and Armenia and established themselves in Baghdad as rulers of the Sunni Muslim world. 1071 was also the year of their most impressive triumph over Christians, the defeat of the Byzantine emperor in a great battle at Manzikert in Turkish Armenia. They then proceeded to overrun much of Asia Minor, pushing their way dangerously near Constantinople.[1]

For the next twenty years Byzantines, Turks, and Shiites fought over the entire region without a clear victory for anyone. By 1095 the Byzantine emperor decided that his Muslim enemies were so weakened by internal fighting that the time had come for an effort to regain lost territory, and on this account he appealed to the French-born pope, Urban II, for aid against the enemies of Christendom. Relations between Byzantine emperors and Roman popes had not been especially cordial over the years, but this time the advantage seemed to lie with the pope, and he agreed to join the battle: he would call on the knights and clergymen of his native France to embark on a holy war of liberation.

Prelude: "God Wills It!"

In November 1095, Urban presided over a council of several hundred clergymen meeting in Clermont, in south-central France. On the twenty-seventh, toward the conclusion of the council, he held a public session, attended by a crowd so large that he spoke not in the cathedral but from a platform in an open field outside of town. In an eloquent, passionately delivered sermon he called upon Christians to take up the cross and journey to Jerusalem, where they would take just revenge for the suffering and humiliation that had been inflicted on the faithful in Christ's own sacred land. One chronicler (known as Robert the Monk) recalled his words as follows:

> Let none of your possessions detain you, no solicitude for your family affairs, since this land which you inhabit, shut in on all sides by the seas and surrounded by the mountain peaks, is too narrow for your large population; nor does it abound in wealth; and it furnishes scarcely enough food for its cultivators. Hence it is that you murder one another, that you wage war, and that frequently you perish by mutual wounds. Let therefore hatred depart from among you, let your quarrels end, let wars cease, and let all dissensions and controversies slumber. Enter upon the road to the Holy Sepulchre; wrest that land from the wicked race, and subject it to yourselves.[2]

We see that the pope was a practical man with more in mind than the holy city of Jerusalem: he spoke with rather surprising frankness of what he hoped to accomplish by directing surplus population into new territory. But the assembled crowd, profoundly stirred and hearing only the call to holy war, responded with shouts of "God wills it!" One bishop knelt before the papal throne, declaring that he was ready for the journey; hundreds immediately followed.

From Clermont the message was carried throughout France and beyond, and within a few months people everywhere were preparing to leave for Jerusalem. Urban had anticipated correctly that his most dependable support would come from the French nobility. By the late eleventh century, the boundaries of numerous small feudal domains had become fairly well fixed, and any number of barons were left with nothing much to anticipate at home in the way of profitable warfare. Land was in short supply at home, but in the Holy Land there was new land for the taking. Moreover, as we have seen, this was a time when many people, particularly among the nobility, were caught up in the wave of Christian piety that accompanied Church reform, and they responded eagerly to the idea of a holy war.

The Jews of France realized that religious excitement of this sort might mean serious trouble for them, but they could hardly have known how serious. By December 1095 they were sending letters to the Jewish communities of the Rhineland, warning them that armies were assembling and might soon be headed in their direction. In one of the three extant Hebrew chronicles of the crusade we are told that the French Jews "were gripped by fear and trembling," and that their letters urged the Rhineland Jews to fast and to beg God for deliverance from their enemies. But things had been going well enough for the Jews of Germany that they were unrealistically optimistic, and they seem not to have appreciated the severity of their situation.[3] The chronicler continues with a description of their response to the warnings: They informed the Jews of France that their leaders had decreed a fast day, and that now they were in God's hands. "We are greatly concerned about your well-being," they continued. "As for ourselves, there is no great cause for fear. We have not heard a word of such matters, nor has it been hinted that our lives are threatened by the sword."[4]

Whether Jewish communities in France were attacked, and if so, how many, is impossible to determine. In September 1096, Duke Robert of Normandy (son of William the Conqueror), about to depart for Jerusalem with an army, may have been responsible for an attack on the Jews of Rouen, but the only account is by a monk with a penchant for fabrication.[5] In any event, it seems certain that the situation for Jews in France never approached that in the Rhineland. In France each region was under the firm control of a powerful duke or count who could insist on discipline and order when armies moved through his territory. But in Germany there was no one of comparable stature locally—

only the emperor, who as it happened, was not even in the country when the crusaders arrived. Thus Jews found themselves confronting vicious mobs with no one but a well-intentioned but almost powerless (and often frightened) bishop to protect them.[6]

The pope had envisioned a holy war conducted by well-disciplined armies under the guidance of bishops, but as it turned out, the nobility took the lead. The armies that assembled in 1096 were led by powerful dukes and counts, and it was men of this stature who eventually reached and conquered Jerusalem. Departing that summer, they traveled mostly through Italy rather than Germany, and they did not harass Jews. In plain contrast were the haphazardly assembled bands of ordinary folk who gathered around a number of lesser barons, eager for change and excitement. Inadequately provisioned from the start, they were bent on getting what they needed through pillage. These people never made it to Jerusalem; most either dropped out, died along the way, or were killed in distant lands by those whom they plundered. It was people of this sort who attacked the Jews of the Rhineland.

Some of these raggle-taggle armies assembled around leaders who were frankly bizarre. One of the first to attract a band of followers was an itinerant French monk known as Peter the Hermit. A short, swarthy man with a lean face and a long grey beard, Peter went about barefoot and in rags, riding an ass and preaching to enthusiastic crowds wherever he appeared. It was said that Jesus himself had appeared to this holy man and handed him a letter instructing him to lead an army of crusaders, and he traveled with the letter on display. Peter attracted a motley crew (including women and children), without property or prospects, who were more than willing to follow anyone who promised adventure, salvation, and riches. Between December 1095 and April 1096 he traveled from France to the Rhineland, gathering an increasingly large and excited following as he proceeded. By April there were some fifteen thousand in his entourage. The fate of Byzantium could hardly have been of much interest to such folk; what moved them was the intoxicating prospect of a dramatic change in the dull routine of their lives, and perhaps the vision of a glorious future in the liberated Holy Land. But until that wonderful time arrived, they had to survive.

Destruction of the Rhineland Communities

Before his departure Peter had secured letters from the Jews of France urging those in the Rhineland to provide him with whatever he required. (The original letters to the Rhineland may have been sent because his followers had been threatening local French Jews.) Marching eastward, he and his entourage arrived at Trier and Cologne in early April, letters in hand. Apparently the Jews gave in to his demands. There was a great deal of excitement and perhaps random violence, but by April 20 he had moved on without further harassment of Jews.

We have seen that most crusading armies, whether legitimately or haphazardly mobilized, were originating in France. But Peter's preaching in the Rhineland now incited several local barons to raise armies of their own, and it was one of these in particular that proved to be catastrophic for the Jewish communities of the region. Among the new enthusiasts was a Count Emicho, a minor landholder in Upper Lorraine, described by a contemporary Christian chronicler as a man "of very ill repute on account of his tyrannical mode of life."[7] Perhaps taking a cue from Peter, Emicho declared that one of the apostles had appeared before him and branded a cross on his body.[8] He attracted a mob of the usual sort, but he had sufficient military reputation to induce a number of experienced French and German knights to join him.

Emicho, who seems to have been an accomplished charlatan, probably claimed that he had been divinely anointed for leadership in the messianic mode. For centuries Europeans had circulated fantasies about a supernatural figure, the "Emperor of the Last Days," who would conquer Jerusalem for Christ.[9] A mighty warrior (in the Jewish messianic style), his body marked between the shoulders with a cross, he would defeat the forces of Islam and establish himself triumphantly in the Holy City. There he would do battle once again, this time destroying the even more powerful army of Antichrist, the satanic son of a Jewish harlot, who aspired to rule the world in the name of the devil.[10] He would reign in Jerusalem amidst peace and contentment until the time arrived for Christ to return and receive from him the imperial crown. Finally, very near the end of worldly time, the Jews would miraculously awaken to the truth; they would be converted, and they too would enter at last into the Kingdom of Heaven. The millennium—a thousand years of glory with Christ as king of the world—would follow.

Emicho probably intended people to believe that he was branded with the cross of the "Emperor of the Last Days" and thus was destined to defeat not only Muslims but Antichrist himself. We can readily understand that in the popular imagination Jews were associated with the Antichrist; hence, that their conversion—or, failing that, their physical destruction—would have been a gratifying feature of a sacred pilgrimage intended to bring about the millennium. As the historian Hans Liebeschütz remarks, only "a small change of emphasis" was needed to transform voluntary conversion of Jews in the millenial age into something more immediately gratifying: "an impulse to bring about the end of Judaism by every means, including violence and murder."[11]

Emicho's army began its career of murder and plunder on May 3, a Saturday, with an attack on Speyer. The Jews took refuge with the bishop, successor to the one who had granted them the charter only twelve years earlier. He held fast to the promises of the charter and managed to save most of the community—perhaps at least in part because they were behind walls that could be defended. One historian says that they paid the bishop a handsome bribe, but a Jewish chronicler says that "the Lord had moved him to keep them alive without taking a bribe." Eleven or twelve Jews, captured and offered conversion, were killed when they refused. One woman committed suicide to escape being raped. Several of the perpetrators were seized, and the bishop ordered that their hands be cut off—possibly the first and last commensurate punishment that was imposed on any of Emicho's followers.[12]

Two weeks later Emicho's band were at Worms. Knowing what had happened at Speyer, the Jews were of course terrified. Some fled to the bishop for refuge and were permitted to remain within his compound. Others, probably reassured by friendly Christians that no harm would come to them, turned their money over to such people for safekeeping and remained hidden at home. We get some sense of their terror, and of their culturally conditioned passivity, from an outstanding Jewish chronicler, Solomon ben Simson:

When the Jewish communities became aware of their intentions, they resorted to the custom of our ancestors, repentance, prayer, and charity. The hands of the Holy Nation turned faint at this time, their hearts melted, and their strength flagged. They hid in their innermost rooms to escape the swirling sword. They subjected themselves to great endurance, abstaining from food and drink for three consecutive days and nights, and then fasting many days from sunrise to sunset, until their skin was shriveled and dry as wood upon their bones. And they cried out loudly and bitterly to God.[13]

Meanwhile, a mob of townspeople and peasants was milling about with the crusaders, waiting for the excitement to begin. Before long there ensued a riot in which some three hundred Jews were murdered. Those who had taken refuge with the bishop were safe for the moment, but the others were massacred: "set upon by the steppe-wolves," says Solomon ben Simson. The mob attacked everyone alike, he continues, male and female, infants to elderly. "They pulled down the stairways and destroyed the houses, looting and plundering; and they took the Torah Scroll, trampled it in the mud, and tore and burned it. The enemy devoured the children of Israel with open maw."[14]

A day or two later, an attack was launched on the bishop's compound, where some five hundred Jews were still gathered, hoping to weather the storm. They had sent clothing for the dead and messages of reassurance (no doubt undelivered) to those who had accepted baptism in order to survive, but they themselves had not ventured out. Apparently the bishop informed the Jews that he could no longer ensure their safety unless they agreed to baptism—not necessarily a case of cynical opportunism, for he was probably urging them to take the only way out. Some Jews asked for time to decide, then killed their families and themselves; others did nothing.[15]

Eventually the mob broke through the gates and perpetrated another grisly massacre. Most victims died without resisting. Whether or not they envisioned their own deaths as voluntary martyrdom, Solomon ben Simson, writing a generation later, did precisely that: the victims had chosen to die, he said, "to sanctify the Name" (kiddush ha-Shem). In his description of the scene, a key document for its time, we see the emergence of martyrdom as a new, all-important theme in European Jewish consciousness:

> The Jews, inspired by the valor of their brethren, similarly chose to be slain in order to sanctify the Name before the eyes of all, and exposed their throats for their heads to be severed for the glory of the Creator. There were also those who took their own lives, thus fulfilling the verse: "The mother was dashed in pieces with her children." Fathers fell upon their sons, being slaughtered upon one another, and they slew one another—each man his kin, his wife and children; bridegrooms slew their betrothed, and merciful women their only children. They all accepted the divine decree wholeheartedly and, as they yielded up their souls to the Creator, cried out: "Hear, O Israel, the Lord is our God, the Lord is One." The enemy stripped them naked, dragged them along, and then cast them off, sparing only a small number whom they forcibly baptized in their profane waters.[16]

We hear little of resistance in these accounts; obviously the Jews were overwhelmingly outnumbered, and despite what we learn about armed resistance at Mainz (to be discussed shortly), no one could have mounted an adequate defense. A few individuals did fight back, but of course not for long. One chronicler tells of a youth named Simcha ha-Cohen, who agreed to accept baptism, then drew a knife and stabbed three Christians before being overwhelmed and slain.[17]

The Jewish chroniclers speak bitterly of the bishop and the townspeople of Worms, all of whom they blame for the catastrophe, but modern historians have concluded that nothing more could have been done. The more civil element of the local population, definitely a minority, could not have stopped Emicho's army, particularly when it was joined by mobs of townspeople, and the bishop was probably being frank when he told Jews that conversion was their only option.[18]

Having by this time massacred some eight hundred people, Emicho and his cohort proceeded to Mainz, where they arrived on May 25, eager to repeat their performance. The town gates were closed, probably by order of the local archbishop, for trouble had already begun. Sometime earlier a predatory mob had gathered outside the town gates, especially excited by the presence of a peasant woman who claimed that her pet goose had miraculous understanding of the crusade and was accompanying her as guide and mascot. A riot had developed, with townspeople fighting crusaders, and one of the latter was killed. Solomon ben Simson says that the Jews were blamed for the death. In any event, when Emicho's band arrived, the mob was already inflamed and no doubt eager to attack Jews.

The Jewish community leaders, led by Rabbi Kalonymos ben Meshullam, decided on what was in truth their only available course of action: they took payments to the archbishop and to a local count and were granted refuge in their palaces. The archbishop and his staff advised the Jews to bring their wealth for safekeeping in the church treasury, which they did—an ironic twist to an always complex relationship. In view of what followed, the Jewish chroniclers interpret the entire affair in the worst light; as Solomon puts it, employing a metaphor from Ecclesiastes, "they gave this advice so as to herd us together and hold us like fish that are caught in an evil net."[19] But again it must be said that the plan was reasonable, even though it failed.[20]

The Jews, perhaps still unable fully to recognize the severity of their situation, sent an emissary to Emicho, bearing a substantial gift of gold and letters for him to present to other Jewish communities along his route. In return he promised not to cause further trouble. But of course the promise was cynical and worthless. At midday on the twenty-seventh, local people opened the town gates, whereupon the entire mob rushed in and headed directly for the archbishop's palace. Leading the attack was an organized force under Emicho's command. Realizing that the situation was already out of control, and probably fearing for his own life, the archbishop fled with his staff to the nearby town of Rudesheim on the opposite bank of the Rhine, where he owned a country villa, leaving the Jews to their fate. "We were not even comparable to Sodom and Gomorrah," laments Solomon, "for in their case they were offered reprieve if they could produce at least ten righteous people, whereas in our case not twenty, not even ten, were sought."[21]

Once again, many Jews accepted death without resistance; it was said that some men sat with their prayer shawls draped over their shoulders and offered their necks to be slashed. But not all were so passive. A few faced their oppressors in the manner of medieval warriors (although surely with a much different mentality): "They donned their armor and their weapons of war," says Solomon, "adults and children alike. . . . But, as a result of their sufferings and fasts, they did not have the strength to withstand the onslaught of the foe," and "as a result of their transgressions the enemy overpowered them and captured the gate."[22] With that, the mob swarmed into the palace for an orgy of murder and pillage. Many hundreds of Jews, possibly a thousand or more, were slaughtered. As usual, some were offered conversion and a few accepted to save their lives, but most either accepted death or, in an act of ultimate defiance, killed one another and themselves. Having to kill children was the supreme torment, but both mothers and fathers did so: "The women girded their loins with strength and slew their own sons and daughters, and then themselves. Many men also mustered their strength and slaughtered their wives and children and infants. The most gentle and tender of women slaughtered the child of her delight. They all arose, man and woman alike, and slew one another."[23]

A day or so later, a mob set fire to the count's palace and massacred the Jews when they tried to escape. At some point in the riots, which probably lasted at least three days, a few Jews made their way to the synagogue and burned it down to save it from being desecrated. Even when all was obviously lost, some Jews struggled on. We learn from another chronicler that "righteous women hurled stones from the windows on the enemy" and taunted them by referring to Jesus as a "putrid corpse." On at least one occasion they caught a crusader and stoned him to death.[24]

A man named David ben Nathaniel engaged in an act of lone defiance. He had hidden with his family in the courtyard of a priest who clearly wanted to do his best for them. Realizing that they were about to be discovered, the priest urged them to convert so that he could announce this and save their lives. David replied that he should tell everyone to come hear him speak, and the priest ran off to relay what he interpreted as good news. As the chronicler tells it, David faced the assembled crowd and spoke as follows:

> Alas, you are children of whoredom, believing as you do in one born of whoredom. As for me—I believe in the Eternally Living God Who dwells in the lofty heavens. In Him have I trusted to this day and in

Him will I trust until my soul departs. If you slay me, my soul will abide in the Garden of Eden—in the light of life. You, however, descend to the deep pit, to eternal obloquy, condemned together with your deity—the son of promiscuity, the crucified one![25]

Whether the man spoke in these words or not, he may well have spoken defiantly, for we are told that he and his entire family were slain immediately. His speech as interpreted by the chronicler can be read as another example of the developing emphasis on martyrdom as an act of affirmation and defiance, embellished in this case with grievous insults to Christians and their faith.

The leader of the Jewish community, Rabbi Kalonymos, had led the initial resistance to the attack on the archbishop's palace, but in the course of the struggle he and fifty-three young men fled into the adjoining cathedral and hid in the sacristy (the storage room for priestly vestments and sacred objects—again, the deepest irony), where they survived for the remainder of the day. Late that night, a messenger arrived to tell them that the archbishop had arranged for boats to carry them across the Rhine to Rudesheim, where he was entrenched with several hundred armed defenders. But by the time the refugees arrived, the mob was already in pursuit. The archbishop, realizing that his men would not risk their lives to protect Jews, declared that he could do no more for them unless they agreed to convert. Some responded by killing themselves; others tried to flee into the surrounding countryside and forest, but most were caught and slain. Kalonymos and his son were among the dead.

All told, the massacre lasted into early June. When it was over, somewhere between seven hundred and thirteen hundred people had been murdered, and the foremost Jewish community of the Rhineland, one of the greatest in European Jewish history, had been all but destroyed.

Emicho and his band remained in Mainz only for the first few days of the riots. Moving on toward their next victims, they now proceeded to Cologne—traveling northwestward, we note, in a direction almost precisely opposite to that of Jerusalem—and arrived there on either May 29 or 30, just at the beginning of the Jewish holiday of Shavuot (Pentecost). News of their approach had reached Cologne the evening before, and the Jews had gone at once to seek refuge in the homes of Christian acquaintances (probably established merchants, people with whom they were on good business terms). Initially there was no serious trouble, but on the first of June the mob broke into the Jewish quarter and looted the empty homes. The synagogue was also looted and burned, and Torah scrolls ripped and trampled upon. One unfortunate man was dragged to the church to be baptized, but he spat and shouted insults and was killed at once. A woman carrying gold and silver to her husband's hiding place was also caught and murdered. These appear to have been the only immediate victims. On June 3 the archbishop arranged for the Jews to be transported to seven neighboring villages, where they remained in hiding for three weeks, praying and fasting, obviously terrified—"daily anticipating their death," says Solomon ben Simson. On June 24, when a crowd of peasants assembled at one of the villages to celebrate a saint's day, the news went around that Jews were hiding nearby. Once again, men, women, and children were massacred. Some were tortured in vain efforts to force them to accept baptism. One man was tortured into unconsciousness, then baptized; when he recovered, he returned briefly to his home in Cologne, then drowned himself in the Rhine.

Over the following week much the same thing happened in five other villages: discovery by mobs, forced conversions, murder, plunder, and suicide. Local Jews were victims along with the refugees from Cologne. Only the few Jews who had hidden in the village of Kerpen survived, because it lay somewhat southwest of Cologne; the other villages were to the north.

Having been responsible for the virtual elimination of the Jewish population of his own region, Emicho now departed for Jerusalem by way of Hungary. But there his predatory army engaged in several battles with Hungarian forces and were eventually killed almost to a man. Emicho's "crusade" was ended; he escaped with a few companions back to Germany. Albert of Aix, a pious Christian chronicler, offered a final commentary: "So the hand of the Lord is believed to have been against the pilgrims, who had sinned by excessive impurity and fornication, and who had slaughtered the exiled Jews through greed of money, rather than for the sake of God's justice, although the Jews were opposed to Christ. The Lord is a just judge and orders no one unwillingly, or under compulsion, to come under the yoke of the Catholic faith."[26]

Some of the crusaders accompanying Emicho had taken off on their own at Mainz and turned westward to attack Jews in the Moselle Valley region, particularly at Trier and Metz. Twenty-two Jews died at Metz and many others accepted conversion, at the hands of either this mob or another. The Jews of Trier had already been forced to bribe Peter the Hermit; but this second threat, coming from people who now knew that they could rob and murder Jews with impunity, was not so readily escaped. Solomon's account of the events at Trier is not clear on chronology, but it appears that some of the townspeople had been threatening Jews in order to obtain bribes, and there had probably been at least one riot even before the outsiders arrived. When they did appear, sometime around the last week of May, the Jews were already demoralized; many had been fasting and praying for weeks, probably ever since the encounter with Peter. Some now panicked and killed their families and themselves almost at once. Women are described as filling their skirts with stones and leaping off the town bridge. Most people tried the familiar tactic: they fled to the archbishop's castle, a well-fortified structure that promised better than average protection.

The archbishop was away at the time, but he returned several days later, in time to face the mob. Sunday, June 8, was Whitsunday, the Christian Pentecost, and a large fair was being held in town, with many peasants in for the day and everyone no doubt aware that the Jews were still in hiding. In the cathedral the archbishop preached a bold sermon urging calm and forbearance. But the crowd responded so virulently that he fled in fright and went into hiding himself for an entire week. When things had quieted down somewhat, he sent word to the Jews urging them to convert promptly; otherwise he could do nothing more for them. It is said that he or his palace guard even went so far as to permit two Jews (one a young man who volunteered) to be led out and killed as warning to the rest. But to Jewish eyes the only message was the glory of martyrdom: "Know that if each of us had ten souls, we would give them up in witness to the Oneness of His Name, rather than let them defile us."[27] A Christian chronicler reports, however, that the community rabbi agreed to convert and advised people to save themselves by doing likewise, which many did. (Interestingly, we learn that this rabbi was the only Trier Jew who did not revert to Judaism soon afterward.)[28]

It appears, then, that although many Jews in the Moselle Valley towns died during these attacks, quite a few, perhaps proportionately more than in the Rhineland, converted and were spared. In 1097, Henry IV returned from Italy and granted formal permission to all forcibly converted Jews to return to Judaism, and the great majority did so promptly. They were welcomed back into the fold, treated not as defectors but as retrieved victims. Incidentally, the only recorded response of Pope Urban to the fate of the Jews during the crusade was a condemnation of Henry for granting remission of baptism.[29]

Less is known about the fate of Jewish communities elsewhere along the path of the crusading armies, but at least two more major assaults occurred, on the important communities of Prague and Regensburg. The Prague community was attacked sometime in May or June by an army led by one Volkmar, another baron from the Rhineland, probably not unlike Emicho in character. They massacred an unknown number of Jews in Prague, once again despite the protests of the bishop, and may have done the same at Magdeburg. The attack on Regensburg, which probably involved mass conversions as well as murder of those who resisted, also took place in May and was perpetrated either by Emicho's army or by still another band of crusaders led by one of Peter's disciples, a man named Gottschalk. According to Solomon ben Simson, the Regensburg Jews were herded into a river (presumably the Danube), then baptized collectively by making the sign of the cross over them.[30] One or another of these same bands may also have been responsible for massacres in other towns of Bohemia and Bavaria. None ever came near Jerusalem; they were all massacred by the Hungarians, who proved less vulnerable than Jews to victimization. The fate of crusaders of this sort "deeply impressed Western Christendom," says one historian. "To most good Christians it appeared as a punishment meted out from on high to the murderers of the Jews."[31]

The Message of the Chronicles

The most complete chronicle of these events, the one I have quoted most often, was composed about 1140 and is attributed to Solomon ben

Simson; some of the material was probably added later by unknown authors.[32] Solomon employs many stock phrases; for example, his wish for such men as Emicho, repeatedly expressed, is "may his bones be ground to dust." He embellishes his account with biblical phrases and at times confines the narrative almost entirely to tales of heroic martyrdom. This was all appropriate for the time. The literary style is not unlike that of contemporary Christian literature, even including the emphasis on martyrdom.[33] But Solomon (and whoever else contributed to his chronicle) is a skillful narrator who not only describes events vividly but also provides us with some sense of how matters were perceived on both sides. The Jews, realizing from the start that they were impossibly outnumbered, and surrounded even in their own towns by people who were mostly hostile or indifferent, turned first (as European Jews almost invariably have done) to men at the top: local bishops, who represented not the Church but public authority. A few fled to the homes of Christians whom they had reason to trust, probably friendly merchants. Some were fortunate enough to find secure refuge, but the majority were not. Many, it seems, were paralyzed with fear and retreated into behavior that, if anything, may have lessened their chances for survival. We recall Solomon's descriptions of people fasting to the point of weakness and exhaustion, their skin "shriveled and dry as wood upon their bones"—hardly the best preparation for the fight of one's life.

As I have already suggested, perhaps the deepest irony in the entire story attaches to the relationship between Jews and bishops. Jews turned repeatedly to these princes of the Church, and bishops consistently did their best to defend and protect Jews, even when this meant no inconsiderable danger to themselves. We envision Jews huddling terrified in cathedral courtyards, crowding for days on end in rooms of an archbishop's palace (surely a place they never expected to see from the inside), racing for their lives into a cathedral sacristy filled with crucifixes and chalices. We see them bringing their wealth to a cathedral treasury for safekeeping, and on at least one occasion bringing even Torah scrolls to a bishop's palace to save them from the mob. The bishops themselves behave with commendable, even astonishing, sympathy and generosity. True, they often urge conversion as the only way out, but with hindsight that advice seems well intended and reasonable. (Had more Jews gone through the motions of conversion, they would have lived to return to Judaism within a year.) To put this somewhat differently, what we would now call social class outweighed religion when a bishop was acting in his political role. After all, most Jews were respectable merchants who contributed to the local economy and behaved properly, and it was in a bishop's best interests to protect such people.

When all hope was lost, some Jews—those who had time to decide on their own fate—accepted martyrdom as their only honorable option. The other option, presumably offered only before rioting became frenzied, was to accept conversion on the spot; but many Jews, possibly the great majority, refused and were killed at once. The dozen or so martyrs of Speyer who "sanctified their Creator on the holy Sabbath"[34] were followed by hundreds, then thousands, of Jews who died "to sanctify the Name." Many victims killed their family members and themselves before the crusaders could reach them—perhaps to ensure that they would not succumb at the last moment to the urge to live. Surely the most dramatic form of martyrdom was the killing of children, an act hard to imagine. Converts to Judaism grasped the opportunity to declare the firmness of their commitment, even if only to those who were going to die with them. Solomon tells of one such man in Mainz, whose mother had not been Jewish: "He called out in a loud voice to all those that stood about him, saying: 'Until now you have scorned me. Now see what I shall do.' And he took the knife which he was holding in his hand and thrust it into his neck in front of all, and he slaughtered himself in the name of the Mighty of Mighties, Whose Name is Lord of Hosts."[35] Some Jews submitted to conversion only to kill themselves soon afterward, but others were fortunate enough to survive until they were permitted to return to their communities with the approval of the emperor as well as local rabbinic authorities.

Up to this point I have cited the Hebrew chronicles, with their emphasis on heroic martyrdom, as essentially accurate historical accounts. But can we assume their entire accuracy? How many Jews did in fact die willingly as martyrs, and how many were helpless victims who had no choice whatever? The chroniclers portray people as not only willing but eager to die for their faith, and repeatedly name individuals who did so: an honor roll for readers' inspiration. But they were writing a generation or more after the events they describe; they were neither eyewitnesses nor survivors, although they may well have spoken with survivors or read letters and chronicles that have been lost. Robert Chazan is convinced that "their commitment to detail and diversity" with regard to the behavior of both Christians and Jews speaks for their reliability.[36]

But there are arguments on the other side. First, there is the question of selective memory: Did the chroniclers record what best suited their purposes and gloss over whatever did not? There can hardly be any question that some Jews died as intentional martyrs. But considering that the victims numbered in the thousands, the martyrs identified by name were obviously a very small minority; for the others we have only the word of the chroniclers that they died bravely and willingly. I find it not difficult to imagine that most people died in terror, torment, and despair, with neither time nor will to make any decision about how or why they were dying. That they wanted above all to live is surely beyond question. The many who fled to bishops for protection obviously had no wish to become martyrs. Even those who slew their families and themselves—beyond challenge or compare as an act of passion—did so to escape what may have been an even more dreadful death at the hands of raging mobs. Perhaps all that can be said in conclusion is that at least some of those who perished may have been able to do so in a manner that made their final moments meaningful and thus bearable.

Second, there can be no escaping the hagiographic character of the narratives—that is, their insistence on the saintliness of the victims. All the Jewish deaths, whether presented as passive acceptance or heroic defiance, are idealized and endowed with significance. These dead were not just casualties; they were sacrificial victims whose deaths served to atone for the sins of all Israel and to attest to the devotion of the Holy Nation to its God. In short, we can hardly accept the chroniclers or their sources as "objective" recorders of historical "facts," because that was not their foremost purpose. Their purpose was to inspire, even to instruct, their readers: This, they were saying, is how Jews must learn to die.

The Christian Perspective

If many Jews perceived their tragic fate as the ultimate challenge to faith, the crusaders—at least those who had something in mind other than murder, rape, and pillage—saw the situation quite differently. They were on the way to liberate Jerusalem and to establish there a Christian domain that would someday become the kingdom of Jesus Christ. Immediately before his return, or perhaps just at that time, would occur the conversion of the Jews, a miraculous awakening that would herald the end of ordinary time and the beginning of the millenium. The Jews of the Rhineland—conveniently concentrated, well established and prosperous, favored even by bishops—were irresistible targets for a conversion effort that—who could tell?—might lead Jews everywhere to realizing that the time for Christ's return was at hand.

It would be going too far to argue that most crusaders had conversion as their first object, and that they killed Jews only when the latter refused to comply. Clearly, many participants in riots were there because they wanted to rape, rob, and murder. But even the Jewish chroniclers recognize that for some crusaders the goal was conversion. Speaking of events at Worms, for example, Solomon says that the crusaders spared "only a small number whom they forcibly baptized in their profane waters."[37] No doubt many Jews, probably most, were never offered conversion: they were the enemies of Christ and had wealth for the taking—reasons enough for slaughtering them without mercy.

In the final analysis, perhaps the entire disaster was inevitable: if Emicho's band, or Volkmar's, or Gottschalk's, had not been the perpetrators, there would have been others. For although Jews and Christians were all "medieval" men and women, the cultural and psychological distance—the differences in perceptions of what the world was about—between the crusaders for Christ and the Jews of Germany could hardly have been more profound among people living in the very same time and place; and the prospect of an unfavorable outcome for the latter could hardly have been more plainly ordained.

The Impact on Jewish Consciousness

These events—peripheral, really, to the events on the main stage and rating at best only a page or two in the work of most historians of the crusades—dealt a blow to Ashkenazic Jewry from which, in a sense, it never recovered. Chazan argues that the aftermath was characterized by a "return to normalcy," and that despite all that had happened, the Jewish communities not only recovered but grew rapidly during the following century.[38] Moreover, he says, there is little reason to conclude that Jews became obsessed with the massacres or that their attitudes toward life in Christian Europe changed very much. He does acknowledge, though, that prayers centering on martyrdom now became an important part of the liturgy.[39]

The three closely related towns of the Rhineland—Speyer, Worms, and Mainz (Cologne was farther north)—were now spoken of collectively by the acronym SHUM (derived from the initial letters of their names) and served as the model of the *kehillah kedoshah* (holy community), defined by its piety and by its readiness for collective martyrdom. Even the year of their tribulation, 1096, became known by the acronym TaTNU, based on the Hebrew letters designating the date in the Jewish calendar—a date to be permanently remembered along with those of other major catastrophes.[40] The seven-week interval between Passover and Shavuot (late April to early June), the most pleasant season of the year, became a formally observed mourning period, incorporating memory of the massacres indelibly into the Jewish consciousness.

By the twelfth century, on the sabbath before Shavuot—anniversary of the attack on Speyer—the names of martyrs were being read out in the synagogue, and a new prayer, the *Av harakhamim* (merciful Father), had entered the liturgy:

> May the merciful Father who dwells on high, in his infinite mercy, remember those saintly, upright and blameless souls, the holy communities who offered their lives for the sanctification of the divine name. They were lovely and amiable in their life, and were not parted after death. They were swifter than eagles and stronger than lions to

do the will of their Master and the desire of their Stronghold. May our God remember them favorably among the other righteous of the world; may He avenge the blood of His servants which has been shed.

The Hebrew chronicles are exemplary tales, handbooks of instruction, as it were, for readers who might someday be called upon to offer themselves as martyrs. Accordingly, the authors are primarily concerned not with what we would call social history—not even with chronologically clear narratives—but with detailed accounts of the suffering and heroic self-sacrifice of named individuals. Jews who converted are mentioned sympathetically but reluctantly; it is those who died on whom the chroniclers want to focus attention, and it is they whom readers are encouraged to admire. Acceptance of martyrdom was an established tradition long before the eleventh century, but now the prospect of personal martyrdom came to have more reality and immediacy than ever before. "The ancient tradition of martyrdom," says the historian Jacob Katz, "became, once again, a reality," and the deeds of the Rhineland martyrs "became a paragon for the generations to come." The act of self-sacrifice was deemed especially fulfilling when performed as an act of defiance, so that Christian tormentors might see for themselves the sustaining power of belief in God's ineffable Oneness.[41]

Thus, from this time onward, readiness for martyrdom emerged as one of the hallmarks of Ashkenazic Jewish culture—what might (ironically) be called an adaptive strategy for a people living in a perilous world.

· 7 ·

CHRISTIAN RENEWAL,
JEWISH DECLINE

The Twelfth Century

Twelfth-century Europeans seem to have known that they were living in an unusual time. The term they most often used to describe their society was *renovatio*, renewal: creating new ways of thinking, new approaches to life's questions and problems. We describe them as Europeans, but they did not yet have that sense of themselves. They did know that they lived in a dynamic civilization extending far beyond their own immediate regions. They knew too that their world was changing. Because the population continued to grow, more and more land had to be cleared. Growth in agricultural knowledge kept pace. All sorts of new inventions and techniques appeared: cast-iron tools, water mills, two-wheeled carts, horse collars, and more. Improved building techniques climaxed in the great Gothic architectural style.

Although the average town still had only a few thousand inhabitants, many more of them were merchants, and towns were becoming lively centers of commerce. By mid-century a number of towns, particularly in Champagne, had become the sites of regularly scheduled commercial fairs that attracted throngs of merchants. The economy was now monetary as never before; currency, says the historian Georges Duby, "was everywhere, dominating everything."[1] Money might be wicked, but Europeans could no longer live without it.

France and Germany remained feudal societies. French kings were still confined mostly to their own royal domains, and much of their energy was taken up with endless struggles to maintain royal authority in the face of challenges from powerful barons as well as external enemies. The political history of the century was dominated by the British Angevin kings, most notably Henry II, who ruled not only England and Normandy but also a huge parcel of western French territory. The situation in Germany was similar: although German kings were emperors of the Holy Roman Empire, their authority too was limited by powerful dukes who controlled their own domains. In 1152, Frederick I, called Frederick Barbarossa, came to the throne, and Germany gained its most forceful leadership since the tenth century, but even he had to come to terms with the dukes. So life in much of western Europe still meant submission to the authority of a regional ruler—a duke, a count, or even a lesser lord—who ruled his own territory with virtually unlimited power.

The one institution that dominated twelfth-century life beyond question was the Church. Bishops were no longer appointed by kings; they were elected and invested by their fellow clergymen, and kings were permitted only to grant them secular authority. This might be called separation of powers, but with the understanding that the Church stood above and beyond all earthly monarchs. By the latter half of the century, the Church had reached a zenith of power and prestige that would be maintained for more than a hundred years. Europe had become, above all else, a Christian world, and people now looked to the Church as a transcendent power that endowed everyone's life with a sense of unity and purpose beyond anything achievable by kings or emperors.

Monasteries were becoming centers of social and economic life, and monks were revered by peasants and lords alike. Many monks were not at all isolated from the give-and-take of everyday life; they ministered to the needs of ordinary people, providing refuge for the weak and food for the hungry. Monks were idealized as models of Christian piety. "The world was full of violence, steeped in mortal sin and depravity," says Frederich Heer; "amid such confusion only a monk could achieve personal perfection."[2] But many monasteries were also productive enterprises, worldly and wealthy, their abbots and monks living as feudal lords supported by the labor of peasants who were bound to monastery lands.

The outstanding clergyman of the century was Bernard of Clairvaux, abbot of a prominent monastery affiliated with the Cistercian order, which had arisen early in the century in reaction to the increasing materialism of older monastic orders. The new order was dedicated to the original monastic principles of poverty, humility, obedience, and manual labor, and under Bernard's guidance its influence spread rapidly. What mattered for Bernard was spiritual enlightenment. Turning away from the image of Jesus as ruler and judge of the universe, he imagined a gentle redeemer dying in agony. He also helped transform the image of the Virgin Mary, who now became the loving mother not only of Jesus but of all humanity—another intercessor with God, infinitely merciful and forgiving.[3]

The century was marked by a new wave of popular piety and religiosity. Everyone was now deemed equal in the sight of God, and the goal of duke and peasant alike was supposedly to transcend worldly concerns and prepare for the life to come—best achieved, of course, through dutiful acceptance of the Church's teachings and participation in its rituals.

During the first half of the century, intellectual life centered on the monasteries, with their strictly traditional approach to sacred texts. But by mid-century, in urban centers throughout Europe, there were appearing schools of an entirely different kind, schools that represented the spirit of *renovatio*. Beginning in association with cathedrals, the most advanced of them were soon evolving into the earliest form of universities, where teachers and students could meet in a new kind of relationship. Although still occupied with theological questions, their approach to knowledge was a radical departure from the past. Rather than accepting texts as beyond question, scholars now set out to examine them logically and rationally. As the philosopher Abelard declared, the new path to knowledge was through open debate, with questions and answers posed in dialectical form until everyone was satisfied that a text had been thoroughly examined and understood. The method was called "disputation," because the pros and cons of an argument were presented, followed by a resolution taking account of opposing interpretations. Classical Greek texts, now available in Latin translations made by Arab and Jewish scholars in Spain, inspired new

standards of mental discipline, and rational inquiry replaced unques-
tioning faith as the hallmark of their scholarship.

In time, the effects of the intellectual renewal extended beyond the
universities. Literacy increased everywhere, and people began to write
in Latin and vernacular languages, not just about religious questions
but about the pleasures and challenges of earthly life. So although
twelfth-century life and thought were still very "medieval" in style,
European civilization was expanding in directions that foreshadowed
the early Renaissance.

Jewish Status in Decline

Even though Jews were participating (in a limited way) in the twelfth-
century "renewal" and even benefiting somewhat from it, the ultimate
outcome for them was to be decidedly negative. The most damaging
element in their situation was that they were being gradually confined
to moneylending. This trend began in northern France; until late in the
century, Jews in southern France and in much of the German empire
continued to be active, prosperous merchants. In southern France they
were even serving as town officials and as financial advisers to local
barons and clergymen.[4] To the east they were participating in a steadily
developing international trade linking Russia to western Europe. The
Bavarian town of Regensburg, a center for this commerce, was home
to a flourishing Jewish community.[5] Aside from the major population
centers—Paris, Orléans, Cologne, Mainz, and a few others—most Jewish communities were still small, numbering only a hundred or so individuals in all. But they had become well established, with firm
leadership and a recognized, if sometimes precarious, position in their
towns. In Paris, Jews were in the center of things, living in crowded,
unattractive neighborhoods but participating in the excitement of urban life.

Jewish intellectual achievements matched, and in a sense paralleled, those of the Christian world. A number of outstanding scholars,
including some descendants of Rashi, developed a mode of biblical
and talmudic scholarship that was obviously similar to that of their
Christian counterparts. Some even met with Christian scholars who
hoped to discover what they called *Hebraica veritas,* the true Hebrew

meaning of biblical passages—the question being, Have we interpreted this correctly, or have we been misguided by poor translations? Also, as mentioned earlier, Jewish scholars in Spain were collaborating with Arabs in translations of classical Greek texts, particularly Aristotle, from Arabic and Hebrew into Latin, for use by Christian scholars—another form of long-distance commerce. It cannot be said that Jews were truly sharing in the new culture; for one thing, they were not to be found in the universities. But they had their own cultural achievements that gained them permanent fame in Jewish history and also attracted the attention of their Christian counterparts.

Nevertheless, it must be said that the overall course of Jewish life in the twelfth century was downhill—that, slowly but surely, as Christians progressed and prospered, Jews became pariahs. The clearest evidence for this trend was in their changing political status. The charters that had been issued to Jews earlier—Louis's ninth century charters to individual Jewish merchants, for example, or the Speyer charter of 1084 to an entire community—had one thing in common: the Jews were assumed to be independent persons, free to decide where they lived and on what terms. But now they were becoming dependent; they were assumed to be helpless, in need of protection and obliged to please their protectors.

The trend was already modestly apparent in 1103, when at an assembly of the German nobility Henry IV ordered that for a period of four years there was to be a "public peace" throughout his realm and that violence was to be punished with mutilation or death. Several kinds of people were singled out as especially vulnerable and in need of particular protection: clergy, merchants, women, and Jews.[6] It is important to note that the first three categories are defined by occupation or gender, while Jew is an ethnic category that in fact crosses two of the others. The discrimination is of a positive kind, but it is discrimination nonetheless.

Everywhere in western Europe but especially throughout northern France, Jewish communities now came under the explicit protection of local lords—but only as long as they proved useful. In effect, they had become the personal property of those whom they served, with no rights other than what they "earned" by supplying money on demand. Barons maintained tight control over "their" Jews, whom they needed

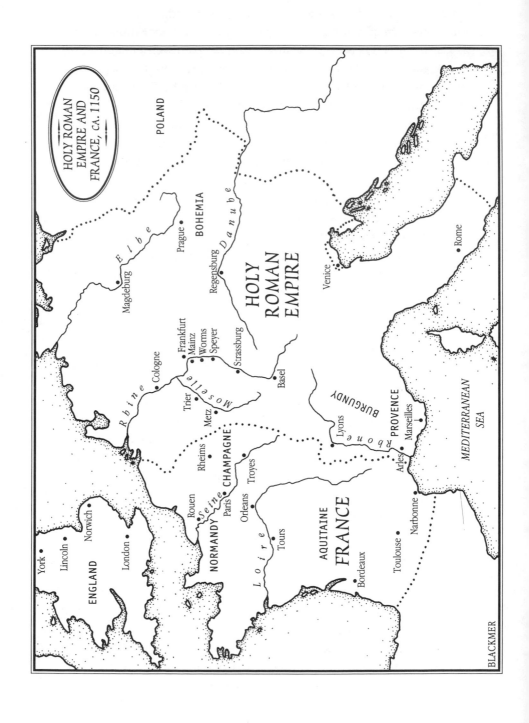

HOLY ROMAN
EMPIRE AND
FRANCE, CA. 1150

POLAND

BOHEMIA

Prague

Elbe

Magdeburg

Danube

Regensburg

HOLY
ROMAN
EMPIRE

Venice

Rome

Frankfurt
Mainz
Worms
Speyer
Strassburg

Cologne

Rhine

Basel

Moselle

Trier

Metz

BURGUNDY

Lyons

PROVENCE

Marseilles

Rhône

Arles

MEDITERRANEAN
SEA

Rheims

CHAMPAGNE

Troyes

Rouen

Seine

Paris

Orleans

NORMANDY

Narbonne

York

Lincoln

Norwich

London

ENGLAND

Loire

Tours

AQUITAINE

FRANCE

Toulouse

Bordeaux

to help finance everything from building construction to warfare. Jews were expected to grant generous loans, of course, either interest-free or on very favorable terms, and to pay whatever taxes or fines the lord saw fit to impose. In return, he guaranteed their safety—or, perhaps more often, simply tolerated their presence. For the relationship was by definition wholly unequal, a "business arrangement" with all the decision-making power on one side. Jewish financiers, no matter how wealthy they might become, could be drained in a moment at the lord's whim. Moreover, to maintain their precarious position they were obliged to loan money to everyone else at rates guaranteed to generate resentment: less-favored clients were routinely charged more than 40 percent interest. Usury of such dimensions was inescapable if they were to meet the lords' incessant demands for tax payments and low-interest loans, but of course it meant that they soon had a reputation for greed and rapacity that confirmed everything said about them in the Gospels. Thus they were caught in a nasty trap: disliked and resented by the general populace because they did no visible work and seemed to flourish on the misfortunes of others; too weak to defend themselves, hence dependent on rapacious lords. Although this state of affairs developed only gradually, the result was that while most Jewish communities had been relatively independent at the beginning of the century, by the end they were not.

"Expecting Nothing Therefrom":
Usury as Sin

We must think more about moneylending and usury. Aside from the charge of deicide, surely no other image of Jews has contributed so much to their rejection and oppression, and no theme is more pervasive in Ashkenazic Jewish history from this time onward.

To begin, we have to distinguish between "lending" and "usury" as these were defined in medieval times, for the difference was between moral behavior and sin. An edict issued in Charlemagne's time stated the matter very clearly, in terms that were still accepted in the twelfth century—at least by everyone except members of the new merchant class. Lending, the edict proclaimed, meant giving something and requiring only that it be returned later; usury meant claiming a return greater than the original loan.[7] In short, any interest whatever constituted usury, and usury was immoral. Even ordinary commercial gain—buying and selling merchandise for profit—was by strict interpretation unacceptable. The same applied to a "mortgage," whereby a creditor received temporary usage of an estate, including receipt of its produce and income, until a loan was repaid: all was usury. These ideas fitted the traditional Germanic "gift economy" grounded in personal relationships and reciprocity, but of course they were unrealistic for what had now become a vibrant commercial economy.

This was not simply a question of social courtesy, and not just a matter for secular law. It was a moral and religious injunction, backed by sacred texts, sanctioned by the Church, standing beyond analysis or challenge by any proper Christian. Among other often quoted texts was the Sermon on the Mount, as recorded in the Gospel of Luke, chapter 6: Jesus tells his disciples to give freely to everyone without expectation of any return whatever; for "if you lend only where you expect to be repaid, what credit is that to you?" Rather, one should "lend without expecting any return" other than heavenly rewards. (v. 34, 35). In the standard Latin translation, the Vulgate, the key phrase, *nihil inde sperantes,* "expecting nothing therefrom," was of course understood quite literally. Old Testament passages were also cited, particularly Deuteronomy 23:20, which permitted charging interest to a "foreigner" but not to a "fellow-countryman." Clearly, Jewish lenders were not treating Christians as their "fellow-countrymen."

But many Christian merchants were no less willing than Jews to lend money, and despite whatever pressure of public opinion they had to endure, they routinely charged interest at the same high rates and earned as much profit as they could. In fact, despite the inescapable connection between Jews and moneylending, they soon came to be outnumbered by their Christian counterparts. Of three major ecclesiastical gatherings (Lateran Councils) in the twelfth century, two made a point of condemning usury. On one such occasion, in 1179, the pope spoke out harshly against Christian lenders, even declaring them ineligible for communion or Christian burial and ordering that clergy who indulged them were to be suspended and investigated.[8]

Given this climate of opinion, it was obviously expedient for many people, including the clergy, to turn to Jews rather than Christians for loans—especially when it was known that a Jew would find difficulty gaining support from the usual authorities when pressing for repayment. Thus, for example, no less eminent a Christian than Peter the Venerable, abbot of the great monastery at Cluny, turned mainly to Jewish lenders when the monastery fell on hard times, handing over to them sacred treasures in pawn.[9]

Compared with ordinary commerce, moneylending is an abstract transaction requiring almost no personal involvement or skills; all that is transferred is money, and it is only the recipient who needs enterprise and creativity. Merchants do not produce in the literal sense, but since they do move goods to where they are needed or wanted, they too are active agents in the economy. Moneylenders move nothing and handle nothing other than money; they are simply sources of liquid capital—"moneybags" on whom others draw for productive enterprises. Moneylending is thus by its very nature a socially isolated and isolating activity; it neither requires nor even permits entry into the larger world of economic activities and relationships. Thus a paradox: For Christian merchants money was now the foundation of entry into the economy; for Jews it was becoming the source and symbol of isolation from the economy.

Jewish moneylenders were burdened with uncertainty and insecurity of a sort almost never experienced by Christian lenders. They were vulnerable to assault and robbery by brigands who knew that they would probably escape punishment. The nobility, ostensibly their protectors, might turn on them at any time with exorbitant demands, refusal to repay loans, and even with threats of expulsion.[10] Locked into an occupation that represented only the husk of what they had once done, many Jews succeeded at it and sometimes even became immensely wealthy. But the wealth was never really their own, and it must have brought them the unease that is the lot of those who have what others want.

"Although They Persist"
Policies of the Church

Only occasionally were Jewish communities granted charters spelling out what was required of them and what they could expect in return,

but interestingly enough, they did receive such a charter from the papacy. Sometime around 1120, Pope Calixtus II issued an edict, *Sicut
Judaeis* (the first two words), which came to be known as the "Constitution of the Jews." Reissued with minor additions or modifications by
a number of his successors, it provides us with a reliable picture of
how the later medieval Church viewed Jews and their rights in Christian society.[11] Until the late twelfth century, popes were cautious about
interfering in the internal affairs of political states, and the edict applied at first only to the Jews of Rome. But with repeated papal affir-
mations it acquired the status of a "Constitution," a statement of
Church policy toward Jews living throughout Christendom.

The statement was grounded in the principle already laid down
in the late sixth century by Pope Gregory I: just as Jews must not over-
step their bounds, so Christians must not arbitrarily mistreat them.
Although Jewish faithlessness must be condemned, it begins, the Jews
must not be unjustly oppressed. Although they persist in their obstinacy and refuse to understand the mysteries of their own scriptures,
Christian charity demands that they be granted papal protection.
Thus, they are not to be forced into baptism; nor may they be injured,
robbed, or persecuted in any manner. No one is to desecrate their cemeteries, or to exhume and plunder bodies. Those who violate these
prohibitions are to be subject to excommunication unless they make
proper amends. But, the edict concludes, the Church extends protection only to those Jews who have not plotted to subvert the Christian
faith.

The essential message here was forbearance. Jews were to be
peacefully encouraged to see the light, but until they did so of their
own free will they were to be tolerated, preserved as a form of testament to Christian truth. As the original owners of a sacred text which
they had transmitted to the world—even though they themselves did
not understand its real significance—they were to be permitted to live
in their own antiquated manner until the time came for them to recognize their error and enter the ranks of the redeemed.

Protection on the one hand and restriction on the other was characteristic of the Church's policy toward Jews, but it could hardly have
been otherwise. Although anti-Jewish decrees were common enough,
they were intended not to sanction oppression but to protect Christian

interests. For example, prohibitions against employment of Christian maids or nurses stemmed from fear that unsophisticated Christians in Jewish homes might be lured into conversion to Judaism. Christian witnesses were encouraged to testify against Jewish litigants; but here again the motive was defensive, since much Jewish litigation consisted of claims by moneylenders, including those with outstanding debts incurred by churches and monasteries. In short, the purpose of papal and clerical legislation was not to oppress Jews but to contain and restrain them.

"Choice Severed Limbs": The Second Crusade, 1146–1147

The Christian conquest of Jerusalem in the First Crusade led to the creation in the Near East of four European-dominated feudal states. The northernmost and most vulnerable was Edessa, a large territory in what is now southeastern Turkey. In the summer of 1145, word reached Europe that while the count of Edessa was away at one of his estates celebrating Christmas, a Muslim army had captured the capital city of Edessa and overrun the entire county. Now they were well situated for further assaults on the neighboring crusader states, including Jerusalem itself.

On the first of December, Pope Eugenius III called for a new crusade. Addressing his letter to King Louis VII of France and his barons, the pope promised high rewards: not only remission of all sins but also remission of all interest on debts and postponement of payment until the crusaders' return. Eager to battle for Christ, Louis assembled his barons and bishops at Christmastime to ask for their support but found that very few shared his enthusiasm. Still determined, he scheduled another assembly to be held in Burgundy just prior to Easter. Meanwhile, he turned for assistance to Bernard of Clairvaux—an aging and sickly man by this time, though at the zenith of his career and still among the most influential men in western Europe. The news that Bernard would appear at the Burgundy gathering attracted people from throughout France; just as when Pope Urban preached the First Crusade, the assembled crowd was so large that Bernard had to speak from a platform outside of town. His audience was so deeply stirred that many vowed at once to go on crusade. So many shouted for crosses to wear that Bernard removed his own outer garments to provide more cloth. From then on, waves of excitement swept over France, and the Second Crusade was under way.

Late that summer, in the midst of a preaching tour, Bernard received letters from the archbishops of Cologne and Mainz urging him to come to the Rhineland to halt persecutions of the Jews. A monk named Radulph, locally well regarded for his piety, had been preaching violence against the Jews, and there had already been a number of murderous assaults, although nothing on a scale matching those of fifty years earlier. Bernard was no friend of the Jews: his sermons and letters are replete with anti-Jewish invective. But he insisted always that Jews had to be dealt with humanely and permitted to live—to demonstrate that those who reject Christ must suffer, but also that they would be present in the flesh when Christ returned to reveal himself and to redeem them.[12] Typical of his attitude towards Jews (although milder in tone than some of his more doctrinaire statements) were the comments in a widely circulated letter calling on the people of Europe to join the Crusade:

> I have heard with great joy of the zeal for God's glory which burns in your midst, but your zeal needs the timely restraint of knowledge. The Jews are not to be persecuted, killed, or even put to flight.... The Jews are for us the living words of Scripture, for they remind us always of what our Lord suffered. They are dispersed all over the world so that by expiating their crime they may be everywhere the living witnesses of our redemption. . . . If the Jews are utterly wiped out, what will become of our hope for their promised salvation, their eventual conversion? . . . It is an act of Christian piety both "to vanquish the proud" and also "to spare the subjected," especially those for whom we have a law and a promise, and whose flesh was shared by Christ whose name be for ever blessed.[13]

Now he wrote to the archbishop of Mainz, declaring in forceful terms his personal distaste for Radulph ("without sense and void of all modesty, . . . a man with a great opinion of himself and full of arrogance") and his insistence that the Jews not be harmed:

Is it not a far better triumph for the Church to convince and convert the Jews than to put them all to the sword? Has that prayer which the Church offers for the Jews, from the rising up of the sun to the going down thereof, that the veil may be taken from their hearts so that they may be led from the darkness of error into the light of truth, been instituted in vain? If she did not hope that they would believe and be converted, it would seem useless and vain for her to pray for them. But with the eye of mercy she considers how the Lord regards with favor him who renders good for evil and love for hatred.[14]

Bernard must have felt some personal responsibility for what was happening. When it became apparent that his warnings were not enough, he himself traveled to the Rhineland to confront Radulph in person. A chronicler of the encounter, Bishop Otto of Freising, reports that, having "found Radulph living there in greatest favor with the people," Bernard admonished him for disobedience and persuaded him to return to his monastery. "The people were very angry," says Otto, "and even wanted to start an insurrection, but they were restrained by regard for Bernard's saintliness."[15] Satisfied that he had done all he could to prevent further violence, Bernard took advantage of his presence in Germany to recruit King Conrad and his barons for the crusade.

But the damage had been done—not only by Radulph but inadvertently by Bernard through his own impassioned preaching. From autumn 1146 though spring 1147, Jews in the Rhineland, and probably in northern France as well, endured repeated assaults—mostly episodic, probably not involving large numbers of assailants, and certainly not as severe as those of the earlier crusade, but painful enough. The most thorough, and almost the only, source for accounts of these misfortunes is a Hebrew chronicle, the "Book of Remembrance" (Sefer Zekhirah) of Ephraim ben Jacob of Bonn, a scholar and poet who says that he was a thirteen-year-old eyewitness of some of the events he describes.[16] The chronicle is a litany of crimes, embellished with liturgical poetry dedicated to the victims. An atmosphere of terror is established at the beginning with descriptions of vicious assaults on harmless individuals: A Jewish traveler on his way by boat from Cologne to Trier refused to accept baptism, whereupon his assailants "severed his head from his body by placing it in a winepress"; a Jewish woman from Speyer who ventured outside of town was attacked by men who cut off her ears and thumbs. Then Ephraim moves to descriptions of what were probably his own experiences. A group of Jews from Cologne and neighboring towns bribed the archbishop to help them find refuge in a fortress outside the city; they also paid the local baron to empty the fortress of all its occupants so that there would be no possibility of betrayal by Christians. Other Jews found refuge in the castles of "Gentile acquaintances"—one of several indications in the chronicle that there were Christians willing, in some cases even determined, to provide protection.[17]

Ephraim portrays Jews mostly as helpless victims, but not always. He describes what happened when two Jewish youths were murdered on their way to visit the fortress:

> Their father wept for them, and he mourned his sons many days. Later it became known who had murdered them, and the community paid the bishop a bribe, and he ordered that the culprit be seized. They gouged out the eyes of the murderer, and three days after he was blinded, the villain's heart ceased and he turned to stone. Thus the Lord struck him down, and he died and turned into a putrid corpse. May all Thine enemies perish thus, O Lord.[18]

The worst episode known to Ephraim in detail took place in northwestern Bavaria, at Würzburg, in February or March of 1147. The Jews of Würzburg "anticipated living in tranquility, but instead they endured distress and destruction." When a man's body was found in the river, the local people accused the Jews of having killed him. Then, says Ephraim, "the errant ones" (that is, those who were about to depart on crusade) and the shiftless ("those who derive joy from things of no consequence") attacked the Jews and killed twenty-two of them. One young woman, dragged to the church for baptism, was beaten and burned when she resisted. She survived, either by pretending to be dead or perhaps because she was unconscious, and was rescued by a Christian woman who carried her away and hid her in her own home. Other Jews also escaped by hiding in the homes of friendly Christians.

The town bishop, apparently badly shaken by the massacre, took the extraordinary step of ordering that the mutilated corpses—"all the choice severed limbs: hips and shoulders, thumbs of hands and feet, sanctified with holy oil, together with everything else that remained of their bodies and limbs"—be interred in a specially consecrated plot in his own garden. "May the generous one be blessed for his bountifulness," Ephraim concludes.[19]

Other massacres, possibly even more severe, appear to have occurred in northern France but are reported only in outline: some 150 people killed in a place called Ham, and many others elsewhere. Ephraim describes in detail one episode from Champagne, happier in outcome but noteworthy because of the identity of the victim. On May 8, 1147, during the holiday of Shavuot, a band of men, ostensibly on their way to join the crusade, arrived at Rameru, some thirty miles northeast of Troyes, home of the famous Rabbi Jacob Tam. Having forced their way into his house, they seized a Torah scroll and ripped it to pieces in the rabbi's presence, then dragged him into a field, intending to torment and probably to kill him. They taunted him with insults, then struck him five times on the head, declaring that since he was leader of the Jews he must receive five wounds in return for the five inflicted on Jesus (i.e., the stigmata of the Crucifixion: the puncture wounds on hands and feet and the stab wound in the chest). They would probably have gone on to kill him had not a local baron happened to pass through the field at just that time. Jacob called out to him for help, promising a valuable horse in return. The baron persuaded the assailants to desist—not with threats or even reproach, but by asking for time to speak with the Jew about conversion. "Perhaps he will be tempted," he said (as Ephraim imagined the event), "and we shall succeed in swaying him. Should he refuse, know that I will hand him back to you tomorrow."[20] Apparently the crusaders let the matter drop, for we learn nothing more about the event. Jacob Tam did not convert, of course; he recovered from his wounds and moved soon afterward to a more secure situation in Troyes—presumably after giving the baron the promised horse.

The crusaders departed for Jerusalem in May and June of 1147. Soon the excitement wore off; by July, Jews were settling back in homes from which they had fled. Some had survived by accepting baptism, but they "returned to the true path" that same year, Ephraim reports, and life resumed as before.

Ephraim's chronicle presents a different picture from those associated with the First Crusade. Most of the assaults this time were perpetrated by individuals or small bands; there were no crusading armies bent specifically on attacking Jews, and apparently no villainous leader to match Emicho. As Ephraim is careful to note, some Christians went out of their way to assist Jews. The actions of the bishop of Würzburg indicate that at least some of the higher clergy dealt benevolently with Jews in their jurisdictions. We do learn of several serious attacks at a distance from Bonn, but Ephraim may have been reporting a mixture of fact and rumor. Compared with the devastation of 1096, these events seem almost negligible; certainly they have received less attention from historians and liturgists. Nevertheless, with benefit of hindsight we can say that they were harbingers of worse misfortunes to come.

"Therefore Be Assured":
The Response to Catastrophe

By the second half of the century, Jews were finding themselves ever more often in dangerous circumstances with little or no dependable protection. In an ironic reversal of what had in fact been happening, it was becoming commonplace to accuse Jews of murdering Christians. The usual pattern of events was the discovery of a corpse—almost always that of a boy or youth—followed by groundless charges against the local Jewish community. On at least one occasion, at Pontoise, a suburb of Paris, the dead youth was venerated as a martyred saint. The best-documented episode, and the most catastrophic, followed a grim comedy of errors involving no corpse whatever. This took place in 1171 at Blois, a prominent city on the Loire River, southwest of Paris, where there was a small but thriving Jewish community numbering some forty adults. One day in the spring of that year, a Jewish man, probably a tanner, was walking along the riverbank with a bundle of untanned hides, when he happened to encounter a Christian of the simpler sort, the servant of a prominent town official. The Christian was either riding or leading a horse. As luck would have it, one of the raw skins came loose and slithered to the ground, perhaps into the water, whereupon the horse became agitated and the servant even more so: he ran off to town and informed his master that he had chanced upon a Jew dumping a boy's corpse into the river. By this time it was accepted as common knowledge that Jews maliciously killed Christian boys by crucifixion, and for reasons of his own the man who heard the story was inclined to accept it at face value.

The Jews of Blois had been involved in local political intrigues, probably more than was in their best interests, and had made enemies, including the man who received the report. In particular, a Jewish woman named Polcelina had aroused resentment because of her influence over Thibaut, the count of Blois, whose mistress she may have been for a time. But at this point his interest in her had waned—surely to the satisfaction of his wife, who was no less than the daughter of King Louis VII and Eleanor of Aquitaine. In any event, thanks to the activities of Polcelina and others, the Jews of Blois were in a vulnerable situation, and without further investigation their enemies pounced: They rushed to inform Thibaut, calling for immediate revenge. The count (known as Thibaut the Good), perhaps urged on by his wife, accepted the charge and ordered that every Jewish adult in town be imprisoned. All except Polcelina were placed in chains, and although she was granted much leniency, her guards saw to it that she was prevented from communicating with the count. The children, meanwhile, were carried off for forcible baptism.

Other Jews in the neighborhood, residents of the county and thus also within Thibaut's jurisdiction, began frantic negotiations and tried to bribe the count with an offer of money and remission of all his outstanding debts, but they made the crucial mistake of offering him far less than he expected. Nevertheless, he must have hesitated at the prospect of punishing people for a murder when everyone knew that there was not even anyone missing, for at this point a priest stepped in to propose the next step. This man, whose identity is unknown—"may he be destroyed and may his memory be uprooted from the land of the living," says the Jewish chronicler—proposed that the witness to the alleged crime submit to an ordeal by immersion in holy water. Ordinarily, truthful or innocent persons sank and others floated; but

on this occasion either the reading was reversed or the chronicler confused, for the story is reported to have been confirmed when the man
floated. In any event, the fate of the Jewish prisoners was sealed. On
May 26 they were taken from prison and presented with the choice of
conversion or death. Some eight or nine may have accepted baptism,
but the rest were herded into a wooden hut and burned to death. Two
or three men escaped and begged to be spared because they had survived an "ordeal by fire." When this proved futile, they grabbed a
Christian and tried to drag him along; but the executioners pulled the
man away, killed the Jews with swords, and shoved their bodies back
into the fire. Most of the adult Jewish community of Blois—thirty-one
or thirty-two individuals, women and men—died that day.[21]

Note the Jewish response. First, they demonstrated customary soli-
darity: although the initial effort to save lives obviously failed, efforts
on behalf of the survivors were well coordinated, and ultimately the
catastrophe was recognized and commemorated throughout the Ashkenazic Jewish world.[22] But from the beginning Jews knew that they
had no prospect of receiving serious redress for the almost complete
destruction of one of their communities. Punishment of the perpetrators was impossible at the local level, of course, since the count himself
had sanctioned the executions; moreover, it would have been unrealistic to expect Louis to take action against a powerful baron who was
also his son-in-law. All that the Jews could reasonably hope for was
to forestall proliferation of rumors and accusations, and to rescue the
surviving prisoners and baptized children. To this end they moved on
several fronts, but in each case with what was now becoming characteristic caution and deference.

The Jews of Paris, being the largest and most influential community, took it upon themselves to approach the king himself and received
a public audience at which Louis behaved graciously: he deplored
what had happened and assured the Jews that he placed no credence
in charges of this sort. In a letter circulated among Jewish communities, the Parisian Jewish elders quoted the king in words that sound
more like their own than his: "Therefore be assured, all you Jews in
my land, that I harbor no such suspicions. Even if a body be discovered
in the city or in the countryside, I shall say nothing to the Jews in that
regard. Therefore be not frightened over this issue."[23]

Another delegation, probably led by Jacob Tam, visited Thibaut's elder brother, the count of Champagne, who ruled over territory containing Troyes and many other Jewish communities. They almost certainly brought the customary monetary gifts and in return received his assurance that he did not and would not accept charges that Jews were conspiring to murder Christians. The most effective negotiator appears to have been Nathan ben Meshullam, member of a family with a reputation for skill in dealing with Christians in difficult situations. He called on Thibaut's other brother, William, a prominent archbishop, and, promising further payments for both William and Thibaut, arranged for the archbishop to persuade his brother to release the remaining prisoners and the baptized children and to declare that he would not permit another such episode. Thibaut agreed but, as Nathan later reported in a letter describing his own efforts, the survivors "escaped the clutches of the wicked one with their clothes only, for he retained possession of all their goods—both capital and loans."[24]

Reflecting on the Jewish community's response to this episode, we find that having suffered a massacre grounded in nothing more substantial than local political feuds, the Jews of northern France paid large sums of money to the man who was mainly responsible (and to his brothers), asking only that the survivors be spared and that nothing comparable happen again. Justice—however that might be defined after more than thirty people had been brutally murdered—was entirely beyond their reach.

⋄ 8 ⋄

ENCOUNTERS AND
REPRESENTATIONS

Jews and Christians in Twelfth-Century Cultural Life

"And If You Were to Say":
Jewish Scholarship

A twelfth-century Christian scholar paused in the course of a commentary on the New Testament to muse on what he had observed of the educational practices of Jews. "If the Christians educate their sons," he remarked, "they do so not for God, but for gain, in order that the one brother, if he be a clerk, may help his father and mother and his other brothers. . . . But the Jews, out of zeal for God and love of the law, put as many sons as they have to letters, that each may understand God's law. . . . A Jew, however poor, if he had ten sons would put them all to letters, not for gain, as the Christians do, but for the understanding of God's law, and not only his sons, but his daughters."[1]

He might have omitted the final phrase, for when it came to formal education, girls certainly did not receive the kind of attention accorded to boys; but otherwise the comments ring true. Although literacy was on the increase everywhere by this time, as a group Jews were still well ahead of everyone else. Every Jewish boy was expected to get an education. Most began elementary schooling by age four or five and continued as long as they could, the best students eventually attending a yeshiva. Since every man was expected to be able at least to read basic prayers, complete illiteracy must have been rare. We have already seen that Jewish communal life was grounded in religious scholarship and that leadership went to the learned. The familiar ritual of initiation into schooling for young children, associating food delicacies with the letters of the Hebrew alphabet, originated at about this time. Ivan Marcus describes this "rite of passage from early childhood to cultural membership." Wrapped in a coat or prayer-shawl, the boy was carried by his father to the synagogue schoolroom or the teacher's home:

> The teacher sat the child on his lap and showed him a slate on which was written the Hebrew alphabet, verses from the Bible, and the sentence, "May the Torah be my occupation." The teacher read each letter and the child repeated it. Then the slate was covered with honey and the child licked it. The child was then given honeycakes and peeled hardboiled eggs on which were written additional Biblical verses. After repeating them aloud following the teacher, the child ate the inscribed cakes and eggs, thereby symbolically incorporating the words of Torah.[2]

No time was wasted. Marcus cites an account from twelfth-century northern France in which a father tells his son's teacher to teach letters (consonants) the first month, vowels the second, and words the third. Then the child was ready to begin studying the laws regarding "purity" in Leviticus—because children were themselves pure! Having mastered biblical studies and prayers, most boys went on to study at least some Talmud. Genuine scholarship was the pursuit of a lifetime and the path to recognition as a community elder, but even men who settled for ordinary careers met when they could for an hour or two of collective study.

Talmudic scholarship was esteemed above all else. In contrast to the Jews of southern France and Spain, who routinely studied natural sciences, philosophy, and other secular subjects, Jews in northern Europe had an advanced curriculum centering almost exclusively on the Talmud, and other subjects were pursued, if at all, only for what they might contribute to understanding Talmudic passages and problems. For example, animal anatomy was studied as an aid to understanding Talmudic commentary on laws regarding kosher food, and history meant learning more about the lives of rabbinic sages.[3] Since the social and political conduct of the community was grounded in rabbinic knowledge, this kind of focused learning was viewed not as detached scholarship but as preparation for everyday life.

Every Jewish community of moderate size had a council of seven learned elders who judged disputes, regulated taxation, ordered punishments, and represented the community in dealings with outsiders. A council's authority was confined for the most part to its own immediate vicinity. But in the upper echelons of the intellectual hierarchy were a few men whose scholarship earned them general recognition, and whose opinions and rulings were accepted throughout the Ashkenazic Jewish world. These men were in regular communication with one another, mainly through letters circulated for commentary and joint approval; they also gathered on occasion for synods.[4] This small coterie of scholars, numbering perhaps a dozen or so, issued legislation and judgments that were accepted as binding by the entire Ashkenazic Jewish community. It might be said, then, that Ashkenazic Jewry was an informal federation, in the sense that although each community was self-regulating, everyone recognized the authority of the most eminent individuals, who functioned as a kind of supreme court.

At the summit of the intellectual hierarchy were scholars whose achievements earned them enduring fame. Several were in the family of the great Rashi. They included two of his sons-in-law (he had no sons), and in the next and greatest generation, two of his grandsons: Samuel (Shmuel) ben Meir (1080–1150), known as Rashbam, and Samuel's younger brother, the foremost leader of twelfth-century Ashkenazic Jewry, Jacob ben Meir (ca. 1100–1171), known as Jacob Tam—the man who escaped death during the Second Crusade. (Here *tam* means a person completed to perfection.) A dogmatic and willful man, always ready to challenge the authority of others, including his own grandfather, Jacob was an accomplished scholar-politician who probably deserves most of the credit for the remarkable political integration of twelfth-century Ashkenazic Jewry. Though he moved in a circle of other outstanding scholars, none could match his talent for leadership. His decisions were undoubtedly disputed and debated at times, for these were men for whom scholarly argument was the breath of life; but he was accorded widespread respect and deference, and he was known even to Christians as a formidable representative of his people.

Rashi had led the way to a scholarly revival that for the first time established western Europe as an intellectual center of world Jewry. His successors built on that achievement, writing *tosafot* ("additions") to his commentaries; hence the scholars are known as tosafists. Their work received the highest honor possible in the world of Jewish religious scholarship: It was added as commentary to the Talmud. A printed page of the Talmud now consists of four sections. In the center are the two components of the original Talmud: the Mishnah (codified rabbinic laws) and Gemara (early commentaries on the Mishnah), both dating from the pre-European period. Along the margins are the commentaries of Rashi and those of the tosafists. We might pause to think about this: half of the foremost product of Jewish intellectual life before modern times was composed not in the ancient Near East but in medieval France and Germany.[5]

Rashi's particular contribution to Talmudic studies had been his careful explanations of the "plain" (clearest and simplest) meaning of the text, called *peshat*. His successors aimed, as one might expect, for a more critical or analytical approach. They looked for alternative interpretations and favored a dialectical style of study: Student poses a question, teacher responds, everyone joins the discussion until all agree on the answer. Their commentaries were written in the same style. They began with a hypothetical question, introduced by the phrase "And if you were to say" (*ve-im tomar*), followed by a neatly rhymed reply, "And then one may answer" (*ve-yesh lomar*).[6]

The correspondence between this kind of scholarship and that of Christian "disputations" is too striking to be written off as coincidence. Few if any Jews read Latin, and even one who did would hardly have been interested in Christian theological discussions. But whatever the explanation, it seems beyond question that Jewish scholars shared in the general intellectual climate of the age. Moreover, a few Christian scholars had become aware of their Jewish counterparts and wanted to know what they were saying. This has been recognized by the historian Beryl Smalley, whose book on the study of the Bible in the Middle Ages takes special note of the tosafists and their influence on Christian scholars. Speaking of several prominent tosafists, particularly Rashbam and two of his disciples, Joseph Bekhor Shor and Eliezer of

Beaugency, she comments on their "most interesting characteristics": first, "a fondness for explaining Scripture by reference to the custom of the country in which they lived," and second, "their freedom and frankness in criticizing and disagreeing with their predecessors and contemporaries." She notes their use of vernacular French, remarking that Bekhor Shor sometimes introduced entire French phrases into his texts. "Most important, perhaps, from our present point of view," she continues, "is their rationalism, or naturalism. Wherever possible they will reduce biblical miracles to normal natural phenomena and they show critical insight which anticipates the scholarship of a later time."[7]

Joseph Bekhor Shor, who came from Orléans but lived for some time in Paris, was an especially independent thinker who accepted miracles only with qualifications and often rejected supernatural explanations for what he regarded as natural phenomena. For example, with regard to the story of the changing of Lot's wife into a pillar of salt at the time of the destruction of Sodom and Gomorrah (Gen. 19:26), he commented: "She tarried and was overtaken by the flow of lava." In another passage he attributes the plague of boils in Egypt to natural causes and stands his ground even where he cannot offer an entirely convincing explanation: "God does not alter the laws of nature and therefore effected the miracle partly according to natural laws. . . . And so you will find with the majority of miracles that God does not alter natural laws." Bekhor Shor's intellectual style, concludes Smalley, "shows us a fresh and little-known side of twelfth-century culture."[8]

"The Surface of the Letter": The Search for *Hebraica veritas*

Obviously, most Jewish and Christian scholars were working independently of one another. After all, even though they were sometimes studying the same texts, the sources and purposes of their scholarship could hardly have differed more. But a few Christians went out of their way to cultivate Jewish contacts for the specific purpose of learning how Jews studied their own Scriptures. What they sought first and foremost was accurate translation: *Hebraica veritas*, the true Hebrew meaning of the texts. Most expected, of course, that once they understood the Hebrew meanings, they would be able to demonstrate even more convincingly that the Old Testament did indeed foretell the coming of Jesus Christ. But a few—a very few, it seems—were prepared to take the next big step and to pay serious attention to Jewish interpretations. Though there is no reason to think that any of these scholars, all deeply immersed in Christian theology, ever wavered in their faith, they were more open to Jewish arguments and perspectives than anyone had ever been before.

The edition of the Bible in use at that time was the Vulgate (from *vulgus*, ordinary people), a fourth-century Latin translation from Old Testament Hebrew and New Testament Greek by Saint Jerome, one of the church fathers. Over time the errors of copyists had accumulated, and by the twelfth century there was so much uncertainty about the correctness of texts that scholars were ready to consult anyone with dependable answers. One of the first to seek help was Stephen Harding, abbot of a monastery at Cîteaux in Champagne, in the early years of the century.[9] In the course of work on what they planned as an authoritative edition of the Bible, the monks of Cîteaux realized that their source texts differed significantly. Aware that there were prominent Jewish scholars in the neighborhood, Stephen consulted with one of them, probably at Troyes, who explained, in French, the meaning of the Hebrew text. Stephen then dictated his own Latin translation to his scribes. How much he may have rephrased the Jewish interpretation we do not know, but even this much consultation with a Jew was a bold step.

The most remarkable instances of Jewish-Christian intellectual exchange took place in Paris, at the Abbey of St. Victor, the leading institution for biblical studies in western Europe. Paris was by this time a major Jewish population center and the home of a number of outstanding scholars. In consulting with them the Christians encouraged not just careful translation but genuine discussion of alternative interpretations: they made it clear that they wanted to understand not just what Jewish scholars knew in the literal sense but what they thought. The first to move in this direction was Hugh of St. Victor, who learned from Jewish scholars, probably in Paris, about the work of Rashi, Rashbam, and others. Where Jewish interpretations conflicted with Christian doctrine, Hugh went so far as to present both in his work, neutrally and without comment—a major departure from conventional practice, to say the least.

But it was one of Hugh's students, Andrew of St. Victor, who probably ventured farther than anyone else along the perilous path of serious dialogue with Jews. Not only did he consult with them regularly, but in his writings he displayed astonishing readiness to accept their interpretations. Andrew was by nature not a theologian but a historical researcher. He intended to learn the literal meanings of biblical passages in their actual historical contexts—even though they might seem to contradict Christian interpretations that read everything in terms of the future appearance of Christ. From the orthodox Christian perspective, his research methods were inherently dangerous. One of Andrew's more important Jewish contacts was probably Joseph Bekhor Shor, who was in Paris during the mid-century years when Andrew was working; his rationalist interpretations appear so frequently in Andrew's work that the two must have known each other.[10]

The most remarkable feature of Andrew's writings is that he weighs Jewish and Christian interpretations equally, judging them mainly on rational grounds, almost always discounting supernatural interpretations on either side. Where there is disagreement he simply presents both sides, the Vulgate with its Christian interpretation and the Hebrew text with its Jewish commentary. But since he can assume that his Christian audience is familiar only with the former, he concentrates on the Jewish material, and at times this leads him along thorny paths. For example, the famous passage in Isaiah referring to "a young woman" who "shall conceive" (7:14) was translated in the Vulgate as "a virgin shall conceive," and of course this was taken to refer to Mary. But Andrew's Jewish consultants interpreted the passage literally, in its immediate historical context, and Andrew, committed as he was to just this kind of approach, found it difficult to challenge their arguments. Obviously uneasy but determined to play the game to the end, Andrew rails at the Jews (perhaps to protect himself) but admits that on logical grounds their arguments hold up well: The Jews, "foes of the truth, rise against us and strive with their battering ram of mockery to break down the stronghold of our faith." He himself seems to have found the battering ram terribly seductive. It would be best not to try to refute them, he warns; rather, accept their "literal" interpretations but hold fast to the faith, even when its foundations have been shaken. Considering his social environment, he displays remarkable candor and makes astonishing concessions:

> These are the darts which the Jews hurl against us, calling us perverters and violent distorters of Holy Writ. There is no need for us to answer them, since others have done so before us; but whether their answer is sufficient, let those who have answered judge. Nor would it be useful [for us to answer]. Were we to enter the lists with strength unequal to the doubtful contest, we might perhaps yield. Then the Jews, victorious, would insult not only us, but those whose sharp and lively skill would have vanquished them easily, had they competed. We have put forth all our strength; so now we leave deeds of bravery to braver men. Let us continue the explanation of the literal sense which we have begun.[11]

Lest we fail to appreciate how far this man ventured out of line, Smalley reminds us that for Andrew "the 'literal sense' is the Jewish explanation." But having said that he wanted only to uncover "the surface of the letter" (the obvious meaning of the text) and to leave deeper "spiritual" explanations to others, Andrew could not escape attending to what Jews had to say. The truth of the matter was that earlier Talmudic scholars had created a vast body of allegorical and metaphorical interpretations equal to any in the Christian world. But Rashi had stuck close to the text and pressed for more rational forms of interpretation, and his followers did the same. So we can understand, Smalley concludes, why in Andrew's mind "Letter, Jews, and Reason" were closely connected.[12]

One of Andrew's colleagues, Richard of St. Victor, though interested in Jewish scholarship himself, felt that Andrew had gone much too far in his willingness to accept Jewish interpretations. In a treatise on this question, Richard refers to Andrew and his students as "our Judaizers" (judaizantes nostri) and sharply rejects their neutral stance. What he finds most offensive, he says, is Andrew's way of citing a Jewish interpretation "as if it were not merely the Jews' but his own—and true." Andrew was forgetting that the Old Testament could never be understood apart from the New, and therefore that no Jewish inter-pretation could ever stand on its own.[13]

Another scholar of Andrew's type, less well known but no less remarkable, was Herbert of Bosham, a man who worked in isolation and probably never achieved much recognition, but who may have been the most accomplished Hebrew and Judaic scholar in the twelfth-century Christian world.[14] Working in a monastery in Picardy (north-ern France), Herbert prepared a commentary on a fourth-century Christian translation of the Book of Psalms. "I am not striving after an understanding of the difficult spiritual senses," he explains in a pref-ace, "but with the animals that walk the earth, I cleave to earth, at-tending only to the lowest sense of the letter of the Psalter."[15] And as he saw it, his preference for "the lowest sense of the letter"—what Andrew had called "the surface"—required that one not only discuss texts with Jews but also learn their languages and read texts as they were reading them, all of which he did with remarkable success. He became an accomplished reader of Hebrew and Aramaic. He spoke with rabbis, studied the Talmud and other rabbinic texts, and devel-oped what the historian Jeremy Cohen characterizes as "remarkable familiarity with the subtleties of rabbinic hermeneutics." Although never as generous as Andrew in his attitude toward Jewish scholar-ship, he could have accomplished little without it. But as Cohen makes clear, Herbert's goals were quite different from those of his Jewish con-temporaries. He wanted to understand "the true, antique religion of biblical Israel," and as he saw it, most rabbinic explanations were heret-ical distortions of the ancient religion in its pure and proper state. Again unlike Andrew, he did not mince words when commenting on Jews: "It is indeed the error of a perverse, depraved generation and its obstinate hatred of the truth," he declared, "which prefers to deviate from its own masters and the authority of its sages, knowingly and intentionally to distort the Scriptures, so as not to espouse their ecclesi-astical interpretations which its own ancient masters actually held!" Which was to say once again that Jews were too stubborn and perverse even to read their own books correctly. But since Herbert devoted his life to scholarship of precisely the kind that he claimed to reject, it is not surprising that he felt obliged to identify himself as a dutiful Christian.[16]

Bovinis intellectus:
The Intellectual Assault on Judaism

Herbert was not the only scholar to insult Jews even while he learned from them; often, in fact, the more Christians came to know about the Judaism of their time, the more hostile they became. What startled them especially was the realization that Judaism was not the fossil they had imagined: that Jews had been working on their own to develop a vigorous cultural and intellectual tradition, and that the Jewish way of life had not stood still all those centuries since the time of Jesus. An implicit principle of Christian belief was that Jews had not changed and would not change—that they were historical relics ("stationary in useless antiquity," as St. Augustine had expressed it) who could be redeemed from their petrified state only by Christian revelation. Over the centuries there had developed a literature of discourses against Jews, some in the style of a "disputation," in which a Christian and a Jew, both fictional, presented arguments and counterarguments. But of course the Jews in these imagined contests were stock characters who presented "Old Testament" arguments that were then handily refuted by the Christian debater. Most of this literature was actually addressed not to Jews but to fellow clergymen who were presumably trying to convert Jews or instructing innocent Christians who might have been exposed to Jewish teachings—and perhaps also to those whose faith needed some shoring up in the face of doubt about the "mysteries" of the resurrection.[17] The arguments in these discourses demonstrate very little knowledge of rabbinic Judaism, Talmudic scholarship, or the social conditions of contemporary Jewish life. The Jews are still as they were in the Gospels: arch-villains in the divine drama, rigid and unyielding, unable to comprehend the spiritual meanings of their own texts.

Toward the end of the eleventh century there appeared a disputation that for the first time portrayed Jews as real and reasonable persons. Composed by Gilbert Crispin, abbot of Westminster, and (rather predictably) entitled "A Disputation Between a Jew and a Christian on the Christian Faith," it was probably the most widely circulated document of its kind in the twelfth century.[18] The Christian protagonist is Gilbert himself, and although the Jew goes unnamed, he is portrayed as a man with personality and intelligence. Whether Gilbert was describing a real individual with whom he had actually spoken is open to question, but in any event the debate is not evenly weighted but resolves into an apologia for Christianity. It consists of seven set speeches on each side, the Jew presenting a brief challenge and Gilbert responding with a lengthy defense and counterattack. The arguments are standard: The Jew insists that the Hebrew Scriptures say nothing about Jesus, whereupon the Christian demonstrates that revelatory statements are everywhere evident if only the Jew could read them correctly. Though the tone is friendly and bland, there is nothing new in the message.

Gilbert Crispin was still able to portray a Jewish antagonist who was presumed to have nothing new to add to the old debate, and who could therefore be comfortably dismissed with a pat on the head like that accorded Priscus five hundred years earlier. But his mid-twelfth-century successors had to contend with more formidable opponents, men with whom they were consulting as intellectual peers—who, it was now becoming clear, were heirs to an interpretive tradition every bit as rich as their own. And with that the challenge to Christianity became far more immediate and disturbing than ever before. The very act of consultation meant acknowledging that Jews had something to contribute. Even if the contribution was only toward better understanding of the "letter of the Law," Christian scholars had already conceded a great deal: that Christianity might not have all the answers, and that in fact Jews, working entirely on their own, had been developing creative new interpretations about which Christians knew nothing.[19]

We have already seen some Christian reactions in the edgy response of Richard of St. Victor to the writings of Andrew, and in Herbert's diatribes against the very interpretations that he found most useful. This was the usual stance. With the possible exception of Andrew, Christians who learned about Jewish scholarship were likely to react with distaste and to declare that contemporary Judaism, rooted as it was in the Talmud as much as in the Scriptures, was nothing better than another heresy, a distortion of the genuine Judaism of the Old Testament—which, antiquated though it was, possessed at least the merit of being familiar and unadulterated, something that one could refute with confidence. But now Christians confronted a challenge of unknown dimensions: self-sufficient Jewish scholars steeped in a complex body of rabbinic literature about which non-Jews knew almost nothing. For the first time in the history of Christian-Jewish relations, the Jewish antagonists emerged as real persons, much more formidable than the nameless villains of the Gospels. Now "the Jews" were talented scholars, living in such places as Paris or Mainz, speaking the vernacular language fluently—and at the same time functioning capably in the turbulent world of commerce and moneylending—despite the Church's teaching that they languished in darkness.

Over the centuries Christians had assumed that in order to penetrate Jewish minds with Gospel truths (and to reassure wavering Christians) the best strategy was persuasion: one cited passages from the Old Testament and explained how to read them correctly—how to discover Jesus beneath the "surface of the letter." But now the rules of the game were changing. It turned out that the Jews had other books, particularly the Talmud, having no legitimacy whatever—books to be rejected, not interpreted—and this change called for a straightforward offense.

The attack began with written diatribes. Ironically, although many tracts attacking Judaism and the Talmud were ostensibly addressed to Jews, the readers must have been almost entirely Christian. One of the best known and also one of the most vitriolic examples of this new literature is the "Treatise Against the Rigid Obstinacy of the Jews," written sometime around mid-century by Peter the Venerable, abbot of the great monastery at Cluny. Peter knew about the Talmud only at second hand, from the polemical writings of Jewish converts to Christianity, but he speaks as though he had read it from cover to cover. It is a nasty book, he says, full of irrational and absurd arguments, an insult to God and to human intelligence. In fact, he wonders whether those who could create a book of this kind—individuals so entirely devoid of spiritual capacity—are even properly human.

The tract opens with a prologue addressed directly to Jews, almost as though they were seated before him and resigned to hearing his polemic: "I speak to you—to you, I say—O Jews, who to this very day deny the Son of God. How much longer, you miserable creatures, will you go on rejecting the truth? How long will you stand against God? How long before your hearts of iron are softened?"[20] The bulk of what follows—four of the five chapters—consists of more or less standard diatribe in which Old Testament passages are interpreted in the usual manner. But Peter seems to imagine that his fictional audience will have none of it, and in his exasperation he switches to a style of argument that we have not heard before. "How long, O Jews," he rages, "will this bovine mentality *(bovinis intellectus)* be embedded in your hearts?"[21] Somewhat further along he returns to this line of attack, remarking that he has to go on with the argument even though he wonders whether Jews have enough human intelligence to understand him, since they seem to recognize neither human reason nor sacred authority. Can anyone be human, he asks, from whom the "heart of stone" has not been removed and replaced with the "heart of flesh," and within whom there dwells no Spirit of God? The image is unmistakable: God breathed his spirit (called "the breath of life" in Genesis 2:7) into Adam but not into animals.

Here and elsewhere in the tract Peter asserts that Jews, although potentially redeemable (else why exhort them so much?), are deficient in a basic human characteristic: they cannot understand abstractions, ideas detached from immediate physical experience. Just beneath the surface we sense a familiar theme: Jews are paralyzed by their own materialism—their focus on commerce, their lack of capacity for spiritual growth. But Peter had problems of his own that may help explain the virulence of his attack. As abbot of the largest and grandest monastery in western Christendom, he had many concerns that were material to the core. Cluny had been founded as a refuge for monks who hoped to reach spiritual heights through rigorous living and self-denial. But by the late eleventh century it had become a lavish establishment, far more splendid than originally envisioned. Peasants now performed the ordinary labor, while monks lived like feudal lords. Massive amounts of wealth flowed in from landholdings and donations, but still expenses overwhelmed the budget. In Peter's time (1122–56) the situation became so acute that he had to borrow money, placing sacred objects in pawn—and, as might be guessed, most of the creditors were

Jews.[22] His portrait of materialistic Jews takes on added meaning when we realize that Bernard of Clairvaux, renowned for piety, accused Cluny of having deteriorated into ostentation and materialism.

In the fifth and final chapter of Peter's treatise, entitled "On the ridiculous and utterly foolish tales of the Jews," he argues even more plainly that Jews are hardly better than mindless animals. Consider, he says to his imaginary Jewish audience, oxen or asses, the stupidest beasts in creation: Does their intelligence really differ from your own? "An ass hears and does not understand; a Jew hears and does not understand." But now, he continues, I'll show the world that you are truly such a beast (*iumentum,* a term for a beast of burden): "In the presence of all, O beastly Jews, I exhibit that book of yours—your book, I say—that Talmud of yours, that esteemed doctrine of yours, which you prefer over the writings of the prophets and all other authentic teachings."[23]

The display of ridiculous material, which occupies most of the rest of the chapter, consists of Talmudic passages of the kind that use metaphor or fable to develop and embellish an interpretation. For example, he cites a statement that God weeps daily over the exile of the Jews—tears fall from his eyes into the sea, and the truly pious can sometimes hear him praying that pity for his people may overcome his anger against them. Such nonsense, says Peter, is appropriate for dogs or swine.[24] So having first been condemned for being too thickheaded to understand metaphor ("spiritual" interpretations), here Jews are caricatured as gullible enough to accept their own metaphors as literal truth.

But despite the obvious Jewish capacity for all kinds of fanciful commentary (which Peter inadvertently demonstrated in his own attack), what infuriated him most was their insistence that biblical texts meant just what they said and not what Christians were reading into them. In their most private moments, did men like Peter the Venerable ever entertain the thought that Jews might be correct—that perhaps texts really did say just what they seemed to say and nothing more? Was their hostility, their insistence that Jews were as irrational as animals, rooted in uncertainty about precisely those Christian teachings (the virgin birth and the fatherhood of God, for example) that so challenged the rational mind?[25]

"Earthly Things": Peter Abelard's Dialogue

The outstanding intellectual figure of the century was Peter Abelard, the most dynamic and controversial philosopher of his time, even though most often remembered now for his passionate love affair with Heloise. Abelard insisted that a critical philosopher could also be a good Christian—rational argument and criticism were not only compatible with Christian faith but could even support it.[26] After a lifetime of conflict with conservative opponents, he retired for what were to be his final two years to the monastery at Cluny, where, under the patronage of Peter the Venerable, he wrote what was probably his final work: an unfinished treatise entitled *Dialogue of a Philosopher with a Jew and a Christian.*[27]

Although the philosopher is obviously Abelard himself, the dialogues are frankly fictional. "I was looking about in a dream," he begins, "and suddenly three men, coming by different paths, stood before me." The three paths correspond to the three great periods of world history as defined by Augustine and still recognized in Abelard's time. First came the period of "natural law," extending from Adam to Moses; then the period of "written law," from Moses to Jesus; and finally that of "grace," from Jesus to the end of time. Corresponding to each period were types of people: pagans, Jews, and Christians. The dialogues pose the philosopher as a representative of "natural law" (but not paganism), meaning morality based on rational principles, against the Jew as spokesman for the "written law" of the Old Testament and the Christian for the "grace" of the New. But it soon turns out that this is not an evenly matched three-sided debate: the Jew stands alone. Abelard's goal is to demonstrate that Christianity is not really in conflict with "natural law" but is in fact its most sublime expression, hence entirely suited to a rational philosopher like himself. Only Judaism represents an earlier "pre-philosophical" (or nonrational) stage of religion. Abelard endows his Jewish character with good sense and sound arguments, so that the Christian position can emerge as superior to that of a solid opponent. But of course the Jew, no matter how resourceful, is destined to lose the argument, for history itself stands against him.[28]

The dialogues focus on the question of which religion, if either, is consistent with "natural law." Does God still require obedience to the "written law" ("the Law"), or has that now been replaced by Christian "grace"? The Jew presents a straightforward argument: God intended the Law to be obeyed eternally, and there is no reason to believe that he has changed his mind. To be sure, being a faithful Jew is not easy:

> Surely, no people is known or is even believed to have endured so much for God as we constantly put up with for him. . . . Dispersed among all the nations, alone, without an earthly king or prince, are we not burdened with such great demands that almost every day of our miserable lives we pay the debt of an intolerable ransom? . . . We are allowed to possess neither fields nor vineyards nor any landed estates because there is no one who can protect them for us from open or occult attack. Consequently, the principal gain that is left for us is that we sustain our miserable lives here by lending money at interest to strangers; but this just makes us most hateful to them who think they are being oppressed by it.[29]

But the philosopher turns this lament against his opponent: Has not the Jew acknowledged, then, that his people are receiving none of the rewards that God supposedly promised them? Besides, the true goal of life should be not material rewards but eternal salvation, and that comes only to those who obey the "natural laws" of morality. Jews, being "a carnal people who knew only earthly things" (terrena), were promised only material rewards because spiritual rewards were beyond their comprehension. But since Jews have fared so poorly even in the realm of earthly rewards, it stands to reason that there must be a higher form of law and a more sublime reward. The Jew responds by insisting that obedience to the Law is the indispensable step toward spiritual rewards. But of course he has been pressed to the wall.

The debate takes an intriguing turn with a discussion of circumcision. The Jew comes up with a surprising argument:

> For the sign of circumcision seems so abhorrent to the Gentiles that if we were to seek their women, the women would in no way give their consent, believing that the truncating of this member is the

height of foulness. . . . Or even if they were to offer us their consent
in this, we would shrink in horror from associating that member with
the foulness of unbelieving women—that member sanctified to the
Lord precisely through that sign by which we enter into a covenant
with him alone.[30]

As the debate develops, he again defends the custom, this time
with a rather bizarre metaphor: God ordered the Jews to sanctify themselves "through the very instrument of their conception"; that is, they
were expected to "cut themselves off" from unbelievers and to become
a new people with a higher culture. God had compared the Jews to a
choice vineyard that yielded only wild grapes. What it required was
pruning, and "through this comparison the cutting away of the fore-
skin signifies the care of the divine husbandry towards us by which
God made a beginning of our cultivation."[31]

Abelard seems inordinately concerned with circumcision, perhaps
because damage to the penis had special meaning for him. The outcome of his notorious love affair with Heloise was a child. He was
eager to marry her; but although she loved him deeply, she was reluctant to marry him, purportedly because marriage might hinder his
career. In any event, one night while Abelard slept, a band of Heloise's
kinsmen attacked him and mutilated his genitals. As Abelard described the episode in his "Tale of Misfortunes" (Historia calamitatum),
his assailants "took cruel vengeance on me of such appalling barbarity
as to shock the whole world; they cut off the parts of my body whereby
I had committed the wrong of which they complained." His mental
anguish surpassed even his physical suffering: "What road could I
take now? How could I show my face in public, to be pointed at by
every finger, derided by every tongue, a monstrous spectacle to all I
met?"[32] He was so overwhelmed by the catastrophe that he entered a
monastery and asked Heloise to enter a convent. (She obeyed and became a distinguished abbess, though at immense personal cost.) It
seems likely that Abelard's elaborate commentary on circumcision was
not unrelated to his personal misfortune.

The philosopher remains unconvinced by any of the Jew's arguments, of course, and this section of the dialogue ends with his declaring that he finds Judaism spiritually deficient on every count, fixated

on external legal observances rather than moral and ethical principles. "The Lord hungers for the sacrifice of the heart," he instructs the Jew, "not the sacrifice of animals." And with a few more observations of this sort he turns to the Christian for a dialogue nearly twice as long as the first.

The core of the Christian's argument is that the "New Law" is "more compelling" because it easily surpasses the Old as a guide to morality and virtue. He assures the philosopher that ethics and religion are one and the same ("What you call ethics we are accustomed to call divinity"), and the philosopher responds with "wholehearted approval" of the "new usage." Soon they have both agreed that the difference between Judaism and Christianity is the difference between materialism and ethical principles, and the language, for all of Abelard's lofty intentions, begins to sound not unlike that of Peter the Venerable: Jews, "being animals and sensual beings endowed with no philosophical capacity enabling them to discourse rationally, are moved toward faith solely by external miracles."[33]

In general, the philosopher seems more comfortable with the Christian than he had been with the Jew: there is more give-and-take in the conversation, and the two are usually in accord. Soon he delivers a high (and self-serving) compliment: "I am certainly learning that you are a first rate philosopher." In contrast to the first dialogue, much of this one is not a debate but a cooperative effort to reach deeper understanding where there is already basic agreement. The philosopher is cautious about literal reading of the Bible (Abelard's own doubts?), but the Christian urges him to read it as a philosopher should: "If you knew how to read Scripture in a prophetic spirit rather than in the manner of the Jews, . . . not literally and in a material sense but mystically through allegory, you would not accept what is said as an unlettered person does." But such minor differences aside, they are kindred souls bent only on reaching better understanding.

The treatise, not quite completed, ends abruptly, but the point has been made. The purpose of this three-person dialogue is to demonstrate that the two aspects of Abelard's own identity, philosopher and Christian, are entirely compatible. Only the Jew—confined as he is to "earthly things," fixated on the "Old Law," unable to grasp spiritual meanings or ethical principles—stands apart.

Peshat and the "Paths of Reason":
The Jewish Counterattack

Despite what Christians claimed, every Jewish scholar understood allegorical interpretation (in Hebrew, *derash*) and knew very well how to extract "hidden" meanings from biblical passages. But since Rashi's time, the preferred method had been to take the opposite—or, more accurately, complementary—approach by focusing on *peshat*, the plain and obvious meaning. We have seen that the usual Christian strategy in polemics against Judaism was to counter the literal "Jewish" sense of the text with the "mystical" Christian sense (following the third-century Christian theologian Origen, who distinguished between *sensus Judaicus* and *sensus mysticus*). The Jewish response was straightforward. We understand, they replied, that there are deeper and less evident meanings, but these are only complementary to literal meanings. In particular, they argued, it was unacceptable to maintain that the divine laws, so clearly laid out in the Torah, could be interpreted as having only allegorical or "mystical" meaning and hence no longer had to be obeyed. Thus Jews took their stand on *peshat* and on what one scholar, Joseph Kimhi of Narbonne, called the "path of reason." Whatever fanciful interpretations might be contrived, one had to keep in mind the plain and simple meaning of the text, and any interpretation that distorted the obvious meaning had to be rejected.[34]

Kimhi is remembered particularly as author of "The Book of the Covenant" *(Sefer ha-Berit)*, one of the first Jewish treatises concerned entirely with polemics against Christianity. Originally from Spain, he had left there in mid-century and settled in Narbonne, the center of Jewish life in southern France and an ideal environment for someone of his critical style: a vigorous Jewish community in a cosmopolitan city, where Christians and Jews debated more freely than they could in northern France or Germany.[35] Like its Christian counterparts, Kimhi's book was really addressed not to the opposition but to those in the home group who might be wavering. Designed as a defense against converts from Judaism who were trying to persuade other Jews to defect, it is presented as a fictional dialogue between a faithful Jew and an apostate, the latter offering tediously conventional arguments that are triumphantly refuted.

Even considering that Kimhi was writing in Hebrew for a Jewish audience, his style is remarkably combative. For example, in response to the convert's insistence that salvation comes only through faith in Jesus as Messiah, the faithful Jew shows what is meant by "paths of reason": How am I to believe, he asks, that the mighty and concealed Creator of the world (the *"Deus absconditus"*) "needlessly entered the womb of a woman, the filthy, foul bowels of a female, compelling the living God to be born of a woman, a child without knowledge or understanding, senseless, unable to distinguish between his right hand and his left, defecating and urinating, sucking his mother's breasts from hunger and thirst, crying when he is thirsty so that his mother will have compassion on him"?[36]

Somewhat further along, the apostate retreats into the oldest and weakest argument: "You understand most of the Torah literally while we understand it figuratively. Your whole reading of the Bible is erroneous, for you resemble him who gnaws at the bone, while we [suck at] the marrow within." Kimhi's faithful Jew is well prepared for this tactic, however, and assures his opponent that not only does he understand both modes of interpretation quite well, but he also knows the proper place for each. Citing passages on "circumcision of the flesh" and "of the heart," favorites with Christians, he moves again to a frontal attack. You are uncircumcised, he says, in both senses—"for whoever transgresses the commandments and murders, fornicates, steals, oppresses, speaks abusively to people, and mocks and robs them is uncircumcised in heart."[37]

As the discourse draws to a close, the author returns on stage with a final word of encouragement for the young student who had asked for guidance: "May He keep you from the way of fools and those who err in their belief."[38]

Joseph Kimhi's polemic was among the most outspoken Jewish counterattacks of the century. The debate became even more heated during the thirteenth century, and one of the most prominent combatants was Joseph's son, David Kimhi.[39] But, for the most part, all these people were talking past one another: Christians were writing in Latin, Jews in Hebrew, and very few on either side were able or even inclined to read one another's polemics.

Res miranda, Res neganda:
Images of Jews in Drama

Among the most striking creations of the twelfth century were religious dramas, based on traditional biblical themes but with remarkably imaginative narrative and character development. Two outstanding examples are a Christmas play and a Passion play, both known from manuscripts in a collection discovered in a Bavarian monastery. I focus on the Christmas play, which was probably first performed during the final quarter of the century. It must have been exciting to watch. Designed for a large cast of actors, and intended for performance inside cathedrals or major churches, it presented once again the conflict between Christian faith and Jewish literalism.[40]

The core of the drama is an encounter between two men, representing Christianity and Judaism: on one side, St. Augustine, speaking for that which must be accepted on faith alone; on the other, an outlandish character called Archisynagogus (Leader of the Jews), who speaks for Jewish skepticism and literalism. They disagree on everything about the Christmas story, of course, but their encounter centers on the dogma of virgin birth—an ideal topic, because it enables them to dispute something as seemingly elementary as the connection between sexual intercourse and pregnancy.

The play opens with Augustine standing at center stage, flanked on the right by Isaiah, Daniel, and other Old Testament luminaries, and on the left by Archisynagogus and a company of Jews. The introductory scene is what is known as a "Procession of Prophets": Isaiah and the others step forward in turn and announce that "a virgin will give birth without the seed of a man." Daniel (performing here, like all the biblical characters, as Augustine's ally) addresses the Jews directly: "Wretched Judaea, dwelling in darkness, cast off the stain of mortal crime, and with joyful delight at such a celebrated birth, be enticed into error no more." Finally, having heard all the arguments, Archisynagogus and his cohort step forth, "clamoring intensely" (*valde obstrepet),* to declare that they accept nothing. Archisynagogus plays his role to the hilt, "shaking his head and his entire body, stamping his foot on the ground, and with his staff imitating all sorts of Jewish gestures" (*gestus Judaei),* he declares his position: "I think I hear it being spread about that a virgin can give birth without intercourse. O, what simplemindedness leads them to be so foolish!"

But after the "shouting and misinterpretation" *(tumultu et errore)* of the Jews have had their moments on stage, the prophets step forward together to lament the spiritual poverty of this people: "The ancient dregs of error still adhere to them. When we speak of Christ, they laugh and put forth arguments based only on their own understanding." Now Augustine, speaking here as throughout the play with calm deliberation clearly intended to contrast with the agitated behavior of the Jews, replies to their challenges with Christian dignity and mildness: "Let those who are concealed in darkness step forth, and let those people bound in error offer themselves to us, that the error may be overcome by revealing it to them, and that the paths of Scripture may be opened for them." But Archisynagogus remains stubborn, of course, and protests with "raucous laughter" *(nimio cachinno):* You are asking us to believe something contrary to reason, he declares, "a confusion of the natural order." Augustine, responding in a "sober and judicious manner," patiently explains that it is wholly possible for a virgin to become pregnant with her "gates of shame *[pudoris ostio]* still unopened": "Just as the sun's rays enter a transparent glass and pass entirely through it without damage, thus into the womb of the virgin the Son of the supreme Father will indeed alight harmlessly." Now, with all their arguments laid out, the two groups defy each other, calling back and forth in chorus: *"Res miranda,"* a marvelous occurrence! *"Res neganda,"* an occurrence to be denied!

All of this has been a prologue to a revised version of the Christmas myth, one that makes Jews responsible for antagonism to Jesus even during his infancy. Herod learns of the birth of Jesus and calls on Archisynagogus for advice on how to deal with the threat of an infant king. The Jew enters with "immense arrogance" *(magna superbia)* and suggests how Herod can wheedle more information from the three kings (Magi) who had come in search of Jesus. Eventually Herod orders that all infants in his realm be killed, for which he is punished with immediate death and carried off by devils. The play ends as Mary and Joseph prepare to flee with their infant.

The central and surely most enduring message of this drama is that Christian faith stands eternally opposed to Jewish skepticism—

Jews lurk in readiness to undermine and ridicule spiritual truths, and Christians must guard against the dangers posed by their sinister challenges. The two sides are brilliantly represented in the persons of Augustine and Archisynagogus: one, a revered saint, intellectually profound, serene and secure in his faith; the other, a vividly imagined villain, embodying what were said to be the characteristics of an entire people: spiteful, perverse, spiritually stunted, unable to grasp the simplest truths of Christian revelation.

With Banner Drooping:
Artistic Representations of Church and Synagogue

Until about the tenth century, portraits of Jews in Christian art were for the most part unremarkable: Jewish characters looked much like everyone else, even when they were portrayed as villains. For example, an illustration in a late tenth-century Gospel Book belonging to Emperor Otto III, showing Jesus driving money merchants from the temple, the face of Jesus is surrounded by a halo but otherwise closely resembles those of the merchants.[41] But soon a few artists began experimenting with a new kind of artistic portrait that would become dominant in the twelfth century. Instead of specific individuals or events, these artists created symbolic representations of Christianity and Judaism, which they portrayed as a contrasting pair of women, one representing Church (*Ecclesia*), the other Synagogue (*Synagoga*). The earliest portraits of this type, dating from the ninth century to the early eleventh, depict the two women as essentially equal in status, even though it is made clear that God's favor has passed from one to the other. For example, a ninth-century carved ivory tablet from Metz depicts the Crucifixion with a number of surrounding figures, some entirely symbolic. At the right side of Jesus stands a woman representing Church; blood pours from the stab wound in his chest, and she holds out a jug or cup (represented by the chalice in Christian communion ritual) to catch the flow. At his left side stands another woman, Synagogue; her body is turned away from the cross but her face still looks toward Jesus, as though she were uncertain about her next move. But she is neither sad nor contrite; she holds a bannered staff firmly in hand, and the expression on her face might be interpreted as brazenness or spite. In another slightly later carving, also from Metz, Church and Synagogue both appear on the left side of the Crucifixion, Church now looking much like Synagogue in the previous carving, a woman with a bannered staff walking away from the cross. In this case, however, she has approached another woman, older and larger, who is seated on a throne and is wearing a halo-like crown resembling the temple at Jerusalem. In her right hand she carries another waving banner, and in her left she holds a large curved circumcision knife. The two women are disputing: Church points at Synagogue's head, signifying that salvation now comes from changes in the mind, not from circumcision; Synagogue looks back at her with an expression of rejection or defiance.[42]

Representations of Synagogue in this style continue into the early eleventh century: Though portrayed as a woman on the losing side, she is self-confident and even defiant. But by the later eleventh century a new image appears. The struggle has ended; the triumph of Church over Synagogue is now complete, and the two women are no longer equal adversaries. Now Synagogue appears with her head cast downward in defeat. Her crown has fallen: sometimes we see it sliding ignominiously from her head; in a few instances Jesus himself has removed it with his left hand (Synagogue is always to his left) while with his right hand he crowns Church. Synagogue now stands with staff broken and banner drooping. Her left hand hangs passively at her side; the tablets of the Law are either about to slip from her hand or have already fallen and lie broken on the ground. Across her eyes is a veil—symbolizing blindness, of course, but also suggesting that she might still be redeemed. In one picture, somewhat more optimistic, Jesus is lifting the veil from her face with his left hand while he crowns Church with his right. But in another, a drawing from the late twelfth century, Synagogue sits with a serpent, symbol of the devil, curled around her head and across her eyes, while opposite sits Church looking on with an expression of disgust.[43] More often Church now appears standing victoriously, her staff with its cross or waving banner held firmly upright and the communion chalice extended confidently toward Jesus. One twelfth-century manuscript illustration sums up the situation neatly: the mouth of Hell, depicted as a monster with crocodilian teeth, yawns at Synagogue's side, while just behind Church stands a large baptismal font, the gateway to salvation.[44]

The finest surviving representations of this theme, especially remarkable for the sympathetic portrait of Synagogue, are two sculpted figures on a facade of the thirteenth-century cathedral at Strasbourg.[45] Synagogue is a handsome woman, bereft of her crown but not of her dignity. She stands in an attitude of quiet resignation, her head tilted downward, her eyes veiled. In her right hand is a broken staff, and from her left hand the Mosaic tablets seem about to slip to the ground. Facing her is a triumphant Church: a rather less attractive woman whose face bears a satisfied, almost smug, expression as she gazes upon her rival with cold condescension. In her right hand is a sturdy staff topped by a cross, and in her left the traditional chalice. Although Church is dressed somewhat more elaborately than Synagogue and stands in an attitude of obvious superiority, the latter is the more compelling figure: a vanquished queen. Who can guess what was in the mind of the masterly sculptor who carved such a memorable portrait of Judaism at one of its lowest moments?

In retrospect, paired figures of this kind appear as a moderate first step toward something far more virulent and vindictive. As we shall see, thirteenth and fourteenth century artists descended to levels of obscenity and indecency that surely would have horrified the sculptor of Strasbourg.

· 9 ·

"THE YOKE OF SERVITUDE"

Late Twelfth and Early Thirteenth Centuries

By the late twelfth century, Jews in France had become so prominent as moneylenders, and so exclusively dependent on moneylending for survival, that anything said about "usury"—invariably negative—was bound to call Jews to mind. Thus they were becoming the very embodiments of sin, more marginalized and more detested than ever before: "moneybags" whose only activity was to dole out loans and receive large repayments.

The heart of the matter, as we have seen, was that Europeans were adopting a new economic system: from a small-scale economy based on kinship, friendship, and relatively modest exchanges, often defined as "gifts," they were shifting to a more complex system involving production of goods for sale and profit. Since everyone participating in the new economy—lords, merchants, workers, even peasants—required capital, if only for tax payments, it was inevitable that the need for money would come to dominate many people's lives. But even the ruling elite had very little notion of monetary policy, and only nascent understanding of investment; rather, money was viewed only in connection with straightforward transactions—as a device enabling people to buy from and sell to one another. And from this perspective Jews were simply sources of coins—rather like fields to be harvested. They were tolerated for their ability to generate a seemingly endless supply of coins, even while the means by which they obtained their wealth was deemed beneath contempt.

Thus the new economy produced an inescapable paradox, and it was the fate of the Jews to be trapped therein. The gift-giving economy might be disappearing, but not the belief system that supported it. Capital accumulation and investment were becoming essential, but people continued to hold traditional beliefs about money: that it was nonproductive, evil, the devil's own substance, and thus no proper Christian should have any more to do with it than he must. Above all, taking interest—any interest, not just interest at high rates—was usury, and usury was a cardinal sin.

That Christians as well as Jews were lending money at interest was well known, and it was also well known that Christian lenders (perhaps because they had less to fear) sometimes charged the highest rates. But they were condemning themselves to hell. Often recalled was a declaration of the fifth-century pope Leo I: *Fenus pecuniae, funus est animae*, "Usurious profit from money is the death of the soul."[1] In line with this reasoning, Christians who did lend money were sometimes called Jews. A prominent late twelfth century clergyman, Peter the Chanter (so-called because he was choir leader at Notre Dame in Paris), composed a popular manual of ethics in which he condemned wealthy lords and bishops who collaborated with both Christian and Jewish usurers. The Christian lenders, he remarked, were veritable leeches, but society treated them as though they were Jews, not subject to the moral standards expected of Christians. Even clergymen were involved in the nasty business—so much so that their clients were referring to them as "our clerical Jews."[2]

Despite the hazards of their situation, many Jews prospered and a few became exceedingly wealthy, at least for a time. But for several reasons Jewish moneylenders, however wealthy, were forever insecure. First, functioning solely as sources of capital, they lost their independent identities and became the property of others, owned in the most literal sense: to be managed, protected, and carefully exploited. The term for them was *Judei nostri*, "our Jews." The highest-ranking nobility, including the king, agreed to respect one another's property rights by neither enticing Jews into their own domains nor accepting those who moved (or fled) from another region. Second, most Jews could expect relentless extortion from their "protectors": frequent requests for loans (not always repaid), heavy taxes, fees and fines of every sort, and at worst, demands so exorbitant that they simply could not be met. The image that comes to mind is of conduits, or pipelines, channeling wealth from the Jewish community into the hands of a ruling lord, always with the prospect of being unable to generate enough flow to satisfy demands at the receiving end.

Finally, there was the fear of outright physical oppression. Jews who could not satisfy their overlords were subject to brutal mistreatment: imprisonment, torture, starvation to death. That this must have happened often is evident from a letter addressed by Pope Gregory IX in 1233 to the archbishops and bishops of France. Despite the perfidy of the Jews, he begins, they must be tolerated and preserved, "for they bear the image of our Savior, and were created by the Creator of all mankind."

> But certain Christians of the French Kingdom, heeding this circumstance not at all, persecute and afflict the said Jews with many kinds of oppressions and with many unbearable burdens. Cruelly raging in their midst, and longing for their property, they torture them horribly by means of hunger and thirst, by the privations of prison and by intolerable tortures of the body. . . . Certain ones of these lords rage among these Jews with such cruelty, that unless they pay them what they ask, they tear their fingernails and extract their teeth, and inflict upon them other kinds of inhuman torments.[3]

No matter how much a lord benefited from his unsavory relationship with "his" Jews, he never granted them anything more than provisional toleration. When Jews had been exploited to the point of impoverishment, or when a lord decided that Jewish usury was too sinful to be tolerated—even though he was its main beneficiary—he might expel them at whim. And the Jews, even if they managed to satisfy the lord's demands, always faced the prospect that the virulent resentment of ordinary debtors might boil over into murderous assault—directed not at the overlord, of course, but at those who served him.

For centuries the word "Jews" had been defined in terms of Christian myth and doctrine; Jews were the enemies of Christ, condemned to suffer for their blindness to the promise of salvation. But now the name took on additional meanings of quite another sort: Jews were, at one and the same time, valuable forms of property and highly visible targets of hatred. They were trapped in a most peculiar and painfully ironic predicament. Living like prosperous gentry, handling more money than most people saw in a lifetime, they were almost as helpless as the poorest peasants—even less fortunate, in a sense, in that they were never immune from the most vicious abuse, physical as well as verbal.

Here we find what appears to be the key not only to medieval Jewish history but to the entire span of European Jewish history thereafter. The connection with money was a condition of Jewish life, and money was the very substance of survival. But money was also the devil's own creation, and handling it with such intimacy only confirmed what the Gospel of John had declared: that Jews were truly children of the devil. With this in mind, one readily understands the pervasive sense of insecurity that came to characterize so much of European Jewish life, even into the twentieth century.

The Reign of Philip Augustus (1180–1223)

There can be no better example of the Jewish predicament than the story of their fate under the French king Philip II, who reigned from 1180 to 1223. Philip had been on the throne less than a year when the Jews of his domain were subjected to treatment unlike anything they had previously experienced from a Frankish or French king. The royal treasury needed boosting. And so, on a Sabbath morning in February 1181, the king's agents entered synagogues, arbitrarily arrested Jews, and confiscated their possessions. A ransom of fifteen thousand marks (an immense sum, equivalent to about eight thousand pounds of silver, possibly more) was demanded for their release. The Jewish community paid.[4] The next year Philip canceled all debts owed to Jews in his domain upon payment of one-fifth of the amount to the royal treasury. Thus a debt of one hundred marks could be eliminated by payment of twenty marks to the treasury—and nothing to the Jewish creditor. By this single act, hardly explainable except as improvidence, Philip impoverished the Jews so thoroughly that they were no longer of any use. Then, rather than making some effort to rehabilitate his own income sources, in 1182 he simply expelled them from the royal domain altogether. To complete the devastation he appropriated their real estate and other fixed property, sending them on their way with virtually nothing. In Paris alone at least two thousand people were forced to abandon a very considerable amount of property, all to be disposed of as Philip chose.[5]

This may not sound like wise policy-making by a capable king, but the fact is that Philip's reign was so distinguished as to earn him the title Augustus. A vigorous and resourceful politician, he eventually regained for the French crown much of the western territory in Normandy and Anjou that had been held by the English, and he also extended his rule northeastward into parts of Champagne and Flanders. But in 1182 the royal domain was still a relatively small territory extending from just north of Paris southward to Orléans and Bourges, and it was from this region alone, not all of France, that Jews were expelled. Most moved no farther than to neighboring regions—to Champagne especially, but also to Blois, Burgundy, and elsewhere, wherever they could gain admittance. The various French barons, though eager for new income, were uneasy about these particular Jews. Philip was a shrewd and ambitious king, intent on extending his authority, and the barons knew quite well that they had to maintain their own power or be swallowed up. Taking in Jews whom the king had expelled was a tactical move with uncertain costs and benefits: they wanted the fresh capital that Jews could provide, but sheltering the king's rejects might antagonize him unnecessarily.

Sixteen years after their expulsion by Philip, many of the same Jews were expelled once again—and by the very men who had accepted them earlier. This time the barons were apparently moved by religious impulses. Since 1195 a priest named Foulques of Neuilly, a gifted preacher and passionate reformer, had been traveling throughout northern France, preaching against every form of spiritual corruption, particularly prostitution and usury. He attracted enthusiastic crowds, and his exhortations on usury seem to have induced some barons to opt for piety over financial gain. But the results must have surprised them. A chronicler of the time, Robert of Auxerre, tells what happened:

In those days, moreover, the Jews were troubled with serious plundering and affliction. For since the lord Foulques demanded the complete extirpation of sins and the implanting of virtues and utterly
abhorred usurers, he detested the Jews in all ways, because many of
us were weakened by infinite and heavy usuries. Hence through his
instigation, and through the efforts of the bishops, it was brought to
pass that half of all debts owed to the Jews were to be repudiated
and half were to be paid at decreed terms. But some of the barons
commanded that they be expelled from their lands; however the expelled were received and retained by the king. Truly that detracted no
little from the king's reputation, when those whom he had expelled a
long time back he admitted again.[6]

One wonders why Jews were so ready to place themselves once
again at the disposal of such a heavy-handed and unpredictable ruler,
but that is what many of them did. Although memory may be short,
they had to reach back only six years, to 1192, to recall the kind of man
with whom they were dealing. In that year a Christian—probably a
knight of middling status, but described in one source as "a vassal of
the king of France"—murdered a Jew in the town of Bray in Champagne. The Jews appealed to the countess of Champagne, offering her
a substantial bribe in return for justice and revenge. She complied,
either by having the culprit hanged or perhaps by turning him over to
the Jews for the same fate. Learning of the incident, Philip raced to the
town, asserted his rights as a feudal lord whose vassal had been killed,
and took revenge by killing most of the Jews of Bray—some eighty or
more individuals. The historian Robert Chazan suggests that Philip
was exploiting an opportunity to assert his power and authority in
Champagne, a region that he coveted perhaps more than any other,
and the deaths of a few score Jews were a negligible by-product of his
political campaign. Another historian, William Chester Jordan, locates
the attack not in Bray but in Brie, somewhat nearer to Paris, where
Philip also wanted his royal authority recognized. Whatever the case,
Philip perpetrated a massacre so brutal that it has been called "the
bloodiest single attack in the history of medieval northern French
Jewry."[7]

This, then, was the king to whose rule and protection Jews submitted once again. The remainder of his long reign, another quarter-

century, was devoted to shrewd political maneuvering and territorial conquest. Capital extracted from Jews undoubtedly provided him (and his adversaries) with essential revenue. Regulation and controlled exploitation of Jews now entered a new phase as Philip and various barons concluded arrangements to respect one another's rights over Jews, agreeing not to abduct or accept Jews from anyone else's domain. The model for these documents was issued by Philip in 1198 for Count Thibaut III:

> Let all whom this letter reaches know that we agree to retain in our land none of the Jews of our most beloved and faithful nephew, Thibaut, count of Troyes, except with his stated consent; and that none of our Jews may lend money to anyone, or seize any person or property in the count's land, except with his stated consent. The same Count Thibaut has granted to us that he will retain none of our Jews in his land, except with our stated consent; and that none of his Jews may lend money to anyone, or seize any person or property, except with our stated consent.[8]

Agreements of this kind followed regularly thereafter, some between king and barons, others among individual barons. In addition to Philip the person most often concerned was Blanche, countess of Champagne, in whose territory were settled a number of prominent Jewish moneylenders. What these agreements meant, in effect, was that Jews were now being dealt with as fixed property, permitted to reside or conduct business outside their appointed districts only with the explicit consent of their overlords.

These restrictions were followed by more systematic procedures for regulating loans. In 1206, Philip issued legislation, with Blanche's consent, that regulated Jewish moneylending much more strictly than was the case for Christians. Interest rates were stabilized at 43 percent, which was more or less standard for the time. Debtors had at least one year to pay, and no debt could be called in earlier unless the debtor had agreed in advance. Debtors could terminate loans before the due date without further interest or penalty, and no penalties for late payment could be added to regular interest. Jews were not to accept sacred religious objects in pawn, nor could they accept ecclesiastical land as security for loans. They were also not to accept suspiciously damp or bloodstained garments. Additional bureaucratic control was instituted by requiring a scribe to write loan documents in each town and two other officials to apply a validating seal.[9]

So by the first decade of the new century Jewish moneylenders in much of France had been incorporated into the fiscal apparatus of the monarchy and nobility, and their financial operations had become anything but their private concern. But of course Jewish financial knowledge and experience were never utilized; only their gold and silver, not their personal abilities, received any consideration. Never were Jews viewed as potential advisors on economic and fiscal policy; they were simply generators of wealth for the royal treasury.

Legal niceties meant nothing when Philip needed money quickly; he took what he wanted, regulations notwithstanding. Moreover, all questions of fairness or justice aside, he seems often to have proceeded too radically and impulsively for his own best interests. In 1210, apparently convinced that Jews were not reporting their financial affairs honestly, he once again ordered Jews arrested and held for ransom, forcing collection of their outstanding loans and diversion of the receipts to his own treasury.[10] At the same time he continued to sponsor legislation designed to protect borrowers from what were generally perceived as the excessive demands of Jewish lenders. In an undated directive issued around 1212, he ordered that each loan run for a clearly stated term with an agreed amount of total interest; if not paid on time, the loan was to accrue penalty interest of 43 percent for one more year, but no longer. After that, the Jewish lender could ask royal officials to enforce payment of the principal, or he could grant an extension without additional penalty.[11] In 1219 an extensive ordinance forbade loans to manual workers and laborers and permitted them to members of the lower clergy only with the permission of their superiors. In addition, it protected debtors from land foreclosures and ordered that Jews must not receive church ornaments or the spoils of robbery as pawn.[12] Much of this legislation seems not unreasonable as attempts to protect working people from being impoverished by excessive borrowing. But as the Jews must have viewed the matter, they were being relentlessly driven to provide money while their sources were being steadily reduced.

Because heavy debts were a hardship for people in every walk of life, Jewish moneylending was bound to aggravate their resentment. Many debtors found themselves committed far beyond their capacity. The poorest ended in prison, those in the middle ranks sank toward poverty, and even the moderately prosperous were sometimes forced to cede or sell valuable real estate or other property. Extremely high interest rates and annual compounding led to crushing debt accumulations. In a letter addressed to Philip in 1205, Pope Innocent III observed bitterly that the Jews extort "not only usury but usury upon usury" (non solum usuras sed usuras usurarum).[13] He may have had in mind hard-pressed clergymen who were pawning everything from cathedral chalices to church-owned real estate; the thought that these were falling into Jewish hands was more than he could bear.

Reflecting on the fate of the Jews during Philip's reign, the historian William Chester Jordan observes that until this time moneylending had received at least "qualified royal support." But, he continues, this is not the heart of the matter. "Leniency in business practice is not the issue. Predictability of social experience is. From the moment Philip Augustus came to the throne in 1179 almost to the very moment of his death in 1223, the Jews had been witnesses to and victims of the erratic policy of the king." They had to endure this. But whenever it seemed that they had reached a tolerable accommodation, "it would always be shattered by the rage or moral posturing or greed" of this most unpredictable king.[14]

When Philip died in 1223, he was succeeded by his son, Louis VIII, who was destined to live only three more years. Like his father and his barons, Louis seems to have been remarkably ambivalent about Jewish moneylenders: they were, on the one hand, a menace to society, but on the other, a most useful source of revenue. Thus, in November 1223, just a few months after reaching the throne, he issued an ordinance, "with the will and assent of the archbishops, bishops, counts, barons, and knights of the French kingdom, those who hold Jews and those who do not," that seems to have been designed not just to control Jewish moneylenders but to eliminate them altogether—only, however, after they had been thoroughly despoiled. Three of the five provisions would lead one to conclude that the plain intent was to terminate Jewish moneylending: No existing debts owed to Jews could continue accumulating interest; all outstanding debts had to be registered by the next February ("prior to the coming Feast of the Purification of the Virgin Mary"), but debts older than five years were altogether invalid; and Jews were no longer permitted to use official seals on their debt documents. The document is unclear, though, about whether future debts could be contracted with interest. Moreover, the other two provisions indicate that neither king nor barons were yet prepared to abandon such lucrative sources of revenue. The first ordered that outstanding debts were to be repaid not to Jewish creditors but to their overlords. The second, perhaps the most telling, was an agreement, to be binding on all overlords throughout France, that no one—"those who have sworn to the ordinance as well as those who have not"—would try improperly to obtain another's Jews. The intention here is clear: Jews who found the legislation unbearably oppressive might try to move to territory controlled by someone who had not signed the decree, but this would not be tolerated. Thibaut IV, count of Champagne, whose domain was already home to many Jews and offered excellent prospects for resettlement, was the most prominent baron who did not sign. But he too agreed to accept Jewish immigrants only on condition that the original overlord was absolved of all debts and could take possession of all immovable property left by the refugees.[15]

"To Me Pertain Matters Relative to the Jews": The Reign of Louis IX

Louis VIII was succeeded by his son, Louis IX (later Saint Louis), one of France's greatest monarchs, honored for his Christian piety as well as his exceptional administrative abilities. His long reign (1226–70) was characterized by substantial territorial gains, administrative reforms, and general prosperity; it was also characterized by increasingly overt persecution of Jews.

Louis was only twelve years old when his father died, and the first eight years of his reign were managed by his mother, Blanche of Castile. Blanche was a capable ruler, respected by the Jewish community for her sense of justice. But her son's notions of what constituted a Christian kingdom included no place for Jews. A story, perhaps apocryphal but not out of character, is told of Louis by his greatest contemporary biographer, Jean de Joinville. The king, Joinville reports, told him of a staged debate between Christian clergy and Jews at the great monastery of Cluny. A crippled and impoverished knight was granted permission to pose one question to the most learned rabbi. The question was whether the rabbi believed "that the Virgin Mary, who bore our Lord in her body and cradled Him in her arms, was a virgin at the time of His birth, and is in truth the Mother of God?" When the rabbi gave the predictable reply, the knight struck him with his crutch, and "all the Jews took to flight." When the monastery abbot reprimanded the knight, the latter replied that the greater folly was to bring Christians and Jews together this way, "because there were many good Christians there who, before the discussion ended, would have gone away with doubts about their own religion through not fully understanding the Jews." Louis then delivered the lesson of the tale and added a touch of his own: "'So I tell you,' said the king, 'that no one, unless he is an expert theologian, should venture to argue with these people. But a layman, whenever he hears the Christian religion abused, should not attempt to defend its tenets, except with his sword, and that he should thrust into the scoundrel's belly, and as far as it will enter.'"[16]

Louis was probably the first French king for whom moral considerations regarding usury so outweighed financial needs that he was prepared to forego monetary gain rather than imperil his immortal soul. He detested Jews on religious grounds alone; as moneylenders they were doubly reprehensible. Some of his advisors objected to his campaigns against Jewish lenders, arguing that since people needed money it was preferable that Jews be the sinful providers; moreover, they noted, Jews were charging less interest than their Christian counterparts. Louis replied:

> Matters relating to Christians who lend money and to their usury seem to be the concern of the prelates of the churches. To me, however, pertain matters relative to the Jews—who are subjected to me by the yoke of servitude—that they might not oppress Christians through usury and that they not be permitted, under the shelter of my protection, to engage in such pursuits and to infect my land with their poison. Let those prelates do what pertains to them concerning those subject Christians, and I must do what pertains to me concern-

ing the Jews. Let them abandon usury or they shall leave my land completely, in order that it no longer be polluted with their filth.[17]

In 1230, when Louis was sixteen years old and Blanche was still regent, an assembly of barons issued in his name an ordinance with significantly new language and provisions. For the first time, the barons declared that they would no longer enforce repayment of debts to Jews. But the ordinance was unevenly observed, and at least some barons maintained their financial connections with local Jews. For example, the third name in the list of signatories was that of Count Hugh of Lusignan; but two years later Hugh accepted two Jewish families who had formerly lived in the royal domain, with the understanding that in return for a fixed annual payment he would enforce repayment of legitimate debts owed to them, and that he would guarantee them a safe journey to the royal domain whenever they chose to return.[18]

In retrospect, the document's most striking provision was the following, because it introduced language that reveals how far Jewish status had declined in a relatively brief time: "Nor can anyone in the whole kingdom retain the Jew of another lord, and wherever anyone may find his Jew he may lawfully seize him just like his own serf, no matter how long the Jew shall have stayed under another lord or in another kingdom."[19]

The key phrase was "just like his own serf" (tanquam proprium servum). As Gavin Langmuir has convincingly demonstrated, this was not a declaration that Jews were serfs or were equated with serfs, but rather that Jews were personal property who belonged to a lord just as did his servi (meaning in the thirteenth century not literal serfs but dependent workers or peasants); hence, any Jew who tried to flee could be apprehended, as if he were a dependent laborer. The Church had long maintained, of course, that, as Pope Innocent III phrased it, Jews were "consigned to perpetual servitude because they crucified the Lord." But the phrase tanquam servum, "like a serf," was not rooted in Christian dogma; rather, it legally defined the status of Jews as individuals denied the right to determine their own residence.[20]

In 1234 a prominent French baron, Archembaud, duke of Bourbon, took the final step against Jewish moneylenders, "with the will and assent" of King Louis. "For my salvation and that of my predecessors," he declared, "I will and order that all Jews who wish to remain hence-forth on my land must live by their own labor and by honest business, abstaining completely from usurious exactions."[21] The following year Louis issued a similar decree, along with statements on other matters that offended his Christian piety:

1. That they live by their own labor or by trade, but without usury.

2. That they must give up Christian prostitutes and nurses.

3. That they shall not be received in taverns except as transients.

4. Concerning Christian servants of the Jews who have been ex-communicated, that the Jews dismiss them.[22]

These strictures seem based on two fundamental assumptions. First, that Louis viewed moneylending as a moral rather than an eco-nomic problem is strongly suggested by the association of the first prohibition with those that follow. Second, both Louis and Archem-baud believed (or at least maintained) that Jews were quite able to sustain themselves by means other than moneylending ("by their own labor or by trade"), an interpretation of the Jewish situation that seems strangely out of touch with reality. Both assumptions seem to reflect a belief that Jews were concentrated in moneylending simply because they had an inherent affinity for it, not because they had been squeezed into it—a belief reinforcing the conviction that because Jews were wicked by nature, only harshly restrictive measures could detach them from usury.

Despite this legislation, however, and despite the steady progres-sion from regulation to restriction to abolition, the king and his barons understood full well that if they were to have ready capital there had to be moneylenders, and that moneylenders, Jewish or Christian, could survive only by lending at interest. In fact, there is good evidence that Jews continued to lend money extensively long after 1235. In 1247, for example, Pope Innocent IV intervened on behalf of the Jews of Champagne, who had complained that Christian debtors were not honoring legitimate loan contracts. And in 1248, Louis himself was still issuing legislation addressing problems connected with Jewish mon-eylending. Even as late as 1254, on his return from a six year crusading expedition, he issued yet another set of restrictive ordinances in which usury now appeared in conjunction with possession of the Talmud and with "blasphemy, magic, and necromancy" as part of a package of

Jewish insults to the Christian social order. Here too, for the first time in his reign, there appeared the threat of expulsion, probably carried out against some Jews.[23]

By the mid-thirteenth century, then, the Jews of France were in the grip of a hostile king and his barons, all of whom viewed them as a despicable people serving an inescapable need. They were subjected on the one hand to strict, often unreasonable, regulation and restraint, and on the other to limitless extortion and vicious mistreatment when they proved unable to comply. The desperation of their position was surely as evident to them as to us; but given their utter powerlessness and severely limited options, they had no choice but to survive as well as they could. Survive they did for another half-century or so, but the pernicious contradictions in their situation heralded the close of the medieval phase of European Jewish history.

"In Their Ancient Manner": Germany, 1182–1197

In 1182, the year in which Philip Augustus expelled Jews from his royal domain, Frederick I (called Frederick Barbarossa), king of Germany and Holy Roman Emperor, issued a charter for the Jews of Regensburg (also called Ratisbon). Jews had lived in Regensburg since at least the sixth century, and for centuries Jewish merchants had played a major role in the international trade that linked Germany with peoples to the east.[24] One of Frederick's predecessors, Henry IV, had granted "privileges" to the Jews of Regensburg in 1097, immediately after the assaults connected with the First Crusade, ensuring that they could live and work there in safety. Now Frederick renewed the charter, adding a revealing introduction. It was his duty, he declared, "as well as a requirement of justice and a demand of reason," that he grant due protection to everyone in his empire, "not only adherents of the Christian faith, but also to those who differ from Our faith and live in accordance with the rites of their ancestral tradition." Therefore, he continued, "deeply concerned with the welfare of all Jews living in Our Empire who are known to belong to the Imperial Chamber by virtue of a special prerogative of Our dignity, We concede to Our Regensburg Jews and confirm with Our imperial authority their good

customs which their ancestors had secured through the grace and favor of Our predecessors until Our time." The charter goes on to guarantee Jews the right to sell precious metals and other wares, and to
pursue their commercial interests in "their ancient manner" (antiquo
more suo).[25]

Frederick, proud to be the heir of Charlemagne and Otto the Great,
declared that his empire would be ruled by their "good customs."[26]
His attitude toward Jews was consistent with this self-image, but also
with the political realities of his reign. He ruled, at least in name, over
a huge territory that included not only German lands from the Rhineland to Bohemia but much of Burgundy and Italy as well. The German
territories were largely under the control of feudal barons: dukes,
counts, and lesser lords who acknowledged nominal fealty to the emperor but in fact ruled over their own domains with all but absolute
power. The Jews of Germany stood outside ordinary social boundaries,
defined not by where they lived but as a distinct population with a
particular economic role. Declaring that Jews were his own subjects—
that they belonged to his imperial court and to no one else—was one
way in which Frederick could maintain that no matter who ruled a
region, he and he alone was emperor of all Germany. But Frederick
was not inclined to exploit Jews with anything resembling the determination of his French counterparts. With enough territory under his personal control to provide him with revenue, he still valued Jews mainly
as merchants, active contributors to the German economy, and not simply as passive sources of capital. Furthermore, his statements regarding them convey much less social distance. The Jews of Regensburg,
like all Jews in his empire, belong to his imperial court. But the language is that of mutual welfare, not unlike that of earlier centuries: the
emperor expects to benefit from the prosperity of his Jewish subjects,
and in return he guarantees them freedom and security.

There was little correspondence, however, between imperial declarations and popular attitudes. The Jews of Germany had long since
come to be recognized as an alien population, profoundly distrusted
and disliked, mutually liable for one another's crimes and misdemeanors, real or imagined. Time and again townspeople erupted against
them with virulent fury. The emperor or his personal representatives
frquently intervened to protect Jews (when they learned what was

happening) or to punish those who attacked them. But, as we see in the following episodes, the gap between popular prejudice and imperial policy was ominously wide.

In February 1187, in Neuss (one of the small Rhineland towns where a massacre had occurred during the First Crusade), a demented Jewish man killed a young Christian woman in the presence of witnesses. A riot ensued in which the murderer was killed along with six other Jews. Their homes were pillaged and their bodies taken to the center of town to be broken on the wheel. Several days later the guilty man's mother and uncle were dragged off and buried alive. A Jewish woman and her three daughters were forcibly baptized, though they were able later to reaffirm their Judaism. The surviving Jews had to bribe the local count and archbishop for protection and for assistance in removing the bodies for burial. Frederick probably knew nothing of these events, and the Jews had recourse only to local authorities, who obviously provided inadequate protection and acted only when paid.[27]

Another episode later the same year, reported by a Jewish chronicler, demonstrates unmistakably the determination of the imperial government to protect Jews against assault whenever it could. The site this time was the great Jewish community of Mainz, and the agitation was probably connected with the fall of Jerusalem to the Egyptian sultan Saladin. When news of this catastrophe reached Germany, says the chronicler, the Christians, identifying Jews as allies of Muslims, began calling for revenge. When he and other Jews heard about this, he continues, "a very great trembling seized us, and we took up the arts of our forefathers, decreeing fasting, weeping, and mourning." In January 1188 a Christian mob attacked the Jewish quarter and was driven off by local authorities. But over the next few weeks, as preparations escalated for another expedition to Palestine (the Third Crusade), the Jews became increasingly anxious and resorted once again to the customary fasting and penitential praying. "Thus we begged tearfully for our lives," says the chronicler, "for our wives, and for our children, lest the wicked kill them or baptize them with their impure waters." By March the Mainz Jews had decided on a more promising strategy; along with Jews from Speyer, Worms, and other towns, most fled to nearby villages or fortifications. By this time Frederick had arrived in Mainz to join the crusade himself, and it was almost certainly owing to his presence that the town marshal and his men finally took positive steps to protect the Jews. The chronicler quotes a letter from a Jew who remained in Mainz, describing what happened on March 26:

> On the Sabbath prior to the month of Nisan, the Crusaders gathered in our street to assault us and to attack us. One arose, with a sword in his hand, and attempted to smite a Jew. Then the marshal came . . . and seized him by the hair, pulling it, and smote him with a staff until his blood spilled to the ground. The rest fled to the marketplace and told their fellow Crusaders what had been done to them on account of the Jews. They all gathered, by the thousands and the ten thousands, and wished to take a standard and advance upon our street. The matter was revealed to the marshal; with a staff in his hand, he took his servants with him and smote the Crusaders and beat them, until they had all dispersed. . . . Blessed is the Lord and may His memory be exalted forever, for He provided relief prior to the blow. The officers understood clearly, saying, "How beloved are the Jews in the eyes of the king!"[28]

Soon thereafter Frederick issued a decree promising swift punishment for offenders: for harming a Jew, loss of a hand; for killing a Jew, the death penalty. He also ordered that Jews receive especially careful protection thereafter. "All of this," notes the chronicler, "was paid for fully." Frederick needed money to finance his crusading expedition, and no doubt he welcomed a generous contribution from the Jews of the Rhineland. This was tribute but not extortion. Even in the passion of preparations for a crusade, Frederick refused to tolerate violence against Jews and went out of his way to protect them.

In June 1190, Frederick drowned in Cilicia (now southern Turkey) while on his way to Palestine. His son, Henry VI (1190–97), an equally proud and ambitious man, regarded himself, says one historian, "as the feudal overlord of the world."[29] During his relatively brief reign, the policy of protection for Jews was maintained, as is illustrated by an episode in which his brother played the principal role. In 1195 the body of a murdered woman was found some three miles from Speyer, and as usual the Jews were blamed. Jewish emissaries appealed for assistance to Henry's brother Otto, duke of Burgundy, paying him the customary bribe, and he agreed to order that no one should be harmed. But the order, if it was received, arrived too late. According to the Jewish chronicler Ephraim of Bonn, the Christians "rose up as if to swallow the Jews alive":

> They removed the corpse of the daughter of Rabbi Isaac ben Asher ha-Levi from its grave during the period of mourning and hung it naked in the marketplace, with a rat hanging in the strands of her hair as a mockery and humiliation to the Jews. Her father ransomed the corpse through bribery and returned it to the grave. The following day the burghers—those men of Sodom—surrounded the rabbi's house, breached it, and killed him, along with eight other Jews. They also burned all the Jews' homes. . . . The enemy despoiled everything in the Jews' homes. They threw books and Torah scrolls into the water and burned the synagogue.

When Otto learned of the riot, says Ephraim,

> he was enraged. He gathered troops and besieged Speyer. He burned all the villages belonging to the wicked bishop and the burghers; he cut down their trees, tore up their vineyards, and trampled their grain totally. . . . Subsequently, the emperor came and captured the murderers, until they paid him great sums of money. They gave the Jews approximately five hundred talents and rebuilt their homes and synagogue as before.

Only a week afterward, further violence erupted in the nearby village of Boppard, where eight more Jews were killed. This time Otto ordered that the murderers be blinded. Later, when Henry arrived on the scene, he ordered the local people to pay a large fine to the Jewish community.[30]

Jewish chroniclers, we should of course remember, wrote mainly about violence and destruction, not about peaceful encounters in everyday life. Most Jews in late twelfth-century Germany were probably living in reasonably good circumstances most of the time. Yet no matter how fairly they may have been treated, they remained a categorically distinct people. To be sure, some legislation was addressed specifically to Jews, but even in documents in which Jewish identity would seem to have no particular bearing, that identity is still noted.

For example, a house in Würzburg is described as belonging to "the Jew Samson," and in Regensburg an abbot signs a contract with "the Jew Abraham."[31] Even when Jews are included as part of a broader policy, they are likely to be singled out for mention. Thus, in 1212, Emperor Frederick II granted the bishop of Worms primary authority in matters relating to townspeople *or* Jews.[32]

Although there is no reason to believe that German emperors particularly liked Jews, they were seeing to it that Jews could continue in their traditional roles as merchants. The economic prosperity of the empire, as well as maintenance of public order, required that this endlessly paradoxical people—prosperous but insecure, useful but helpless—be designated the emperor's own protected "servants."

"Servants of the Court": The Reign of Frederick II

Henry VI died in 1197, leaving a three-year-old son, Frederick. For the next fifteen years, two rival political factions claimed the throne, but at the age of eighteen Frederick was elected to succeed his father. Frederick II was not the kind of man one would imagine as a German emperor. Born in Italy, heir through his mother to the Norman kingdom of Sicily (which included the southern half of Italy), he had grown up in the cosmopolitan city of Palermo, where Christians, Muslims, and Jews mingled familiarly. Frederick thrived in this social atmosphere and remained all his life a heterodox thinker and religious skeptic. A more striking contrast to his French counterpart, Louis IX, can hardly be imagined. Politically astute enough to realize that the best way to gain papal favor was to cooperate in the escalating battle against heresy, in the early years of his reign he freely issued legislation threatening heretics with severe punishment. But, in fact, much of his time and energy went into struggles with the popes themselves, for he was determined to incorporate all of Italy (except for the papal domain) into his empire—a goal acceptable neither to the Vatican nor to the northern Italian city-states, which were by this time second to none in Europe as commercial centers. Germany itself held few attractions for Frederick. Preoccupied with political and military affairs in Italy, and by temperament a southern European, he remained most of the time in Italy, leaving Germany to be ruled by his sons.

Frederick treated Jews mildly for the most part, not because he especially favored them but because he recognized their usefulness. The Jews of Italy and Sicily viewed him with definite approval, and the Jews of Germany also trusted him to act with goodwill. Following the policies of his predecessors, Frederick was disinclined to exploit Jews, trusting rather that Jewish merchants, fairly treated, would contribute to the prosperity of the empire.

Representative of his imperial style was his response to an episode in the town of Fulda in 1236. When several boys were found murdered there, townspeople leveled what was in effect a new accusation against the Jews: that they had killed the boys to obtain blood for ritual consumption. For nearly a century Jews had often been charged with ritual murders—specifically, with abducting and killing Christian boys in imitation of the crucifixion of Jesus. But the Fulda accusation included an ominous new twist; now the charge was not just ritual murder but ritual cannibalism.[33] The grim irony (it was Christians, after all, who drank symbolic blood at communion) seems not to have bothered the accusers. In the riot that ensued, thirty-two Jews were murdered. Realizing that similar accusations would soon spring up elsewhere, Frederick acted with characteristic good sense. Consulting with German barons and bishops, he gained their agreement to a conference of experts on Judaism, particularly Jewish converts to Christianity, who would determine whether Jews actually required blood for religious rituals. Learned men from many parts of Europe attended the conference. Their conclusions, which absolved the Jews completely, were summarized in an imperial decree:

> [I]t was clear that it was not indicated in the Old Testament or in the New that Jews lust for the drinking of human blood. Rather, precisely the opposite, they guard against the intake of all blood, as we find expressly in the biblical book which is called in Hebrew, "Bereshit," in the laws given by Moses, and in the Jewish decrees which are called in Hebrew, "Talmud." We can surely assume that for those to whom even the blood of permitted animals is forbidden, the desire for human blood cannot exist, as a result of the horror of the matter,

the prohibition of nature, and the common bond of the human species in which they also join Christians.[34]

In the same decree Frederick spelled out clearly his own position regarding Jews: as "servants" (servi) of his court, under his personal protection, they were not to be subjected to slander or physical harm. Jews, as he diplomatically defined them, were a "special group" of "non-believers": "although it is fitting, for the protection of the faith which stems from celestial dispensation, to treat the faithful of Christ with special favor, nonetheless, for the proper management of justice, it is required that we rule the non-believers properly and protect them justly, as a special group committed to our care." This document is another landmark in the evolution of Jewish political status, demonstrating that even in the most benign circumstances Jews had become categorically viewed as a vulnerable and defenseless people.[35]

Above all, Frederick was a practical politician who chose whatever maneuver best suited his needs of the moment. Just a year after the decree discussed above, he issued another, for the city of Vienna, which shows clearly that his dealings with Jews were based entirely on expedience. Vienna was the capital city of the domain of the powerful duke of Austria, also named Frederick II but known as "Frederick the Belligerent." This man had earned his sobriquet by opposing the domination of the emperor until the latter, overcoming him by force, asserted imperial control over the city. Apparently the duke had not only granted generous privileges to Jewish merchants but, despite popular opposition, had also appointed Jews to public office. Now the king's Vienna decree of 1237, which granted privileges to the townspeople in appreciation for having supported the emperor, included a provision forbidding Jews to function as public officials. The stated reason was a familiar one: that they had been "condemned to perpetual servitude" (the usual phrase in papal letters) and must not hold power over Christians.[36]

Only one year later we find Frederick issuing yet another decree, this one a charter addressed specifically to the Jews of Vienna and almost certainly intended to reiterate the essential point that control over a region meant ownership of its Jews. "We wish to announce to the entire world," he declared with characteristic modesty, "that we take the Jews of Vienna, servants of Our court, under the protection of Ourselves and of Our Empire." The charter follows the customary language of its predecessors, but with omissions that may signify that Frederick recognized public objections to Jewish commercial prominence. On the positive side, baptism of Jewish children against their parents' wishes was expressly prohibited and punishable by a heavy fine. Furthermore, Jews were not to be condemned on Christian testimony alone, and killing or assaulting a Jew was to be punished by a fine equivalent to that imposed for the same offense against a Christian. Jews were granted all essential freedoms and complete autonomy in their internal affairs. But the document permitted less than usual in the way of commercial privileges, probably in deference to local sentiment. Overall, however, there was little cause for Jewish complaint; Frederick dealt with Jews everywhere more generously than did any of his contemporaries.[37]

Before leaving Vienna we should note another landmark charter, granted to all Austrian Jews in 1244 by Duke Frederick, who had by then regained hegemony over the region. The charter is clearly intended to encourage Jews to engage in commerce and moneylending under the duke's protection. Matters connected with moneylending and pawnbroking are addressed in detail; lenders and borrowers are guaranteed rights and security, with exceptional consideration for the Jewish lender in some circumstances. For example, one section provides for cases in which a Christian claimed that items stolen from him were accepted by a Jew as pledge for a loan; if the Jewish lender swore that he had been unaware of the origin of the items, the Christian was required to pay the principal and interest in return for the stolen goods. Jews were to be protected from harsh treatment, and Jewish women received particular protection: "[I]f a Christian raises his hand in violence against a Jewess," states one section, "we order that the hand of that person be cut off." The oaths of Jews were to be respected in court, and Jews were generally to be accorded rights and privileges consistent with a policy of generous acceptance. This charter was to play an especially important role in eastern European Jewish history because it was eventually adopted with only minor changes by rulers in Poland, Hungary, and elsewhere.[38]

We have seen that under German emperors Jews were enjoying considerably more security than their counterparts in France. Their well-being, however, was almost entirely contingent on the favor of a few high political authorities; and because they depended so heavily on such favor, they were perceived by the populace as a privileged minority who deserved nothing of the kind. Moreover, the religious atmosphere was certainly not developing in their favor: In a society in which the Church, here as throughout Europe, was becoming increasingly more influential, everything pointed to the prospect of mounting oppression. Despite their temporary advantages over the Jews of France, the Jews of Germany were also living on borrowed time.

· 10 ·

"REVEAL NO SECRETS"

Maintaining a Culture in a Hostile World

By the twelfth century most Jews in France and Germany were living in tightly organized communities, almost entirely responsible for their own maintenance. Everyone accepted collective responsibility for every aspect of life, from taxes and charity to education and legal disputes. Typically, a few hundred Jews lived together in a neighborhood within a city, interacting daily with Gentiles but with a firm sense of themselves as a people destined to remain apart. When it came to the more personal kinds of social interaction, Talmudic regulations regarding food and wine were rigorous enough to ensure that Jews would eat and drink only with one another. Each community controlled settlement rights to protect members from unwelcome economic competition; Jewish refugees and wayfarers, however, were granted shelter and assistance. Everyone recognized ties to other Jewish communities, of course, but there was no centralized administration other than the rulings of prominent rabbis who were accepted as authorities. The communities were egalitarian and supportive, at least to the degree that everyone had the right to be heard, and to be protected against physical harm, personal insults, poverty, and social isolation. Moreover, everyone was obliged to serve the common welfare by respecting community secrets and not providing information to powerful Gentiles.

Their essential concerns can be summarized in three words: *education, cooperation,* and *security.* The outstanding educational centers were in northern France, in such cities as Paris, Orléans, and Troyes, but wherever Ashkenazic Jews lived there were schools of every kind, from elementary schools to yeshivas. It was taken for granted that every man would try to study throughout his life, and even those whose days were taken up with mundane labor looked forward to evenings around a table with an open Talmud and a group of like-minded friends. Books were esteemed as spiritual objects, and a man's library was his most precious possession.[1]

More than ever, communal welfare depended on the absolute loyalty and cooperation of every individual. One had to be generous with personal wealth, honest in business affairs, willing to pay a fair share of heavy taxes, charitable toward the needy, ready to help defend anyone who was threatened or endangered. Antisocial behavior, such as lying or stealing, rumor mongering, inappropriate fraternization with Gentiles, or careless public accusations against other Jews could lead to *kherem*, excommunication. Leadership was in the hands of a small group of respected men who were likely to be prosperous merchants or moneylenders as well as learned students of rabbinic law. Though they probably decided most issues among themselves, they had to be responsive to the will of the general community. These men also served as intercessors with the authorities in the case of conflict with Gentiles or oppressive actions by the authorities themselves. In effect, they were the community's legislative, judicial, and executive bodies, issuing rulings and ordinances *(takkanot)*, passing judgment on crimes and transgressions, and enforcing the communal will with the threat of boycott or excommunication.

At times the leaders of several communities met to issue legislation applying to everyone under their jurisdiction. Such a council, or synod, convened at Mainz in 1220, and its regulations provide a glimpse of communal life as well as relations with outsiders. Here are a few:

> No one shall put his wine in the vessels of Gentiles unless they are properly purified. . . .
> No one shall permit a Gentile to make his wine; nor shall one eat what is cooked by Gentiles. . . .
> An anathema should be declared against informers on every Sabbath. . . .

No Jew shall through recourse to Gentiles free himself of his communal obligations. . . .

Nor shall anyone reveal any secrets to Gentiles. . . .

No one shall call his neighbor "bastard" or revile him with any other blemish of birth. . . .

Every man shall set aside a definite time for study. If he is unable to study Talmud, he shall read Scripture, the weekly portion, or the Midrash according to his ability. He who does much and he who does little are alike.[2]

The Righteous Ones: *Hasidei Ashkenaz*

Despite social isolation, Jewish religious life responded to cultural currents in the Christian environment. During the middle of the twelfth century there appeared in the Rhineland communities a religious movement that seems to have paralleled trends in the Christian world. A small group of men, who came to be called *Hasidei Ashkenaz*, the Pious (or Righteous) of Germany, set new standards for what they declared to be a properly led Jewish life. Insisting that Jews should practice uncompromising piety, asceticism, self-denial, and humility, they themselves aimed to achieve holiness in daily life well beyond that prescribed by rabbinic law. Having identified themselves as "the Righteous," they wrote and spoke of other Jews, no matter how observant in the conventional sense, as "the Wicked" or "the Evil Ones," maintaining that only their own version of piety ensured rewards in the hereafter; the rewards, they declared, would be "proportional to the pain." The historian Ivan Marcus calls them the "Puritans" of their time, but as he recognizes, they had contemporary Christian counterparts.[3]

The movement corresponded so closely to comparable developments in the Christian world that a connection seems likely—not through direct borrowing, but because Jews and Christians must all have been responding to a social and religious climate favoring mysticism, asceticism, and challenges to religious complacency. Asceticism was gaining prominence in monastic life in reaction to the excesses of splendor and luxury characteristic of the great monasteries of the eleventh and early twelfth centuries. More immediately, the Church was now being challenged by vigorous heretical movements, particularly the dualistic doctrine called Catharism. These heretics practiced extreme asceticism in the form of constant fasting and prayer, took vows of celibacy and poverty, and identified themselves as the only truly pious people—the "Perfect" or the "Elect," as they called themselves.[4] It seems likely that the Hasidei Ashkenaz were responding, however indirectly, to the same social and religious climate that gave rise to the Cathars and other heretics.

Their theology was unsystematic and in places contradictory, but that was of no concern to them. God was said to be infinite and wholly spiritual but also immanent (physically present) in the entire world, including all living beings. God's first creation had been his own revealed aspect, the divine emanation called *kavod*. This was all that humans could even begin to apprehend, because God never revealed himself directly; instead, he "maintains His silence and carries the universe."[5] Magic, mystical interpretations of sacred texts, and even demonology were all manifestations of God's power to transcend the natural laws of his own creation in order to reveal his deepest will. But only the initiated could share in such esoteric knowledge or the mystical experience to which it led.

The movement was initiated by members of a single family, named Kalonymos, which had been prominent in the cities of the Rhineland since the time of Charlemagne. The founder was Samuel ben Kalonymos (known as Samuel the Hasid), born in Speyer early in the twelfth century. His son, Judah ben Samuel of Worms (Judah the Hasid), who lived until 1217, was the principal author of the movement's key text, *Sefer Hasidim*, "Book of the Righteous." Judah was a stern sectarian who envisioned a utopian community that would adhere to standards of utmost piety and asceticism, guided and sustained by sages like himself. Because they were to provide a model for other Jews, they would accept as brethren only those who were prepared to acknowledge their sinfulness and to lead exemplary lives thereafter. It goes without saying that women had no significant place in Judah's world. The movement did not advocate celibacy; to the contrary, it maintained (in characteristic Jewish manner) that a life of absolute piety required marriage and family. But only men could aspire to complete righteousness.

Embedded in Judah's religious philosophy was a critique of Jewish communal life. He did not hesitate to declare that most rabbis and community leaders fell far short of his standards for the genuinely righteous. Moreover, he condemned distinctions based on wealth. Although he considered it possible that poverty was punishment for sin, wealth in itself implied no particular merit, and he insisted that prosperous men should give generously to the poor. According to the "Book of the Righteous," when everyone in a community was taxed an equal amount, wealthy men should "return to the poor in secret all that the latter give, without the evil people knowing about it."[6] Likewise, rabbinic learning in itself meant nothing; only those who were righteous, charitable, and humble would find favor in the eyes of God.

Orthodox Judaism centers on visible behavior (prayers, observance of the Sabbath, and charitable acts, for example) as the core of religious life. The Hasidei Ashkenaz insisted that obedience to the Law was only the beginning of acknowledgment of the divine will. Equally or more important was one's inward state, which demanded a depth of cultivation that could never be achieved by routine observances. Men had to be scrupulous in recognizing sinful thoughts and inclinations, the urgings of the "evil impulse" (yetzer hara), so that they might undertake penance and strive toward ever higher levels of perfection. God's will was not immediately evident in Torah or Talmud—not on the surface, in any event. One had to search for deeper meanings, sometimes veiled in the numerological mysteries of letter combinations (in Hebrew, numbers are signified by letters), to reveal the true intent of the divine commandments. To ensure that everyone not only met the ordinary expectations of the Law but advanced well beyond them, it was necessary to create new "fences," or safeguards, around each requirement, to avoid coming anywhere near a violation. Thus righteousness did not entail challenges to traditional observance; rather, scrupulous observance became the essential part of a program of complete personal transformation.

Men seeking admission to the fellowship of the righteous had to undergo an initiatory ritual involving confession of sin to a sage, public contrition, and performance of suitable penitential acts. Sexual misdemeanors were probably among the sins most frequently acknowledged. A man who confessed to an adulterous relationship had first to avoid the woman entirely for a year; only then was he eligible for acts of penance that would gain him entry into the fellowship. Here is the penance prescribed in the "Book of the Righteous" for an adulterer: "[I]f it is winter when he comes to inquire and there is ice on the river, if he wishes, he should break the ice and sit in the water up to his mouth or nose for the same amount of time from when he [first] spoke to [the woman] about the sin until its completion."

The penance for intercourse with a Christian woman was less daunting but rigorous enough: "If he did it even once, he should fast for three consecutive days, night and day, not eat during the day nor during the night, for three years. If he should prefer [to do this] three times, for three days and nights, within the same year, it is enough."[7]

Judah's vision of a sectarian community was never realized, probably because even his most devoted followers were reluctant to sever themselves entirely from Jewish communal life. His designated successor was one of his pupils, Eleazar ben Judah (ben Kalonymos), also of Worms, a man equally pious but more realistic about human nature. Realizing that "righteousness" had to be somehow accessible to everyone, he advocated a more outgoing form of revivalism that would encourage deeper personal piety for every Jew in the community. This is the theme of his principal work, *Sefer ha-Rokeah*, "Book of the Perfumer," a title meant to connote soothing qualities and encouragement. Rather than demanding public confession of sins and humiliating penance, Eleazar urged Jews to confess inwardly and to atone by becoming more pious in their daily lives. The movement, says Ivan Marcus (being candid about his own sympathies), was thereby transformed "from a program of an obnoxious group of extremists into a religious blueprint for the spiritual amelioration of the average law-abiding Jew." Thus Eleazar, a modest man who called himself "Eleazar the Insignificant," had more impact than his predecessors on Jewish religious life.[8] Incidentally, Eleazar believed that the Messiah would appear in the year 1240 and would punish Christians for having oppressed Jews.

"Such Disorder Has Developed"

In July 1205, Pope Innocent III addressed a letter to the bishop of Paris and the archbishop of Sens, instructing them on matters that had come to his attention pertaining to the Jews of northern France. Jews, he reminded the bishops, "are consigned to perpetual servitude because they crucified the Lord" and dwell among Christians only on sufferance; therefore they "ought not be ungrateful to us, and not requite Christian favor with contumely and intimacy with contempt." But that was precisely what they were doing: turning on those who were generous enough to tolerate their presence, and becoming

> so insolent that they hurl unbridled insults at the Christian faith, insults which it is an abomination not only to utter but even to keep in mind. Thus, whenever it happens that on the day of the Lord's Resurrection the Christian women who are nurses for the children of Jews take in the body and blood of Jesus Christ, the Jews make these women pour their milk into the latrine for three days before they again give suck to the children. Besides, they perform other detestable and unheard of things against the Catholic faith, as a result of which the faithful should fear that they are incurring divine wrath when they permit the Jews to perpetrate unpunished such deeds as bring confusion upon our faith.[9]

The letter, with its emphasis on order and control, says much about the pope and the time. Innocent III had become pope in 1198, a vigorous man still in his thirties, well trained in law, and a resourceful politician whose overriding purpose was to assert his supremacy over any and all who challenged the absolute authority of Church and papacy. He inherited a Church that had been sliding ominously in efficiency and esteem. The clergy had grown lazy, most of them more attached to luxury than to theology, out of touch with ordinary people. Challenged by everyone from arrogant monarchs to bold theologians and outright heretics, and preceded by several weak popes who had damaged the Church's prestige, Innocent was determined to reverse the course of events. He created a more efficient administration, answerable to him alone. He insisted on absolute control over clerical appointments. Most importantly, he stood firm against every kind of rebelliousness, from kings, clergy, and townspeople alike. Repeatedly he stood up to the most powerful monarchs of his day—Otto IV of Germany, John of England, Philip Augustus of France—and forced them to accede to his demands. His most decisive victory came in 1214, when at the Battle of Bouvines (in Flanders) armies mobilized on his behalf defeated and deposed Otto IV as punishment for having invaded northern Italy.

Perhaps the most demanding challenge of all was posed by the spread of heretical ideas that seemed to threaten the very foundations of Christianity—particularly the doctrines of the Cathars, whose teachings were sharply contrary to Christian orthodoxy. By the beginning of the thirteenth century, Catharism, or Albigensianism, had found widespread acceptance in much of western Europe, but especially in northern Italy and southern France, in the region called Languedoc, where it attracted adherents from every social class. The Cathars viewed the universe as a battleground between a spiritual world created by God and a material world created by Satan. The spiritual world was goodness, virtue and light; the material world was evil, sin and darkness. They declared that the Old Testament was a wicked, materially oriented book, and that "the devil, in the form of a calf, gave the Law to the Jews."[10] In defiance of the Nicene Creed, they taught that Jesus did not share in God's divine nature but was his spiritual emissary and had never assumed a truly physical body. The essential elements of Christian ritual—communion wafers, wine, baptismal water—were nothing more, they insisted, than evil matter. Even the sacrament of marriage should be condemned, because it led to the entrapment of spiritual souls in material bodies subject to sin and wickedness. Those who were admitted into their membership, known as "Good Men," embarked on lives of asceticism; the vegetarianism and celibacy of these wandering mendicants posed stark alternatives to the decadence of the Catholic clergy. Many who found the movement attractive but were unable to adopt its rigorous strictures were admitted as "Believers" who renounced Catholic Christianity, lived as far as possible according to Catharist doctrine, and pledged themselves to full conversion at the end of their lives.[11]

In 1208, when a papal legate was murdered in southern France, blame naturally fell on the Cathars. Innocent called upon Philip Augustus to confiscate lands of the powerful count Raymond of Toulouse as punishment. Though Philip was not averse to that prospect, he was too heavily engaged in other skirmishes to be diverted. Not to be thwarted, Innocent preached a crusade to liberate France from heresy. In response, in 1209 a vast army assembled at Lyons and marched southward, massacring and pillaging heretics and faithful Christians alike; the record of brutality matches that for the Rhineland in 1096. In Béziers they massacred people indiscriminately, burned a church crowded with refugees, and also burned the cathedral and many homes. A gratified archbishop, one of the crusade leaders, reported (probably with exaggeration) that his army had killed some fifteen thousand people, "showing mercy neither to order nor age nor sex," and characterized the victory as "miraculous."[12] The struggle lasted until 1229, thirteen years after Innocent's death. The ultimate result was the incorporation of Languedoc into the royal domain.

In contrast to those in northern France, Jews in southern France were enjoying relatively favorable treatment at this time; their services as merchants and lenders were encouraged, and some even reached prominence as public officials. The fate of their communities was incidental to the crusade, in that they were not singled out for attack; their relatively comfortable status as allies of the local authorities, however, became untenable. Most probably escaped the Béziers massacre when they and other noncombatants accompanied the local viscount who fled to Carcassonne just before the main assault.[13] But the Church authorities, aware of how well many Jews had been faring, determined to institute changes. In 1209, Raymond and other barons swore to obey a set of injunctions dictated by the papal legate. Most had to do with the status of Cathars and other heretics, but one specifically addressed the role of Jews in public office, ordering Raymond "to remove the Jews from the administration of public and private affairs in all your lands" and never "to restore them to the same or to other offices, nor to take any Jews for any administrative office, nor ever to use their advice against Christians."[14]

That heretics and Jews were closely associated in the minds of the clergy is also apparent from an edict issued at an ecclesiastical council convened in 1212 at Pamiers, in Provence. It declared that no heretical Christian should be appointed to public office or permitted to testify in a lawsuit. The same also applied to Jews, except that one Jew might testify against another.[15] Whether this edict was obeyed is open to question, since Raymond's successor, another Raymond, was in 1229 again ordered to expel Jews from public office.[16]

The papacy of Innocent III culminated in 1215, when more than four hundred bishops and hundreds of other clerical and secular dignitaries gathered in Rome for the Fourth Lateran Council, a legislative assembly that laid down an extensive program designed to create a unified, orthodox, and obedient Christendom. Among its edicts (or "titles") were five referring specifically to Jews. One of two edicts addressed to the problem of "heavy and immoderate" usury suggests that Jews were still providing essential capital at high rates of interest and gaining ownership of valuable properties when debtors defaulted. The second orders that "the secular powers shall compel the Jews to remit their usury, and until the Jews have done so they shall be denied commercial intercourse with Christians," adding that men are not to be charged interest while away on crusade.

Another edict repeats the standard injunction against appointing those "who blaspheme against Christ" to public office, "since this offers them the pretext to vent their wrath against the Christians." A fourth addresses the question of how to deal with converts who appear insincere; they are in effect heretics, for even though they "voluntarily approached the baptismal font," they had not "completely driven out the old self in order the more perfectly to bring in the new." To ensure that they do not "retain remnants of their former faith" and "tarnish the beauty of the Christian religion by such a mixture," the edict orders that they be held "by compulsion" to unadulterated Christian observance: "For there is less evil in not recognizing the way of the Lord than in backsliding after having recognized it."[17]

None of these provisions broke new ground, but a fifth one did precisely that. The first paragraph of Title 68 initiated a new era in European Jewish history:

Whereas in some provinces of the Church a difference in clothing distinguishes Jews and Saracens, in certain other lands such disorder has developed that no differences are discernible. Thus it sometimes happens that Christians mistakenly have intercourse with Jewish or Saracen women, and Jews or Saracens with Christian women. Therefore, lest these people, under pretext of such error, seek to excuse the sin of such intercourse, we decree that these people of both sexes, in all Christian provinces and at all times, shall be readily distinguishable from everyone else by their type of clothing.[18]

Such radical legislation suggests that many thirteenth-century Jews must have been virtually indistinguishable from Christians, and that despite all social obstacles, Jews and Christians still interacted frequently, with occasional sexual relationships an inevitable outcome. Assimilation had probably proceeded less smoothly in northern France and Germany, however, than in Spain and southern France, and it may be that the edict was directed mainly at the latter. The Jews of northern France and Germany, the most conservative in Europe, were probably already distinguishable by beards, earlocks, and clothing. The Jews of Paris may have been required to wear a distinctive badge for a time, but there is no definite evidence for a badge requirement in northern France until considerably later.[19]

For a time some Jews passively resisted the order. In 1221, Innocent's successor, Pope Honorius III, informed the bishops of Bordeaux province that he had heard of some Jews in the region "that they scorn to wear the prescribed signs by which they are to be distinguishable from Christians through a difference in their clothing [*diversitate habitus*], as was decreed by the General Council," with the unfortunate result "that Christians mingle [*commiscentur*] with Jewish women, and Jews wickedly mingle with Christian women."[20] Twelve years later his successor, Gregory IX, protested in a bitterly worded letter to the bishops of Germany that nothing had changed there. He seems to have emphasized his annoyance by repeating the wording of the original edict: "Although it was announced that Jews of either sex should, in all Christian provinces and at all times, be distinguished from others by the nature of their clothes, yet [such disorder has developed] in some parts of Germany that no difference is discernible."[21]

It appears that where Jews were seen to be adopting styles of clothing and personal appearance not unlike that of other relatively prosperous people, they were required to wear badges. But in those regions, particularly central France and most of Germany, where they were maintaining a more distinctive appearance—growing earlocks and beards, wearing clothing that was recognizably Jewish in style—the badge was not required. So, for example, we find that while the Jews of Paris may have been wearing badges as early as 1216 or 1217, those in other parts of France probably were not required to do so until much later. An ecclesiastical council held at Rouen (in Normandy) in 1231 ordered, probably for the first time in that region, that Jews wear "an easily distinguishable badge" on their chests.[22] A council convened at Albi (in Languedoc) in 1254 issued an edict requiring that Jews not wear "round capes" similar to those of Christian clergy, because they were being mistaken for priests and the "respect due to the clergy" was thus being "seriously impaired." They also insisted that Jews "continually and publicly" wear a circular badge on their chests.[23] It was not until 1270 that Jews in the German empire were required to wear distinguishing clothing, when they donned an item that became recognizable for centuries thereafter: the pointed cap, which is often seen in late medieval and early modern representations of Jews.[24]

The Ultimate Goal: Conversion

As we have noted, by the early thirteenth century all Europe was conceived as Christendom, a single community of the faithful, transcending all regional and national boundaries, presided over by a pope who was beholden to no earthly ruler. Christian society was said to be the earthly equivalent of the mystical body of Christ (*Corpus Christi*), eternal and indestructible, endowed like its heavenly counterpart with spiritual power surpassing ordinary comprehension. Nothing was more vital to this vision of Christendom than the idea of order; thus no heresy, no deviation of any sort from designated roles and statuses could be tolerated.

But it was becoming evident that Jews were doing just that: deviating from their proper roles far beyond the limits of toleration. For centuries Jews had been subscribers, as it were, to an implicit contract granting them conditional acceptance as bearers of the "Old Testament"—benighted and misguided bearers, to be sure, but heirs nevertheless to an indispensable antecedent of Christianity, and destined ultimately, despite their infuriating stubbornness, to achieve redemption and entry into the Christian community. By now, however, it was apparent that rabbinic Judaism, evolving for centuries along its own path, had created a corpus of writings, particularly the Talmud, that interpreted and expanded on the Hebrew Scriptures just as surely as Christians had done—not, however, in the service of Christian revelation but quite to the contrary. For this reason Jews were now being regarded as veritable heretics who had rejected their divinely appointed role and had chosen for themselves a path that was unmistakably the devil's.[25]

The obvious solution was to step up the effort to eliminate Judaism entirely by converting each and every Jew—by peaceful persuasion, if possible (a point on which popes had always insisted), but by more vigorous means if necessary. The campaign was spearheaded by the Dominican and Franciscan friars, who had emerged around 1215 as militant orders dedicated to relentless missionizing and inquisitorial persecution of anyone whose beliefs and practices challenged the supremacy of the Church. A favorite tactic was to deliver sermons to Jews in forced attendance; but since a congregation of Jews at a Christian sermon was still a congregation of Jews, under such circumstances very few were likely to break ranks. And so the task became conversion of individuals, but with more attendant problems than may have been anticipated. For one thing, since papal policy dictated that converts must not suffer any material losses, particularly through disinheritance by outraged kinsmen, Jews were forbidden to appropriate a convert's property. But that was precisely what the nobility who "owned" such Jews wanted to see happen. Since Jews who converted were, in effect, lost to their erstwhile patrons, it was greatly preferable that their personal property should remain with the Jewish community, still available for extraction. Some lords even went so far as to treat converts as rebellious vassals who had severed the "feudal" relationship of master and Jew!

Conversion was not without its attractions. Promising at least the prospect of acceptance as a full-fledged member of society, it led in any event to release from the various forms of confinement that were part and parcel of Jewish identity. Some, perhaps most, converts left the Jewish community not because they found Christianity compelling on theological grounds but with more material, even cynical, motives. Since it was Church policy that converts should be granted sustenance and support as encouragement, some attached themselves to the Church in order to receive benefits. Some behaved in such a leech-like manner as to cause more trouble than they were worth. One family of converts in Mainz badgered the local cathedral clergy for grants and support over a period of some twenty-five years, until they eventually garnered the income from a clergyman's stipend in Mainz and two parish churches outside of town. Not a few Jews who chose more conventional routes became regular members of the clergy.[26]

Although the Church tried to reward Jews who seemed to be sincere converts, it dealt firmly with those who converted only to "backslide" into the ancestral religion. We have already noted the edict of the Fourth Lateran Council stating that such individuals were to be held to Christian observance "by compulsion." Converts who refused to remain faithful to their Christian vows were treated as heretics. By the latter part of the century, popes were declaring that such individuals should be burned at the stake.[27]

The Devil's Own

In one of the most dramatic scenes in the Gospel of John (8:37–44, cited in chapter 1) Jesus declares that the Jews who scorn him are the veritable offspring and heirs not of Abraham but of the devil. Although this message must have rested in the minds of countless Christians throughout the centuries, in the thirteenth it erupted into public discourse as never before, and imagery associated with the idea reached new depths of virulence. Jewish deficiencies were now attributed not just to willfulness or confusion but to intrinsic (what we would now call genetic) qualities: Jews were wicked because their father and teacher was none other than the devil. Every genre from folklore and drama to clerical and scholarly literature portrayed Jews as cursed with physical characteristics and capacities revealing their tainted ancestry: repulsive infirmities along with unnatural power to harm others. Tiny horns, hidden by hair but detectable to the touch, sprouted from their heads. Their faces and bodies were ugly, blemished and deformed;

some even had tails, carefully hidden. Many had red hair, revealing their devilish ancestry, and the men wore goatees recalling that of their father. Indeed, Jews resembled goats, for they exuded a foul, goatish odor, *foetor Judaicus;* moreover, the goat, with its devilish qualities—lechery, greed, aggressiveness—was an apt symbol for Jews and matters Jewish. Ironically enough, the pig was another animal appearing in vicious portraits of Jews: the fat *Judensau,* giving suck to its voracious Jewish offspring (portrayed as adults). This image later evolved into the most obscene of all, a sow giving suck to Jews while another Jew squats behind, feeding on her feces.[28]

Jews were said to suffer from illnesses characterized by the unnatural flow of blood (excessive menstruation in women, bleeding of a menstrual sort in men), physical deficiencies that could be remedied only by consuming or bathing in Christian blood. But the obverse of their unnatural infirmities was unnatural power. As legacy from their wicked father, Jews had access to knowledge and skills beyond the ken of decent Christians: techniques of sorcery, poisons and their uses, magical spells and curses. Information on such matters was hidden in the Talmud and other arcane Jewish texts, all composed in the Hebrew language, itself a repository of mystery and witchcraft. Thus, a familiar paradox—Jewish vulnerability (the reality) fused with Jewish power (the fantasy)—now emerged with an especially malignant twist: the very same people who were cursed with illnesses and deformities indicative of their satanic ancestry were endowed by that same ancestry with magical powers of frightening dimensions.[29]

Closely connected with these beliefs were legends about Antichrist, the supreme leader of Satan's army, whom Jesus would overcome in the final battle between good and evil that would precede the Millennium. Antichrist was often portrayed as the child of a Jewish harlot, his father either a Jew, an evil spirit, or the devil himself. He was not only the ultimate opponent of Jesus Christ but the image of Christ in reverse: a pseudo-messiah whose career stood in diabolical counterpoint to that of the Savior. Aside from the obvious parody in his birth to a whore, he had preached, gained disciples, performed miracles, even pretended to have died and been resurrected—all in evil mockery of the life of the true Messiah. And at the end of time he would assemble an army of Christ's enemies for the final struggle that he was fated to lose. The core of his army, according to some versions of the legend, would be the ten "lost tribes" of Israel, whom he would readily convert and mobilize for the battle against Christendom. For, in the final analysis, who could be better qualified than Jews to serve in the armies of Antichrist?[30]

Thus Jews became, more than ever before, the ultimate outsiders, embodiments of all that was unseemly, illegitimate, un-Christian. They had come to represent a reversal or denial of the social order as it was intended to be. They provided a diabolically framed window, as it were, through which proper Christians might contemplate images of the fate of human beings who bound themselves to the devil.

"Matter So Abusive and So Unspeakable": The Assault on the Talmud

In 1236, Pope Gregory IX granted an audience to a man named Nicholas Donin, a convert to Christianity who was already well known in the Jewish community as a troublemaker. Donin had spent his youth in La Rochelle, a port town on the western coast of France, where he gained a reputation as a clever but contentious man who had angered his teachers by challenging rabbinic traditions and the authority of the Talmud. Why he was such a rebel is an unanswered question. He may have been influenced by doctrines holding that the Torah was the only valid source of authority, or he may have been attracted to the writings of contemporary rationalist philosophers, particularly Maimonides. But it seems equally likely that he was the sort of person who enjoys dissent for its own sake—a judgment that his later career would seem to confirm. As early as 1220, Donin had probably begun to challenge his elders and to reject Talmudic scholarship as a blemish on what he defined as authentic (that is, biblical) Judaism. By 1225, having so enraged the local rabbis that they excommunicated him, this maverick embarked on a career as the Jewish community's nemesis. He may have been involved (on the side of the accusers) in at least one ritual murder accusation; and, like a number of other well-educated converts, he was viewed by Jews as potentially a more dangerous enemy than any ordinary Christian antagonist. At some point before 1236 he had not only converted but had probably joined the order of Franciscan friars.[31]

Donin presented to the pope a list of thirty-five charges against rabbinic Judaism—that is, Judaism as it had been understood and practiced since the first century; a religion that, as we have seen, was not the fossilized creed imagined by Christians but a way of life, grounded in ongoing scholarship and commentary, rooted in but not confined to Torah and Talmud. But as Donin insisted to the pope, the Talmud and all other products of the "oral tradition"—for example, the commentaries of Rashi—were illegitimate, heretical documents, which the Jews, in their usual perverse manner, had not only accepted but had granted status equal to that of the Hebrew scriptures. These books, Donin assured the pope, were immensely wicked and sinful, a compound of all sorts of nonsensical commentary with outright slander and insult directed against Christianity. Most egregiously, they were replete with nasty references to Jesus Christ and his virgin mother—maintaining, for instance, that Jesus was conceived in adultery.

More specifically, Donin leveled five charges against the Talmud. First, the Jews claim that it is a divinely ordained document, transmitted by God to the rabbis as a new legacy, superior even to the Torah as a guide to behavior. Second, it demeans Christians and recommends that they be treated with guile and contempt. Third, it even insults and demeans the deity; for example, it claims that God weeps and curses himself for sins against the Jews, particularly the destruction of the Temple, and moreover, that he studies the Talmud and once lost an argument over a legal question with some learned rabbis. Fourth, it libels and reviles not only Jesus and Mary, but the disciples, the pope, and the Christian faith, and teaches that obscene language is acceptable when applied to the Church. Finally, it contains any number of tales, fables, and ordinances that are not only ridiculous but blasphemous.[32]

Whether or not the pope was surprised to learn that Jewish commentary was sometimes hostile to Christianity, Donin's charges must have caused him some anxiety. For centuries Christian clergy had proceeded on the premise that the Judaism of the Old Testament was the only legitimate Judaism—or, in any event, the only temporarily tolerable form of Judaism—and that it had been succeeded, of course, not by a new form of Judaism but by its divinely ordained replacement, the New Israel. The only acceptable image of Judaism was of a static religion ("stationary in useless antiquity," as Saint Augustine had phrased it), the stale superstition of a blinded people whose only prospect was to endure as testimony until the time arrived for their awakening and redemption. The proposition that Judaism was not at all stationary but was in fact a dynamically evolving religion based on learned discourse of a specifically Jewish character was completely at odds with Christian doctrine: an unacceptable challenge to the idea that the Hebrew Scriptures could be properly interpreted only as a "foreshadowing" of the arrival of Jesus Christ. The suggestion that for more than a thousand years Jews had been amassing their own interpretations of what was, after all, their own part of the Bible, could not have been welcome news to the pope.[33]

Should he have been surprised? Had Christian scholars not already realized that Jewish intellectual life was as vigorous and Jewish biblical exegesis as lively and imaginative as their own? The apparent answer is that only a few scholars were even partially aware of the extent and quality of rabbinic scholarship. The vast majority of Christian clergy must still have perceived Jews as a spiritually bankrupt people, miserably wedded to a wicked legacy, waiting in intellectual and religious limbo until they would receive revelation.

Donin's charges thus constituted a serious challenge for the pope. But for reasons of his own, Gregory was hesitant about taking action against Jews at that particular time. A militant pope despite advanced age, he was nevertheless fair-minded with regard to Jews and disinclined to harass them arbitrarily, believing that although they were an arrogant and deceitful people, it was the duty of the Church to practice Christian tolerance and forbearance until the time when they would recognize their error and willingly enter the fold. That he passionately disliked Jews seems beyond question. In March 1233 he addressed a papal letter to the bishops of Germany, warning them about Jews who "have become insolent to such a degree that they are not afraid to commit excesses insulting to the Christian faith, such as it is sinful not only to mention but even to think of." Among these "excesses" were conversion of slaves (still part of the social scene in some regions), intimacy with female Christian servants ("enormities that are an abomination and a horror to hear"), and the wearing of clothing like that of everyone else, so that (quoting the language of the ordinance of 1215) "no difference is discernible." To ensure that Jews "should not again dare to straighten their necks bent under the yoke of perpetual slavery in insult against the Redeemer," he ordered the bishops "to prohibit most stringently that they should at any time dare to dispute with Christians about their faith or their rites, lest under pretext of such disputation the simple-minded slide into a snare of error, which God forbid."[34]

But, like all medieval popes, Gregory drew the line at physical persecution. Only a month later we find him writing to the bishops of France in a different tone, urging that they restrain French lords who were not only breaking loan repayment contracts but imprisoning and torturing Jews to extort even more money from them. "Although the perfidy of the Jews is to be condemned," he begins, "nevertheless their relation with Christians is useful and, in a way, necessary; for they bear the image of our Savior, and were created by the Creator of all mankind. They are therefore not to be destroyed, God forbid, by His own creatures, especially by believers in Christ, for no matter how perverse their midway position may be, their fathers were made friends of God, and also their remnant shall be saved." The bishops were instructed to "warn all the faithful Christians in your dioceses and to induce them not to harm the Jews in their persons nor to dare rob them of their property, nor for the sake of plunder to drive them from their lands, without some reasonable cause or clear guilt on their part, but rather to permit them to live in pursuance of their laws and their former status, as long as they do not presume to insult the Christian Faith."[35]

In 1235, shortly before Donin appeared with his list of charges, word had reached Gregory through "a tearful and pitiful complaint" from Jewish petitioners that rioting bands of "crusaders" were massacring large numbers of Jews, possibly as many as three thousand, in parts of central and western France. He was deeply disturbed by this information. In September 1236 he addressed two letters, one to the bishops of the region and another to the king, Louis IX, urging in passionate language that such assaults not be tolerated and that the offenders be required to pay recompense to the afflicted Jewish communities.[36]

For whatever reasons—probably his awareness that Jews were being persecuted and his personal inclination toward fairness and moderation—Gregory procrastinated in responding to Donin's charges, and it was not until several years later, in June 1239, that he finally acted. Although there is no specific evidence that Donin continued to press the matter, it seems likely that this was the case, for he was available when the time arrived. The pope sent Donin himself as bearer of a letter to the bishop of Paris, along with Donin's list of accusations and a request that the bishop transmit other papal letters to the archbishops and kings of several countries, including France. All the letters were worded similarly. The one addressed to the archbishops read in part as follows:

> If what is said about the Jews of France and of the other lands is true, no punishment would be sufficiently great or sufficiently worthy of their crime. For they, so we have heard, are not content with the Old Law which God gave to Moses in writing: they even ignore it completely and affirm that God gave another Law which is called "Talmud," that is "Teaching," handed down to Moses orally. . . . In this is contained matter so abusive and so unspeakable that it arouses shame in those who mention it and horror in those who hear it.
>
> Wherefore, since this is said to be the chief cause that holds the Jews obstinate in their perfidy, we thought that your Fraternity should be warned and urged, and we herewith order you by Apostolic Letters, that on the first Saturday of the Lent to come, in the morning, while the Jews are gathered in the synagogues, you shall, by our order, seize all the books of the Jews who live in your districts, and have these books carefully guarded in the possession of the Dominican and Franciscan friars.[37]

Later the same month Gregory issued a second letter addressed to the bishop of Paris and to the friars in that city, directing that those books found to be offensive should be burned at the stake (*incendio concremari*, "completely incinerated").[38] The letter was obviously intended to apply very widely—it refers to "Jews who live in the Kingdoms of France, England, Aragon, Navarre, Castile, Leon and Portugal"—but the investigation was to be conducted in Paris. The pope's instructions were carried out precisely: on a Saturday in March 1240, books were confiscated from synagogues and handed over to the friars and clergymen for scrutiny. Louis IX, sensing perhaps that a public spectacle might be exemplary, directed that before books were burned there should be a debate of sorts—in effect, a "show trial" in which Jews would play the role of defendants with predetermined guilt.[39]

And so, in June of 1240, there took place a staged encounter between Nicholas Donin, playing the role of chief prosecutor, and the leading rabbi of Paris, Yechiel ben Joseph, who was required to respond to Donin's charges. Held at the royal court in Paris, presided over by the Queen Mother, Blanche of Castile, and attended by a host of prominent clerical officials and noblemen, the entire event epitomized the declining status of Jews in that century and their transformation in Christian minds into little more than embodiments of blasphemous doctrine. Nevertheless, if we are to believe the most informative surviving source—a Hebrew document, the *Vikuach* ("Debate") of Rabbi Yechiel, composed by one of his students—the rabbi maintained his poise and dignity, and defended the Talmud with adroit argumentation. (The chronicler is not unbiased, of course; he refers to Donin as an "insect" and wishes for him the greatest of Jewish misfortunes: that he be childless.) Here is Yechiel in battle, as presented by his student:

> The faithful emissary girded himself with courage and said to the heretic: "On what grounds do you contend against me, and what do you ask?" The heretic then replied: "I ask you about an old matter. For I do not deny that the Talmud is four hundred years old." The rabbi replied: "It is more than fifteen hundred years old." He then said to the queen: "Please, my lady! Do not compel me to answer his charges, since he admits that the Talmud is very old and thus far no charges have been brought against it. . . . If there is wrong in it, it would not have been left unscathed till now. Were there not before now churchmen and converts as capable as these? Yet no allegations have been brought throughout these fifteen hundred years."[40]

Yechiel went on to say that Nicholas Donin was not only an apostate from Judaism but a heretical interpreter of its traditions. Every one of Donin's charges, the rabbi insisted, was a distortion rooted in personal vindictiveness: "From the day that you left our community fifteen years ago," he told Donin, "you have looked for a pretense to impugn us with malicious slander."[41] The Talmud, he explained, had to be understood as an ancient document embodying the historical experience of Jews over many hundreds of years, and nothing in it should be carelessly (or, as in Donin's case, intentionally) misinterpreted or applied to situations for which it was not intended. Donin charged, for example, that the Talmud preached hostility toward Gentiles and dishonesty in dealings with them; but Yechiel insisted that the references were to ancient enemies of the Hebrews, not to contemporary Christians, and that in fact the Talmud taught that righteous Christians could achieve salvation and should be treated with friendship and acceptance. Donin made much of Talmudic fables and homilies, particularly some representing God as a human-like being with ordinary weaknesses. To this, Yechiel replied that Jews were bound to accept only the Talmud's legal principles, not its fables, which were obviously intended to be understood figuratively.

The most damaging charges—and the most difficult to refute— were those having to do with insulting references to Jesus, Mary, and other New Testament figures. Particularly offensive was a passage declaring that Jesus was condemned to an eternity in hell, immersed in "boiling excrement."[42] Yechiel naturally tried to maneuver away from this assertion, though unsuccessfully, by maintaining that the references were to another Jesus, remarking (with astonishing boldness) that "not every Louis born in France is the king of France." But, he continued, the fact was that the rabbis who created the Talmud had good reason for rejecting the teachings of Jesus, for he had tried to undermine the Law, the foundation of Judaism: in the words of the *Vikuach*, "he deceived and beguiled Israel, purported to be God, and denied the essence of the faith."[43]

The Hebrew chronicle suggests that Yechiel had enough fortitude to defend the Talmud capably against formidable opposition and before an almost uniformly unsympathetic audience. A Christian chronicler, however, probably summarizing the proceedings for ecclesiastical records, presents the story much more drily and with no recognition whatever of Yechiel's defense. In his words, the encounter reduces to a "confession." Regarding references to Jesus, he comments: "He said that Jesus Nosri is Jesus the Nazarene, son of Mary, who was crucified on the eve of Passover. Concerning this Jesus, he confessed that he was born out of adultery and that he is punished in hell in boiling excrement and that he lived at the time of Titus. Then he says that this Jesus is different from our Jesus. However, he is unable to say who he was, whence it is clear that he lied."[44]

This public performance was probably followed soon afterward by a more formal proceeding in which Yechiel and several other prominent rabbis were summoned before a clerical court presided over by a dogmatically anti-Jewish clergyman, the chancellor of the University of Paris, Odo (or Eudes) de Chateauroux, who was also the papal legate in France.[45] They first interrogated Yechiel alone, then Rabbi Judah ben David of Melun; and when it was concluded that these two had presented consistent testimony, the others were dismissed. The court found the Talmud guilty on all charges and condemned it to be burned. Somehow the Jews managed to bribe one of the clerical judges—probably Walter, archbishop of Sens, who was known to be relatively sympathetic—and he intervened successfully to postpone the book burning. But soon afterwards Walter fell ill and died: an obvious portent, the meaning of which was not lost on anyone, including Louis IX. He sent a directive to the friars, ordering that all copies of the Talmud be burned without further delay.[46]

In June 1242, some twenty or more wagonloads of manuscripts, probably more than ten thousand volumes, were destroyed in a public bonfire that burned for a day and a half in a prominent town square in Paris. The Jews of northern France and the Rhineland rightly perceived the event as a terrible omen. From now on, they realized, they were going to be held culpable not only for the persecution of Jesus some twelve hundred years earlier but also for their contemporary religious doctrines and practices, which were being condemned as heretical deviations from genuine (that is, biblical) Judaism.[47]

The events at Paris were only the beginning of a concentrated campaign against rabbinic Judaism that was to become a featured policy of the two orders of friars, part of their comprehensive campaign against heresies of every sort. But as an event calculated to devastate the Jewish community, nothing could have exceeded the mass burning of thousands of volumes of Talmudic and other rabbinic writings. From then on, the Jews of Europe knew that harsh times were ahead.

Just two years later, in May 1244, the attack was renewed by Gregory's successor, Innocent IV. In a letter addressed to Louis IX, the pope urged that all remaining copies of the Talmud and similar volumes be sought out and burned. Louis must have responded energetically, for soon afterward the Jews of France sent a personal appeal to the pope. In late 1244, Innocent IV moved from Rome to Lyons, fearing an attack by Emperor Frederick II, with whom he was engaged in a bitter dispute over Frederick's claims to much of Italy. Lyons was within the German imperial domain at that time, but very near the border with France, and Jewish leaders probably traveled there to petition the pope directly, arguing that the destruction of their sacred literature was undermining the foundations of their daily existence. Despite his obvious personal sentiments, the pope decided that the matter merited reconsideration, and in August 1247 he wrote again to Louis, but this time with a remarkable change in tone, directing that a further investigation be conducted to determine which Jewish books deserved destruction and which might be restored to their owners:

> When, therefore, the Jewish masters of your kingdom recently asserted before us and our brothers, that without that book which in Hebrew is called "Talmut" they cannot understand the Bible and their other statutes and laws in accordance with their faith, we then, bound as we are by the Divine command to tolerate them in their Law, thought fit to have the answer given them that we do not want to deprive them of their books if as a result we should be depriving them of their Law. Whereupon we directed our letters to our venerable brother, the Bishop of Tusculum, Legate of the Apostolic Throne, ordering him to cause the Talmud as well as other books to be shown to him, and to have them carefully inspected; of these he should tolerate such as he will find may be tolerated . . . and he shall restore them to the Jewish masters.[48]

The letter was not as favorable to the Jewish cause as might appear, for the bishop of Tusculum was the same Odo of Chateauroux who had proved to be a passionate ideologue when he headed the investigation of 1240. Now the decision of that tribunal was in effect being called into question, and Odo's response to the pope intimated what could be anticipated as his second decision on the matter. Lest "anyone be fooled in this affair by the shrewdness and falsehoods of the Jews," he wanted to assure the pope that he and his colleagues had inspected the Talmud thoroughly in their initial investigation and had found it a despicable document, containing "so many unspeakable insults that it arouses shame in those who read it and horror in those who hear it" (a slightly amended quotation from Pope Gregory's initial letter). It was evident, he concluded, that the Jews had lied to the pope, and it would be "most disgraceful, and a cause of shame for the Apostolic Throne, if books that had been so solemnly and so justly burned in the presence of all the scholars, and of the clergy, and of the populace of Paris, were to be given back to the masters of the Jews at the order of the pope—for such tolerance would seem to mean approval."[49]

The outcome of the new investigation was thus entirely predictable. In May 1248, Odo issued a public declaration that stood in a sense as a final seal of condemnation for rabbinic Judaism, hence for Ashkenazic Jewry:

> Certain books by the name of Talmut having been presented by the Jewish masters to us, . . . we have examined these books and caused them to be carefully examined by men of discretion, expert in these matters, God-fearing, and zealous for the Christian Faith. Whereas we found that these books were full of innumerable errors, abuses, blasphemies and wickedness such as arouse shame in those who speak of them and horrify the hearer, . . . we pronounced that the said books are unworthy of tolerance, and that they are not to be restored to the Jewish masters, and we decisively condemn them.[50]

The Talmud had thus emerged as the foremost symbol of everything that medieval Christians feared and detested in Jews. The campaign against it continued throughout the thirteenth century and long thereafter. Louis IX remained in the forefront of the battle throughout his long reign, renewing orders for book burnings and cooperating enthusiastically with friars and clergy whenever they launched renewed investigations. Their Jewish victims, harassed and discouraged, reduced to defensive strategies in a hopeless struggle, had to acknowledge that what had always been a precarious existence was now becoming all but impossible.[51]

As for the man who began it all, Nicholas Donin ended his life rejected by Christians and Jews alike. In 1287, a malcontent to the last, he was condemned by the pope for writing a tract critical of the Franciscan order, of which he was probably a member. A letter written by a Venetian rabbi, Jacob ben Elijah, comments on Donin's life and death, suggesting that he probably died violently:

> Do you not know, or have you not heard what happened to Donin the apostate, who became a convert from the laws of God and his Torah, and did not even believe in the Roman religion? . . . This wicked man sought to destroy us and gave a sword in the hands of the king to kill us. He lied to him. But God returned to him double his iniquity. . . . and the day of misfortune came upon him because he had sent forth his tongue against the wise men. He was struck and he died and there was none to avenge. . . . So may perish all thine enemies, Lord.[52]

· II ·

"OUR PROPERTY"

Jews in Twelfth- and Thirteenth-Century England

"That Precious and Desirable Treasure"

In early twelfth-century England, Norwich ranked with London and York as one of the nation's leading commercial centers. With a population of some three or four thousand, it was a small town, but at that time even London had no more than seventeen or eighteen thousand people. The town included a small community of Jews, perhaps a hundred or so, clustered mostly in a Jewish district on the western side in a pocket between the marketplace and the local castle. Jews had begun to settle in England in the late eleventh century, following the Norman conquest, but at first only in London; so the Jews of Norwich were almost certainly newcomers. They were aliens and strangers in every respect. Though associated in the minds of the English with the Norman conquerors, they were vastly different from the Normans in culture and social identity. Probably speakers of French and Yiddish as native languages, they would have managed English only with obviously foreign accents. The western section of town, where they were concentrated, was called "new town" (*novus burgus*). This district was occupied mainly by Normans, who were also relatively recent immigrants, of course, and the castle was supervised by a Norman sheriff, the king's local representative.[1]

The Jews of Norwich followed expectable occupational pursuits: most were moneylenders or pawnbrokers, one or two may have been physicians, and a few probably engaged at least part of the time in commercial activities. Some were undoubtedly wealthy, but most were not. Although many dealt with Christians on an everyday basis, their social interaction must have been confined to practical matters.

In a village near Norwich lived a prosperous farmer named Wenstan and his wife Elviva; they had several children, including a son named William. Born in 1132 or 1133, William left home in 1141 to be apprenticed in Norwich to a skinner, a man who processed animal hides. The skinner came into fairly frequent contact with Jews, for whom he apparently repaired garments. On the Monday before Easter in 1144 (two days before Passover), William appeared at home in the company of a man who identified himself as cook for the archdeacon of Norwich and offered to give the boy kitchen employment if he would begin at once. This was a step up for William and he was eager to make the move, but his mother hesitated because she did not recognize the man. A gift of a few shillings brought her around, and William departed with the cook. The next day, for reasons unknown, the man brought William for a visit to his mother's sister, Leviva, the wife of a local priest named Godwin Sturt. She must have been equally uneasy about the man, for when the pair left she told her daughter to follow them. The girl reported that they entered the home of a prominent Norwich Jew, a man named Eleazar. William was not seen again until that Saturday, the day before Easter, when his mutilated body was found in a local forest called Thorpe Wood.[2]

The news spread rapidly, of course. When William's mother was notified, she screamed that the Jews had killed her son. Most townspeople, however, did not attribute the crime to the Jews, and in fact the matter seems to have been largely forgotten in a very short time. There is no record of an investigation of the kind that might be expected in the wake of the murder of a child, and no evidence that Jews were held to account.

Sometime in mid-April, several weeks after the murder, in the course of a meeting of local clergy, Godwin Sturt publicly charged the Jews of Norwich with the crime. The bishop proceeded cautiously, but he did summon the Jews to appear and speak for themselves. They responded with understandable anxiety, turning to the sheriff for assistance, and he advised the bishop that Jews were subject only to royal authority and need not submit to questioning by anyone else. Eventually both sheriff and Jews relented to the point of discussing the charge with the bishop, but they left without any resolution. This encounter was followed by enough public talk that the sheriff decided to convey the Jews to the castle for a time. But the episode must have amounted to little more than mob rumbling and empty threats, for there is no record of violence or looting.

The dead boy was rescued from almost certain oblivion when a visiting clergyman, rather more foresighted than his Norwich colleagues, requested permission to remove the body to his monastery, where he said it would be venerated. The point was not lost on the bishop, who refused the request and instead ordered on April 24—a full month after the boy's death—that the body be exhumed and reburied in the local monks' cemetery. But it is evident that even a month after his death William was viewed as nothing more than the victim of a murder, possibly by a Jew or Jews.

William would almost certainly have lain forever in the obscurity of the monks' cemetery had it not been for the imagination and enterprise of one Thomas of Monmouth, who joined the Norwich monastery years later, probably in 1148 or 1149. Thomas was fascinated to the point of obsession with William's story. Not only was he absolutely convinced that Jews had murdered the boy, but he conceived—independently, it would seem, and entirely through the workings of his own mind—a lurid account of how William had been cruelly tortured and crucified in fulfillment of a religious obligation connected with the Passover season. He thereby became the creator of the myth of ritual murder.

Soon after his arrival in Norwich, Thomas began investigating the story of William's death, interviewing people and even inspecting the house in which the murder had allegedly taken place. (The original owner, Eleazar, had himself been murdered by men in the employ of one of his debtors.) By 1150 he had composed the first of seven "books" (chapters) of a treatise, "The Life and Miracles of St. William of Norwich," declaring himself prepared "to sacrifice my own modesty rather than that the many and great virtues of the holy martyr William should pass away in oblivion or through the rust of ignorance."[3]

As Thomas told the story of William's life and death, the boy was divinely destined for martyrdom, and evidence for his appointment was manifest even before his birth: his pregnant mother received a vision "which revealed to her how great should be the sanctity and dignity of him whom she bore in her womb." She reported the dream to her father, a man with "much experience in the expounding of visions," and he interpreted it in a scene reminiscent of the angel's annunciation to Mary: "[I]n very truth thou shalt bring forth a son who shall attain to highest honor in the earth, and after being raised above the clouds shall be exalted exceedingly in heaven. Know, too, that when thy son shall have attained to twelve years, then he shall be raised to this pitch of glory."[4]

This was only a taste of what Thomas's fertile mind could imagine. He reported that as a young child William was already performing miracles and behaving in a manner in itself quite miraculous for a little boy: touching a man's iron fetters, which thereupon "shivered into pieces"; fasting several days each week and giving much of his food to the poor. One is left wondering why such an extraordinary child should have been apprenticed to an animal skinner. But what interested Thomas most was the boy's contact with Jews:

> Now, while he was staying in Norwich, the Jews who were settled there and required their cloaks or their robes or other garments (whether pledged to them, or their own property) to be repaired, preferred him before all other skinners. For they esteemed him to be especially fit for their work, either because they had learnt that he was guileless and skillful, or because attracted to him by their avarice they thought they could bargain with him for a lower price. Or, as I rather believe, because by the ordering of divine providence he had been predestined to martyrdom from the beginning of time, and gradually step by step was drawn on, and chosen to be made a mock of and to be put to death by the Jews, in scorn of the Lord's passion, as one of little foresight, and so the more fit for them.[5]

As Thomas interpreted the events of March 1144, then, the mysterious stranger who seduced the boy away from his mother had obviously been hired by Jews for just that purpose. The heart of the matter, of course, was the question of what happened to the boy between Tuesday and Saturday of the fateful week, and Thomas confidently provided a dramatic answer: a detailed reconstruction of the first ritual murder—circumstantial, to be sure, but based on the reports of reliable witnesses, he insisted, and entirely consistent with what he knew about Jewish religious practices before Passover.

The boy was kept at Eleazar's home, Thomas reported, treated kindly at first, to put him off guard while they prepared to offer him as a Passover sacrifice. On Wednesday, the first day of Passover, "after the singing of the hymns appointed for the day in the synagogue," they seized the boy and tortured him to death in imitation of the crucifixion of Jesus. First they "introduced an instrument of torture which is called a teazle," a device designed to apply intense pressure to the head and jaws, described by Thomas in minute detail. "But not even yet," he continued, "could the cruelty of the torturers be satisfied without adding even more severe pains."

> Having shaved his head, they stabbed it with countless thorn-points, and made the blood come horribly from the wounds they made. . . . And thus, while these enemies of the Christian name were rioting in the spirit of malignity around the boy, some of those present adjudged him to be fixed to a cross in mockery of the Lord's passion, as though they would say, "Even as we condemned the Christ to a shameful death, so let us also condemn the Christian, so that, uniting the Lord and his servant in like punishment, we may retort upon themselves the pain of that reproach which they impute to us."[6]

Finally they crucified the boy; not on a cross, however, but on a set of posts, and with the right hand and foot bound rather than pierced with nails—all details cleverly designed to throw Christians off the track. "Thus then," concludes Thomas, "the glorious boy and martyr of Christ, William, dying the death of time in reproach of the Lord's death, but, crowned with the blood of a glorious martyrdom, entered into the kingdom of glory on high to live for ever."[7]

How was Thomas able to deduce so much about a murder that had occurred five or six years earlier? For one thing, he inspected the house in question "and discovered some most certain marks in it of what had been done there." He also spoke with a Christian servant woman who had been in Eleazar's home that day. She had peeped through the door chink and had seen the boy nailed to a post: "She could not see it with both eyes, but she did manage to see it with one. And when she had seen it, with horror at the sight she shut that one eye and then shut the door." Fearful of losing employment—or worse, being attacked herself—she said nothing, but later she found some of the boy's belongings and noted on the timbers of the house "the marks of the martyrdom."[8]

But the ultimate confirmation of Thomas's story came from one Theobald, a Jew who had converted to Christianity and became a monk after hearing about the martyrdom of William. He explained to Thomas an essential feature of the Passover celebration:

> that the Jews, without the shedding of human blood, could neither obtain their freedom, nor could they ever return to their fatherland. Hence it was laid down by them in ancient times that every year they must sacrifice a Christian in some part of the world to the Most High God in scorn and contempt of Christ, so that they might avenge their sufferings on Him; inasmuch as it was because of Christ's death that they had been shut out from their own country, and were in exile as slaves in a foreign land.

Prominent Jews assembled each year at Narbonne, explained Theobald, to "cast lots for all the countries which the Jews inhabit." Jews of the selected country had then to choose a town by the same method. In 1144 "it happened that the lot fell upon the Norwich Jews, and all the synagogues in England signified, by letter or by message, their consent that the wickedness should be carried out at Norwich." So it was not just a few Norwich Jews who were responsible for the martyr's death; the crime had been ordained by world Jewry.[9]

Continuing to embellish the story at every point, Thomas described the discovery of the body as another divinely ordained event, when "a fiery light suddenly flashed down from heaven," and those who performed the burial experienced a miracle that would be repeated whenever the body was exposed: "a fragrant perfume filled the nostrils of the bystanders as if there had been growing there a great mass of sweet-smelling herbs and flowers." A month afterward, when the boy's body—"that precious and desirable treasure" (*thesaurus ille preciosus ac desiderabilis)*—was transported at the bishop's bidding to the monks' cemetery, "he was found to be unchanged and without corruption in any part." And when the body lay exposed in its sepulchre just before interment, people noted once again "the sweet-smelling fragrance" of the young martyr.[10]

In 1150, Thomas was instructed in a vision that William's body should be moved into a building adjacent to the cathedral, where it might receive proper veneration. It was not long before monks were reporting miracles at the new tomb. One monk reported seeing the Virgin Mary, seated on a golden throne and attended by William himself, who bowed as she placed on his head a crown of flowers that she had personally woven for him. Soon the boy was receiving steady attention, and a gratified Thomas was duly reporting miracles in the later books of his treatise. Dying children were snatched back to life and health. A youth who had swallowed a live viper several years before and suffered intense abdominal pain drank water mixed with scrapings from the tomb and was promptly delivered of the viper and two of its young. Even animals benefited; a poor woman whose hog was dying burned a candle at the tomb and returned home to find the creature restored to health.[11]

In July 1151, as the young saint's reputation spread, the body was moved yet again—this time into the cathedral itself, to a tomb near the high altar. Finally, on Easter Monday of 1154, perhaps to stimulate public interest in what had become a lucrative pilgrimage enterprise, William went to his final resting place in the martyr's chapel, a position of high honor that was quite fitting; for as it turned out, he was the first in a long line of children whose deaths were to provide fuel for accusations of ritual murder, one of the most enduring myths in European culture.

England in the Early Twelfth Century

Although Jews reached medieval England only in the late eleventh century and were expelled before the close of the thirteenth, that period of some two hundred years was a remarkable episode in European Jewish history.[12] A few Jews entered England soon after the

Conquest and established a modest presence in London. Most came from Normandy or elsewhere in northern France; others drifted in from as far away as the Rhineland. These earliest settlers were joined by a larger number of new immigrants after the massacres of 1096, and by 1100 there was a small but vital Jewish community in London— perhaps two or three hundred people all told. During the next several decades, as the community grew by natural increase and further immigration, a few Jews ventured into other locations; and by 1140 there were a number of small communities, located mostly in towns in the populous eastern part of the country, where they found security in the presence of a royal castle and a sheriff. The total Jewish population of England by then was some two thousand, hence about eight hundred adult men and women, of whom most still lived in London. As was the case on the Continent, they lived near one another in neighborhoods that were recognizably Jewish. These were not ghettos in the strict sense; a few Christians also resided in the same neighborhoods, and it would seem that Jews and Christians interacted in a reasonably amicable manner. But in light of the sharply marginal role of Jews in English society, the two groups were probably guarded in their dealings with one another. Certainly evidence from later in the century and thereafter indicates that anti-Jewish sentiment was widespread.

Having arrived at a time when Jews in France were already moving into moneylending in large numbers, the Jews of England specialized from the start in that occupation, with the inevitable result that they were inescapably associated with the image of wealth obtained without productive labor. Not all were moneylenders, however, and relatively few became truly wealthy. Jews also worked as physicians or as dealers in such basic commodities as wine, cheese, and wheat. Nonetheless, there can be little question that most were inclined—and, in effect, required—to function as financiers, large or small. Just about everyone used their services, including members of the higher clergy, who often borrowed money with pledges of sacred vessels or even relics of saints. But their foremost role, the one that gained them essential protection even though it also placed them in a profoundly precarious situation, was to provide revenue for the royal treasury. They were already serving this function during the reign of Henry I (1100–35), but it was during the reign of his illustrious grandson, Henry II (1154–89), that Jewish capital came to be the virtual foundation of the royal treasury.

Henry I was probably the first English monarch to have issued a protective charter declaring that Jews and all their possessions belonged to the king, hence that his lieges and marshals were required to ensure their safety and well-being. Although the charter is not extant, Henry II issued a similar document that seems to have been modeled on a predecessor. It guaranteed residential rights, free movement for merchants, exemption from customs and tolls, inheritance rights, and the right to a fair trial in a court under royal jurisdiction. In other words, although Jews were permitted to live as free persons in English society, their freedom derived not from membership in the society but from their status as royal property. Already by 1130, however, they were experiencing the perils of existence as protected aliens. In or about that year the Jews of London, blamed for the death of a man who had probably been treated by a Jewish physician, were fined two thousand pounds (roughly equivalent in contemporary buying power to at least $150,000). In 1141, while Stephen and Mathilda were contending for the crown, the latter occupied the town of Oxford and demanded a large sum from the resident Jews, which they paid. Soon afterward, Stephen captured the town and demanded a much larger sum as punishment for their having given money to his rival. The Jews tried to withhold payment whereupon he set fire to a large Jewish home and forced them to yield. But despite episodes of this sort (and, as we shall see, worse to follow), most Jews seem to have fared reasonably well during the twelfth century, and a few became famously wealthy.

Relations with the Christian clergy were surprisingly cordial (one might almost say intimate). The historian Cecil Roth notes that not only did Jews regularly lend money to the clergy, but they also placed women and children in monasteries for safety, kept business deeds in cathedral treasuries, and at times even tried to influence elections of monastery abbots. "They were familiar figures in St. Paul's Cathedral in London," he continues, "to which they resorted to seek their debtors. Jews and clerics rode together on journeys, and jested together in bad French."[13]

During the earlier years of the reign of Henry II, Jews were frequently called upon for loans to the royal treasury, with at least the formal expectation that these would be repaid. For a time the king dealt with consortia of wealthy Jews, some four or five of whom would finance loans beyond the capacity of any individual. In 1177, for example, a single loan from such a consortium provided the royal treasury with more than 3,800 pounds (equivalent to about $300,000 or more today). But by the final years of his reign, Henry had abandoned even the pretense that loans were going to be repaid and had turned to outright taxation as his principal source of revenue. From that time onward it was understood that Jews must pay, and pay heavily, for the right to exist in England. For the century thereafter English kings taxed Jews relentlessly, fined them exorbitantly for minor or perhaps nonexistent crimes, and generally exploited them so mercilessly that their ultimate fate might well have been predicted. That a few Jews became exceedingly wealthy should not obscure the fact that most did not. Moreover, the wealthiest must have endured more than their share of uncertainty and anxiety, for they were never beyond the royal gaze.

The century's most prominent financier was Aaron of Lincoln, with loans and investments in twenty-five counties, who probably financed the construction of more abbeys and cathedrals than any other man in England. When Aaron died, about 1186, his entire estate was claimed for the royal treasury. (The gold and negotiable items were sent by ship to France to help finance a war against Philip Augustus, but the ship sank in the Channel with all its cargo.) To manage collection of his outstanding debts (about fifteen thousand pounds, owed by some 430 debtors), there was created a new branch of the Exchequer (registry for the royal treasury) called the *Scaccarium Aaronis*, in which four men worked for nearly five years to organize records and initiate collections. The king's realization that liquid capital could most readily be obtained by direct expropriation from Jews seems to date from this time, for in 1188, when, to help finance the Third Crusade, the entire nation was assessed at one-tenth of property value, the Jews had already been assessed at one-fourth. The anticipated income was sixty thousand pounds from Jews and seventy thousand from everyone else in the nation—probably exaggerated on the Jewish side, but indicative of images of Jewish wealth. Thus by the time of Henry's death in 1189, he had laid the foundations of a royal "Jewish policy": frequent and efficient extraction of large amounts of wealth.[14]

A Pivotal Year

Despite these developments, the fact is that throughout the reign of Henry II, Jews were probably better situated financially than at any time in the century that followed.[15] However, they still faced occasional threats to their security. In the aftermath of the events at Norwich, accusations of a similar sort emerged from time to time. In 1168 the Jews of Gloucester were accused of torturing and murdering a child whose body had been found in the Severn River, and similar charges were leveled in Bury St. Edmunds in 1181 and Bristol in 1183. As usual, the alleged victims were all boys; some were later venerated as martyrs. But knowledge that Jews were under royal protection was apparently enough to ensure that they were not attacked.

When Henry died in 1189, the Jews had good reason to anticipate that his son and successor would also find them useful enough to merit protection, and that their lives would continue to be pleasantly uneventful. But instead, this was a turning point in their history, the preamble to a downward slide from which they would never recover. On the afternoon of September 3, the coronation ceremony for the new king, Richard I, known as the Lion-Hearted, was approaching its climax, and a crowd of excited spectators had gathered outside Westminster Abbey to be as near as possible to the events inside and perhaps to gain a glimpse of the young king. In the gathering was a small delegation of prominent Jews who had come bearing valuable gifts, no doubt in the hope and expectation that the new king would follow in his father's footsteps. Among them was Benedict of York, a leader of the Jewish community and one of the wealthiest men in England. The Jews had been denied entry to the main hall; a proclamation issued before the coronation prohibited attendance by women or Jews—presumably because they might exercise their powers of sorcery. At the conclusion of the ceremony and mass, the new king was escorted to the palace for a celebratory banquet. What happened next was recounted by a leading chronicler of the time, William of Newburgh, a clergyman from the vicinity of York:

When the mass had been celebrated, the king, splendidly arrayed, proceeded to the banquet amidst a magnificent procession. But it happened that while he was seated with the noble assembly, the crowd of onlookers around the palace became very excited. Some Jews among the crowd thus passed through the palace doors. It is said that a certain Christian became indignant at this and, with the royal edict in mind, struck a Jew with the palm of his hand to force him away from the door. Aroused by his example, others now began insulting the Jews and beating them back. The situation became tumultuous; the disorderly mob, assuming that they were following the king's own wishes and acting, as it were, by his authority, rushed to attack the Jews who were watching events at the doorway. At first they beat them viciously with their fists, but as they became more enraged they used sticks and stones. The Jews fled; but some were caught and beaten to death, while others were trampled to death. Among the group were two distinguished Jews from York, named Joce and Benedict; the former escaped, but the latter was unable to run because he was being beaten. To avoid being killed, he was forced to declare that he would become a Christian; whereupon he was taken to a church and immediately baptized.
Meanwhile a gratifying rumor—that the king had ordered the extermination of all Jews—spread throughout London with amazing rapidity. Soon there gathered a huge unruly mob, composed of townsfolk along with many from the provinces who had been attracted by the coronation ceremony, heavily armed, eager to kill and plunder the despised people whom God had condemned. Then the Jewish citizens, many of whom live in London, together with those who had gathered from elsewhere, took refuge in their own homes. A surging mob surrounded their homes and laid siege to them from mid-afternoon until sunset. But they were too well built to be broken into, and the infuriated assailants had no assault devices; so they hurled torches onto the roofs, creating terribly destructive fires that overwhelmed the struggling Jews but provided useful light to the enraged Christians as they went about their night's work. Nor did the flames harm only the Jews, though intended for them alone, but

recognizing no distinctions, spread to the homes of neighboring Christians. One saw the finest parts of the city miserably consumed in fires set by townspeople acting as though they were enemies. The Jews were either burned to death in their homes or, when they tried to escape, were slain with swords. Much blood was quickly shed. But the growing desire for plunder soon induced people to abandon the slaughter; avarice replaced cruelty and the massacre ended, as their rage and greed led them to plunder homes and seize wealth.[16]

A few Jews escaped to safety in the Tower of London or in the homes of friendly Christians. A Jewish chronicler, Ephraim of Bonn, says that about thirty Jews were killed, including an eminent rabbi who had recently immigrated from Orléans, and that some men killed their own wives and children.[17]

King Richard responded to these events with what may be generously described as restraint. Upon being notified during the banquet that a riot had begun, he dispatched several prominent officials to the scene. But when some members of the mob began to threaten these worthies, they promptly withdrew, and the riot raged on until the following morning without further attempt at interference. It ended, says the chronicler, when they became too exhausted to continue, not because they respected the king's wishes.

Richard was angry over the blemish on his coronation and at the defiance expressed toward his representatives, but he was hard pressed to decide how to respond and whom to blame among the multitude of ordinary townsfolk and even nobility who had participated. He ordered three men hanged—not for crimes against Jews but for having destroyed Christian homes. Apparently the royal gatekeeper was also executed (scapegoated?) for having made light of the affair; Ephraim of Bonn says that the man was dragged through the streets by horses until he died.[18]

The day after the coronation the newly baptized Benedict (now called William) was brought before Richard for a personal interrogation. In attendance along with others was the archbishop of Canterbury, presumably anticipating a gratifying demonstration of the power of Christian persuasion. An account of the episode was written by a contemporary Christian chronicler, Roger of Howden (or Hoveden).

"Who are you?" Richard asked. "I am Benedict the Jew, from York," the convert replied. Turning to the embarrassed archbishop, Richard asked what was to be done. "Since he does not wish to be a Christian," came the angry reply, "let him be the Devil's man." And so, continues the chronicler, "since there was no one to prevent him, the said William returned to the Jewish depravity." Benedict went for a time to Northampton, where he died soon thereafter, probably from his injuries. It is said that his body was rejected for burial in both the Jewish and Christian cemeteries.[19]

The London riot alerted Richard to the precarious status of Jews with whom he intended to maintain a profitable connection. In March 1190, when he had already departed for France to help organize the Third Crusade, he issued a charter, very similar to that of Henry II, granting basic legal rights to the Jews of his realm, twice referring to them as "our property." Addressed to "the archbishops, bishops, abbots, counts, barons, viscounts, ministers, and to all his faithful in England and Normandy," the charter confirms rights specifically for one prominent individual, Isaac ben Josce, but extends them to "his children and their men," and in several clauses refers simply to "a Jew" or "the Jews." The charter grants Jews rights to travel freely without payment of customs and tolls, to take oaths on the Hebrew Scriptures, to be tried only in royal courts, and to purchase anything brought to them ("except those which belong to the Church and bloodstained cloth"); and it orders the addressed persons to "guard and defend and protect them."[20]

Richard was to be away from England for several years (he was captured on crusade and for a time was held for ransom). Whatever may have been his intentions and expectations, the charter was not nearly sufficient protection, for during the next two years the Jews of England experienced a series of murderous attacks that left them anxious and demoralized. If any year can be singled out as pivotal, the year 1190, falling exactly a century before their expulsion, stands out as the time when Jews experienced an ominous and essentially irreversible change in their social status: from that of a protected, although plainly disliked, commercial class to that of openly exploited and roundly despised aliens, tolerated only insofar as they served the interests of their royal masters.

The Riots of 1190

The trouble began in February of the fateful year, in Lynn (later King's Lynn), a port town in Norfolk county, where a hostile encounter between local Jews and a recent convert to Christianity erupted into a riot, possibly led by foreign sailors. The chronicler, William of Newburgh, portrays the Jewish community as prominent and prosperous. When several Jews physically attacked the convert as he passed in the street, he ran into a nearby church for refuge. Surprisingly enough, the Jews tried to force their way into the church, with the result that they soon found themselves under assault by an angry mob. Some were killed as they fled. The mob made its way to Jewish homes, which they pillaged and burned, killing more victims in the process. In fact, the Jewish community was almost entirely eliminated in the course of a few hours. The next day a prominent Jewish physician, a man who was liked and admired by Christians for his "skill and modesty," protested so vehemently that the people were aroused to renewed fury, and he became their final victim. When royal officials arrived to investigate the massacre, the townspeople insisted that the perpetrators had been not themselves but the foreign sailors, who by then had conveniently sailed away.[21]

About a month later, in early March, people gathered for an annual Lenten fair at Stamford, in Lincolnshire; among them were a number of young men preparing to go on crusade. "Indignant that the enemies of the cross of Christ who dwelt there should possess so much when they had not enough for the expenses of so great a journey," they launched an attack that resulted in several deaths before the Jews could escape into the local castle, after which a mob thoroughly pillaged Jewish homes.[22]

Similar attacks took place within the next month or two at a number of other locations, including Lincoln and several smaller towns where the Jewish community must have consisted of only a few isolated families. At Dunstable an entire small community was said to have escaped massacre only by accepting baptism.[23]

These events were chronicled by William of Newburgh, to whom we are indebted for the most complete account of Jewish tribulations in 1190. Another chronicler, Richard of Devizes, presents a brief account of the same events, including the London riot, and offers an explanation for why the townspeople of Winchester did not attack local Jews. The tone of his commentary says all that need be said about the climate of the times:

> Winchester alone spared its worms. They were a prudent and far-sighted people and a city that always behaved in a civilised manner. They never did anything over-hastily, for fear they might repent of it later, and they looked to the end of things rather than to the beginnings. They did not want partially to vomit forth the undigested mass violently and at their peril, even though they were urged to do so, when they were not ready. They hid it in their bowels, modestly (or naturally) dissimulating their disgust meanwhile, till at an opportune time for remedies they could cast out all the morbid matter once and for all.[24]

In March 1190 a massacre of such proportions took place at York that the city gained "enduring fame as the *locus classicus* of medieval English anti-semitism."[25] The chief perpetrators were probably a small band of middle-level nobility, moderately wealthy landowners who were heavily indebted to Jewish moneylenders, and who held chronic grievances against the royal government for what they correctly perceived to be exorbitant taxation. One night early in March a fire broke out in the town, perhaps started by the same individuals. In any event, taking advantage of the excitement and distraction, these men, led by one Richard Malebisse, forced their way into the home of Benedict (who by this time had died), murdered his widow and daughters (the sons escaped), plundered the house and set it afire.

Next day, after thoroughly terrified Jews consulted with the man who was now indisputably the wealthiest in the community, Josce of York, he successfully petitioned the royal constable for an escorted withdrawal into the local castle. A few nights later, Josce's home, a massive, solidly constructed edifice, was attacked and plundered in a riot that lasted into the next day. The few Jews who were unfortunate or unwise enough to have remained in town were presented with the usual choice: baptism or death.

At this juncture the Jews in the castle made a crucial tactical error. The constable had been the only person entering and leaving the castle freely; but now, wracked with anxiety and foreboding, and fearing that the constable might accede to the mob and evict them, the Jews refused to permit him to reenter. The frustrated constable consulted with the Yorkshire sheriff, who responded impetuously with an order that the Jews be forcibly removed at once. When the town rabble heard about this, they of course rushed to the scene to join the fray. A hermit from a nearby monastery, possibly in the employ of Malebisse and his cohort, goaded the mob into a frenzy.

The Jews appear to have defended themselves with determination for several days. A large rock rolled over the castle wall crushed the hermit to death; but as it turned out, he was the only Christian casualty in an uneven contest. On Friday, March 16, the eve of Shabbat ha-Gadol, the Great Sabbath just before Passover, the attackers brought in siege machines capable of breaking through the stout walls of the castle, and the Jews realized that they were doomed. Rabbi Yom-Tov ben Isaac, a sage who had come from France to provide spiritual leadership for the community, now called upon everyone to prepare for *kiddush ha-Shem*, death by martyrdom. Josce may have been the first to do what each of the men had to do in turn: cut the throats of wife and children, then submit to the same fate at the hands of the rabbi, who finally killed himself. Before dying, the men started a fire that eventually engulfed not only their possessions but many bodies as well. A few of the besieged Jews apparently refused to accept self-slaughter, and the next morning appealed for mercy, promising to accept baptism; but when they emerged from the castle, they were immediately murdered.[26]

Malebisse and his accomplices went at once to York Minster, demanded all Jewish bonds on deposit, and burned them in the church. Several then departed to join the Third Crusade, and the others returned to their country estates.

By the end of March, Richard, who was then in Normandy, had been notified of the massacre and ordered the new chancellor, William of Longchamp, to punish the offenders. William reached York early in May, accompanied by a large royal militia. The perpetrators had been forewarned, however, and had left the area, abandoning their lands and property. William dismissed the York constable and county sheriff, but there was no one else to punish individually. He levied heavy fines on the entire town based on wealth alone—thereby almost certainly punishing respectable townsmen who had not participated in the massacre. That appears to have been the full measure of penalty exacted for these crimes. The historian who has studied these events most thoroughly, R. B. Dobson, comments that the reasons for this leniency "must certainly include the unpopularity which would be incurred by any medieval ruler prepared to take extreme measures against Christian persecutors of the Jews."[27]

Controlling Jewish Finances:
The *Archae Judeorum*

Richard spent most of his brief reign (1189–99) away from England, first as a prominent participant in the Third Crusade, then in warfare on the Continent. In 1192, on his way home from the crusade, he was captured by the duke of Austria, who turned him over to the German emperor, Henry VI. Henry demanded a ransom of 150,000 marks, equal to about one hundred thousand pounds, and acknowledgment of fealty from Richard, both of which were granted. The ransom money was still being raised in 1194, and the Jews of England were assessed five thousand marks. Although this amount may seem modest if defined as only one-thirtieth of the total, it was triple the amount levied on the Christian citizens of London, by far the nation's wealthiest city. (The rough equivalent in purchasing power today would be four hundred thousand dollars.) Jewish representatives met at Northampton to assess each community, the largest amounts being levied on London, Lincoln, Canterbury, Northampton, and Gloucester, each with some twenty to forty donors. They were able to raise only about half the total assessment, but apparently this was accepted without penalty.[28]

In Richard's absence the kingdom was managed by a team of administrators, among whose achievements was the creation of a formal apparatus for recording the business affairs of Jewish moneylenders and for extracting their wealth efficiently whenever the royal treasury neeeded replenishment. The idea for an institution devoted specifically to Jewish affairs evolved gradually over a decade or so. It seems to have originated in 1194, when a number of offices for registry of Jewish bonds and deeds, called *Archae Judeorum* (presumably modeled on the *Scaccarium Aaronis*), were established in all towns with substantial Jewish communities, specifically for the purpose of recording debts to Jews and controlling Jewish financial affairs. The principal officials, first called Keepers of the Jews, later Justices of the Jews, oversaw operations at six or seven registries, each managed by a small team of Christian and Jewish supervisors, assisted and monitored by royal clerks. All bonds and other contracts belonging to Jews had to be written in duplicate on a strip of parchment with the word *Chirographum* (bond manuscript) written in bold letters between the two copies. The document was then divided by cutting in an irregular line through this word; one copy went to the Jewish creditor, the other to the debtor or was deposited in a locked chest in the registry. After each transaction the Jew had to swear on the Hebrew Scriptures that he would dutifully register all future transactions and would report evasions or other illegal practices to the royal authorities.[29]

Thus, by the middle of Richard's reign, the Jews of England had lost much of the autonomy that they had enjoyed under his predecessors. The registry provided modest advantages for them, of course, in the form of insurance against defaulting debtors. More importantly, though, they now had to endure steady appropriation of their wealth, sometimes to the point of impoverishment. In effect they were becoming "the royal milch-cow": conduits for the transfer of wealth from the king's subjects to the king's treasury.

The Exchequer of the Jews

Richard, killed in battle in 1199, was succeeded by his brother John, who ruled until 1216. It was during his reign that exploitation of Jews was refined into an efficiently managed operation serving as probably the most important single source of revenue for the royal treasury. Sometime around 1200 the *archae* system became a branch of the Royal Exchequer (registry for the royal treasury) called *Scaccarium Judeorum*, Exchequer of the Jews, which now not only oversaw registry of all Jewish bonds but also supervised collection of special taxes levied on Jews and adjudicated financial disputes involving Jews.[30] Not surprisingly, the adoption of this efficient method for overseeing and controlling Jewish financial transactions was the prelude to a level of extortion beyond anything previously attempted. Much of John's reign was taken up with failed military campaigns, most notably his unsuccessful struggle to retain territory in western France against the determined onslaught of Philip Augustus. The campaigns in France, and others in Scotland, Wales, and Ireland, drained the royal treasury, and everyone was taxed beyond reason; but Jews especially were subjected to ruinous demands in the form of impossibly high fines for real or concocted misdemeanors, arbitrary taxes, and outright appropriation of bonds and property. Forced to pay ever larger sums, and with their resources depleted, Jewish creditors were obliged to foreclose on debtors who would otherwise have been granted more time to pay—and received all the anger and resentment that ought to have been directed at the king.

Since all Jewish bonds and deeds were now registered with the Exchequer, it was a relatively simple matter to assess the wealth of prominent Jews and tax them accordingly. Also, royal authorities could now call in bonds for payment as they chose. The usual practice was to demand immediate, but discounted, payment of overdue debts, with part of the proceeds going to the Jewish creditor, the rest confiscated as a fine paid to the crown. Jewish lenders may have benefited modestly from this practice in that they were able to collect something on bad debts, but in the final analysis they were simply intermediaries in an extractive process that was draining the nation of its wealth.[31]

Although John renewed the charter issued by Richard, granting "to all the Jews of England and Normandy the right to reside in our land freely and honorably," and to "enjoy more fully and quietly and honorably all their liberties and customs," he intended that they would reside in his land for one purpose only. In return for the charter he demanded payment of four thousand marks, an amount that the Jews were able to pay only in installments, and he taxed them so regularly and remorselessly that they in turn were driven to demand payment from their debtors. By 1203 antagonism toward Jews in London had reached such a pitch that John had to instruct the mayor to protect them. "We say this not only for our Jews," he declared, "but also for our peace, for if we gave our peace to a dog it should be inviolably observed."[32]

In 1204–5 John lost Normandy to the French. As a result, the Jews of England, who had always maintained close ties with relatives and friends across the Channel, were cut adrift, not only culturally but also economically. Now, among other disadvantages, they found it more difficult to arrange for outside financial assistance when John's demands exceeded their ability to pay.

With John steadily engaged in costly military campaigns, no year was a good one, but 1210 stands out as probably the worst in his seventeen-year reign. Returning from a failed campaign in Ireland, John ordered all Jewish males with property to be imprisoned immediately, on the grounds that they were hiding assets and not recording all debts. There may have been some truth to the claim, but the punishment exceeded anything previously imposed on the Jewish community. The Jews, says Cecil Roth, were fined "a tallage of unprecedented magnitude, which was exacted with the utmost barbarity."[33] Those who could not pay had their property seized. Many were imprisoned and tortured, and a few were hanged. Even the poorest Jews were fined forty shillings, and those who could not pay were expelled from the country—a procedure well calculated to pare the community down to those who knew how to earn large sums. Isaac of Norwich, a very wealthy man, gained his freedom by promising to pay the spectacular sum of ten thousand marks at the rate of one mark (roughly equal to seventy or eighty dollars today) daily for nearly thirty years.[34]

The period 1213–15 found English barons at war with John over his fiscal policies, and, as usual, Jews were seen not as fellow victims of the king's extravagance but as his agents and allies. During riots in London in May 1215, homes in the Jewish quarter were pillaged and destroyed. Later, when John capitulated and signed the Magna Carta, that famous document included two clauses addressed to grievances arising from the practices of Jews and other moneylenders. One stated that minors inheriting debts were not to be charged interest until they reached adulthood; another stated that a deceased debtor's estate must first repay his widow's dowry and provide for her children before any other claims were honored. Both clauses were revoked a few years later during the regency period of John's son and successor, but their inclusion in the charter reveals the resentment that moneylending activities generated.

Adversity and Decline

When John died, his son, Henry III, was still a child and could not assume full responsibility as king until 1227. During those years the kingdom was managed by regents who ruled with more providence and good sense than either John before them or Henry after. Their foremost goal during that decade or so was to restore order in the kingdom and confidence in the government, and that meant that they were inclined to treat Jews with moderation. They released Jews whom John had imprisoned, restored bonds to their proper owners, and took steps to ensure that arbitrary harassment and persecution of Jews would end. In each city with a significant Jewish population, they instructed the royal agents to appoint twenty-four prominent citizens who were to be personally responsible for the safety and security of local Jews. Harbor wardens were instructed to admit Jewish immigrants freely, the only requirement being that they register promptly with the Exchequer of the Jews. Jews were not permitted to leave the country, however, without an offficial permit.

The power of the regents was limited when their plans came into conflict with the will of the clergy, and Jews experienced more than enough harassment from that quarter. In 1218, with the archbishop of Canterbury leading the attack, Jews were ordered to wear prominent badges on their clothing—among the first such orders after the edict issued by the Lateran Council of 1215. In Worcester the bishop ordered that Jews were not to employ Christian servants or nurses, not to take sacred objects in pledge for loans, and not to store money in churches for safekeeping. At an ecclesiastical council convened at Oxford in 1222, the clergy again demonstrated how bitterly opposed they were to the Jewish presence in England. A deacon who had studied Hebrew, then converted to Judaism and married a Jewish woman, was condemned by the council and turned over to the local sheriff for punishment as he saw fit. The sheriff, swearing "by the throat of God" that he would punish the man properly and that he regretted not having the woman in hand as well, promptly ordered the victim burned at the stake. The council members followed suit by passing new legislation designed to restrict and confine Jews. Once again, Jews were to have no Christian servants; they were not to enter churches for any purpose;

they were not to build new synagogues; they were to pay tithes to the local priest; and they were to wear badges, as previously ordered. Finally, Christians who associated with Jews in a friendly manner or who sold them basic provisions would be excommunicated. Secular officials did not try to interfere with most of these edicts, but for obvious reasons they drew the line at clerical efforts to control Jewish moneylending operations; there they insisted on preserving the right of Jews to lend money without interference or restrictive legislation. They also reversed the order regarding supply of provisions, since this would have reduced the Jewish community literally to starvation.[35]

Henry grew into a pious but impetuous young man, deferential to the clergy but inclined to extravagant tastes and profligate spending—all in all, an ominous combination of personality traits when seen from the Jewish perspective. And indeed his reign proved disastrous for the Jewish community. Henry reached his majority in 1227, and from that time on, the Jewish community experienced a decline from which it would never recover. He taxed everyone heavily and improvidently, but Jews above all endured impossibly large assessments and brutal mistreatment, including imprisonment of entire families, when they were unable to satisfy his demands. In addition, corrupt Exchequer officials managed to extract still more money for themselves. As an example of how immense were this king's demands, in 1241–42 he assessed the Jewish community twenty thousand marks, and in 1244 sixty thousand—a total of what would be at least five or six million dollars today. By this time most of the burden was falling on the very wealthiest Jews, the only ones who still had enough money to make a difference. But these two tallages, says the historian Robert Stacey, "ruined the Jewish magnates" and "effectively decapitated the class structure of medieval Anglo-Jewry."[36]

By 1254 the situation had become so intolerable that prominent Jews were literally begging for permission to leave the country; but this was never granted, and indeed port wardens were instructed to be on the lookout for anyone attempting to escape. It was only prosperous Jews, however, who were wanted; the others had already been expelled from one town after another. In 1231, Jews were expelled from Leicester by Simon de Montfort, the baron who would later lead the revolt against Henry. Between 1233 and 1243 they were expelled from a number of entire counties and districts, and finally, in 1253, an order was issued that Jews were not to settle anywhere without permission and only where there was an established community. This was but one item in a thoroughly punitive edict instructing the Justices of the Jews on conditions for tolerating the Jews' presence. The edict bears repetition in full as a summary of the royal attitude toward Jews at mid-century.

1. That no Jew remain in England unless he do the king service, and that from the hour of birth every Jew, whether male or female, serve us in some way.

2. That there be no synagogues of the Jews in England, save in those places in which such synagogues were in the time of King John, the king's father.

3. That in their synagogues the Jews, one and all, subdue their voices in performing their ritual offices, that Christians may not hear them.

4. That all Jews answer to the rector of the church of the parish in which they dwell touching all parochial dues relating to their houses.

5. That no Christian man or woman serve any Jew or Jewess or eat with them or tarry in their houses.

6. That no Jew or Jewess eat or buy meat during Lent.

7. That no Jew disparage the Christian faith or publicly dispute concerning the same.

8. That no Jew have secret familiar intercourse with any Christian woman, and no Christian man with a Jewess.

9. That every Jew wear his badge conspicuously on his breast.

10. That no Jew enter any church or chapel save for the purpose of transit or linger in them in dishonor of Christ.

11. That no Jew place any hindrance in the way of another Jew desirous of turning to the Christian faith.

12. That no Jew be received in any town but by special license of the king, save only in those towns in which Jews have been wont to dwell.[37]

By 1255, realizing that he had reduced the Jews to virtual poverty, Henry mortgaged the entire community to his brother, Richard of Cornwall (a more temperate man, who had treated Jews with relative moderation), in return for a loan of five thousand marks. The official chronicler of Henry's reign commented that Richard "was thus permitted to disembowel those whom the King had flayed."[38] Some years later Richard mortgaged them again to Henry's son, the future King Edward, who soon mortgaged them yet again to the Cahorsins, French moneylenders who were by that time replacing the Jews. The entire Jewish community was thus being managed and transferred as a commercial property, with no more independence than a herd of cattle.[39]

"Little St. Hugh" of Lincoln

Perhaps at no time was Henry's impetuous nature and poor judgment with regard to his Jewish subjects more in evidence than in the infamous episode associated with the creation of yet another boy martyr supposedly murdered by Jews. In 1255 the decomposing body of an eight-year-old boy named Hugh, the son of a widow, was found in a well in Lincoln. As it happened, a large number of Jews from throughout the country had recently assembled to celebrate a wedding, and soon rumors were circulating that the child had been murdered by Jews. After a canon of Lincoln Cathedral declared that the Jews must have ritually crucified the boy, the body was taken to the cathedral, accompanied by a long procession of chanting clergy, for burial and veneration as that of a martyr. The canon, John de Lexinton, was a member of the town's leading clerical family and a man with much to gain from the presence of a martyr in his cathedral.[40] He singled out a Jew named Copin and forced him to confess to the usual events associated with the fantasy of ritual murder, promising him immunity from punishment if he revealed the "truth." Soon afterward, Henry, who happened by chance to arrive in Lincoln, immediately ordered that Copin be executed. The unfortunate man was dragged through the streets by a horse, then hanged. Dozens of other Jews were imprisoned in London, and when eighteen of them objected to trial by an all-Christian jury, they too were hanged forthwith on presumption of guilt. The others were eventually released (probably after payment of the customary bribes). Perhaps Henry realized that the case against them was weak and circumstantial.

The child became known as "Little St. Hugh" to distinguish him from a sainted bishop of the same name. His body rested for centuries in an elaborate shrine in Lincoln Cathedral, where it was venerated and worked miraculous cures.[41] Chaucer enshrined the child's memory—and the belief in ritual murder—in his *Canterbury Tales*, when at the close of the *Prioress's Tale*, about another boy martyred by Jews, he called upon "yonge Hugh of Lyncoln" to pray for "we synful folk unstable" that Jesus might be merciful for "reverence of his moder Marie."[42]

"A Ruined Community"

The years just before and during the so-called Barons' War, when the nobility, in protest against Henry's improvident financial policies, tried to gain control of the government, were especially difficult for the Jewish population: even though Jews were more heavily exploited than other people, they were viewed as "the king's men," his allies rather than his victims. Riots resulting in murder and pillage occurred in a number of cities, including London, Gloucester, Worcester, and Lincoln, and in that time of anarchy the Jews had no recourse. The leader of the barons, Simon de Montfort, who controlled the government for a year or so in 1264–65, soon realized, like others before him in similar circumstances, that it was in his interest to protect Jews. They were permitted to return to the homes from which they had been driven and assured that they would be able to live unharmed. But Simon was killed in battle in 1265, and the situation soon returned to prewar normality—that is, maximal exploitation, minimal protection.

Jews who were unable to collect on debts often held in bond land that they could not personally own, and the most efficient way to retrieve at least part of such loans was to transfer the land to a wealthy Christian who paid the debt. Thus small landholders of declining fortunes were were being replaced by wealthy merchants or squires who were able to accumulate large landholdings and the feudal power that went with them. Since this development represented a serious threat to the centralized power of the monarchy, Henry now acted to curtail Jewish dealings in land. In 1269 an edict entitled Provisions of Jewry declared that Jews might no longer contract debts with land as surety and that all contracts of this kind were cancelled. Moreover, transferal of land from Jew to Christian in return for debt payment was to be treated as a capital offense, and in fact no debt could be assumed by another party without an official permit. The Jews, trying somehow to recover their potential losses, petitioned for permission to own land (which they had been granted in twelfth-century charters). But after considerable political maneuvering, the petition was rejected with explicit regulations designed to hedge the Jews in even more: they were to have no permanent rights to any land whatever, no matter how obtained, nor could they own any houses in towns other than those in which they personally resided or those rented to other Jews for residence.[43]

Henry was still taxing Jews inordinately in 1272, the last year of his life. Summing up the Jewish predicament under his rule, Cecil Roth remarks that "Jews were like a sponge, sucking up the floating capital of the country, to be squeezed from time to time into the Treasury; while the king, high above them and sublimely contemptuous of their transactions, was in fact the arch-usurer of the realm." At Henry's death, Roth concludes, they were "a ruined community," drained beyond their capacity to recover.[44]

The Final Years of Medieval English Jewry:
1272–1290

Edward I, away on crusade when his father died, did not return until 1274. But already by then his ministers had levied yet another brutal tax on Jews, the heaviest in more than thirty years. Several more followed, and in 1278, Edward ordered all Jews arrested and their homes searched for evidence that they were concealing wealth. Some were declared guilty and hanged as punishment. The Jewish community had always included many poor families, but by this time probably most had reached the point of ruin. As a last resort some sold their homes, while others were banished and their homes and property appropriated for sale by the royal treasury. The community had been reduced to some three thousand persons, perhaps six hundred adult couples, most impoverished or nearly so. Twenty or thirty families, once wealthy but now reduced to near penury, were carrying practically all the burden of taxation during Edward's reign.

The situation was not only desperate but even grimly comic. In 1274, an ecclesiastical council meeting in France under the pope's sponsorship urged that usury be abolished entirely and that Jews in particular be forced into "productive" labor. Edward, an uncommonly pious man, obeyed promptly. In 1275 he issued a "Statute of the Jews" declaring that they were no longer to lend money but were to be permitted to become merchants and artisans—a rather ridiculous expectation for people who had been socially ostracized so completely for so long. That the isolation would continue was ensured by the inclusion in the same statute of a repeated order that all Jews above age seven wear a badge on their clothing.

A few Jews tried commerce in wool, wheat, or jewelry on a modest scale, but most were already too impoverished and too demoralized to venture seriously into new occupations. Others resorted to desperate actions. One path was conversion, from which some then tried to retreat, only to be punished severely. A number turned to crime, with similar prospects. Aside from outright robbery, which was not unknown, many Jews engaged in "coin clipping"—shaving small amounts of silver from coins and melting this into bars for sale. The penalty for clipping had been banishment, but now it was changed to execution; and although more Christians than Jews were involved in this practice, it was more often Jews who were arrested and severely punished.

To add to their despair, Jews were enduring more persecution for imagined crimes (ritual murder and blasphemy against Christianity, for example) than ever before, and there were frequent riots in which Jews were murdered and their homes pillaged. A number of towns had expelled them altogether, and others had issued explicit prohibitions against their settling, so that by this time there were fewer than twenty Jewish communities in all of England.

Most significantly, the Jews were no longer consequential contributors to the royal coffers. They were paying about one-fourth of what they had been able to pay in the late twelfth century, and whereas that had constituted nearly fifteen percent of the total intake, their present contribution was little more than one percent. Foreign consortia from France and Italy were now operating far more effectively in England than the Jews ever had, being better equipped to finance large loans and to collect on them effectively. Clearly the time was at hand for the final chapter of Jewish history in medieval England.

In 1289, Edward ordered the arrest of all Jews in Gascony, the region of southwestern France that was still under English hegemony, after which their property and assets were seized and they were expelled altogether. The experiment, such as it was, worked to his satisfaction, and the next step was to order the same for the Jews of England. On July 18, 1290, he ordered that all Jews were to leave the country by November 1, and that any Jew who remained thereafter was to be executed. Until that time the sheriffs were to see to it that they were not mistreated, and they were to be permitted to take all movable property. Their outstanding debts were to be paid to the royal treasury—but without interest, because the fiction was that they were being expelled because they had violated the statute prohibiting moneylending.

Whatever their personal sentiments may have been about the loss of this familiar source of ready money, most English citizens were outwardly joyful at the news of the forthcoming expulsion. Parliament expressed its pleasure by voting to grant special tax revenues to the king. The process soon moved into high gear, with Jewish homes being sold to generate the last bit of revenue that could be extracted from the refugees. Some of this money was assigned to completion of a tomb for Henry III; another portion paid for stained-glass windows in Westminster Abbey.

A contingent of some of the poorest members of the London Jewish community journeyed in October to the coast, where they boarded a ship for France. Not far out, the ship was anchored at a sandbank and the captain invited (or perhaps ordered) the Jews to leave the ship and walk about for a while. When the tide began to rise, he returned to the ship but refused to let them aboard, taunting them by suggesting that they ask Moses to control the seas as he had done before, and then sailing away. The entire group drowned. (The incident was observed and reported, and the captain and his crew were hanged.) Other Jews fared little better. Some died when ships were wrecked by storms at sea; others, barely more fortunate, were discharged on the French coast with almost nothing to their names.

They left behind little evidence of their two-hundred-year sojourn: a few stone homes of unusually sturdy construction, here and there a synagogue, streets or neighborhoods known as Jewries. "As their memory faded from the minds of Englishmen," remarks one historian, "they became an evil thing, unknown, dreaded and accursed."[45] For most English people of a later age, Jews perhaps existed only as Marlowe's "Jew of Malta," or as the complex character—part villain, part victim—created by Shakespeare in "The Merchant of Venice." But of course Marlowe's and Shakespeare's archetypal Jews were residents not of England but of distant Mediterranean ports—perhaps because by that time their audiences would have found it difficult even to imagine Jews in England.[46]

◦ 12 ◦

"ODIOUS TO GOD AND MEN"

Persecutions and Expulsions

"Let Them Abandon Usury": France

For the Jews of France, the latter half of the thirteenth century brought only continuation and aggravation of the restrictions and persecutions that had already become their expectable lot. Three men ruled France during this time: Louis IX (1226–70), his son Philip III (1270–85), and his grandson Philip IV (1285–1314), and their policies toward Jews were virtually indistinguishable. Louis IX remained on the throne for another twenty years after mid-century, establishing the reputation for probity and piety that eventually gained him sainthood; but, as we have seen, the saintly king had no compassion for Jews. Robert Chazan characterizes his reign as the beginning of the end for the Jews of France, concluding that "by the end of this reign, French Jewry had lost the vigor, strength, and intellectual prowess that had been its pride since the late eleventh century."[1] And yet Chazan also observes that this very same reign "represents a high-water mark in the history of medieval France," and nearly all other historians agree. What better evidence can there be for the unwelcome conclusion that Jewish prosperity and security in medieval Europe were inversely proportional to the development and flourishing of European civilization?

It was during the thirteenth century that Louis and his immediate successors were able to convert France from an assemblage of loosely linked feudal territories into a true state, with a centralized administration and a population that was developing a sense of national identity.[2]

The foundations for this process lay in fundamental changes in social and economic life: the feudal social order, localized and hierarchical, was being replaced by a new national polity, increasingly dependent on production for sale and export, and increasingly dominated by the urban merchants who had been steadily gaining power and prominence for some two hundred years. These men, ambitious entrepreneurs with capital of their own, resented Jewish competition and looked upon Jews as anachronistic nuisances.

There were grounds for their disdain. Since money borrowers were likely to be spendthrift nobility, impoverished peasants and laborers, or people in similarly precarious circumstances, much of the money borrowed from Jews went into immediate consumption, not productive enterprise. Moreover, the profits flowed ultimately into royal or ducal treasuries. This rickety system was maintained by exorbitant interest rates that could lead ordinary people into financial ruin, and of course many debtors defaulted or went bankrupt. None of this was in the best interests of urban merchants trying to build a thriving economy.

Thus Jews were disparaged on two main counts. They still faced the familiar charge, of course, that there should be no place in Christian society for people who had rejected and scorned the Savior. Now there was the additional charge that these same people were leading the least productive members of society into ruin by encouraging them to consume beyond their means. For a long time, as James Parkes observes, while kings needed Jews as a source of capital, usury secured for them "official protection at the price of public detestation."[3] But that situation could not last indefinitely. By the end of the century French kings, and soon thereafter many of their counterparts elsewhere in continental Europe, were recognizing that the destiny of their nations lay in production, commerce, and export. When this stage—the first stirrings of mercantilism—was reached, it was inevitable that Jews would be deemed superfluous. In short, the Jews of medieval Europe were victims of progress.

Louis IX: The Later Years

As we have noted, Louis IX was genuinely committed to social, economic and religious reform. By "purifying" France—eliminating all forms of vice and dishonesty—he hoped to create a nation that would be a model of Christian virtue. His policies toward Jews have to be understood as a minor feature of a much larger picture. That he detested Jews seems beyond question, but his reasons for adopting particular policies remain obscure. Louis had a demanding conscience; he felt responsible for abuses connected with usury, whether exacted by Jews or Christians, and he would have liked to eliminate it entirely. Though he realized, of course, that his own treasury benefited substantially from Jewish tax payments, he was prepared to make sacrifices in the service of Christian principles. Probably the main obstacle in his path was his own reluctance to confront the powerful barons who also benefited from the presence of Jews in their domains but did not always share his standards of rectitude. It was more politic to settle for limitations on usury and to hold the Jews responsible for engaging in an occupation that everyone supposedly rejected. Such ambivalence seems to characterize his policies and those of his successors: maintaining fairly tight restrictions on moneylending but never really abolishing it entirely, even when legislation appears to be designed precisely for that purpose.

Although Louis's edict of 1235 had explicitly prohibited moneylending (ordering that Jews "live by their own labor or by trade, but without usury"), the practice obviously continued throughout the kingdom. Thus, nearly twenty years later, in 1253, while Louis was on his way home following a bitter defeat on crusade, we find him issuing a stern warning to all Jews: either abandon usury or leave France. One of his biographers described this edict in a paragraph that says a great deal about personal motives. Part of the passage was quoted earlier, but it bears repetition here.

> The Jews, odious to God and men, he detested so much that he was unable to look upon them. He wished that none of their goods be transformed for his use, claiming that he did not wish to retain their poison. He wished that they not practice usury, but rather that they

earn their food by labor or by proper commerce, as used to be done in other areas. Many of his counselors advised him to the contrary, claiming that without lending the populace could not exist, nor the land be cultivated, nor labor and commerce be pursued. They said that it was better and more tolerable that the Jews, who were damned already, exercise this function of damnation rather than Christians, who under these circumstances oppress the populace with heavier usury. This good Catholic responded to these contentions: "The matter of Christian usurers and their usury seems to pertain to the prelates of the Church. The matter of the Jews, who are subjected to me by the yoke of servitude, pertains to me, lest they oppress Christians by their usury, and lest, under the shelter of my protection, they be permitted to do this and to infect my land with their poison. . . . Let them abandon usury, or let them leave my land completely, lest it be further defiled by their filth." He had their goods seized along with them, not with the intention of retaining these goods, but so that through proper proof they might be restored to those from whom they had been extorted by usurious depravity.[4]

Reading between the lines somewhat, we can see that Louis probably faced opposition not only from his own counselors but also from the higher clergy, many of whom were too dependent on capital provided by moneylenders, Christian as well as Jewish, to want to campaign against them. If the edict had been obeyed to the letter, the Jews would have been promptly pauperized. As William Chester Jordan points out, Louis did not anticipate that Jews would take up occupations to serve the Christian community; his intention was that they abandon their only viable source of income and, "by taking up crafts that had a very restricted market (limited to other Jews), condemn themselves to grinding poverty."[5]

Louis's religiosity goes a long way toward explaining his commitment to policies that were not especially popular, particularly not with people in the upper echelons of society. That same religiosity induced him to support efforts to convert Jews by encouraging the activities of Dominican and Franciscan friars and also by overlooking the actions of those who abandoned all restraint in campaigns to coerce Jews or to punish them for imaginary crimes.

A single example should suffice to show what was possible (and, in effect, permissible) during those years. In March 1247 a two-year-old girl disappeared one evening in the town of Valréas, in the Jura region of eastern France. Her mother was told that the child had been seen wandering in the town's Jewish street, and that was enough to arouse everyone's suspicion. The next day the child's body, said to have possessed a fragrant aroma, was found in a ditch and brought to the marketplace. There were wounds on the forehead and hands, and small holes in each foot—more than enough evidence, of course, that Jews had ritually crucified the child. She was ceremonially buried under the floor of the church. The grieving mother remarked that her pain and sadness were mitigated by "the miracles that God did for my little girl."

The local baron refused to order that Jews be interrogated, but it happened that two Franciscan friars were in town at the time, and they took charge of the proceedings. Three Jews were arrested and tortured for days until they confessed to the crime, each implicating different accomplices; the confessions consisted of acquiescence to questions phrased by the friars. They acknowledged that Jews assembled each year to select a place for a ritual murder, that the blood was distributed to neighboring communities (probably for use at Passover), and that on Good Friday the body was hung in the manner of the Crucifixion. The baron then took charge and had the Jews brought to the marketplace, where they again confessed in the same manner. According to a letter from Pope Innocent IV condemning the entire incident and blaming the baron in particular, many Jews were brutally murdered: "without admitting the legitimate protestation and defense of their innocence, he cut some of them in two, others he burned at the stake, of others he castrated the men and tore out the breasts of the women. He afflicted them with other diverse kinds of torture, until, as it is said, they confessed with their mouth what their conscience did not dictate, choosing to be killed in one moment of agony than to live and be afflicted with torments and tortures."

After townspeople committed further violence against Jews, in Valréas and the vicinity, the pope responded with two letters of reprimand, both dated the same day, stating that some Jews, "despoiled of all their possessions, were even driven out from their territory." Even a local bishop had participated: he and several members of the nobility, "taking advantage of an excuse of this kind, threw into prison whatever Jews dwell in their lands and dominions, after having robbed these Jews of all their property." In addition, children had been forcibly baptized, "contrary to custom with regard to children born into freedom of a free mother." The pope demanded that imprisoned Jews be released, that property be returned, and that Jews be permitted to dwell freely and without fear of persecution.[6]

Innocent IV wrote these letters in response to a petition from "the Jews of the entire province of Vienne." What is perhaps most remarkable here is that a Jewish community in France—subjected to torture, murder, and dispossession by a number of men in authority, including barons, friars, and a bishop—saw fit to appeal not to the French but to the papal throne. There is nothing in the historical record to suggest that Louis took any action against the perpetrators of the crimes or made any attempt to ensure that surviving Jews were properly treated and adequately compensated; he may very well not even have known about the case. But by 1247 the Jews of France had surely long since learned that no redress was to be expected from this king, and that it would be useless to petition him.

From the Jewish perspective the reign of the saintly king, particularly in its final years, was a time of constant torment. We have already discussed the assault on the Talmud that began in 1239, and the debate that followed in 1240. Other staged debates, or "disputations," probably took place thereafter. Some Jews converted to escape the burdens of pariahdom; at times the conversions were enthusiastically sponsored by the king himself. Jordan comments on the situation just after mid-century:

> All of the ancient rhetoric was given new life that was to some degree sustained for years after Louis's reign came to an end. Pensions were offered adult male converts. These pensions were not necessarily extinguished at death. If the convert left a widow, she received half. The royal archives show mounting numbers of recipients. The king actively pursued his role as sponsor at christenings, appearing himself and rejoicing in the *Ludovici baptisati* (children) and *Ludovici conversi* (adults) he brought to the font. Jewish orphans were cared for,

having been baptized into the faith. By 1260 a crescendo of conversions already necessitated special orders to facilitate the new Christians' integration into local society.[7]

Converts who "relapsed" into Judaism were severely punished. Chazan cites one such case from 1268, described by an anonymous contemporary, in which a Jew who had lived ostensibly as a convert to Christianity and a clergyman for some twenty years was found to have had his sons circumcised and instructed in Judaism:

> On the Sunday prior to the Feast of St. Vincent, at St. Anthony near Paris, with a multitude of good men in attendance—for those who attended received major indulgences from the bishop—the accused was stripped of orders by the bishop, was degraded, and was turned over to the secular court. On the following Thursday—after he had chosen for himself fire rather than to return to the Christian faith, asserting that if all the kindling of Paris were gathered and ignited and he thrown into the midst he would not be burned by that fire— he was led into the square where hogs were sold in Paris and there, bound fast, he was totally consumed by the fire, so that nothing remained unburned either of his body or of his limbs. Then his ashes were strewn throughout the adjacent fields.[8]

That same year, Louis ordered a general confiscation of Jewish property in his own domain and in Champagne and Poitiers, probably as part of a campaign to finance yet another crusading effort. Even cemetery lands were appropriated, and Jews themselves were seized, probably as hostages until all property had been yielded up.[9]

That year also saw the arrival in Paris of Pablo Christiani (or Paul Chrétien), a convert from Montpellier who had become a Dominican friar. A zealous pursuer of Jews, he had made his reputation in 1263 when he engaged in a disputation with the distinguished rabbi Moses ben Nahman (Nahmanides). Urged on by the friar, Louis ordered that all Jews must now wear a distinctive badge—"a circle of felt or yellow cloth, stitched upon the outer garment in front and in back . . . its area must be the size of a palm"—in effect, enforcement of the Lateran Council edict of 1215. And in July 1269, Louis ordered his administrators to compel Jews to attend Pablo Christiani's sermons: "to hear from him and without objection the word of the Lord and present their books as the aforesaid brother shall require. You shall compel the Jews to respond fully, without calumny and subterfuge, on those matters which relate to their law, concerning which the aforesaid brother might interrogate them, whether in sermons in their synagogues or elsewhere." Pablo probably met with the particular disdain reserved for converts. A Hebrew text of the time boasts that although a thousand or more Jews were "pelted with stones" of conversionist rhetoric, "not one of us turned to the religion of vanity and lies."[10]

Characterizing Louis's entire four decades as "an unmitigated disaster" for the Jews of France, Chazan remarks that the final years of his reign "represent unquestionably the nadir of Jewish fortunes."[11] They were a nadir from which there was to be no significant ascent.

Two Philips: 1270–1314

Louis was succeeded by his son, Philip III (1270–85), whose reign has been described as a relatively placid time during which Jews experienced a modest social and economic recovery—but it was indeed modest.[12] Although not as dynamic a ruler as his father or his son, Philip III (called "Philip the Bold") earned a place in Jewish history by not only maintaining all restrictions imposed by his predecessors but also adding some of his own, including one of considerable significance. Along with repetitions of the familiar regulations prohibiting usury and demanding general submission, Philip's parliament revived the old prohibition against Christian women serving Jews as nurses or servants. A far more profound restriction came in 1276, when Philip issued a decree expelling Jews from all French villages and requiring that they live only in the largest towns—the reasoning being that in villages they were living on unacceptably intimate terms with impressionable peasants.

Philip's Jewish policy was summarized in an edict of 1283 that, somewhat puzzlingly, omits mention of usury while otherwise imposing rigorous restrictions: two badges to be worn, one on the chest, another on the back; no Christian nurses or servants, female or male; no new cemeteries or synagogues ("nor may they chant loudly"); residence only in large towns; and no copies of the Talmud or other condemned books ("rather they must be publicly burned").[13] The omission of usury has been taken to mean that Philip was easing restrictions in this domain, but it seems more probable that he considered himself to have dealt adequately with usury already and was now addressing social and religious matters. The prohibitions regarding cemeteries and synagogues suggest that Philip neither desired nor anticipated Jewish population growth. In 1278 he had censured the bishop of Béziers for permitting Jews to build a new synagogue and had ordered the structure demolished—but not simply out of Christian piety. The bishop, probably with personal financial benefits in mind, had encouraged Jews to move from the Jewish quarter under royal jurisdiction to another under his own, and to build the new synagogue there. A parliament assembled by Philip demanded that the Jews be returned to the royal quarter, where they could be properly taxed.[14]

Philip was his father's son, but with a turn in the direction of pragmatism over piety; his own son, Philip IV (1285–1314), was to display that inclination more clearly and, from the perspective of his Jewish subjects, with even more devastating effects. In this king's reign, when "royal power in France arguably reached its medieval apogee,"[15] we encounter the ultimate demonstration of how completely the situation of French Jews had deteriorated. For Philip IV, called "Philip the Fair" and remembered in French history as second in eminence only to his sainted grandfather, first taxed his Jewish "vassals" to the limits of their capacity to pay and then expelled them altogether, so that he might auction off their homes and possessions for a final contribution to his relentlessly demanding treasury. Nowhere, perhaps, in the history of later medieval Europe do we see revealed more clearly the profound ambivalence that characterized relations between lords and Jews—not because Philip (or any other French lord) felt any empathy with Jews, but because he was torn between, on the one hand, the desire to confirm his status as a pious Christian by restricting usury, and, on the other, by the demands of a rapidly expanding and immensely expensive administration. Financial affairs, remarks one historian, were "the center of his attention"; his agents "scoured the kingdom exploiting every claim the king could possibly make upon the resources of his subjects."[16] Jews and their wealth were an integral part of the picture, though in the final analysis only a minor part; they were never more than one among many sources to be exploited, and they never provided more than a small fraction of Philip's annual income. What distinguished them from everyone else, of course, was their occupation as well as their religion: not only were they Jews but they were usurious Jews.

As Philip's biographer, Joseph Strayer, has pointed out, it was during this king's reign that France came fully into its own as a state— that is, as a country with clearly established boundaries, within which everyone owed primary and exclusive allegiance to the crown. But true allegiance, he observes, derives not from fear or self-interest but from "genuine respect, admiration, and, if possible, love for the object of loyalty."[17] To elicit such allegiance, thirteenth-century French kings surrounded themselves and their nation with an aura of sanctity: they were sacred kings ruling a holy land, and their subjects were God's new chosen people—a label adopted by all Christians, of course, but appropriated here to add special significance; the people of France were the most devout of all Christians, France was the heart and soul of Christendom, and its ruler was "the most Christian king." Some French writers even suggested that the king was a "type" (that is, a contemporary representation) of Jesus Christ himself, and that France was an earthly form of the heavenly kingdom.[18] Even a pope, Clement V, writing during the final years of Philip's reign, declared that the French were God's own favored people: "The King of Glory formed different kingdoms within the circuit of this world and established governments for diverse peoples according to differences of language and race. Among those, like the people of Israel . . . , the kingdom of France, as a peculiar people chosen by the Lord to carry out the orders of Heaven, is distinguished by marks of special honor and grace."[19]

Given his country's self-image, it is not surprising that Philip was uneasy about the very presence of Jews, even though he coveted the wealth that their moneylending generated. Could this "most Christian king," ruling over the most sacred land in Christendom, accept in his realm such a "raw spot among the New Chosen People": those who had scorned Christ and continued, by their religious profession as well as by their principal occupation, to deny the legitimacy and validity of Christ's own ministry?[20] And yet, what was he to do? For the most

Christian king was burdened with most oppressive expenses, and he had to find money where he could. He found it not only in Jewish pockets, of course; everyone was subjected to relentless taxation, and some, the clergy in particular, protested as much as they dared. But Jews posed a unique problem, for Christian piety required that they be rejected even while financial needs demanded that he maintain as firm a hold on them as possible. Thus at every turn in the history of this twisted relationship we encounter a degree of ambivalence and inconsistency that must have left many Jews baffled as to what to expect next.

Philip's overriding purpose with regard to Jews was to maintain absolute control over them and their financial affairs. No one was permitted to exercise authority over any Jew in his jurisdiction without the king's express permission—and that included friars who presumed to oppress Jews without royal sanction. Philip was on unfriendly terms with the pope during some of his reign, and his policies regarding Jews were shaped in part by the state of his relationship with the Church at particular times. Always the uppermost consideration was how best to ensure that Jews would continue to funnel wealth from their debtors into his own treasury; he was prepared to make concessions to clergy or friars when this was expedient, but always with his own financial situation in mind. Soon after assuming the throne in 1285, for example, he confirmed the order that Jews must wear badges, then added instructions authorizing the government to sell the badges.[21]

By 1293, in the midst of a heated dispute with Pope Boniface VIII over royal rights to tax French clergy, Philip boldly turned on the Church and issued a stern warning to friars regarding their zealous missionizing and persecution of Jews. His objections were of course purely pragmatic: the friars were interfering with royal property and threatening royal revenues. Six years later, however, the political climate had changed. Boniface VIII, responding to a ban on French exports of gold and silver to the papal court, accepted Philip's right to tax clergy and seemed to be retreating from what had become the traditional papal position on absolute supremacy of Church over State. As a further mark of goodwill, he had sainted Louis IX—a way of acknowledging, perhaps, that France was indeed a sacred land ruled by extraordinary kings. And so in 1299 we find Philip issuing an edict that essentially reverses that of 1293. Now he is not only fully accepting whatever the "inquisitors of heretical depravity" choose to say or do, but also instructing members of his own administration to carry out the friars' orders:

> We understand that the Jews in diverse parts of the kingdom solicit Christians on behalf of heresy and ensnare many with their wiles and with their promises and bribes. In this way they receive from many and dare to handle wretchedly the most holy body of Christ and blaspheme the other sacraments of our faith. They seduce many simple folk and circumcise those whom they have seduced. They receive and conceal fugitive heretics. To the scandal of our faith, they build new synagogues, chanting in a loud voice as though they were officiating in a Church service. They multiply copies of the condemned books called Talmud, containing innumerable blasphemies concerning the most glorious Virgin Mary, and teach an immoderate disparagement of the Christian faith. . . .
>
> In order that such reprehensible misdeeds not go unpunished and in order that the enemies of our faith not be able during our times to gain advantage for their perfidy, we order all of you and each of you that, at the order of the inquisitors of heretical depravity who show the present letter, you seize suspects, imprison them, transfer them from prison to prison, and punish them according to the tenor of the canons of the Apostolic Throne enacted concerning this matter, whenever you are so requested by the aforesaid inquisitors.[22]

The reference to "the most holy body of Christ" is particularly noteworthy here: Philip was accusing the Jews of desecration of the Host, that is, torture inflicted on communion wafers in imitation of the tormenting of Jesus on the cross. Though this was a new charge, dating only from about 1290, it had already led to Jewish deaths.[23]

But the Jews—pawns of little consequence in this ongoing game between king and pope—had only to wait for yet another reversal of policy. In 1301, Philip ordered a disloyal bishop in southern France to be imprisoned; the pope refused to support the action and instead issued a bull (Unam Sanctam) reasserting the absolute primacy of church over state. Further conflict followed: Philip remained defiant, and in 1303 Boniface declared him excommunicated, whereupon the king accused the pope of heresy, sorcery, and sodomy. Eventually Philip's agents tried to abduct the pope while he was visiting his birthplace in Anagni, intending to bring him to France for trial. They were intercepted and Boniface returned to Rome, where he died shortly thereafter.[24]

Understood in the context of that bitter struggle, an edict issued in 1302 means more than is immediately apparent. Here Philip returns to his earlier position and orders his officials to limit very strictly the authority and privileges of the friars:

> [I]f the aforementioned inquisitors involve themselves or attempt in any way to involve themselves against the Jews of our kingdom in questions of usury, blasphemy, or other issues which do not pertain to these inquisitors by virtue of their role of inquisitor, you shall at their insistence or request seize no Jew nor cause him to be seized or molested in any way on the aforesaid charges, nor shall you extend aid or favor in connection with these Jews to these inquisitors.[25]

Obviously, the statement was not a declaration that Jews had the right to be free of molestation; it was simply another assertion of royal power and authority, and of refusal to accept interference by the Church in royal affairs.

We have already noted that by the beginning of the century the nobility had begun treating Jews as movable property. By the end of the century, this had become a more or less routine practice, and Philip himself engaged frequently in transactions involving Jews and in disputes over ownership—not only with other feudal lords but also with archbishops, abbots, and the like. In 1296 he presented to his brother Charles, count of Valois, a human gift: a wealthy Jew and his six children. But for the next several years Charles quarreled with Philip over ownership of other Jews, until the matter was settled in 1299, when Charles, pressed for income, sold all of his Jews to the king for twenty thousand pounds. The sale took place in June; and by December, Philip's treasury was already receiving substantial income from one of the Jews in the transaction.[26]

The inevitable conclusion to the entire story came in 1306, when Philip, under heavy financial pressure as always, issued an edict expelling all Jews from France, including territories still possessed by lesser lords, and ordered that their entire property—"all lands, houses, vineyards, and other possessions"—be sold at public auction. The proceeds were to go, of course, to the royal treasury. Some 125,000 Jews were affected by the order. They were given no warning, so that they would have no time to convert property into cash or to conceal anything. Suddenly they were arrested, their property was confiscated, and they were summarily expelled. Those from southern France sought refuge with Jewish communities in other Mediterranean countries; those from the north did likewise in Germany.[27]

Although Philip was prepared to reward lords who cooperated by expelling Jews from their personal domains, he intended to be the main beneficiary of the expulsion order. But whatever other objections the nobility may have presented, remarks Jordan, "they insisted on their fair share of the loot."[28] As was to be expected, with a windfall of these dimensions suddenly available, everyone who could get a hand into the till did so. Some petty local officials accepted bribes from Jews who hoped to salvage something for the future. Others sequestered property or embezzled—presumably an easy matter when so many were being abruptly dispossessed of unknown amounts of wealth. The few who were caught appear to have gotten off rather lightly: fines and loss of office, for example, but no physical punishments. Ordinary townsfolk also took what they could, particularly when delays by public officials provided them with opportunities to express righteous indignation by attacking and looting Jewish homes.

People were certain that Jews had vast sums hidden away, and the search for "treasure" went on for years. Thus, says Jordan, "we must try to imagine the local officials going about, checking here, checking there, digging, opening, prying, tapping for hollow places, while always at the same time trying not to diminish the value of the property before it could be auctioned." Moreover, discovering a few caches of jewelry or the like "stimulated the imagination to believe that there were more and more and more. It was a feeling that would not go away."[29]

Although financial considerations probably led Philip to expel the Jews, he also benefited in other ways. As we have noted, thirteenth-century French men and women were gradually gaining a sense of shared national identity, and it was in the king's interest to promote the idea—still far from accomplished fact—that France was a nation of people who were socially linked and culturally alike. Expelling Jews, surely the most prominent alien element in the population, was certain to win widespread approval from those who wanted to see France become "as pure as the golden lily that was its emblem." Moreover, whatever opposition may have come from clergy who had depended on Jewish loans, here was undeniable evidence that the king was a pious man who despised the enemies of Christ.[30] All in all, Philip stood to gain more than he lost by carrying exploitation of Jews to its limit.

But Philip died in 1314, and a year later, only nine years after the expulsion, his son and successor, Louis X (who lived only until 1316), readmitted a small number of Jews into the country. His motives were, as usual, financial: he needed money, and readmitting Jews was preferable to increasing taxes. Moreover, despite the objections that the action undoubtedly evoked from some quarters, it would have been in accord with the desires of those who needed ready cash and knew that the high interest rates charged by Jewish lenders were nevertheless often lower than those of their Christian counterparts. The benefits to Louis's own treasury were both immediate and potential: for the privilege of returning to a country where they knew themselves to be objects of disdain, Jews paid 22,500 pounds and pledged an additional 10,000 pounds annually.

The returnees, perhaps the most notable optimists in medieval Jewish history, received a charter, the first of its kind in France, that controlled their activities while providing necessary guarantees—acknowledgment on both sides that they were strictly provisional residents in a country they would never be able to call their own. The charter contained twenty clauses, mostly predictable but with a few innovations. The Jews were guaranteed residence for twelve years, possibly renewable (although, as it turned out, they were destined not to last even that long), and were to receive a year's notice before another forced departure. They could settle only in towns where Jews had resided previously, with the same privileges earlier accorded them. Communal properties—synagogues, cemeteries, and the like—were to be returned to them (at a price); otherwise they were to be permitted to purchase replacement properties. Their religious books, except for the Talmud and other prohibited volumes, were to be returned where possible. They were permitted, even encouraged, to collect on old debts, but with the provision that two-thirds of all payments were to go into the royal treasury. They were required to wear badges at all times, and under no circumstances were they to engage in religious discussions with Christians. The demand that they abandon usury entirely and subsist only by manual labor or honest commerce was repeated, but with the disingenuous provision that should they "by chance" (par aventure) happen to lend money, they could charge no more than two "deniers per livre" (two pennies per pound) per week—in effect, some 43 percent annually, the customary rate at the time. But although the royal treasury obviously stood to benefit substantially from taxes imposed on Jews, the courts were not to assist them in recovering bad debts—another case of the familiar ambivalence characteristic of thirteenth-century French royalty in these matters.

Most of the resettled Jews turned at once to moneylending, of course, particularly as pawnbrokers. Not surprisingly, they were persecuted from the start: subjected to heavy fines, property seizures, and even imprisonment for relatively minor offenses; arrested for such "crimes" as not wearing a badge while working in a vineyard.[31]

Early in the reign of Louis's successor, his brother Philip V (1316–22), it was more than evident that the prospects for these remnants of French Jewry were anything but favorable. For some years the principal inquisitor in France had been a Dominican friar named Bernard Gui. Inquisitor of Toulouse and author of a manual of inquisitorial practice, Gui was a dedicated pursuer of heretics and deviants, and matters relating to Jews were well within his sphere of attention. For some indication of his state of mind, we may consider an order he issued in 1317. A Jewish convert who had "relapsed" and declared that he wanted to remain a Jew apparently died before he could be brought before an inquisitorial court. Bernard Gui ordered that the man's body be removed from the grave and burned, as befitted a heretic. By 1319 he was conducting a concerted attack on the Talmud, and in November of that year the books were publicly burned, "with great fanfare": "On November 28, 1319, two wagons filled with volumes of the Talmud rolled through the streets of Toulouse, preceded by royal officials and criers who proclaimed the blasphemies contained therein. The books were then consigned to the flames."[32]

But not only books were destroyed during these years; many people died. The first major assault came in 1320, when a large assemblage of so-called Shepherds (*Pastoureaux*) launched a "crusade"—in reality an uprising of the dispossessed—which resulted in death and destruction for a number of Jewish communities, particularly in southern France: Aquitaine, Languedoc, and neighboring regions. Historians find it difficult to explain why this particular kind of behavior erupted when it did, but it is known that between 1315 and 1317 (just when the Jews were returning) France experienced crop failure and severe famine. Moreover, for several years Philip V had been somewhat recklessly declaring his intention to mount a new crusade and collecting money for the purpose; but, as one historian observes, "the chief consequence for most people had been an increase in financial burdens," not a triumphant crusade.[33] In any event, the times were characterized by a great deal of religious fervor: millenarian prophecies, penitential processions, expectations that something important was going to happen soon. So there was enough general discontent and excitement to ensure an enthusiastic response to anyone who declared readiness to act decisively—even if that mainly meant attacking Jews, which turned out to be the case.

The affair began early in 1320, in northern France, when groups of what a chronicler of the time described as "shepherds and simple men" declared that they had received revelations from angels commanding them to liberate the Holy Land. Their numbers grew rapidly as they were joined by derelicts and fugitives of every description, but the majority appear to have been naïve youths who had abandoned their work as shepherds or laborers in favor of loftier pursuits. Soon they were marching into Paris, an undisciplined army of thousands, demanding that the king join and lead them, and rioting when he refused. They caused enough mayhem to have justified immediate repression, but the authorities seem to have decided against taking action, and the mob departed "unharmed and unhindered."[34]

Turning southward, they made their way toward Aquitaine, now attacking Jewish communities along the way—murdering, looting, and forcibly converting people in proper crusade fashion, usually with acquiescence and even warm support from local populations. By May or early June, they had reached Toulouse and other southern communities, where they attacked not only Jews but probably also churches and monasteries, presumably because these too were symbols of an oppressive economic structure. That summer Pope John XXII sent several letters to southern French bishops and secular authorities, urging that they take all necessary measures to protect Jews and to "persuade or compel" the "crusaders" to desist from their "evil actions" until the king was ready to lead a proper crusade.[35] Despite the popularity of the Shepherds with most townspeople, the authorities had been antagonistic to them from the beginning. By autumn a local southern official had assembled an army that readily overwhelmed the Shepherds, who were "captured in relatively small groups and were hung in tens, twenties, and thirties from gibbets and trees wherever they were found." Their movement had lasted only seven or eight months, but in that time they had severely damaged what little remained of the Jewish presence in France.[36]

A German Jew named Baruch, residing in Toulouse when the Shepherds attacked, was forcibly baptized but "returned" to Judaism when the danger had passed. He achieved a place in Jewish history when he was hauled before an inquisitorial court and forced into a "disputation" with the bishop of Pamiers, Jacques Fournier, who would later become Pope Benedict XII. The case was a noteworthy example of the Church's doctrine that even forced conversion was legitimate if the victim had "accepted" it willingly—that is, had not actively protested during the baptismal rite. Baruch had barely escaped with his life and had agreed to baptism while under extreme duress (he saw other Jews being killed in his immediate presence), but that was of no consequence: he was a heretic, a Christian who had been caught engaging in Judaic practices. After weeks of hopeless effort, Baruch gave in; according to the Christian chronicler, he recognized the truth of his new faith and agreed to conduct himself accordingly:

> He said, moreover, that he believed this faith from the heart and that he would believe it and teach it henceforth. And he said he believed that the persecution, as a result of which he was baptized, had come upon him for the good of his soul and that he had not been induced

to believe the Catholic faith through fear of death or of torture, or by the force of imprisonment, threats, terrors, blandishments, or promises, but rather through the Holy Scriptures as explained to him by the Lord Bishop.[37]

As Jordan remarks, the Shepherds' Crusade, and the support accorded to the mobs when they attacked Jewish communities, revealed how deeply ordinary people resented the return of the Jews to France.[38] That was underscored the following year, when, in an outbreak of terror rooted in the wildest of fantasies, Jews were accused of collusion with lepers in a "plot to overthrow Christendom."[39] Two Muslim kings, so the story went, had paid Jews to persuade lepers to contaminate wells with poisons of a sort that would induce leprosy in the entire population, thus leaving the Christian world ripe for conquest.[40] Lepers were arrested and tortured until they confessed to the "crime." Many were murdered, often by burning, as were Jews. One chronicler reported that "the Jews in some parts were burnt indiscriminately and especially in Aquitaine," and that at Chinon, near Tours, 160 Jews were burned to death in a large pit.[41] Many other Jewish communities, including the one in Paris, came under attack. Philip V, who appears to have believed in the tale himself, responded by appropriating the property of the victims.

Philip died during the following year (1322) and was succeeded by his brother, Charles IV, the last Capetian king. One of his earliest acts was again to expel all Jews from France—five years before the end of the period guaranteed to them by Louis X. His reasons were, as always, pragmatic: the few Jews who remained were surely so battered and impoverished that it was most expedient to appropriate their debts and some property and to send them on their way, useless relics of a bygone era. "After 1322," says Jordan, "there were virtually no Jews in France."[42]

"The Expected Good Treatment": Germany

In 1241 the Jewish community of Frankfurt numbered about two hundred. When a young Jewish man in Frankfurt decided that year to accept baptism, his parents and friends tried to persuade him not to take the irrevocable step. Arguments between Christians and Jews led to physical violence that caused at least several Christian casualties. The result was a full-scale riot in which possibly as many as 180 Jews were killed, some directly, others in fires that they themselves started in their homes. The fires eventually destroyed about half of the town, and of course the Jews were blamed. The few surviving Jews, obviously terrified, followed their rabbi in accepting conversion. No one was punished for the massacre. Five years later Conrad IV (king while his father was still emperor) issued a special order pardoning the burghers of Frankfurt, "in consideration of their loyalty and service," for all injuries and damages that they had inflicted on the king's Jews, more by "neglect and accident" than by intention.[43]

This sequence of events was typical of what Jews could expect in thirteenth-century Germany. Episodes similar to that in Frankfurt were common throughout the century, and it was evident that Jews could no longer count on royalty for even basic protection. After the death of Frederick II in 1250, Germany entered a period of dissolution and decentralization from which it would not fully recover for many centuries. Although some German kings thereafter received the title of emperor, no one again ruled with imperial authority, and most of Frederick's successors were barely able to maintain the fiction that they ruled supreme as kings of Germany. For the political reality was that both local lords and townspeople were vying with kings and one another for control over their own territories. The lords—dukes, counts, and even lesser figures—ruled independently over their own territories, nominally owing loyalty to the king but actually granting that only in return for freedom to rule as they pleased. They themselves had to recognize the authority of local bishops, but both were being challenged by the emerging class of prosperous burghers, who were now insisting on the right to control their own towns—which meant, first and foremost, to levy taxes and to spend the income as they saw fit.

The effect of all this upheaval on Jewish life can be readily imagined. While kings continued to insist that Jews were their personal property, both barons and town officials maneuvered to direct Jewish taxes into their own treasuries. On a number of occasions, kings willingly relinquished their rights over Jews in order to maintain favorable relationships with regional barons. Thus, with no one exercising undisputed authority, Jews found themselves in a precarious position, uncertain of their status and with even less security than before against exploitation and violence.

Everyone fought over Jews because the stakes were high: while providing an indispensable service, they were also a dependable source of income from taxation. In Regensburg, the dukes of Bavaria and the town bishops struggled with one another, with the emperor, and with the municipal councilors for rights to tax Jews, and agreements among these parties sometimes involved substantial sums of money. Raphael Straus, a chronicler of Regensburg Jewish history, remarks that "questions relating to Jewish revenues together with those regarding jurisdiction over the Jews served repeatedly as grounds for political conflicts and reconciliations." Obviously, to be worth so much attention, the Jews must have been engaged in major transactions. Straus characterizes Jewish business activities in Regensburg in the late thirteenth and early fourteenth centuries as "along banking lines of extended scope," and he provides details of a number of major transactions involving loans granted by Jews to barons, archbishops, and convents, as well as prominent townspeople.[44]

At their most fortunate, Jews were able to negotiate the kind of charter that had always provided their most dependable protection. In 1252, for example, the archbishop of Cologne granted rights to the Jews of the city in a way that acknowledged their value and guaranteed them protection. In return for the usual payment, he promised never to oppress Jews personally or to permit oppression by others. His language is reminiscent of that of the bishop of Speyer some 170 years earlier. Nonetheless, there is a detectable shift in the direction of more emphasis on control and protection:

> We believe that it will contribute much to Our welfare and Our honor if the Jews, who confide in Us and submit themselves to Our dominion in the hope of Our protection and Our grace, should receive from Us the expected good treatment. . . . In order that the Jews who already reside in the city the more willingly remain with Us and that foreign Jews be induced to settle here by the example of the good treatment of those residents, We order Our faithful officials . . . that

you grant the Jews protection, aid, and help to the extent of your ability and not tolerate that they be injured or offended by anyone.[45]

Aside from several categories of major crime—theft, counterfeiting, violent assault, and adultery involving Jewish or Christian women— Jewish courts in Cologne were granted authority over Jewish communal affairs. Although the city council contested his rights over Jews, the archbishop succeeded in maintaining his position of authority and renewed the charter several times. But by 1271 the townspeople had gained independence from clerical control and were taxing the Jews themselves.[46]

An especially revealing document is a 1265 "peace treaty," issued by the archbishop of Mainz, several counts, and the town authorities of Frankfurt and three lesser towns, ensuring fair treatment to everyone in their jurisdictions—"even to the Jews," for whom explicit protection was guaranteed:

> Since some lawless persons in the cities, defying God's will, in the memory of whose passion His sacred Church maintains the Jews, nor even deferring to the Empire to whose Chamber the Jews are known to belong, frequently are prone to riot against them and to insult them, sometimes even inhumanely and miserably to murder them, it is decreed that whosoever will be guilty of such riot and insult against them be punished as the public breaker of the peace.[47]

The period between 1250 and 1273, known as the "Interregnum" because no one ruled with general consent, was a time of particular instability, but even after that, the men who sat on the German throne did so with little of the power and authority of their predecessors. Rudolph I, emperor from 1273 to 1291, tried to maintain the fiction that he owned the Jews of the realm along with everything else, though relatively few were under his actual control.[48] Those he did "own" were treated much like those under the control of French kings—that is, as transferrable property. For example, in 1279–80 he mortgaged Jews of the dioceses of Basel and Strasbourg to the bishop of Basel as a reward for services rendered. Similarly, in 1298 his successor, Adolph I, mortgaged to the municipal authorities of Speyer all imperial revenue from the Jews of that town.[49]

In 1284, Rudolph levied an exceptionally heavy tax on all Jewish communities under his jurisdiction, so burdensome that many Jews fled the country. Rudolph, still insisting on the absolute ownership that had been the emperor's traditional prerogative, declared that since the Jews had acted illegally by fleeing, their entire remaining property was forfeited to the imperial treasury:

> Since the Jews, collectively and individually, in their capacity as servants of Our court, specifically belong to Us with their persons and all their property, just as some belong to princes to whom they have been transferred as a feudal benefice by Us and the Empire, it is right and proper . . . that if any such Jews become fugitives . . . and thus alienate themselves from their true lord, that We as the lord to whom they belong may freely enter into all their possessions . . . wherever they may be found and not undeservedly take them under Our control.[50]

By 1286 so many Jews had departed that Rudolph took vindictive action: he ordered the arrest of Meir of Rothenburg, the most distinguished German rabbi of the century and the acknowledged leader of German Jewry. Meir was destined to spend the remainder of his life in prison, victim of Rudolph's intransigence on the question of his rights over Jews. The Jewish communities rallied quickly and offered a large sum of money for Meir's release, but Rudolph insisted that the money was payment of the tax levy, nothing more, and demanded still more money as ransom for the rabbi. Apparently the demand exceeded the Jews' capacity to pay, for Meir remained a prisoner. Even the pope, Nicholas IV, responding to an appeal from a German Jewish delegation after Meir had already been held prisoner for several years, urged Rudolph to grant clemency ("because there should be no punishment where there was no crime") but to no avail. Meir appears to have been treated with some consideration—he was permitted regular visits from his students and followers—but his imprisonment was clearly perceived as an outrage, confirming for German Jews that their situation had deteriorated severely. Meir died a prisoner in 1293, and it was not until years later that a wealthy German Jew was able to secure release of the body for proper burial in a Jewish cemetery.[51]

Absence of dependable protection at the political summit also meant that local populations could assault Jews with relative impunity. Observing that the situation was much worse here than anywhere else, Salo Baron characterizes Germany as "the scene of the most extensive slaughter of Jews and the wholesale destruction of communities, far exceeding in both frequency and geographic extension anything that happened in neighboring lands." But there was nothing comparable to the overwhelming taxation and sudden mass expulsions promulgated by French kings: "the Empire was too diverse and decentralized a structure to allow for any simultaneity of anti-Jewish action extending beyond certain regions."[52] Even so, the average Jewish community knew that at any time it might be subjected to vicious persecution based on fabricated charges of ritual murder or Host desecration. The latter charge was particularly frequent by the end of the century and, of course, impossible to refute.

As an example of what could and did happen, in 1285 the Jews of Munich were accused of ritually murdering a Christian child. When they took refuge in the synagogue, the mob set it on fire, killing dozens of people. Reports on casualties differ, but the total number of deaths in the riot may have reached 180.

By this time the tradition of accepting martyrdom was well established, and Jews sometimes killed one another, then committed suicide, rather than be faced with the choice of conversion or death at the hands of the mob. Ten or twelve Jews died in a riot in Koblenz in 1265. Afterward, Meir of Rothenburg received a letter from a man who said that he had killed his wife and four sons at their request, but was rescued by friendly Gentiles before he could kill himself. He asked whether he should do penance for his sin. Meir replied that one "is indeed permitted to take his own life for the sanctification of God's name; but whether one is permitted to take the lives of others, even for a deeply pious reason, is questionable." Nevertheless, he concluded, since many of his predecessors had "martyrized" their own sons and daughters, he feared that to order penance would be to insult their memories.[53]

The century, among the most miserable in Jewish history, ended catastrophically. Early in 1298, the Jews of Roettingen, a small town near Würzburg in Franconia, were accused of Host desecration. A minor nobleman named Rindfleisch (Beef), probably deeply in debt to Jews, declared that he had received a message from heaven instructing him to punish the Jews for their crime. He soon assembled an army of the usual sort, which proceeded to attack the Jews of Roettingen, then others in Rothenburg, Würzburg, Nuremberg, and numerous other towns in southern Germany—according to the best estimate, 146 in all. The casualties were disastrous: about nine hundred dead in Würzburg, where the Jewish community was completely destroyed; more than seven hundred in Nuremberg. The total number of deaths may have reached twenty thousand. Of the major Jewish communities in Franconia, Bavaria, and neighboring parts of Austria, only those of Regensburg and Augsburg escaped harm, thanks entirely to firm protection by local burghers. Rindfleisch was probably able to continue his course as long as he did because the political situation was in even more disarray than usual: Albert I, son of Rudolph, was at that time at war with the reigning king, Adolph, whom he defeated and succeeded. Albert later imposed heavy fines on Würzburg, Nuremberg, and other towns because they had done nothing to protect Jews and had even appropriated the possessions of the victims. There is apparently no record that Rindfleisch himself was ever punished.[54]

During the first half of the fourteenth century, German Jews were still being made to feel reasonably welcome by town authorities who found them economically useful. Nonetheless, it was evident that they could look forward only to persistent exploitation and oppression. Henry VII (1308–13) and Louis III (1314–47), following their predecessors in viewing Jews strictly as sources of revenue, were too weak or indifferent to provide anything more than nominal protection. Henry regularly used Jews as pawns in his efforts to please or reward powerful barons and clergymen, granting rights to taxation or canceling debts as he saw fit. Louis, chronically in need of money for military campaigns, decreed in 1342 that every Jewish male or widow aged twelve or over was to pay an annual tax, in return for which he rather gratuitously promised better protection than he had provided until then.

This must have been small comfort indeed to the Jews, who had just experienced a wave of massacres that, lasting from 1336 to 1339, had once again decimated their communities. The perpetrators this time were bands of peasants calling themselves Armleder, because they wore leather armbands, supposedly to distinguish themselves from knights who wore armor. Led, like the Pastoureaux, by men who claimed to have received divine messages, they swarmed throughout Franconia, Alsace, Swabia, and Bavaria, attacking about 120 Jewish communities and murdering thousands of people. Some townspeople, notably those of Würzburg and once again Regensburg, successfully resisted the marauders and protected their Jewish residents, but in many other towns the local response was precisely the opposite. By 1338 some of the Alsatian towns that had done nothing to protect their Jews now had second thoughts when it became apparent that the Armleder were not above attacking Christians as well. The towns formed defensive alliances with local lords and the bishop of Strasbourg to ward off further assaults—but of course by then the damage to Jews had been done.

The situation at Colmar, a prominent town in Alsace, demonstrates how little power the emperor possessed to overcome the marauders. When the townspeople refused to surrender their Jewish inhabitants, the Armleder placed the town under siege. Louis sent troops, who drove the attackers away; he then ceded "his" Jews to the town for a substantial payment, and departed the scene—whereupon the Armleder returned and resumed their harassment in the region. The leader of the Armleder also escaped punishment; by 1339 sufficient resistance had developed that he was ready to agree to an armistice guaranteeing him amnesty in exchange for peace. For the Jews that came much too late.[55]

Troubled Hearts:
Popes and Jews in the Thirteenth Century

Although popes urged that Christians be protected against pernicious Jewish influence, they always insisted that Jews not be subjected to physical mistreatment. This long-established principle, formally expressed in *Sicut Judaeis*, the twelfth-century papal bull discussed earlier, had been routinely reaffirmed by each pope thereafter. Also known as the Constitution of the Jews, the bull granted broad protection against physical violence, forcible conversion, disruption of religious ceremonies, and desecration of cemeteries.[56] But by the beginning of the thirteenth century, the provision against forcible conversion had in effect been reversed. The groundwork for this change had long since been laid, only about twenty years after the appearance of *Sicut Judaeis*, by a statement in the *Decretum*, an authoritative codification of Church policy, completed around 1142 by a monk named Gratian. Citing a much earlier ruling that "just as Jews are not to be forced into the faith, so too, once converted, they are not permitted to leave it," Gratian proceeded to draw broad, and ominous, conclusions:

> Thus, in order that they be converted by the free exercise of will and not by force, they are to be persuaded but not impelled. However, as for those who have already been forced into Christianity . . . , since it is manifest that they have linked themselves with the divine sacraments, and have accepted the grace of baptism, and have been anointed with the oil, and have been participants in the body of the Lord, it is necessary that they be forced to uphold the faith which they accepted under duress or by necessity, lest the name of the Lord be brought into disrepute, and the faith which they accepted be held vile and contemptible.[57]

The argument, as it was to evolve on the basis of this statement, ran as follows: Regardless of why a person accepted baptism, once he or she had done so, the sacred rite could not be negated; to do so would be an insult to Christ and to Christianity. Anyone who genuinely resisted baptism—that is, anyone who protested loudly and explicitly during the ceremony (not afterward)—could legitimately claim that there had been excessive coercion; but no one else could, not even someone who had accepted baptism only to escape being murdered on the spot. Since under these conditions there were no living protesters, all Jews who had been forcibly converted were deemed Christians, hence subject to prosecution as heretics if they tried to live as Jews.

It remained only for a pope to act on Gratian's statement, and this Innocent III did in a ruling issued in 1201—even though he himself had issued the traditional repetition of *Sicut Judaeis* only two years earlier. The archbishop of Arles, probably recognizing the conflict between Gratian's statement and the protection afforded by *Sicut Judaeis*, asked the pope whether forcible baptism was legitimate and binding. Innocent replied that it was, since only those who objected vigorously and audibly could claim that they had offered genuine resistance. Those who consented "in the slightest degree" had in effect consented. As Grayzel comments, not only did Innocent's ruling negate *Sicut Judaeis*, "it all but made rioting a holy endeavor."[58]

Even individuals who assisted or harbored heretical converts were liable to prosecution as "patrons" (*fautores*), or "protectors," which meant that unconverted Jews were also in danger. Local barons often confiscated the debt records and other property of converts, and sometimes turned these over to the converts' relatives, so that they might continue to prosper and pay taxes. The barons were not inclined to object to inquisitorial actions against converts (whose property was no longer in question), but they did object when other Jews fell into the net on charges of aiding and abetting converts seeking to reenter the Jewish fold. Hence, the matter was not without political significance for relations between secular authorities and clergy at every level, and inquisitors were bound to come into conflict at times with local barons who did not want to see their Jews being molested.[59]

The situation climaxed in 1267, when Pope Clement IV addressed to the Dominican and Franciscan friars a bull known as *Turbato corde*, "With troubled heart," stating unambiguously the new papal position: Christians who had "defected" to Judaism (that is, converts who reasserted Jewish identity) were to be punished as heretics.

> With troubled heart we have heard and relate that many reprobate Christians have abandoned the true Christian faith and have damnably transferred themselves to the rites of the Jews. This is recognized to be especially reprehensible because the most holy name of Christ can be carelessly blasphemed by enemies from within his own family. . . . We command your organization . . . to inquire diligently and truthfully into the matter regarding Christians as well as Jews. Against guilty Christians you shall proceed as you do against heretics. Jews who are guilty of having induced Christians of either sex

to participate in their execrable rites, or who do so in the future, shall be properly punished. All who oppose you shall be silenced by ecclesiastical censure, with secular assistance if necessary.[60]

That the matter continued to trouble papal hearts is evidenced by revised versions of *Turbato corde* issued by Clement's successors. In 1274, Pope Gregory X issued the bull with an additional warning: Not only were converts sliding away from "the light of Christian faith," but even some Christians by birth had "wickedly transferred themselves to the rites of Judaism." Of course, Gregory wanted both kinds of heretics, along with those who seduced or encouraged them to adopt such an "execrable rite," to be prosecuted vigorously.[61]

The uneven struggle never ended. Gregory's successors reissued the bull several more times during the remainder of the century. That they felt compelled to do so says a great deal about what had long since become a definitive characteristic of medieval European Jews: in the view of their Christian antagonists, their wicked stubbornness; in their own view, their unyielding faith.

Desecration of the Host

The Lateran Council of 1215, which we have already encountered as the originator of the Jewish badge, addressed itself to another question that might at first have seemed irrelevant to Jewish concerns. The Council formally announced the doctrine of transubstantiation, meaning that during the celebration of that part of the mass called the Eucharist, the "substances" of consecrated bread and wine are miraculously transformed into the "substance" (or the "true presence") of Jesus Christ, even though the bread and wine retain their ordinary form and taste. The bread, in the form of small wafers (called the "Host," and unleavened in recollection of the Last Supper) is eaten as communion by each member of the congregation; the wine is usually drunk only by the officiating priest. Ordinary people had understandable difficulties with the theological subtleties and were probably inclined to believe simply that the wafers and wine became the body and blood of Christ. The "mystery" was a subject of great interest to many people, clerical and lay, who apparently were both entranced and puzzled by the thought of Christ being literally present and literally consumed. If the Host was indeed the body of Jesus, could it bleed as he did? An occasional Christian was charged with stealing a consecrated wafer, perhaps for magical purposes or perhaps to test for himself the reality of the transformation. In 1264 a priest reported that on pilgrimage to Rome he had witnessed a bleeding Host. The testimony was accepted by the pope, Urban IV, who proclaimed that thenceforth there would be a feast day each year—*Corpus Christi*, "body of Christ"—consecrated to celebration of the miracle of transubstantiation. The faithful might go on wondering how the miraculous transformation took place, but there could be no further questions about its absolute reality.

Having for two centuries been faced with accusations of ritual crucifixion and blood consumption, Jews now found themselves confronting an even more fantastic, and wholly irrefutable, charge: that they were stealing consecrated wafers and stabbing them to cause suffering and bleeding. By charging Jews with "desecration of the Host," Christians thus not only invented a new and dependably inflammatory justification for murder and robbery, but also provided themselves with satisfying proof of the truth of transubstantiation, hence of the validity of the weekly communion ritual that contributed so much to their prospects for salvation.[62]

Like charges of ritual cannibalism (blood consumption), charges of Host desecration erupted most often in Germany and its immediate vicinity, occasionally in northern France, much less in the Mediterranean region.[63] One of the most spectacular and best-recorded episodes occurred in Paris, in 1290. A rumor arose that a Parisian Jew had acquired a consecrated wafer, either by purchase or by canceling a debt, in order to test its supposed qualities as divine substance. He stabbed it, then threw it into boiling water (some said also into icy cold water), whereupon, so the story went, the water turned red with blood. According to one version, the stabbed wafer divided into three parts, symbolic of the Trinity, and a part thrown into boiling water turned to flesh and blood. Some said that a Jewish family had witnessed the miracle and (understandably) converted at once to Christianity.

The Parisian story was widely circulated and everywhere accepted. In 1295, Pope Boniface VIII addressed a letter to the bishop of

Paris favoring the petition of a Parisian man who proposed to erect a chapel on the site where the desecration was said to have occurred. The chapel was dedicated in a public procession in which the wafer (mysteriously preserved) was carried through the streets. It soon became such a popular pilgrimage site that the wafer had to be moved to a larger church to accommodate the crowds. The entire episode was remembered for centuries and was still being commemorated a hundred years ago. It is important to note, however, that despite all the publicity and excitement, no one rioted or attacked Jews; none of the numerous chronicle accounts speaks of violence.[64]

But that was not the case elsewhere. From 1290 on, charges of Host desecration were leveled frequently, particularly in German territories, and often these were followed by riots in which many Jews died. Accusations of this kind, along with charges that Jews practiced sorcery and dealt in poisons, set the stage for the concluding phase of medieval Jewish history: the massacres and expulsions associated with the plague known as the Black Death.

"A Powder in a Thin Sewn Leather Bag": The Black Death Massacres

In the latter months of 1346, word began to spread in European port towns that a severe plague had struck the Orient and people were dying in droves. By 1347 what had begun as rumor was coming home to those same towns as dreadful reality. In October of that year, a fleet of Genoese ships, on their way home from the Crimea, sailed into the Sicilian harbor of Messina, their entire crews dead or dying of plague. Soon ships of this kind, carrying the infected rats and fleas that transmitted the disease, docked at ports throughout the Mediterranean. Within weeks the entire region was afflicted with what came to be called the Black Death, and unprecedented numbers of people were dying in agony everywhere. The disease, now spreading like wildfire, soon reached Germany and made its way steadily northward, extending throughout virtually all of Europe. By late 1350, when it had nearly run its course, some twenty-five million people—about one European in three—had died: a demographic and social disaster of unparalleled scope.

The most learned physicians and intellectuals of the time were inclined to explain the disaster in terms of astrological theories about contamination of the air. A few recognized contagion as the problem and urged better sanitation practices. Many of these people also believed, however, that poisons, perhaps intentionally deposited in wells, could produce or propagate plague—presumably if astrological conditions had already set the stage.[65]

Such were the attempts of the learned to explain what was to remain inexplicable for many centuries thereafter. But to the great majority of people the matter was all too clear: outcasts of some sort were spreading poison about. "Everywhere," says one historian, "the blame was placed on those residents of the city who were not of the majority group."[66] Among those who were accused were lepers, cripples, gravediggers, itinerant monks, or members of whatever ethnic group happened to be present in small numbers. But overwhelmingly, and more exclusively as time went on, blame fell on the Jews. In May 1348 the Jews in a number of towns in Provence, most notably Narbonne and Carcassonne, were slaughtered; and from then on, accusations and murderous assaults erupted everywhere. In September ten Jews were arrested at Chillon, on Lake Geneva, and tortured until they confessed to participation in a conspiracy to destroy Christendom. The text of one confession, that of a surgeon named Balavignus, was copied and widely distributed to such nearby towns as Basel, Berne, and Strasbourg. It affords a glimpse into the atmosphere of ignorance, fear, and hatred with which fourteenth-century Jews had to contend.

> Balavignus the Jew . . . was only placed on the rack for a short time, and when he had been taken off he confessed after some considerable time that about six weeks ago Master Jacob, who since Easter had been staying at Chambéry, in accordance with orders, and who had come from Toledo, sent him to Thonon by a Jew boy poison in an eggshell; this was a powder in a thin sewn leather bag, together with a letter, in which he was ordered on pain of ban and in obedience to their law to put this same poison into the larger and smaller wells of his town, as much as was required to poison the people who fetched their water from there, and that he should reveal this to no one on

pain of the above punishment. Further, in the same letter he was instructed to forward the same order to several other places by command of the Jewish Rabbis or masters of their law; and he confessed
that he had secretly placed the quantity of poison or powder indicated in a well on the lake shore near Thonon one evening beneath a
stone. He confessed further that the above-mentioned boy had
brought him more letters dealing with the same matter which were
addressed to many other Jews. . . . Further, he confessed that when he
had placed the poison mentioned in the well at Thonon, he expressly
forbade his wife and children to make further use of the well, but
refused to tell them the reason. He swore by his law and by all contained in the Pentateuch, in the presence of several reliable witnesses,
that all he had confessed was entirely true.

The confession continues with comments suggesting that some ob-
servers came close to understanding that the essential problem was
contagion.

Balavignus alleged, further, that as a surgeon he knew that if anyone
was affected by this poison and anyone touched him in this condition,
when overcome by weakness, he was sweating, that by this contact
he might easily be infected, as also by the breath of anyone infected;
and of this he was convinced, as he had heard it from experienced
medical men, and he was further convinced that the Jews could not
deny these charges, as they were fully conscious that they were guilty
of the actions with which they were charged. The said Balavignus
was taken across the lake . . . to verify and point out the well into
which, as he alleged, he had placed the poison. When he arrived he
was made to get out of the boat, and when he saw the place and the
well where he had deposited the poison he said: "That is the well in
which I put the poison." This well was examined in his presence, and
the linen bag in which the poison was wrapped was found in the
mouth of the well by a public notary. . . . He then admitted and confessed that this was the linen cloth in which the poison had been, and
that he had placed it in the open well, and that it was parti-colored,
black and red. This linen cloth was taken away and is preserved as
evidence.[67]

Thereafter, one after another, townspeople throughout the entire Rhineland attacked their Jewish populations mercilessly. In Basel, as in many other towns, the local authorities tried to discourage riots, but they were overridden by merchants and artisans who wanted Jews out of the way and were more than ready to capitalize on plague hysteria. Some six hundred individuals, the entire adult Jewish population, were herded onto an island in the Rhine and forced into a shack, which was then torched. Surviving children were converted. The town council then issued a decree declaring that no Jews were to be allowed entry for at least two hundred years.

Much the same pattern was followed at such localities as Freiburg, Stuttgart, and Speyer. In Strasbourg, home to one of the largest Jewish communities of the time, at least two thousand people, possibly many more, were murdered by a mob aroused to fury by a particularly vindictive bishop. Hauled off to the Jewish burial ground to be burned, the victims were assaulted on the way by townspeople who tore the clothing from their backs and ripped it to pieces searching for concealed coins or gems. The occasional Jew who accepted instant conversion was spared, as were a few young women, but those were the limits of mercy. Jews who escaped the flames were chased down and murdered on the spot. Afterward, the town council ordered cancellation of all debts owing to the victims and distributed what remained of their property among the local citizenry. Bricks from destroyed Jewish homes, and even Jewish gravestones, were used for church construction and repairs.[68]

Many of the very same people who scapegoated Jews believed that the plague was divine punishment visited upon a sinful world. In the latter months of 1348, processions of penitents, sometimes numbering in the hundreds, began to assemble in Germany, making their way from town to town, acquiring new members as they traveled. In the grip of millenarian fantasies, they posed as world redeemers and called themselves "Bearers of the Cross" or "Brotherhood of the Flagellants"—the latter because of their remarkable practice of collectively scourging themselves with leather thongs tipped with sharp metal spikes. Performances were conducted in town squares, where fascinated crowds watched as the Flagellants rhythmically whipped themselves until the blood ran, meanwhile singing hymns to Christ and the Virgin Mary.[69]

If the Jews of a town had not yet been attacked, the appearance of the Flagellants was almost certain to spell trouble. In July 1349, for example, when a procession of penitents reached Frankfurt, "they rushed directly to the Jewish quarter and led the local population in wholesale slaughter."[70] In August they were in Mainz, again instigating attacks on Jews. This time the Jews, in actions of resistance recalling events during the First Crusade, not only set fire to their own homes but also fought back, with bloody but, as always, uneven consequences. About two hundred Christians died in the counterattack, but so did thousands of Jews; some accounts place the number as high as twelve thousand, but three is a more likely estimate. The community barely recovered thereafter and never again achieved its status as a major center of Jewish life and culture.

Similar fates befell other Jewish communities: Worms, Cologne, and many other settlements, large and small, throughout Germany. In all, more than three hundred communities were destroyed and countless thousands killed. A contemporary Hebrew account, reading much like the chronicles of crusade massacres, portrays the Jews of one German town, Nordhausen, going to their deaths as true martyrs:

> [T]hey joyfully arrayed themselves in their prayer shawls and shrouds, both men and women. . . . They took each other by the hand, both men and women, and danced and leapt with their whole strength before God. . . . Singing and dancing they entered the grave, and when all had entered, R. Meir jumped out and walked around to make certain that none had stayed outside. When the burghers saw him they asked him to save his life [by apostasy]. He answered: "This now is the end of our troubles, you see me only for a while, and then I shall be no more." He returned to the grave; they set fire to the scaffolding; they died all of them together and not a cry was heard.[71]

The account is almost certainly imaginative, a continuation of the tradition of exemplary martyrology, but surely the massacre it portrays was real enough.

Despite persistent speculation that Jews suffered less than average from the plague, it is likely that they were afflicted as much as anyone else. Some of the more objective contemporary reports note that Jews were also perishing in large numbers from the disease they were accused of causing. The net result was that, while the Black Death was disastrous for all of Europe, for the Jews it was catastrophic to a point beyond recovery.

A few communities, though not many, behaved rationally. Several, notably Vienna, Schaffhausen (now in northern Switzerland), and the often dependable Regensburg, defended their Jews successfully, no doubt because the town authorities were forceful enough to protect valuable human resources. Pope Clement VI also spoke out, maintaining the traditional papal position that Jews must not be physically abused. In September 1348 he issued a statement remarkable for its humanity and good sense:

> [C]ertain Christians, seduced by that liar the devil, are imputing to poisonings by Jews the pestilence with which God is afflicting the Christian people. . . . These same Jews are prepared to submit to judgment before a competent judge on the false allegation of this sort of crime, but the violence of those Christians has not grown cool on this account; rather, their fury rages all the more against them; where they offer no resistance, their aberration is taken to be proved!
>
> Now, if the Jews were guilty . . . We would wish them struck by a penalty of suitable severity. . . . Still, since this pestilence, all but universal everywhere, by a mysterious judgment of God has afflicted, and does now afflict, throughout the diverse regions of the earth, both Jews and many other nations to whom life in common with Jews is unknown, that the Jews have provided the occasion or the cause for such a crime has no plausibility.[72]

The same argument was concretely supported by a prominent clergyman and writer on scientific matters, Konrad of Megenberg: "But I know that there were more Jews in Vienna than in any other German city familiar to me, and so many of them died of the plague that they were obliged to enlarge their cemetery."[73] But, of course, such appeals to reason did nothing whatever to prevent frenzied mobs from attacking and murdering Jews.

To the extent that we can or need to explain these events—events that in effect signaled the end of medieval European Jewish history—

we face questions very like those associated with the massacres of the late eleventh century. One historian has argued that envy of Jewish wealth and indebtedness to Jews, "rather than matters of faith and religion," were the real motivating force behind the massacres. He perceives in these events "an atmosphere of cold calculation, without the religious fervor and zeal for the faith" associated with the First Crusade, and cites a contemporary Christian chronicler who commented, "Had the Jews been poor they would not have been burned."[74] There is something to be said for this argument, but it hardly explains everything. The viciousness and vindictiveness of the attacks, the bizarre behavior of the flagellants, the mob psychology that prevailed at such scenes as the Strasbourg or Mainz massacres: these do not seem to have been products of "cold calculation." Likewise, the fact that a few converts—admittedly only a few—were spared suggests that, even in conditions of extreme fear and panic, at least some Christians were still prepared to accept Jews who agreed to abandon their identities as people apart, even while all other Jews were anathema. The weight of evidence seems to argue that although oppression of Jews was intimately linked to their role in the economy, it did not stem from economic foundations alone.[75]

Terminal Years

Not much needs to be said about the period between about 1350 and 1500, for these were terminal years for western European Jewry, years characterized for the most part by steady decline in population and very difficult social circumstances. As we have seen, Jews were already gone from most of France by the early fourteenth century. A few communities of significant size remained in Provence and in the eastern border regions, but the great centers of Jewish life in northern France were now gone. In 1337, France began the prolonged struggle with England that came to be known as the Hundred Years' War, and in 1356 the French king, John II, was captured by the English at the Battle of Poitiers and held for an immense ransom. Not coincidentally, in 1359 a small group of Jews from the eastern border (Franche-Comté) were granted provisional entry into the royal domain, and one year later their financial resources contributed to John's ransom. The immigrants were guaranteed residence for twenty years, later extended to 1401 had the contract been honored. They were maintained in very small settlements within the main towns, segregated and protected, participants in daily life only as moneylenders: "pure outsiders" in every sense.[76] Lacking the customary security and sanctions of firmly established communities, these settlers squabbled with one another and did little to encourage the government to retain them. Moreover, they had been granted permission to charge interest rates exceeding 86 percent; and although they may well have needed to collect such extraordinary amounts to satisfy the demands of their protectors, the inevitable result was widespread bitterness and hostility toward them.

By 1365, John's son, Charles V, was already being pressured to expel the Jews; though he went so far as to sign a decree of expulsion, it was never put into effect. Charles's death in 1380 was the occasion for popular uprisings in Paris and elsewhere, originating in resentment at the economic hardships caused by the continuing war. In riots that year and again in 1382, Jewish moneylenders were among the prime targets—once again victims of murder, robbery, and forced conversions.

By this time many Jews were so overtaxed and harassed that they were reduced to beggary and crime, which of course made their situation even more precarious. Aggravating the problem were Sephardic refugees from Spanish persecution who were making their way into France and adding to what was becoming a Jewish underworld. The inevitable climax came in 1394, when Charles VI issued a final decree of expulsion. This left Jews remaining only in peripheral lands not under direct royal control: in the south, parts of Provence, and in the east, parts of Lorraine and Franche-Comté. Some Jews, by this time probably out of touch with the communal bonds that preserved a firm sense of identity, chose to convert rather than try to begin anew in strange lands. But most of the refugees moved eastward, toward Franche-Comté, Savoy, or Swiss territories. As they traveled, some were attacked by bands of Christians eager to pillage them.[77]

The Jews of Provence, throughout the medieval period almost always better situated than their brethren to the north, fared uncommonly well for much of the fifteenth century. In 1423 the reigning queen, Yolanda, issued a statute granting Jews basic freedoms and protection, and this was confirmed by her successor, King René. A cultured and urbane man, René treated Jews with benevolence remarkable for the time, and during his long reign (1434–80) Jewish life flowered for one last time. But after his death most of Provence was ceded to the French crown; and without the protection to which they had become accustomed, the Jews found themselves subjected to the usual forms of persecution, everything from hostile sermons to violent assaults. In 1493 they were expelled from Arles, then in 1500 from all of Provence, except for papal territories in and near Avignon. Thus ended the history of one of the most prosperous and culturally distinguished Jewish communities in medieval Europe.

In Germany, following the devastation associated with the Black Death, some Jewish communities were partly reconstituted but existed only precariously: never with anything better than provisional charters granting a measure of tolerance in return for large payments on entry and regular financial services. They were there because many people still found them useful, for Jews could still be induced to lend money on better terms than the average Christian usurer, and with less power to force repayment. But invariably they were made to understand that they were present on sufferance: that they belonged to the town authorities who granted them admittance, and that they could expect to remain only if money continued to flow in the right direction. In 1352 the Speyer town council issued a statement declaring that the emperor had granted the town complete ownership of the Jews whom they had just agreed to readmit—Jews who "shall belong to us and to our city, and shall be ours in respect of body and property."[78] This was 268 years after the bishop of Speyer had declared that he was inviting Jews into his town to "add greatly to its honor." As for the Jewish self-image at this time, one might consider a petition submitted to the town authorities of Strasbourg in 1369: "To the honorable Burgomaster and Council of Strasbourg we, poor Jews, offer our services. We herewith request you that you may graciously allow us to live with you, as our forefathers had lived with your forefathers . . . in consideration of the great sufferings and tragedy we have sustained without guilt."[79] Eventually, when the town's merchant and artisan guilds had agreed, six families were granted residence for five years.

Interestingly, there is evidence that at least a few Jews were now exploring sources of income other than moneylending. As the larger urban centers became increasingly dependent on rural supplies for food, some Jews found places for themselves as middlemen, purchasing food from agricultural estates for sale in urban markets. Others, facing, as it were, in the opposite direction, peddled manufactured goods in rural areas. Some of these people lived in rural areas, either in villages or on estates. A few Jews took up handicrafts, probably mostly associated with clothing manufacture. These were the beginnings of residential and occupational patterns that would become more characteristic of Jewish life in later centuries, particularly in Eastern Europe.[80]

The newly established Jewish communities were destined to survive for no more than a few generations. By the first half of the fifteenth century, expulsions had become the pattern everywhere in Germany. Sometimes these were brought about simply by nonrenewal of temporary charters, but in other cases it was the customary libels that led first to massacre, then to expulsion. In 1421 a charge of Host desecration in Vienna led to the burning of more than two hundred Jewish women and men. Their children were converted and sent off to be raised in monasteries and convents. The remaining Jews of Vienna and of all Austria were then banished "forever."[81] From then on, there were expulsions everywhere: in 1424, from Cologne; in 1435, from Speyer; in 1438, from Mainz; and so on, until the German lands were virtually emptied of Jews. Small pockets of Jewish population lingered on here and there; and an occasional community readmitted Jews yet again, only again to expel them. In Mainz they were readmitted, expelled again in 1462, readmitted still again, expelled finally in 1471.[82]

By 1450 the medieval phase of Jewish history in Germany and France had effectually ended. There was now under way an eastward migration that over the next hundred years or so would shift the center of Ashkenazic Jewish life to Poland and Lithuania. By 1500 there were probably between fifteen and twenty-five thousand Jews in Poland; by 1600 the number had reached eighty to one hundred thousand.[83]

By 1570 Jews were again being readmitted to Western European cities, this time with generally better guarantees, and the next phase of the region's Jewish history had already begun.[84] But that is another story.

Looking Backward

The singular nature of Jewish experience in late medieval Europe comes down to the fact that their relationships with everyone—kings, barons, clergy, townspeople, peasants—were defined almost entirely in financial terms. Jews were neither neighbors nor countrymen; they were sources of income. People at the top of the social hierarchy squabbled over rights to tax Jews and to borrow from them at favorable rates; and having borrowed, they often sought ways to avoid not only payment of interest but repayment of principal. Those in the middle—merchants especially—were generally inclined to look upon Jews as despised competition, although they were not usually the ringleaders in riots and at times even went out of their way to assist potential victims. Those on the bottom—workers, peasants—encountered Jews primarily as lenders of desperately needed money at high rates of interest. And of course all these people, instructed and encouraged by the clergy, knew that Jews were the descendants of those who had rejected and villified the Lord, then demanded his execution on the cross.

The Jews had no overall strategy for confronting this situation, if indeed there could have been one; all they had were tactics for surviving individual confrontations, threats, and assaults. That they were eventually expelled from most of Western Europe is less remarkable than that they survived as long as they did. The reason for their survival, of course, was that they were useful—often all but indispensable—as sources of liquid capital. But once that usefulness declined, they were doomed. The antagonism rooted not only in traditional religious hatred but also in resentment of the very fact that they were useful led to dizzying oscillations in official policy toward them. For while everyone wanted Jewish money, proper Christian conduct required that Jews themselves be despised and ostracized. This pathological situation reached its inevitable conclusion when it became evident that Jews could no longer keep up with the financial demands to which they were relentlessly subjected. When that time came, they were maligned, persecuted, and ultimately expelled.

NOTES

WORKS CITED

INDEX

NOTES

Preface

1. F. L. Ganshof, *Feudalism*, 3d Eng. ed. (New York: Harper and Row, 1964), xvii.

1. Abraham's Heirs

1. W. J. Ferrar, ed. and trans., *The Proof of the Gospel. Being the "Demonstratio Evangelica" of Eusebius of Caesarea*, vol. 1, bk. 1 (New York: Macmillan, 1920), 25, 33.

2. Ibid., bk. 1, chaps. 6, 7.

3. The Christian roots of antisemitism are analyzed in Rosemary Ruether, *Faith and Fratricide* (New York: Seabury, 1974), a book that attracted considerable attention. See also Alan Davies, ed., *Antisemitism and the Foundations of Christianity* (New York: Paulist, 1979), especially the first five essays. The classic history is James Parkes, *The Conflict of the Church and the Synagogue* (London: Soncino, 1934). On the Church as the "true Israel" an essential reference is Marcel Simon, *Verus Israel* (Oxford: Oxford Univ. Press, 1964), especially chaps. 3 and 6.

4. A concise statement of how Jewish and Christian conceptions of the Messiah differ (but with a clearly Jewish bias) is in the appendix to Joseph Klausner, *The Messianic Idea in Israel*, 3d ed. (New York: Macmillan, 1955), 519–31.

5. *New English Bible* (hereafter NEB): Acts 9:4, 17–19.

6. Rom. 11:13; Rom. 3:29–30 NEB. The literature on Paul is enormous, but the following touch directly on our subject: William D. Davies, *Paul and Rabbinic Judaism*, rev. ed. (London: S.P.C.K. Press, 1955), argues that Paul never departed from his Jewish origins, and that his plan for a mission to the "Gentiles" came about only when he became convinced that most Jews would never accept his message; see also "Paul and the People of Israel," in William D. Davies, *Jewish and Pauline Studies* (Philadelphia: Fortress, 1984). Gregory Dix, *Jew and Greek: A Study in the Primitive Church* (London: Dacre Press, 1953), explains how and why a movement within Judaism was transformed into a new religion for non-Jews. Francis Watson, *Paul, Judaism, and the Gentiles: A Sociological*

Approach (Cambridge: Cambridge Univ. Press, 1986), is an excellent example of recent scholarship emphasizing social history over theology.

7. Gal. 3:10–14 NEB.

8. Rom. 9:3; Rom. 11:15 NEB.

9. Rom. 4:13–17 NEB.

10. John Gager, *The Origins of Anti-Semitism* (New York: Oxford Univ. Press, 1983), discusses the division between Judaism and Christianity and presents a challenging reinterpretation of Paul's message. See also Gager's earlier volume, *Kingdom and Community* (Englewood Cliffs, N.J.: Prentice-Hall, 1975), a portrait of Christianity as a millenarian movement. Two useful studies of a more general nature are Samuel Sandmel, *Anti-Semitism in the New Testament?* (Philadelphia: Fortress, 1978), which answers the question with a moderately phrased affirmative, and Charlotte Klein, *Anti-Judaism in Christian Theology* (Philadelphia: Fortress, 1978).

11. A helpful introduction to the New Testament is Howard C. Kee et al., *Understanding the New Testament*, 4th ed. (Englewood Cliffs, N.J.: Prentice-Hall, 1983). For a Jewish perspective see Samuel Sandmel, *A Jewish Understanding of the New Testament* (Cincinnati: Hebrew Union College Press, 1956).

12. Matt. 2:15, Hos. 11:1–2 NEB.

13. Matt. 23:27–28; Matt. 27:20, 22, 25 NEB.

14. John 8:47, 31–32 NEB.

15. John 8:33–47 NEB.

16. John 8:48, 53, 56–59 NEB.

17. Samuel Sandmel, *Judaism and Christian Beginnings* (New York: Oxford Univ. Press, 1978), 16.

18. On the restructuring of Jewish society after the fall of Jerusalem, see also Salo W. Baron, *A Social and Religious History of the Jews*, 2d ed. (New York: Columbia Univ. Press, 1952–83) vol. 2, chaps. 11 & 12; Gerson D. Cohen, "The Talmudic Age," in *Great Ages and Ideas of the Jewish People*, ed. Leo W. Schwarz (New York: Random House, 1956), 141–212; Judah Goldin, "The Period of the Talmud," in *The Jews: Their History*, 4th ed., ed. Louis Finkelstein (New York: Schocken, 1970), 119–224; Jacob Neusner, "Judaism after the Destruction of the Temple," in *Israelite and Judaean History*, ed. John H. Hayes and J. Maxwell Miller (Philadelphia: Westminster, 1977), 663–77. Alan F. Segal, *Rebecca's Children: Judaism and Christianity in the Roman World* (Cambridge, Mass.: Harvard Univ. Press, 1986), explains the emergence of Christianity and rabbinic Judaism as parallel responses to social and political challenges in first century Palestine.

19. The most remarkable diatribes against Jews and "Judaizing" are eight sermons by the great fourth-century preacher John Chrysostom, called in the usual manner *Adversus Judaeos*, "In Opposition to the Jews," available in English translation as *Discourses Against Judaizing Christians*, trans. Paul W. Harkins (Washington, D.C.: Catholic Univ. of America Press, 1979). See also Robert L. Wilken, *John Chrysostom and the Jews* (Berkeley: Univ. of California Press, 1983).

20. Justin Martyr, "Dialogue with Trypho," in *Writings of St. Justin Martyr*, ed. and trans. Thomas B. Falls (Washington, D.C.: Catholic Univ. Press, 1948), 160.

21. Ibid., 162.

22. Arthur Lukyn Williams, *Adversus Judaeos: A Bird's-Eye View of Christian Apologiae until the Renaissance* (Cambridge: Cambridge Univ. Press, 1935).

23. Jean Daniélou, *A History of Early Christian Doctrine Before the Council of Nicaea,* vol. 2, Gospel Message and Hellenistic Culture, ed. and trans. John A. Baker (London: Darton, Longman and Todd, 1973), chap. 8.

24. Justin Martyr, "Dialogue with Trypho", 211.

25. Ibid., 291–92.

26. Ibid., 173.

27. Ibid., 191.

28. Ibid., 175–76.

29. Ibid., 187–88.

30. Ibid., 186.

31. Ibid., 331–32.

32. Augustine, "In Answer to the Jews," in *Saint Augustine: Treatises on Marriage and Other Subjects,* trans. Sister Marie Liguori (New York: Fathers of the Church, 1955), 400.

33. Ibid., 405–7.

34. Augustine, *The City of God Against the Pagans,* trans. H. Bettenson (Harmondsworth, England: Penguin, 1972), 827–28.

2. The First European Jews

1. Brian Tierney and Sidney Painter, *Western Europe in the Middle Ages, 300–1475,* 4th ed. (New York: Knopf, 1982), 29.

2. The best general introduction to Merovingian history is Patrick J. Geary, *Before France and Germany: The Creation and Transformation of the Merovingian World* (New York: Oxford Univ. Press, 1988), but he does not mention Jews. The same applies to the chapters on the Franks in another standard volume, J. M. Wallace-Hadrill, *The Barbarian West: The Early Middle Ages A.D. 400–1000,* 2d ed. (London: Hutchinson, 1962); however, another study by Wallace-Hadrill, *The Frankish Church* (Oxford: Clarendon Press, 1983), includes an excellent section on "The Jews and Their Religion."

3. Harry J. Leon, *The Jews of Ancient Rome* (Philadelphia: Jewish Publication Society, 1960), chap. 1; Michael Grant, *The Jews in the Roman World* (New York: Scribner's, 1973), chap. 4.

4. Cecil Roth, "The Jews in the Middle Ages," in *The Cambridge Medieval History* (Cambridge: Cambridge Univ. Press, 1932), 7:632–33. Although outdated in some respects, this essay is still worth reading for an introductory overview and for a sense of what was being emphasized at the time. Yosef Hayim Yerushalmi has remarked, in his introduction to *Bibliographical Essays in Medieval Jewish Studies* (New York: Anti-Defamation League of B'nai B'rith, 1976), 8–9, that Roth's essay was a landmark publication: "On the one hand, medieval Jewry was thus granted a recognition it had rarely received before in a work of general scholarship. On the other, the whole of medieval Jewry was placed in splendid isolation, immured between a chapter on 'Russia, 1015–

1462' and another entitled 'Medieval Estates.'" The chapter, he concluded, was in "an historiographical ghetto."

5. Robert Latouche, *The Birth of Western Economy: Economic Aspects of the Dark Ages,* 2d ed. (London: Methuen, 1967), 40–42.

6. Amnon Linder, *The Jews in Roman Imperial Legislation* (Detroit: Wayne State Univ. Press, 1987), 122.

7. Latouche, *Birth of Western Economy,* 103.

8. N. J. G. Pounds, *An Economic History of Medieval Europe* (London: Longman, 1974), 69. In addition to the volumes by Latouche and Pounds, the role of Jewish merchants is also discussed in Robert-Henri Bautier, *The Economic Development of Medieval Europe* (London: Thames and Hudson, 1971), and Georges Duby, *The Early Growth of the European Economy* (Ithaca: Cornell Univ. Press, 1974).

9. Latouche, *Birth of Western Economy,* 123.

10. J. M. Wallace-Hadrill, *Frankish Church,* 390, 53.

11. Ibid., 392.

12. Bernhard Blumenkranz, *Juifs et chrétiens dans le monde occidental 430–1096* (Paris: Mouton, 1960), 377–80. Blumenkranz's outstanding study is somewhat weakened by an underlying tone of apology; the author seems intent on demonstrating that Jews in early medieval Europe were much like everyone else in most respects other than religion.

13. Edward James, *The Origins of France: From Clovis to the Capetians, 500–1000* (New York: St. Martin's, 1982), 101.

14. A number of basic sources for Jewish history have provided background information and orientation for much of my work. Simon Dubnow's five volume *History of the Jews* (South Brunswick, N.J.: Thomas Yoseloff, 1967–73) is written by the outstanding Jewish historian of the early twentieth century; although still valuable, it tends to focus on catastrophic events. Salo W. Baron's multi-volume *Social and Religious History of the Jews* is unrivalled in scholarship but written in densely detailed style that invites perusal rather than steady reading. H. H. Ben-Sasson, ed., *A History of the Jewish People* (Cambridge, Mass.: Harvard Univ. Press, 1976), includes a substantial section on the medieval period by the editor. A noteworthy recent volume on medieval Jewry in western Europe is Kenneth R. Stow, *Alienated Minority: The Jews of Medieval Latin Europe* (Cambridge, Mass.: Harvard Univ. Press, 1992). Mark R. Cohen, *Under Crescent and Cross: The Jews in the Middle Ages* (Princeton: Princeton Univ. Press, 1994), is a comparative study of medieval Jewish societies in the Islamic and Christian worlds. For bibliographic guidance to all aspects of medieval Jewish history see Ivan G. Marcus, "The Jews in Western Europe: Fourth to Sixteenth Century," and Kenneth R. Stow, "The Church and the Jews: From Saint Paul to Paul IV," both in *Bibliographical Essays in Medieval Jewish Studies* (New York: Anti-Defamation League of B'nai B'rith, 1976).

15. Regarding attitudes toward Jews and Judaism in the pre-Christian Roman Empire, see the contrasting arguments of John C. Meagher, "As the Twig Was Bent: Antisemitism in Greco-Roman and Earliest Christian Times," in Davies, *Antisemitism and the Foundations of Christianity,* 1–26, and Gager, *Origins of Anti-Semitism,* pt. 2. Meagher main-

tains that Christian antisemitism arose on well-established pagan foundations, while Gager argues that relations between pagans and Jews were generally positive.

16. Clyde Pharr et al., eds. and trans., *The Theodosian Code and Novels and the Sirmondian Constitution* (Princeton: Princeton Univ. Press, 1952), 467.

17. Theodosian Code, book 16, title 9, in Pharr et al., *Theodosian Code*, 471–72.

18. Pharr et al., *Theodosian Code*, 472.

19. Charles [Karl] Joseph Hefele, *A History of the Councils of the Church* (Edinburgh: T. and T. Clark, 1895), 4:405.

20. Pharr et al., *Theodosian Code*, 70.

21. Hefele, *Councils of the Church*, 4:187, 207.

22. Bernard S. Bachrach, *Early Medieval Jewish Policy in Western Europe* (Minneapolis: Univ. of Minnesota Press, 1977a), 64. Bachrach judiciously reviews his subject from the fifth to ninth centuries, arguing that most early medieval rulers were favorably disposed toward Jews and resisted efforts by the clergy to oppress or restrict them. Bachrach has edited an introductory collection of translated primary sources, *Jews in Barbarian Europe* (Lawrence, Kans.: Coronado Press, 1977), designed mainly for undergraduate courses; the editor notes that some items are paraphrases rather than exact translations, but the book is dependable for general readers.

23. Solomon Katz, *The Jews in the Visigothic and Frankish Kingdoms of Spain and Gaul* (Cambridge, Mass: Medieval Academy of America, 1937), 61.

24. Bernard S. Bachrach, *Jews in Barbarian Europe*, 31.

25. Hefele, *Councils of the Church*, 4·404

26. Pharr et al., *Theodosian Code*, 467–71.

27. Gregory of Tours, *The History of the Franks*, trans. Lewis Thorpe (Harmondsworth, England: Penguin, 1974), 329–33.

28. Ibid., 347–48.

29. John 10:1–16 NEB.

30. Gregory of Tours, *History of the Franks*, 265–67.

31. Jacob R. Marcus, ed. *The Jew in the Medieval World* (Philadelphia: Jewish Publication Society, 1938), 112.

32. Bachrach, *Early Medieval Jewish Policy*, 60–63.

3. "They Display Documents": Jewish Life in the Carolingian Empire

1. S. Katz, *Jews in Spain and Gaul*, 152–54.

2. Max Weinreich, *History of the Yiddish Language*, trans. S. Noble and J. A. Fishman (Chicago: Univ. of Chicago Press, 1980), 329–30.

3. Bachrach, *Early Medieval Jewish Policy*, 69–72.

4. F. L. Ganshof, *Feudalism*, 3d Eng. ed. (New York: Harper and Row), 30.

5. Irving A. Agus, *The Heroic Age of Franco-German Jewry* (New York: Yeshiva Univ. Press, 1969), 9; Irving A. Agus, *Urban Civilization in Pre-Crusade Europe* (New York: Yeshiva Univ. Press, 1965), 13. The earlier publication provides translated texts and discus-

sions of rabbinic responsa (replies to questions on legal and ritual matters). The later one, which presents this material in narrative form, is an indispensable study of Jewish life in France and Germany during the tenth and eleventh centuries. As the titles of both books suggest, Agus was somewhat inclined to hyperbole and probably exaggerated the prominence of Jews in medieval Europe, but he served European Jewish history well by demonstrating how much information was available in rabbinic sources. The fourth chapter, on business, and the eleventh, on relations between Christians and Jews, are especially recommended, but the entire book provided foundations for much of my discussion of Jewish community life.

6. S. Schwarzfuchs, "France and Germany Under the Carolingians," in *The Dark Ages,* ed. Cecil Roth (New Brunswick, N.J.: Rutgers Univ. Press, 1966), 134.

7. James Parkes, *The Jew in the Medieval Community,* 2d ed. (New York: Hermon, 1976), 44.

8. Robert S. Lopez, "The Trade of Medieval Europe: The South," in *The Cambridge Economic History of Europe,* vol. 2, Trade and Industry in the Middle Ages, ed. M. Postan and E. E. Rich (Cambridge: Cambridge Univ. Press, 1952), 260–61.

9. Henri Pirenne, *Mohammed and Charlemagne* (New York: Norton, 1939), 258–59.

10. Schwarzfuchs, "France and Germany," 130–33; Baron, *Social and Religious History of the Jews,* 4:193–94.

11. Marc Bloch, *Slavery and Serfdom in the Middle Ages,* trans. W. R. Beer (Berkeley: Univ. of California Press, 1975), 10–15.

12. Agus, *Heroic Age,* 174.

13. Ibid., 177–78.

14. Ibid., 161–69.

15. Jacob Katz, *Exclusiveness and Tolerance: Jewish-Gentile Relations in Medieval and Modern Times* (Oxford: Oxford Univ. Press, 1961).

16. Bachrach, *Early Medieval Jewish Policy,* 66–67.

17. Arthur J. Zuckerman, *A Jewish Princedom in Feudal France, 768–900* (New York: Columbia Univ. Press, 1972), 50; Julius Aronius, *Regesten zur Geschichte der Juden im fränkischen und deutschen Reiche bis zum Jahre 1273* (Berlin: L. Simion, 1902; reprint, Hildesheim: Georg Olms, 1970), 24–25, no. 67.

18. Bachrach, *Early Medieval Jewish Policy,* 75–76; Parkes, *Conflict of the Church and the Synagogue,* 337–39.

19. My version of the oath, based on Bachrach, *Early Medieval Jewish Policy,* 77, and Parkes, *Conflict of the Church and the Synagogue,* 338. The references here are to biblical episodes that would have been familiar to ninth-century Jews. Naaman was a Syrian military officer who was cured of leprosy by the prophet Elisha. Dathan and Abiron, or Abiram, joined Korah in a rebellion against Moses and were punished by death in a fiery earthquake.

20. Bachrach, *Early Medieval Jewish Policy,* 74; Agus, *Heroic Age,* 37.

21. Bachrach, *Early Medieval Jewish Policy,* 78–79.

22. Ibid., 90–96; Howard L. Adelson, ed. *Medieval Commerce* (Princeton: Van Nostrand, 1962), 124–25.

23. Bachrach, *Early Medieval Jewish Policy,* 84–85.

24. Ibid., 86–89.

25. Ibid., 89.

26. Bernhard Blumenkranz, *Les auteurs chrétiens latins du moyen âge sur les juifs et le judaïsme* (Paris: Mouton, 1963), 155–57; *Patrologia Latina,* ed. J.-P. Migne, (Paris, 1844–64), vol. 104, col. 100–106.

27. Arthur J. Zuckerman, "The Political Uses of Theology: The Conflict of Bishop Agobard and the Jews of Lyons," in *Studies in Medieval Culture III,* ed. John R. Sommerfeldt (Kalamazoo: Medieval Institute, Western Michigan Univ., 1970), 25.

28. Zuckerman, "Political Uses of Theology," 29; Blumenkranz, *Les auteurs chrétiens latins,* 157–58; *Patrologia Latina,* vol. 104, col. 100–106.

29. Blumenkranz, *Les auteurs chrétiens latins,* 160–63; *Patrologia Latina,* vol. 104, col. 69–76. The passages cited here were translated by Sean Smith with my revisions and with final editing and correction by Theodore Steinberg.

30. *Patrologia Latina,* vol. 104, col. 77–100; Blumenkranz, *Les auteurs chrétiens latins,* 163–67.

31. Allen Cabaniss, "Bodo-Eleazar: A Famous Jewish Convert," *Jewish Quarterly Review,* n.s., 43 (1953):319.

32. Zuckerman, *Jewish Princedom,* 274–84; Eliyahu Ashtor, *The Jews of Moslem Spain* (Philadelphia: Jewish Publication Society, 1973), 1:70–79; Cabaniss, "Bodo-Eleazar." The primary source is translated in J. R. Marcus, *Jew in the Medieval World,* 353–54.

4. Cultural Counterpoint: Later Ninth and Tenth Centuries

1. Bachrach, *Early Medieval Jewish Policy,* 114–16.

2. Aronius, *Regesten,* 20, nos. 55, 56.

3. Blumenkranz, *Juifs et chrétiens,* 21–22.

4. Aronius, *Regesten,* 54, no. 125; Edward A. Synan, *The Popes and the Jews in the Middle Ages* (New York: Macmillan, 1965), 60.

5. On the early development of Yiddish, the language of Ashkenazic Jewry for about a thousand years, see Weinreich, *History of the Yiddish Language.*

6. Ganshof, *Feudalism,* xvii. In addition to Ganshof, my discussion of feudalism is based on Georges Duby, *The Three Orders: Feudal Society Imagined,* trans. Arthur Goldhammer (Chicago: Univ. of Chicago Press, 1980), chap. 13; Duby, *Early Growth of the European Economy,* chap. 6; Geoffrey Barraclough, *The Crucible of Europe: The Ninth and Tenth Centuries in European History* (Berkeley: Univ. of California Press, 1976), 86–91; Norman F. Cantor, *Medieval History,* 2d ed. (New York: Macmillan, 1969), 214–23; and Jacques Le Goff, *Your Money or Your Life: Economy and Religion in the Middle Ages,* trans. P. Ranum (New York: Zone Books, 1988), 90–95.

7. Irving A. Agus, "Rabbinic Scholarship in Northern Europe," in *The Dark Ages: Jews in Christian Europe 711–1096,* ed. Cecil Roth (New Brunswick, N.J.: Rutgers Univ. Press, 1966), 190. I am indebted to this author's work, particularly *Heroic Age,* for much of the description of Jewish life in this chapter.

8. Agus, "Rabbinic Scholarship," 195.

9. Agus, *Heroic Age,* especially chaps. 1 and 4.

10. Ibid., especially chap. 9.

11. Ibid., 223; Agus, *Urban Civilization,* 590.

12. S. Schwarzfuchs, "France Under the Early Capets," in *The Dark Ages: Jews in Christian Europe 711–1096,* ed. Cecil Roth (New Brunswick: Rutgers Univ. Press, 1966), 148.

13. James Parkes, *Jew in the Medieval Community,* 42–43.

14. James, *Origins of France,* 71.

15. Robert Chazan, "The Persecution of 992," *Revue des études juives* 129 (1970): 219; and Chazan, *Medieval Jewry in Northern France: A Political and Social History* (Baltimore: Johns Hopkins Univ. Press, 1973), 12.

16. Agus, *Heroic Age,* 350–52.

17. Ibid., 353.

18. J. Katz, *Exclusiveness and Tolerance,* 40.

5. "To Make a City of My Village": The Pivotal Eleventh Century

1. In "1007–1012: Initial Crisis for Northern European Jewry," *Proceedings of the American Academy for Jewish Research* (1970–71): 101–18, Robert Chazan describes a number of eleventh-century episodes expressive of serious antagonism toward Jews. He interprets the Jewish responses as harbingers of "the willingness to accept martyrdom" associated with the period after 1096 (117).

2. Aryeh Grabois, "Les juifs et leurs seigneurs dans la France septentrionale aux XIe et XIIe siècles," in *Les juifs dans l'histoire de France,* ed. Myriam Yardeni (Leiden: E. J. Brill, 1980), 14–15.

3. Irving A. Agus, "Rashi and His School," in *The Dark Ages: Jews in Christian Europe 711–1096,* ed. Cecil Roth (New Brunswick, N.J.: Rutgers Univ. Press, 1966), 215–19; Salo W. Baron, *Ancient and Medieval Jewish History* (New Brunswick, N.J.: Rutgers Univ. Press, 1972), 276.

4. Robert S. Lopez, *The Commercial Revolution of the Middle Ages, 950–1350* (Englewood Cliffs, N.J.: Prentice Hall, 1971).

5. Lester K. Little, *Religious Poverty and the Profit Economy in Medieval Europe* (Ithaca: Cornell Univ. Press, 1978), chap. 1. The third chapter, "The Jews in Christian Europe," presents an excellent overview.

6. Ibid., 56.

7. Chap. 12, "The Gregorian World Revolution," in Cantor's *Medieval History* is especially instructive on matters relating to the situation of the Jews. Gerd Tellenbach, *Church, State, and Christian Society at the Time of the Investiture Contest* (Oxford: Basil Blackwell, 1940), especially 126–37, is deeply instructive on the idea of order in the Christian world.

8. R. W. Southern, *The Making of the Middle Ages* (New Haven: Yale Univ. Press), 125–27.

9. Horst Fuhrmann, *Germany in the High Middle Ages c. 1050–1200* (Cambridge: Cambridge Univ. Press, 1986), 58.

10. Edward Peters, *Europe: The World of the Middle Ages* (Englewood Cliffs, N.J.: Prentice-Hall, 1977), 333; Duby, *Early Growth of the European Economy*, 162–64.

11. Allan Cutler and Helen E. Cutler, *The Jew as Ally of the Muslim: Medieval Roots of Anti-Semitism* (Notre Dame, Ind.: Univ. of Notre Dame Press, 1986).

12. Robert Chazan, *Church, State, and Jew in the Middle Ages* (New York: Behrman House, 1980), 59.

13. Jeremy duQuesnay Adams, *Patterns of Medieval Society* (Englewood Cliffs, N.J.: Prentice-Hall, 1969), 65; translated text also in Chazan, *Church, State, and Jew*, 58–59.

14. Bernhard Blumenkranz, "Germany, 843–1096," in *The Dark Ages: Jews in Christian Europe 711–1096*, ed. Cecil Roth (New Brunswick, N.J.: Rutgers Univ. Press, 1966), 165.

15. Chazan, *Church, State, and Jew*, 60–63.

16. Parkes, *Jew in the Medieval Community*, 161.

6. "In Witness to the Oneness": The First Crusade and the Jews of the Rhineland

1. Steven Runciman, *A History of the Crusades* (Cambridge: Cambridge Univ. Press, 1951), 1:60–63.

2. Edward Peters, ed., *The First Crusade: The Chronicle of Fulcher of Chartres and Other Source Materials* (Philadelphia: Univ. of Pennsylvania Press, 1971), 3.

3. Hans Liebeschütz, "The Crusading Movement in Its Bearing on the Christian Attitude towards Jewry," *Journal of Jewish Studies* 10 (1959): 104–6.

4. Shlomo Eidelberg, ed. and trans., *The Jews and the Crusaders: The Hebrew Chronicles of the First and Second Crusades* (Madison: Univ. of Wisconsin Press, 1977), 99–100.

5. John F. Benton, ed., *Self and Society in Medieval France: The Memoirs of Abbot Guibert of Nogent (1064?–c. 1125)*, trans. C. C. S. Bland, rev. John F. Benton (New York: Harper and Row, 1970), 134–35; Stow, *Alienated Minority*, 37. A controversial paper by Norman Golb, "New Light on the Persecution of French Jews at the Time of the First Crusade," *Proceedings of the American Academy for Jewish Research* 34 (1966), 1–45, argues that there were more persecutions in France than is generally recognized.

6. Robert Chazan, *European Jewry and the First Crusade* (Berkeley: Univ. of California Press, 1987), 91–93; Chazan, *Medieval Jewry in Northern France*, 25–27. The volume on the First Crusade includes translations of the chronicle of Solomon ben Simson (which Chazan designates L) and another known as Mainz Anonymous (S); these translations bring out the style of the narratives and show how they incorporate biblical passages.

7. A. C. Krey, ed., *The First Crusade: The Accounts of Eye-Witnesses and Participants* (Princeton: Princeton Univ. Press, 1921), 53.

8. Runciman, *History of the Crusades*, 1:137; Eidelberg, *Jews and the Crusaders*, 28.

9. Norman Cohn, *The Pursuit of the Millennium*, 3d ed. (New York: Oxford Univ. Press, 1970), 71–73.

10. R. K. Emmerson, *Antichrist in the Middle Ages* (Seattle: Univ. of Washington Press, 1981).

11. Liebeschütz, "Crusading Movement", 104. Jonathan Riley-Smith, *The First Crusade and the Idea of Crusading* (Philadelphia: Univ. of Pennsylvania Press, 1986), 50–56, argues that the principal motive for the attacks on Jewish communities was vengeance for the Crucifixion. Riley-Smith's general study, *The Crusades: A Short History* (New Haven: Yale Univ. Press, 1987), is perhaps the best introduction. The Jewish experience is summarized in S. Schwarzfuchs, "Crusades," *Encyclopaedia Judaica* (Jerusalem: Keter, 1971), 5:1135–45.

12. Runciman, *History of the Crusades*, 1:137; Eidelberg, *Jews and the Crusaders*, 22, 101.

13. Eidelberg, *Jews and the Crusaders*, 22.

14. Ibid., 23.

15. Parkes, *Jew in the Medieval Community*, 70. See Chazan's discussion of "efforts to preserve Jewish lives," *European Jewry and the First Crusade*, 85–99.

16. Eidelberg, *Jews and the Crusaders*, 23.

17. Ibid., 104.

18. Chazan, *European Jewry and the First Crusade*, 85–89; Parkes, *Jew in the Medieval Community*, 71.

19. Eidelberg, *Jews and the Crusaders*, 24.

20. Chazan, *European Jewry and the First Crusade*, 94.

21. Eidelberg, *Jews and the Crusaders*, 29.

22. Ibid., 30.

23. Ibid., 32.

24. Ibid., 111, 113.

25. Ibid., 38, 113–14.

26. Krey, *First Crusade: Accounts*, 56; Peters, *First Crusade: Chronicle of Fulcher*, 104.

27. Eidelberg, *Jews and the Crusaders*, 64.

28. Ibid., 62–67; Parkes, *Jew in the Medieval Community*, 77.

29. Parkes, *Jew in the Medieval Community*, 85.

30. Eidelberg, *Jews and the Crusaders*, 67.

31. Runciman, *History of the Crusades*, 1:136, 140–41.

32. Eidelberg, *Jews and the Crusaders*, 15.

33. Chazan, *European Jewry and the First Crusade*, 3.

34. Eidelberg, *Jews and the Crusaders*, 22.

35. Ibid., 37.

36. Chazan, *European Jewry and the First Crusade*, 44–45.

37. Eidelberg, *Jews and the Crusaders*, 23.

38. Chazan, *European Jewry and the First Crusade*, chap. 5.

39. Ibid., 144–45.

40. David Roskies, *Against the Apocalypse: Responses to Catastrophe in Modern Jewish Culture* (Cambridge, Mass.: Harvard Univ. Press, 1984), 41–45.

41. J. Katz, *Exclusiveness and Tolerance*, 84–85, 88, 91–92.

7. Christian Renewal, Jewish Decline: The Twelfth Century

1. Georges Duby, "The Culture of the Knightly Class: Audience and Patronage," in *Renaissance and Renewal in the Twelfth Century*, ed. Robert L. Benson and Giles Constable (Cambridge, Mass: Harvard Univ. Press, 1982), 249.

2. Friedrich Heer, *The Medieval World: Europe 1100–1350*, trans. Janet Sondheimer (London: Weidenfeld and Nicolson, 1962), 40.

3. Marina Warner, *Alone of All Her Sex: The Myth and the Cult of the Virgin Mary* (New York: Knopf, 1976), pt. 4; Cantor, *Medieval History*, 372.

4. Heer, *Medieval World*, 58.

5. Raphael Straus, *Regensburg and Augsburg* (Philadelphia: Jewish Publication Society, 1939).

6. Fuhrmann, *Germany in the High Middle Ages*, 85; Guido Kisch, *The Jews in Medieval Germany: A Study of Their Legal and Social Status* (Chicago: Univ. of Chicago Press, 1949), 109.

7. Duby, *Early Growth of the European Economy*, 109.

8. Parkes, *Jew in the Medieval Community*, 282.

9. Duby, *Early Growth of the European Economy*, 218.

10. Parkes, *Jew in the Medieval Community*, 352.

11. Summary of edict is based on translation in Solomon Grayzel, *The Church and the Jews in the XIIIth Century*, rev. ed. (New York: Hermon, 1966), 92–95. See also Synan, *Popes and the Jews*, 229–32; Solomon Grayzel, *The Church and the Jews in the XIIIth Century*, vol. 2, *1254–1314*, ed. Kenneth R. Stow (Detroit: Wayne State Univ. Press, 1989), 3–7; Baron, *Ancient and Medieval Jewish History*, 287–88; Parkes, *Jew in the Medieval Community*, 211–13.

12. David Berger, "The Attitude of St. Bernard of Clairvaux toward the Jews," *Proceedings of the American Academy of Jewish Research* 40 (1972): 89–108.

13. Bernard of Clairvaux, *The Letters of St. Bernard of Clairvaux*, trans. Bruno James (Chicago: Henry Regnery, 1953), 462–63. For a more complete sample of Bernard's statements on Jews, see *The Works of Benrard of Clairvaux*, vol. 2, *On the Song of Songs I.* (Shannon: Irish Univ. Press, 1971), sermon 14.

14. Ibid., 465–66. Both of Bernard's letters are reprinted in Chazan, *Church, State, and Jew*, 101–5.

15. Chazan, *Church, State, and Jew*, 107.

16. Eidelberg, *Jews and the Crusaders*, 117–33.

17. Ibid., 123–24.

18. Ibid., 124.

19. Ibid., 127–28.

20. Ibid., 130–31.

21. Marcus, *Jew in the Medieval World*, 127–29.

22. Robert Chazan, "The Blois Incident of 1171: A Study in Jewish Intercommunal Organization," *Proceedings of the American Academy for Jewish Research* 36 (1968): 13–31. In *Medieval Jewry in Northern France*, 56–60, Chazan discusses what can be learned from the episode about Jewish political organization at the time.

23. Chazan, *Church, State, and Jew*, 115–16.

24. Ibid., 117.

8. Encounters and Representations:
Jews and Christians in Twelfth-Century Cultural Life

1. Beryl Smalley, *The Study of the Bible in the Middle Ages*, 2d ed. (Oxford: Basil Blackwell, 1952), 78.

2. Ivan G. Marcus, "Jewish Schools in Medieval Europe," *Melton Journal* 21 (1987): 5–6.

3. Louis Rabinowitz, *The Social Life of the Jews of Northern France in the XII to XIV Centuries, as Reflected in the Rabbinic Literature of the Period*, 2d ed. (New York: Hermon, 1972), 213–24.

4. Chazan, "Blois Incident," 30.

5. On the tosafists see Agus, "Rashi and His School," and Adin Steinsaltz, *The Essential Talmud* (New York: Basic Books, 1976), 69–71. For a picture of a representatiave page of Talmud, showing the commentaries of Rashi and the tosafists, see Robert Goldenberg, "Talmud," in *Back to the Sources: Reading the Classic Jewish Texts*, ed. Barry W. Holtz (New York: Summit, 1984), 140–42, or Jacob Neusner, *Invitation to the Talmud*, rev. ed. (New York: Harper and Row, 1984), 172–73.

6. Israel M. Ta-Shma, "Tosafot," in *Encyclopaedia Judaica*, 15:1278–83.

7. Smalley, *Study of the Bible*, 152.

8. Ibid., 153–54.

9. Aryeh Grabois, "The *Hebraica veritas* and Jewish-Christian Intellectual Relations in the Twelfth Century," *Speculum* 50 (1975): 617–19.

10. Smalley, *Study of the Bible*, 155–56.

11. Ibid., 163; phrase bracketed by Smalley.

12. Ibid., 149–72; quoted passages: 163, 172.

13. Jeremy Cohen, "Scholarship and Intolerance in the Medieval Academy: The Study and Evaluation of Judaism in European Christendom," *American Historical Review* 91 (1986): 599–600; Smalley, *Study of the Bible*, 156–57.

14. Smalley, *Study of the Bible*, 186–95; Grabois, "The *Hebraica veritas*," 630–31; Jeremy Cohen, "Scholarship and Intolerance," 601–2.

15. Smalley, *Study of the Bible*, 188.

16. J. Cohen, "Scholarship and Intolerance," 601–2.

17. Blumenkranz interprets "anti-Jewish polemics and legislation" as responses to

what was perceived as threatening Jewish influence and "powers of attractiveness." Bernhard Blumenkranz, "Anti-Jewish Polemics and Legislation in the Middle Ages: Literary Fiction or Reality?" *Journal of Jewish Studies* 15 (1964): 125–40.

18. Blumenkranz, *Les auteurs chrétiens latins*, 279–87; Williams, *Adversus Judaeos*, 375–80.

19. J. Cohen, "Scholarship and Intolerance," 599.

20. *Patrologia Latina*, vol. 189, col. 507. On Peter's "Treatise" see also Williams, *Adversus Judaeos*, 384–93, and J. Cohen, "Scholarship and Intolerance," 602–4.

21. *Patrologia Latina*, vol. 189, col. 539.

22. Duby, *Early Growth of the European Economy*, 216–18.

23. *Patrologia Latina*, vol. 189, col. 602.

24. Williams, *Adversus Judaeos*, 390.

25. Gavin Langmuir, *Toward a Definition of Antisemitism* (Berkeley: Univ. of California Press, 1990), chap. 8.

26. Gordon Leff, *Medieval Thought: St. Augustine to Ockham* (Harmondsworth, England: Penguin, 1958), 107.

27. Peter Abelard, *Dialogus inter Philosophum, Judaeum et Christianum*, ed. Rudolf Thomas (Stuttgart: F. Frommann, 1970); and Abelard, *A Dialogue of a Philosopher with a Jew and a Christian*, trans. P. J. Payer (Toronto: Pontifical Institute of Mediaeval Studies, 1979).

28. Hans Liebeschütz, "The Significance of Judaism in Peter Abaelard's Dialogus," *Journal of Jewish Studies* 12 (1961): 1–18.

29. Abelard, *Dialogue*, 32–33.

30. Ibid., 47.

31. Ibid., 49–50.

32. Betty Radice, ed. and trans., *The Letters of Abelard and Heloise* (Harmondsworth, England: Penguin, 1974), 75–76.

33. Abelard, *Dialogus*, 90; my translation. Cf. Abelard, *Dialogue*, 78.

34. Erwin I. J. Rosenthal, "Anti-Christian Polemics in Medieval Bible Commentaries," *Journal of Jewish Studies* 11 (1960): 115–35.

35. Joseph Kimhi, *The Book of the Covenant*, trans. Frank E. Talmage (Toronto: Pontifical Institute of Mediaeval Studies, 1972), 16–17.

36. Ibid., 36.

37. Ibid., 46–48.

38. Ibid., 67.

39. E. Rosenthal, "Anti-Christian Polemics," 121–22, 127–33; Frank E. Talmage, ed., *Disputation and Dialogue: Readings in the Christian-Jewish Encounter* (New York: Ktav, 1975), 71–81.

40. David Bevington, ed., *Medieval Drama* (Boston: Houghton Mifflin, 1975), 178–79. Translated passages are based on the Latin text in Bevington, 180–201.

41. Bernhard Blumenkranz, *Juden und Judentum in der mittelalterlichen Kunst* (Stuttgart: W. Kohlhammer, 1965), 16; Bernhard Blumenkranz, *Le juif médiéval au miroir de l'art chrétien* (Paris: Études Augustiennes, 1966), 18. Other early illustrations follow in these texts.

42. Wolfgang S. Seiferth, *Synagogue and Church in the Middle Ages* (New York: Ungar, 1970), figs. 3 and 6.

43. Ibid., fig. 22.

44. Blumenkranz, *Juden und Judentum*, 55–57; Blumenkranz, *Le juif médiéval*, 105–7; Seiferth, *Synagogue and Church*, figs. 23–27, 29; Henry Kraus, *The Living Theatre of Medieval Art* (Bloomington: Indiana Univ. Press, 1967), 151; Joseph Reider, "Jews in Medieval Art," in *Essays on Antisemitism*, 2d ed., ed. Koppel Pinson (New York: Conference on Jewish Relations, 1946), 94.

45. Seiferth, *Synagogue and Church*, 115–16, and fig. 35.

9. "The Yoke of Servitude": Late Twelfth and Early Thirteenth Centuries

1. Le Goff, *Your Money or Your Life*, 32.

2. John W. Baldwin, *Masters, Princes, and Merchants: The Social Views of Peter the Chanter and His Circle*. (Princeton: Princeton Univ. Press, 1970), 1:298–300.

3. Grayzel, *Church and the Jews*, 200–203.

4. Most historians cite the date as February 1180. I follow William Chester Jordan, *The French Monarchy and the Jews* (Philadelphia: Univ. of Pennsylvania Press, 1989), 30.

5. Chazan, *Medieval Jewry in Northern France*, 64–65; Jordan, *French Monarchy and the Jews*, 30–32.

6. Chazan, *Medieval Jewry in Northern France*, 74–75; Langmuir, *Toward a Definition of Antisemitism*, 142–43. I have accepted Jordan's substitution of "retained" for "returned" in the penultimate sentence (*French Monarchy and the Jews*, 272) and changed Fulk to Foulques.

7. Robert Chazan, "The Bray Incident of 1192: *Realpolitik* and Folk Slander," *Proceedings of the American Academy for Jewish Research* 37 (1969): 1–18; Chazan, *Medieval Jewry in Northern France*, 69; Jordan, *French Monarchy and the Jews*, 35–37.

8. Translation adapted from Chazan, *Medieval Jewry in Northern France*, 75, and Langmuir, *Toward a Definition of Antisemitism*, 185.

9. Chazan, *Church, State, and Jew*, 206–7; Jordan, *French Monarchy and the Jews*, 61–63.

10. Chazan, *Medieval Jewry in Northern France*, 79–80; Jordan, *French Monarchy and the Jews*, 66–69.

11. Jordan, *French Monarchy and the Jews*, 74–75.

12. Chazan, *Church, State, and Jew*, 207–10; Jordan, *French Monarchy and the Jews*, 81–87.

13. Grayzel, *Church and the Jews*, 106–7.

14. Jordan, *French Monarchy and the Jews*, 89.

15. Chazan, *Medieval Jewry in Northern France*, 104–7; Chazan, *Church, State, and Jew*, 211–12; Langmuir, *Toward a Definition of Antisemitism*, 146–52; Jordan, *French Monarchy and the Jews*, 93–99.

16. M. R. B. Shaw, ed. and trans., *Joinville & Villehardouin: Chronicles of the Crusades* (Harmondsworth, England: Penguin, 1963), 175.

17. Chazan, *Medieval Jewry in Northern France*, 103; Chazan, *Church, State, and Jew*, 217.

18. Chazan, *Church, State, and Jew*, 213–15; Langmuir, *Toward a Definition of Antisemitism*, 162.

19. Langmuir, *Toward a Definition of Antisemitism*, 167.

20. Ibid., 187–89; Jordan, *French Monarchy and the Jews*, 131–33; Grayzel, *Church and the Jews*, 114–15.

21. Chazan, *Medieval Jewry in Northern France*, 112.

22. Chazan, *Church, State, and Jew*, 216.

23. Chazan, *Medieval Jewry in Northern France*, 118–22; Grayzel, *Church and the Jews*, 268–69; Shlomo Simonsohn, *The Apostolic See and the Jews: History* (Toronto: Pontifical Institute of Mediaeval Studies, 1991), 54.

24. Baron, *Social and Religious History of the Jews*, 9:229–30.

25. Baron, *Ancient and Medieval Jewish History*, 299; Aronius, *Regesten*, 139, no. 314a. Baron has *Ratisbon* for *Regensburg*.

26. Fuhrmann, *Germany in the High Middle Ages*, 153.

27. Aronius, *Regesten*, 144–45, no. 322.

28. Chazan, *Church, State, and Jew*, 118–22.

29. R. H. C. Davis, *A History of Medieval Europe*, rev. ed. (London: Longman, 1970), 339.

30. Chazan, *Church, State, and Jew*, 163–65; Aronius, *Regesten*, 151–52, no. 337.

31. Aronius, *Regesten*, 135, no. 313, and 168–69, no. 381.

32. Ibid., 171, no. 385.

33. Langmuir, *Toward a Definition of Antisemitism*, chap. 11.

34. Chazan, *Church, State, and Jew*, 125–26.

35. Ibid., 123–26; Baron, *Ancient and Medieval Jewish History*, 303; Aronius, *Regesten*, 216–17, no. 497.

36. Baron, *Ancient and Medieval Jewish History*, 302–3; Aronius, *Regesten*, 220, no. 509.

37. Baron, *Ancient and Medieval Jewish History*, 303; Aronius, *Regesten*, 222–23, no. 518; Parkes, *Jew in the Medieval Community*, 167.

38. Chazan, *Church, State, and Jew*, 84–88; Marcus, *Jew in the Medieval World*, 28–32.

10. "Reveal No Secrets": Maintaining a Culture in a Hostile World

1. Ben-Sasson, "The Middle Ages," 524–25.

2. Louis Finkelstein, *Jewish Self-Government in the Middle Ages*, rev. ed. (New York: Philipp Feldheim, 1964), 234, 235, 241, 243, 247, 248.

3. Ivan G. Marcus, *Piety and Society: The Jewish Pietists of Medieval Germany* (Leiden: E. J. Brill, 1981), 12, 16. Marcus discusses all aspects of pietist history and doctrine. The entries by Joseph Dan et al. on "Hasidei Ashkenaz" in *Encyclopaedia Judaica*, 7:1377–83, provide a thorough introduction. The section on this topic by Ben-Sasson in "The Middle Ages," 545–53, is instructive on pietist doctrines regarding inequality. Gershom Scholem

situated the Hasidei Ashkenaz in Jewish history in the third chapter of *Major Trends in Jewish Mysticism*, 3d ed. (New York: Schocken, 1954).

4. Walter Wakefield and Austin Evans, *Heresies of the High Middle Ages* (New York: Columbia Univ. Press, 1969), 41–44.

5. Scholem, *Major Trends in Jewish Mysticism*, 112.

6. Ben-Sasson, "Middle Ages," 551.

7. I. G. Marcus, *Piety and Society*, 79; phrases bracketed by Marcus.

8. Ibid., 131–32.

9. Grayzel, *Church and the Jews*, 114–15.

10. John M. O'Brien, "Jews and Cathari in Medieval France," *Comparative Studies in Society and History* 10 (1968): 216.

11. Walter L. Wakefield, *Heresy, Crusade, and Inquisition in Southern France, 1100–1250* (Berkeley: Univ. of California Press, 1974).

12. Ibid., 102.

13. Ibid., 101–2.

14. Grayzel, *Church and the Jews*, 302–3.

15. Ibid., 304–5.

16. Wakefield, *Heresy, Crusade, and Inquisition*, 128.

17. Grayzel, *Church and the Jews*, 306–13.

18. Ibid., 308–9; translation based on Grayzel's Latin text.

19. Ibid., 65–66.

20. Ibid., 166–67.

21. Ibid., 198–99; I have translated *inolevit confusio* as "such disorder has developed."

22. Ibid., 322–25.

23. Ibid., 335.

24. Ibid., 60–70; Stow, *Alienated Minority*, 248–51.

25. On the role of the friars as initiators of the new doctrine, see especially Jeremy Cohen, *The Friars and the Jews: The Evolution of Medieval Anti-Judaism* (Ithaca, N.Y.: Cornell Univ. Press, 1982). "Living according to the teachings of the Talmud," he writes, "the Jews did not fulfill their proper function in Christian society." Hence, "they had lost the right to exist in Christendom previously accorded them because of their adherence to ancient, biblical Judaism" (256–57).

26. Grayzel, *Church and the Jews*, chap. 4.

27. Ibid., 15.

28. Joshua Trachtenberg, *The Devil and the Jews* (New Haven: Yale Univ. Press, 1943), chap. 3.

29. Trachtenberg, *Devil and the Jews*, 50–52 and chap. 4. The frontispiece to this volume is a picture of the *Judensau*; the book's other illustrations are also noteworthy.

30. On the Antichrist legend, see Emmerson, *Antichrist in the Middle Ages*, especially chaps. 1 and 3; and Trachtenberg, *Devil and the Jews*, chap. 2.

31. J. Cohen, *Friars and the Jews*, 60–76; Chazan, *Medieval Jewry in Northern France,*

124–31; Hyam Maccoby, ed., *Judaism on Trial: Jewish-Christian Disputations in the Middle Ages* (Rutherford, N.J.: Fairleigh Dickinson Univ. Press, 1982), 19–38.

32. Judah M. Rosenthal, "The Talmud on Trial," *Jewish Quarterly Review,* n.s., 47 (1956): 145–66. The thirty-five charges are listed in Latin, with French translations, in Isidore Loeb, "La controverse de 1240 sur le Talmud," *Revue des études juives* 1 (1880): 247–61; 2 (1881) 248–60; 3 (1881): 39–57.

33. Maccoby, *Judaism on Trial,* 23–25. Benjamin Z. Kedar, "Canon Law and the Burning of the Talmud," *Bulletin of Medieval Canon Law* 9 (1979): 79–82, argues that the pope was conceived to be punishing Jews not for transgressions against Christianity but for failure to adhere properly to their own Mosaic law.

34. Grayzel, *Church and the Jews,* 199, 201.

35. Ibid., 200–3.

36. Ibid., 227, 229.

37. Ibid., 241.

38. Ibid., 242–43.

39. J. Cohen, *Friars and the Jews,* 62.

40. Chazan, *Church, State, and Jew,* 225–27.

41. J. Cohen, *Friars and the Jews,* 71.

42. Ibid.; Maccoby, *Judaism on Trial,* 165.

43. J. Cohen, *Friars and the Jews,* 70–71. Maccoby, *Judaism on Trial,* 26–30 presents another account of these events.

44. Chazan, *Church, State, and Jew,* 228.

45. J. Cohen, *Friars and the Jews,* 63; Kenneth R. Stow, *The "1007 Anonymous" and Papal Sovereignty: Jewish Perceptions of the Papacy and Papal Policy in the High Middle Ages* (Cincinnati: Hebrew Union College, 1984), 39.

46. J. R. Marcus, *Jew in the Medieval World,* 149.

47. J. Cohen, *Friars and the Jews,* 76.

48. Grayzel, *Church and the Jews,* 274–79. The events connected with the letter are discussed in Chazan, *Medieval Jewry in Northern France,* 129–30.

49. Grayzel, *Church and the Jews,* 277–78.

50. Ibid., 279.

51. J. Cohen, *Friars and the Jews,* 78–80; Chazan, *Medieval Jewry in Northern France,* 131–32.

52. Grayzel, *Church and the Jews,* 339.

11. "Our Property": Jews in Twelfth- and Thirteenth-Century England

1. W. Hudson, "Note," in *The Life and Miracles of St. William of Norwich, by Thomas of Monmouth,* ed. Augustus Jessopp and Montague R. James (Cambridge: Cambridge Univ. Press, 1896), xlv–xlix; Vivian D. Lipman, *The Jews of Mediaeval Norwich* (London: Jewish Historical Society of England, 1967), chaps. 1 and 2.

2. The principal accounts of the entire episode are in Jessopp and James, *St. William of Norwich*, and in Langmuir, *Toward a Definition of Antisemitism*, chap. 9.

3. Jessopp and James, *St. William of Norwich*, 3–4.

4. Ibid., 10–12.

5. Ibid., 15.

6. Ibid., 20–21.

7. Ibid., 21–23.

8. Ibid., 21, 90–91.

9. Ibid., 93–94.

10. Ibid., 31, 37, 50, 52, 54.

11. Ibid., 152–53.

12. Paul Hyams, "The Jewish Minority in Medieval England, 1066–1290," *Journal of Jewish Studies* 25 (1974): 270–93, is an excellent overview article, as is Zefira E. Rokeah, "The State, the Church, and the Jews in Medieval England," in *Antisemitism Through the Ages*, ed. Shmuel Almog (New York: Pergamon, 1988), 99–125, with an especially useful bibliography.

13. Cecil Roth, *A History of the Jews in England*, 3d ed. (Oxford: Clarendon Press, 1964), 11. The first five chapters of this book are a standard source for the medieval phase. Roth has been criticized for occasional carelessness and incompleteness, but his book remains the best narrative history to date. Also of interest are his essays in *Essays and Portraits in Anglo-Jewish History* (Philadelphia: Jewish Publication Society, 1962), particularly the chapter on physicians and the one entitled "A Day in the Life of a Medieval English Jew."

14. Ibid., chap. 1.

15. H. G. Richardson, *The English Jewry under Angevin Kings* (London: Methuen, 1960), 87; Roth, *Jews in England*, 13–14. Gavin I. Langmuir, "The Jews and the Archives of Angevin England: Reflections on Medieval Anti-semitism," *Traditio* 19 (1963), 183–244, is a penetrating critical review of Richardson's book, applicable to more than its immediate subject.

16. Latin text in Richard Howlett, ed., *William of Newburgh. Chronicles of the Reigns of Stephen, Henry II and Richard I*, Rolls Series 82, vol. 1, 1066–1194 (London: Longman, 1884), 295–96. See also Joseph Stevenson's translation in Chazan, *Church, State, and Jew*, 159–60, and Joseph Jacobs, *The Jews of Angevin England: Documents and Records* (London: G. P. Putnam's Sons, 1893), 100–102.

17. Roth, *Jews in England*, 19; Chazan, *Church, State, and Jew*, 161.

18. Howlett, *William of Newburgh*, 297–99; Chazan, *Church, State, and Jew*, 160–61; Jacobs, *Jews of Angevin England*, 102–5.

19. Jacobs, *Jews of Angevin England*, 105–6. See also Richard B. Dobson, *The Jews of Medieval York and the Massacre of March 1190* (York: St. Anthony's Press, 1974), 24–25.

20. Chazan, *Church, State, and Jew*, 67–68.

21. Howlett, *William of Newburgh*, 308–10. Part of the Latin text is translated in Jacobs, *Jews of Angevin England*, 113–15. For another account see Roth, *Jews in England*, 21.

22. Howlett, *William of Newburgh*, 310–11; translation in Jacobs, *Jews of Angevin England*, 115.

23. Roth, *Jews in England*, 21–22; Dobson, *Jews of Medieval York*, 25; Jacobs, *Jews of Angevin England*, 112–13.

24. John T. Appleby, ed. and trans., *The Chronicle of Richard of Devizes* (London: Thomas Nelson and Sons, 1963), 4.

25. Dobson, *Jews of Medieval York*, 26.

26. Ibid., 26–28.

27. Ibid., 29.

28. Roth, *Jews in England*, 27–28. In 1200, an English mark was equivalent to 13 shillings, 4 pence; hence, three marks equaled about two pounds.

29. Ibid., 29, 110.

30. My discussion of the Exchequer of the Jews is based mainly on Richardson, *English Jewry under Angevin Kings*, especially chap. 7, and Roth, *Jews in England*, 43–53 and 105–13.

31. Roth, *Jews in England*, 31–37.

32. Chazan, *Church, State, and Jew*, 77–78, 123. See also Roth, *Jews in England*, 32.

33. Roth, *Jews in England*, 35.

34. Ibid., 33.

35. Ibid., 38–43.

36. Ibid., 43–46; Robert C. Stacey, *Politics, Policy and Finance under Henry III, 1216–45* (New York: Oxford Univ. Press, 1987), 154.

37. Chazan, *Church, State, and Jew*, 188–89.

38. Roth, *Jews in England*, 47.

39. Ibid., 43–53.

40. Langmuir, *Toward a Definition of Antisemitism*, chap. 10.

41. Roth, *Jews in England*, 56–57. The story of Hugh of Lincoln is also told in J. W. Francis Hill, *Medieval Lincoln* (Cambridge: Cambridge Univ. Press, 1965), 224–31.

42. Geoffrey Chaucer, *The Tales of Canterbury*, ed. Robert A. Pratt (Boston: Houghton Mifflin, 1974), 159–60.

43. Roth, *Jews in England*, 58–59.

44. Ibid., 52, 67.

45. Richardson, *English Jewry under Angevin Kings*, 232.

46. Roth, *Jews in England*, chap. 4.

12. "Odious to God and Men": Persecutions and Expulsions

1. Chazan, *Medieval Jewry in Northern France*, 101.

2. Joseph Strayer, "France: The Holy Land, the Chosen People, and the Most Christian King," in *Action and Conviction in Early Modern Europe*, ed. Theodore K. Rabb and Jerrold E. Seigel (Princeton: Princeton Univ. Press, 1969), 3–16.

3. Parkes, *Jew in the Medieval Community*, 385.

4. Chazan, *Church, State, and Jew,* 217.

5. Jordan, *French Monarchy and the Jews,* 148–49.

6. Grayzel, *Church and the Jews,* 263, 267.

7. Jordan, *French Monarchy and the Jews,* 149–50.

8. Chazan, *Medieval Jewry in Northern France,* 146–47.

9. Ibid., 148–49.

10. Ibid., 150–51; quotation from Hebrew source also in Chazan, *Medieval Jewry in Northern France,* 152.

11. Ibid., 153.

12. Ibid., 155–61; Jordan, *French Monarchy and the Jews,* 150–52.

13. Chazan, *Medieval Jewry in Northern France,* 156. The complete text is in Chazan, *Church, State, and Jew,* 186.

14. Baron, *Social and Religious History,* 9:11.

15. Elizabeth Hallam, *Capetian France 987–1328* (London: Longman, 1980), 278.

16. Peters, *Europe,* 471.

17. Strayer, "France," 4.

18. Ibid., 3.

19. Ibid., 15.

20. Jordan, *French Monarchy and the Jews,* 198.

21. Ibid., 187.

22. Chazan, *Church, State, and Jew,* 187–88. See also Chazan, *Medieval Jewry in Northern France,* 178.

23. Grayzel, *Church and the Jews in the XIIIth Century,* 2: 196–99; Chazan, *Medieval Jewry in Northern France,* 181–82; Jordan, *French Monarchy and the Jews,* 192–94.

24. Joseph Strayer, *The Reign of Philip the Fair* (Princeton: Princeton Univ. Press, 1980), 262–81; Cantor, *Medieval History,* 525.

25. Chazan, *Church, State, and Jew,* 183.

26. Chazan, *Medieval Jewry in Northern France,* 174–75.

27. Chazan, *Church, State, and Jew,* 290; Chazan, *Medieval Jewry in Northern France,* 193–96; Jordan, *French Monarchy and the Jews,* 200–213; Baron, *Social and Religious History,* 10:66–67.

28. Jordan, *French Monarchy and the Jews,* 204.

29. Ibid., 207–8. In two subtly argued papers Sophia Menache has proposed that the expulsions of the Jews from both France and England mainly served the interests of kings aiming to centralize their own power and therefore were not uniformly popular: "Faith, Myth, and Politics—The Stereotype of the Jews and their Expulsion from England and France," *Jewish Quarterly Review* 75 (1985), 351–74; "The King, the Church, and the Jews," *Journal of Medieval History* 13 (1987), 223–36.

30. Jordan, *French Monarchy and the Jews,* 209. See also Baron, *Social and Religious History,* 11:217; and Gustave Saige, *Les juifs du Languedoc antérieurement au XIVe siècle* (Paris: A. Picard, 1881), 88.

31. Chazan, *Medieval Jewry in Northern France,* 200–203; Jordan, *French Monarchy and*

the Jews, 240–42; Parkes, *Jew in the Medieval Community,* 170–78; Baron, *Social and Religious History,* 11:218–19.

32. Yosef Hayim Yerushalmi, "The Inquisition and the Jews of France in the Time of Bernard Gui," *Harvard Theological Review* 63 (1970): 325–26.

33. Malcolm Barber, "The Pastoureaux of 1320," *Journal of Ecclesiastical History* 32 (1981): 161.

34. Ibid., 144, 146.

35. Grayzel, *Church and the Jews* 2:310.

36. Barber, "Pastoureaux," 148. See also Jordan, *French Monarchy and the Jews,* 243–45; Cohn, *Pursuit of the Millennium,* 102–4.

37. Solomon Grayzel, "The Confession of a Medieval Jewish Convert," *Historia Judaica* 17, pt. 2 (1955): 119.

38. Jordan, *French Monarchy and the Jews,* 244.

39. Malcolm Barber, "Lepers, Jews and Muslims: The Plot to Overthrow Christendom in 1321," *History* 66 (1981): 1–17.

40. Salo Baron points out that the tale was especially credible because of a popular belief that lepers were descended from Elisha's servant, Gehazi, and hence "somehow related to Jews." Baron, *Social and Religious History,* 11:220. As the tale is recounted in II Kings, Gehazi deceptively requested payment from a Syrian whom Elisha had cured of leprosy, and as punishment became a leper himself. For a study of how Jews, lepers, and heretics were equated in medieval thought, see R. I. Moore, *The Formation of a Persecuting Society: Power and Deviance in Western Europe, 950–1250* (Oxford: Oxford Univ. Press, 1987). "For all imaginative purposes," says Moore, the three were equivalent: "They had the same qualities, from the same source, and they presented the same threat: through them the Devil was at work to subvert the Christian order and bring the world to chaos" (65).

41. Barber, "Lepers, Jews and Muslims," 5.

42. Jordan, *French Monarchy and the Jews,* 248.

43. Aronius, *Regesten,* 226, no. 529, and 238, no. 554; Baron, *Social and Religious History,* 11:264.

44. Straus, *Regensburg and Augsburg,* 93, 99.

45. Baron, *Social and Religious History,* 9:173.

46. Adolf Kober, *Cologne,* trans. Solomon Grayzel (Philadelphia: Jewish Publication Society, 1940), 40–44.

47. Aronius, *Regesten,* 291, no. 706; Baron, *Social and Religious History,* 9:151.

48. Irving A. Agus, *Rabbi Meir of Rothenburg,* 2d ed. (New York: Ktav, 1970), 138.

49. Baron, *Social and Religious History,* 9:154.

50. Ibid., 153–54; Baron's phrase, "serfs of Our Chamber" has been changed to "servants of Our court."

51. Agus, *Rabbi Meir of Rothenburg,* 143–55; papal statement in Grayzel, *Church and the Jews,* 2:167.

52. Baron, *Social and Religious History,* 11:264.

53. Agus, *Rabbi Meir of Rothenburg*, 679.

54. Baron, *Social and Religious History*, 11:265–66; Reuven Michael, "Rindfleisch," in *Encyclopaedia Judaica*, 14:188; S. Mannheimer, "Rindfleisch," in *Jewish Encyclopedia*, 10:427.

55. Baron, *Social and Religious History*, 9:155–57, and 11:267; Georges Weill, "Armleder," in *Encyclopaedia Judaica*, 3:483–84.

56. Grayzel, *Church and the Jews*, 92–95.

57. Chazan, *Church, State, and Jew*, 20–21.

58. Grayzel, *Church and the Jews*, 2:7.

59. Ibid., 14–15.

60. Latin text in Grayzel, *Church and the Jews*, 2:103. See also page 15 in this volume, and Synan, *Popes and the Jews*, 118.

61. Grayzel, *Church and the Jews*, 2:16, 122.

62. Baron, *Social and Religious History*, 11:166–67; Trachtenberg, *Devil and the Jews*, 109–17.

63. Gavin Langmuir, "L'absence d'accusation de meurte rituel à l'ouest du Rhône," in *Juifs et judaïsme de Languedoc*, Cahiers de Fanjeaux, vol. 12, ed. M.-H. Vicaire and B. Blumenkranz (Toulouse: Édouard Privat, 1977), 235–49; Langmuir, *Toward a Definition of Antisemitism*, 308.

64. Jordan, *French Monarchy and the Jews*, 192–94; Grayzel, *Church and the Jews*, 2:196–99; Baron, *Social and Religious History*, 11:168.

65. Seraphine Guerchberg discusses fourteenth century scientific knowledge in relation to the accusations against the Jews: "The Controversy over the Alleged Sowers of the Black Death in the Contemporary Treatises on Plague," in *Change in Medieval Society*, ed. Sylvia L. Thrupp (New York: Appleton-Century Crofts, 1964), 208–24.

66. Mordechai Breuer, "The 'Black Death' and Antisemitism," in *Antisemitism Through the Ages*, ed. Shmuel Almog (New York: Pergamon, 1988), 143.

67. J. Nohl, *The Black Death: A Chronicle of the Plague* (London: Allen and Unwin, 1961), 198–200.

68. Nohl, *Black Death: Chronicle*, chap. 8; George Deaux, *The Black Death: 1347* (New York: Weybright and Talley, 1969), 172–73; Philip Ziegler, *The Black Death* (New York: John Day, 1969), 103; J. R. Marcus, *Jew in the Medieval World*, 43–47.

69. Ziegler, *Black Death*, chap. 5.

70. Ibid., 106.

71. H. H. Ben-Sasson, "Black Death," in *Encyclopaedia Judaica*, 4:1067.

72. Synan, *Popes and the Jews*, 133.

73. Ben-Sasson, "Black Death," 1067.

74. Breuer, "'Black Death' and Antisemitism," 148–50.

75. In addition to the authors cited, discussion of events connected with the Black Death drew on Cohn, *Pursuit of the Millennium*, 136–39, and Baron, *Social and Religious History*, 11:160–64, 268–70.

76. Jordan, *French Monarchy and the Jews*, 248–49.

77. Ibid., 248–50; Baron, *Social and Religious History*, 11:222–24.

78. Ben-Sasson, "Middle Ages," 563.

79. Baron, *Social and Religious History,* 11:273.

80. Ben-Sasson, "Middle Ages," 566.

81. Baron, *Social and Religious History,* 11:275–76.

82. Parkes, *Jew in the Medieval Community,* 228–29.

83. Bernard Weinryb, *The Jews of Poland* (Philadelphia: Jewish Publication Society, 1973), 115; Jonathan Israel, *European Jewry in the Age of Mercantilism 1550–1750,* 2d ed. (Oxford: Clarendon Press, 1989), 5.

84. Israel, *European Jewry,* chap. 2.

WORKS CITED

Abelard, Peter. *A Dialogue of a Philosopher with a Jew and a Christian*. Translated by P. J. Payer. Toronto: Pontifical Institute of Mediaeval Studies, 1979.

———. *Dialogus inter Philosophum, Judaeum et Christianum*. Edited by Rudolf Thomas. Stuttgart: F. Frommann, 1970.

Adams, Jeremy duQuesnay. *Patterns of Medieval Society*. Englewood Cliffs, N.J.: Prentice-Hall, 1969.

Adelson, Howard L., ed. *Medieval Commerce*. Princeton: Van Nostrand, 1962.

Agus, Irving A. *The Heroic Age of Franco-German Jewry*. New York: Yeshiva Univ. Press, 1969.

———. *Rabbi Meir of Rothenburg*. 2d ed. New York: Ktav, 1970.

———. "Rabbinic Scholarship in Northern Europe." In *The Dark Ages: Jews in Christian Europe 711–1096*, edited by Cecil Roth, 189–209. New Brunswick, N.J.: Rutgers Univ. Press, 1966.

———. "Rashi and His School." In *The Dark Ages: Jews in Christian Europe 711–1096*, edited by Cecil Roth, 210–48. New Brunswick, N.J.: Rutgers Univ. Press, 1966.

———. *Urban Civilization in Pre-Crusade Europe*. 2 vols. New York: Yeshiva Univ. Press, 1965.

Appleby, John T., ed. and trans. *The Chronicle of Richard of Devizes*. London: Thomas Nelson and Sons, 1963.

Aronius, Julius. *Regesten zur Geschichte der Juden im fränkischen und deutschen Reiche bis zum Jahre 1273*. Berlin: L. Simion, 1902. Reprint, Hildesheim: Georg Olms, 1970.

Ashtor, Eliyahu. *The Jews of Moslem Spain*. 3 vols. Philadelphia: Jewish Publication Society, 1973–84.

Augustine. *The City of God Against the Pagans*. Translated by H. Bettenson. Harmondsworth, England: Penguin, 1972.

———. "In Answer to the Jews." In *Saint Augustine: Treatises on Marriage and Other Subjects*. Translated by Sister Marie Liguori, 387–414. New York: Fathers of the Church, 1955.

Bachrach, Bernard S. *Early Medieval Jewish Policy in Western Europe*. Minneapolis: Univ. of Minnesota Press, 1977.

———, ed. *Jews in Barbarian Europe*. Lawrence, Kans.: Coronado, 1977.

Baldwin, John W. *Masters, Princes, and Merchants: The Social Views of Peter the Chanter and His Circle*. 2 vols. Princeton: Princeton Univ. Press, 1970.

Barber, Malcolm. "Lepers, Jews and Muslims: The Plot to Overthrow Christendom in 1321." *History* 66 (1981): 1–17.

———. "The Pastoureaux of 1320." *Journal of Ecclesiastical History* 32 (1981): 143–66.

Baron, Salo W. *Ancient and Medieval Jewish History*. New Brunswick, N.J.: Rutgers Univ. Press, 1972.

———. *A Social and Religious History of the Jews*. 2d ed. 18 vols. New York: Columbia Univ. Press, 1952–1983.

Barraclough, Geoffrey. *The Crucible of Europe: The Ninth and Tenth Centuries in European History*. Berkeley: Univ. of California Press, 1976.

Bautier, Robert-Henri. *The Economic Development of Medieval Europe*. Translated by H. Karolyi. London: Thames and Hudson, 1971.

Ben-Sasson, H. H. "Black Death." In *Encyclopaedia Judaica*, vol. 4, 1063–68. Jerusalem: Keter, 1971.

———. "The Middle Ages." In *A History of the Jewish People*, edited by H. H. Ben-Sasson, 383–723. Cambridge, Mass.: Harvard Univ. Press, 1976.

Benton, John F., ed. *Self and Society in Medieval France: The Memoirs of Abbot Guibert of Nogent (1064?–c. 1125)*. Translated by C. C. S. Bland, revised by John F. Benton. New York: Harper and Row, 1970.

Berger, David. "The Attitude of St. Bernard of Clairvaux Toward the Jews." *Proceedings of the American Academy of Jewish Research* 40 (1972): 89–108.

Bernard of Clairvaux. *The Letters of St. Bernard of Clairvaux*. Translated by Bruno James. Chicago: Henry Regnery, 1953.

———. *The Works of Bernard of Clairvaux*. Volume Two: *On the Song of Songs I*. Translated by Killian Walsh. Shannon: Irish Univ. Press, 1971.

Bevington, David, ed. *Medieval Drama*. Boston: Houghton Mifflin, 1975.

Bloch, Marc. *Slavery and Serfdom in the Middle Ages*. Translated by W. R. Beer. Berkeley: Univ. of California Press, 1975.

Blumenkranz, Bernhard. "Anti-Jewish Polemics and Legislation in the Middle Ages: Literary Fiction or Reality?" *Journal of Jewish Studies* 15 (1964): 125–40.

———. *Les auteurs chrétiens latins du moyen âge sur les juifs et le judaïsme.* Paris: Mouton, 1963.

———. "Germany, 843–1096." In *The Dark Ages: Jews in Christian Europe 711–1096,* edited by Cecil Roth, 162–74. New Brunswick, N.J.: Rutgers Univ. Press, 1966.

———. *Juden und Judentum in der mittelalterlichen Kunst.* Stuttgart: W. Kohlhammer, 1965.

———. *Le juif médiéval au miroir de l'art chrétien.* Paris: Études Augustiennes, 1966.

———. *Juifs et chrétiens dans le monde occidental 430–1096.* Paris: Mouton, 1960.

Breuer, Mordechai. "The 'Black Death' and Antisemitism." In *Antisemitism through the Ages,* edited by Shmuel Almog, 139–51. New York: Pergamon, 1988.

Cabaniss, Allen. "Bodo-Eleazar: A Famous Jewish Convert." *Jewish Quarterly Review,* n.s., 43 (1953): 313–28.

Cantor, Norman F. *Medieval History.* 2d ed. New York: Macmillan, 1969.

Chaucer, Geoffrey. *The Tales of Canterbury.* Edited by Robert A. Pratt. Boston: Houghton Mifflin, 1974.

Chazan, Robert. "The Blois Incident of 1171: A Study in Jewish Intercommunal Organization." *Proceedings of the American Academy for Jewish Research* 36 (1968): 13–31.

———. "The Bray Incident of 1192: *Realpolitik* and Folk Slander." *Proceedings of the American Academy for Jewish Research* 37 (1969): 1–18.

———. *Church, State, and Jew in the Middle Ages.* New York: Behrman House, 1980.

———. *European Jewry and the First Crusade.* Berkeley: Univ. of California Press, 1987.

———. *Medieval Jewry in Northern France: A Political and Social History.* Baltimore: Johns Hopkins Univ. Press, 1973.

———. "The Persecution of 992." *Revue des études juives* 129 (1970): 217–21.

———. "1007–1012: Initial Crisis for Northern European Jewry." *Proceedings of the American Academy for Jewish Research* 38–39 (1970–71): 101–18.

———. ed., *Medieval Jewish Life.* New York: Ktav, 1976.

Cohen, Gerson D. "The Talmudic Age." In *Great Ages and Ideas of the Jewish People,* edited by Leo W. Schwarz, 141–212. New York: Random House, 1956.

Cohen, Jeremy. *The Friars and the Jews: The Evolution of Medieval Anti-Judaism.* Ithaca, N.Y.: Cornell Univ. Press, 1982.

————. "Scholarship and Intolerance in the Medieval Academy: The Study and Evaluation of Judaism in European Christendom." *American Historical Review* 91 (1986): 592–613.

Cohen, Mark R. *Under Crescent and Cross: The Jews in the Middle Ages.* Princeton: Princeton Univ. Press, 1994.

Cohn, Norman. *The Pursuit of the Millennium.* 3d ed. New York: Oxford Univ. Press, 1970.

Cutler, Allan, and Helen E. Cutler. *The Jew as Ally of the Muslim: Medieval Roots of Anti-Semitism.* Notre Dame, Ind.: Univ. of Notre Dame Press, 1986.

Dan, Joseph, et al. "Hasidei Ashkenaz." In *Encyclopaedia Judaica,* vol. 7, 1377–83. Jerusalem: Keter, 1971.

Daniélou, Jean. *A History of Early Christian Doctrine Before the Council of Nicaea.* Volume Two: *Gospel Message and Hellenistic Culture.* Edited and translated by John A. Baker. London: Darton, Longman and Todd, 1973.

Davies, Alan, ed. *Antisemitism and the Foundations of Christianity.* New York: Paulist, 1979.

Davies, William D. *Jewish and Pauline Studies.* Philadelphia: Fortress, 1984.

————. *Paul and Rabbinic Judaism.* Rev. ed. London: S.P.C.K., 1955.

Davis, R. H. C. *A History of Medieval Europe.* Rev. ed. London: Longman, 1970.

Deaux, George. *The Black Death: 1347.* New York: Weybright and Talley, 1969.

Dix, Gregory. *Jew and Greek: A Study in the Primitive Church.* London: Dacre, 1953.

Dobson, Richard B. *The Jews of Medieval York and the Massacre of March 1190.* York: St. Anthony's, 1974.

Dubnow, Simon. *History of the Jews.* 5 vols. South Brunswick, N.J.: Thomas Yoseloff, 1967–73.

Duby, Georges. "The Culture of the Knightly Class: Audience and Patronage." In *Renaissance and Renewal in the Twelfth Century,* edited by Robert L. Benson and Giles Constable, 248–62. Cambridge, Mass.: Harvard Univ. Press, 1982.

————. *The Early Growth of the European Economy.* Translated by Howard B. Clarke. Ithaca, N.Y.: Cornell Univ. Press, 1974.

————. *The Three Orders: Feudal Society Imagined.* Translated by Arthur Goldhammer. Chicago: Univ. of Chicago Press, 1980.

Eidelberg, Shlomo, ed. and trans. *The Jews and the Crusaders: The Hebrew Chronicles of the First and Second Crusades.* Madison: Univ. of Wisconsin Press, 1977.

Emmerson, R. K. *Antichrist in the Middle Ages.* Seattle: Univ. of Washington Press, 1981.

Ferrar, W. J., ed. and trans. *The Proof of the Gospel. Being the "Demonstratio Evangelica" of Eusebius of Caesarea.* Vol. 1. New York: Macmillan, 1920.

Finkelstein, Louis. *Jewish Self-Government in the Middle Ages.* Rev. ed. New York: Philipp Feldheim, 1964.

Fuhrmann, Horst. *Germany in the High Middle Ages c. 1050–1200.* Cambridge: Cambridge Univ. Press, 1986.

Gager, John G. *Kingdom and Community: The Social World of Early Christianity.* Englewood Cliffs, N.J.: Prentice-Hall, 1975.

———. *The Origins of Anti-Semitism: Attitudes Toward Judaism in Pagan and Christian Antiquity.* New York: Oxford Univ. Press, 1983.

Ganshof, F. L. *Feudalism.* 3d Eng. ed. New York: Harper and Row, 1964.

Geary, Patrick J. *Before France and Germany: The Creation and Transformation of the Merovingian World.* New York: Oxford Univ. Press, 1988.

Golb, Norman. "New Light on the Persecution of French Jews at the Time of the First Crusade." *Proceedings of the American Academy for Jewish Research,* 34 (1966): 1–45. Reprinted in *Medieval Jewish Life,* edited by Robert Chazan (New York: Ktav, 1976).

Goldenberg, Robert. "Talmud." In *Back to the Sources: Reading the Classic Jewish Texts,* edited by Barry W. Holtz, 129–75. New York: Summit, 1984.

Goldin, Judah. "The Period of the Talmud." In *The Jews: Their History,* 4th ed., edited by Louis Finkelstein, 119–224. New York: Schocken, 1970.

Grabois, Aryeh. "The *Hebraica veritas* and Jewish-Christian Intellectual Relations in the Twelfth Century." *Speculum* 50 (1975): 613–34.

———. "Les juifs et leurs seigneurs dans la France septentrionale aux XIe et XIIe siècles." In *Les juifs dans l'histoire de France,* edited by Myriam Yardeni, 11–23. Leiden: E. J. Brill, 1980.

Grant, Michael. *The Jews in the Roman World.* New York: Scribner's, 1973.

Grayzel, Solomon. "The Confession of a Medieval Jewish Convert." *Historia Judaica* 17, pt. 2 (1955): 89–120.

———. *The Church and the Jews in the XIIIth Century.* Rev. ed. New York: Hermon, 1966.

———. *The Church and the Jews in the XIIIth Century. Vol. 2: 1254–1314.* Edited by Kenneth R. Stow. Detroit: Wayne State Univ. Press, 1989.

Gregory of Tours. *The History of the Franks.* Translated by Lewis Thorpe. Harmondsworth, England: Penguin, 1974.

Guerchberg, Seraphine. "The Controversy over the Alleged Sowers of the Black Death in the Contemporary Treatises on Plague." In *Change in Medieval Society,* edited by Sylvia L. Thrupp, 208–24. New York: Appleton-Century-Crofts, 1964.

Hallam, Elizabeth. *Capetian France 987–1328*. London: Longman, 1980.

Heer, Friedrich. *The Medieval World: Europe 1100–1350*. Translated by Janet Sondheimer. London: Weidenfeld and Nicolson, 1962.

Hefele, Charles [Karl] Joseph. *A History of the Councils of the Church*. 5 vols. Translated by William R. Clark. Edinburgh: T. and T. Clark, 1895.

Hill, J. W. Francis. *Medieval Lincoln*. Cambridge: Cambridge Univ. Press, 1965.

Howlett, Richard, ed. *William of Newburgh*. *Chronicles of the Reigns of Stephen, Henry II and Richard I*. Rolls Series 82. Vol. 1: 1066–1194. London: Longman, 1884.

Hyams, Paul. "The Jewish Minority in Medieval England, 1066–1290." *Journal of Jewish Studies* 25 (1974): 270–93.

Israel, Jonathan L. *European Jewry in the Age of Mercantilism 1550–1750*. 2d ed. Oxford: Clarendon, 1989.

Jacobs, Joseph. *The Jews of Angevin England: Documents and Records*. London: G. P. Putnam's Sons, 1893.

James, Edward. *The Origins of France: From Clovis to the Capetians, 500–1000*. New York: St. Martin's, 1982.

Jessopp, Augustus, and Montague R. James, eds. *The Life and Miracles of St. William of Norwich, by Thomas of Monmouth*. Cambridge: Cambridge Univ. Press, 1896.

John Chrysostom. *Discourses Against Judaizing Christians*. Translated by Paul W. Harkins. Washington, D.C.: Catholic Univ. of America Press, 1979.

Jordan, William Chester. *The French Monarchy and the Jews: From Philip Augustus to the Last Capetians*. Philadelphia: Univ. of Pennsylvania Press, 1989.

Justin Martyr. "Dialogue with Trypho." In *Writings of St. Justin Martyr*, edited and translated by Thomas B. Falls. Washington, D.C.: Catholic Univ. Press, 1948.

Katz, Jacob. *Exclusiveness and Tolerance: Jewish-Gentile Relations in Medieval and Modern Times*. Oxford: Oxford Univ. Press, 1961.

Katz, Solomon. *The Jews in the Visigothic and Frankish Kingdoms of Spain and Gaul*. Cambridge, Mass.: Medieval Academy of America, 1937.

Kedar, Benjamin Z. "Canon Law and the Burning of the Talmud." *Bulletin of Medieval Canon Law* 9 (1979): 79–82.

Kee, Howard C., et al. *Understanding the New Testament*. 4th ed. Englewood Cliffs, N.J.: Prentice-Hall, 1983.

Kimhi, Joseph. *The Book of the Covenant*. Translated by Frank E. Talmage. Toronto: Pontifical Institute of Mediaeval Studies, 1972.

Kisch, Guido. *The Jews in Medieval Germany: A Study of Their Legal and Social Status*. Chicago: Univ. of Chicago Press, 1949.

Klausner, Joseph. *The Messianic Idea in Israel*. 3d ed. Translated by W. F. Stinespring. New York: Macmillan, 1955.

Klein, Charlotte. *Anti-Judaism in Christian Theology*. Philadelphia: Fortress, 1978.

Kober, Adolf. *Cologne*. Translated by Solomon Grayzel. Philadelphia: Jewish Publication Society, 1940.

Kraus, Henry. *The Living Theatre of Medieval Art*. Bloomington: Indiana Univ. Press, 1967.

Krey, A. C., ed. *The First Crusade: The Accounts of Eye-Witnesses and Participants*. Princeton: Princeton Univ. Press, 1921.

Langmuir, Gavin I. "L'absence d'accusation de meurtre rituel à l'ouest du Rhône." In *Juifs et judaïsme de Languedoc*, Cahiers de Fanjeaux, vol. 12, edited by M.-H. Vicaire and B. Blumenkranz, 235–49. Toulouse: Édouard Privat, 1977.

———. "The Jews and the Archives of Angevin England: Reflections on Medieval Anti-semitism." *Traditio* 19 (1963): 183–244.

———. *Toward a Definition of Antisemitism*. Berkeley: Univ. of California Press, 1990.

Latouche, Robert. *The Birth of Western Economy: Economic Aspects of the Dark Ages*. 2d ed. London: Methuen, 1967.

Leff, Gordon. *Medieval Thought: St. Augustine to Ockham*. Harmondsworth, England: Penguin, 1958

Le Goff, Jacques. *Your Money or Your Life: Economy and Religion in the Middle Ages*. Translated by P. Ranum. New York: Zone Books, 1988.

Leon, Harry J. *The Jews of Ancient Rome*. Philadelphia: Jewish Publication Society, 1960.

Liebeschütz, Hans. "The Crusading Movement in Its Bearing on the Christian Attitude towards Jewry." *Journal of Jewish Studies* 10 (1959): 97–111.

———. "The Significance of Judaism in Peter Abaelard's Dialogus." *Journal of Jewish Studies* 12 (1961): 1–18.

Linder, Amnon. *The Jews in Roman Imperial Legislation*. Detroit: Wayne State Univ. Press, 1987.

Lipman, Vivian D. *The Jews of Mediaeval Norwich*. London: Jewish Historical Society of England, 1967.

Little, Lester K. *Religious Poverty and the Profit Economy in Medieval Europe*. Ithaca, N.Y.: Cornell Univ. Press, 1978.

Loeb, Isidore. "La controverse de 1240 sur le Talmud." *Revue des études juives* 1 (1880): 247–61; 2 (1881): 248–60; 3 (1881): 39–57.

Lopez, Robert. *The Commercial Revolution of the Middle Ages, 950–1350*. Englewood Cliffs, N.J.: Prentice-Hall, 1971.

————. "The Trade of Medieval Europe: The South." In *The Cambridge Economic History of Europe*. Vol. 2: *Trade and Industry in the Middle Ages*, edited by M. Postan and E. E. Rich, 257–354. Cambridge: Cambridge Univ. Press, 1952.

Maccoby, Hyam, ed. *Judaism on Trial: Jewish-Christian Disputations in the Middle Ages*. Rutherford, N.J.: Fairleigh Dickinson Univ. Press, 1982.

Mannheimer, S. "Rindfleisch." In *Jewish Encyclopedia*, vol. 10, 427. New York: Funk and Wagnalls, 1905–1916.

Marcus, Ivan G. "Jewish Schools in Medieval Europe." *Melton Journal* 21 (1987): 5–6.

————. "The Jews in Western Europe: Fourth to Sixteenth Century." In *Bibliographical Essays in Medieval Jewish Studies*, 15–105. New York: Anti-Defamation League of B'nai B'rith, 1976.

————. *Piety and Society: The Jewish Pietists of Medieval Germany*. Leiden: E. J. Brill, 1981.

Marcus, Jacob R., ed. *The Jew in the Medieval World*. Philadelphia: Jewish Publication Society, 1938.

Meagher, John C. "As the Twig Was Bent: Antisemitism in Greco-Roman and Earliest Christian Times." In *Antisemitism and the Foundations of Christianity*, edited by Alan T. Davies, 1–27. New York: Paulist, 1979.

Menache, Sophia. "Faith, Myth, and Politics—The Stereotype of the Jews and their Expulsion from England and France." *Jewish Quarterly Review* 75 (1985): 351–74.

————. "The King, the Church, and the Jews." *Journal of Medieval History* 13 (1987): 223–36.

Michael, Reuven. "Rindfleisch." In *Encyclopaedia Judaica*, vol. 14, 188. Jerusalem: Keter, 1971.

Moore, R. I. *The Formation of a Persecuting Society: Power and Deviance in Western Europe, 950–1250*. Oxford: Oxford Univ. Press, 1987.

Neusner, Jacob. *Invitation to the Talmud*. Rev. ed. New York: Harper and Row, 1984.

————. "Judaism after the Destruction of the Temple." In *Israelite and Judaean History*, edited by John H. Hayes and J. Maxwell Miller, 663–77. Philadelphia: Westminster, 1977.

New English Bible: New Testament. Oxford: Oxford Univ. Press, 1961.

New English Bible: Old Testament. Oxford: Oxford Univ. Press, 1970.

Nohl, J. *The Black Death: A Chronicle of the Plague*. London: Allen and Unwin, 1961.

O'Brien, John M. "Jews and Cathari in Medieval France." *Comparative Studies in Society and History* 10 (1968): 215–20.

Parkes, James. *The Conflict of the Church and the Synagogue.* London: Soncino, 1934.

———. *The Jew in the Medieval Community.* 2d ed. New York: Hermon, 1976.

Patrologia Latina. Edited by J.-P. Migne. 221 vols. Paris, 1844–1864.

Peters, Edward. *Europe: The World of the Middle Ages.* Englewood Cliffs, N.J.: Prentice-Hall, 1977.

———, ed. *The First Crusade: The Chronicle of Fulcher of Chartres and Other Source Materials.* Philadelphia: Univ. of Pennsylvania Press, 1971.

Pharr, Clyde, et al., eds. and translators. *The Theodosian Code and Novels and the Sirmondian Constitution.* Princeton: Princeton Univ. Press, 1952.

Pirenne, Henri. *Mohammed and Charlemagne.* New York: Norton, 1939.

Pounds, N. J. G. *An Economic History of Medieval Europe.* London: Longman, 1974.

Rabinowitz, Louis. *The Social Life of the Jews of Northern France in the XII to XIV Centuries, as Reflected in the Rabbinic Literature of the Period.* 2d ed. New York: Hermon, 1972.

Radice, Betty, ed. and trans. *The Letters of Abelard and Heloise.* Harmondsworth, England: Penguin, 1974.

Reider, Joseph. "Jews in Medieval Art." In *Essays on Antisemitism,* 2d ed., edited by Koppel Pinson, 93–102. New York: Conference on Jewish Relations, 1946.

Richardson, H. G. *The English Jewry under Angevin Kings.* London: Methuen, 1960.

Riley-Smith, Jonathan. *The Crusades: A Short History.* New Haven: Yale Univ. Press, 1987.

———. *The First Crusade and the Idea of Crusading.* Philadelphia: Univ. of Pennsylvania Press, 1986.

Rokeah, Zefira E. "The State, the Church and the Jews in Medieval England." In *Antisemitism Through the Ages,* edited by Shmuel Almog, 99–125. New York: Pergamon, 1988.

Rosenthal, Erwin I. J. "Anti-Christian Polemics in Medieval Bible Commentaries." *Journal of Jewish Studies* 11 (1960): 115–35.

Rosenthal, Judah M. "The Talmud on Trial." *Jewish Quarterly Review,* n. s., 47 (1956): 58–76, 145–69.

Roskies, David. *Against the Apocalypse: Responses to Catastrophe in Modern Jewish Culture.* Cambridge, Mass.: Harvard Univ. Press, 1984.

Roth, Cecil. *Essays and Portraits in Anglo-Jewish History.* Philadelphia: Jewish Publication Society, 1962.

———. *A History of the Jews in England.* 3d ed. Oxford: Clarendon Press, 1964.

————. "The Jews in the Middle Ages." In *The Cambridge Medieval History*, Vol. 7, 632–63. Cambridge: Cambridge Univ. Press, 1932.

————, ed. *The Dark Ages: Jews in Christian Europe 711–1096*. New Brunswick, N.J.: Rutgers Univ. Press, 1966.

Ruether, Rosemary. *Faith and Fratricide: The Christian Theological Roots of Anti-Semitism*. New York: Seabury, 1974.

Runciman, Steven. *A History of the Crusades*. 3 vols. Cambridge: Cambridge Univ. Press, 1951.

Saige, Gustave. *Les juifs du Languedoc antérieurement au XIVe siècle*. Paris: A. Picard, 1881.

Sandmel, Samuel. *Anti-Semitism in the New Testament?* Philadelphia: Fortress, 1978.

————. *A Jewish Understanding of the New Testament*. Cincinnati: Hebrew Union College Press, 1956.

————. *Judaism and Christian Beginnings*. New York: Oxford Univ. Press, 1978.

Scholem, Gershom G. *Major Trends in Jewish Mysticism*. 3d ed. New York: Schocken, 1954.

Schwarzfuchs, S. "Crusades." In *Encyclopaedia Judaica*, vol. 5, 1135–45. Jerusalem: Keter, 1971.

————. "France and Germany Under the Carolingians." In *The Dark Ages: Jews in Christian Europe 711–1096*, edited by Cecil Roth, 122–42. New Brunswick, N.J.: Rutgers Univ. Press, 1966.

————. "France Under the Early Capets." In *The Dark Ages: Jews in Christian Europe 711–1096*, edited by Cecil Roth, 143–61. New Brunswick, N.J.: Rutgers Univ. Press, 1966.

Segal, Alan F. *Rebecca's Children: Judaism and Christianity in the Roman World*. Cambridge, Mass.: Harvard Univ. Press, 1986.

Seiferth, Wolfgang S. *Synagogue and Church in the Middle Ages*. New York: Ungar, 1970.

Shaw, M. R. B., ed. and trans. *Joinville and Villehardouin: Chronicles of the Crusades*. Harmondsworth, England: Penguin, 1963.

Simon, Marcel. *Verus Israel: A Study of the Relations between Christians and Jews in the Roman Empire (135–425)*. Translated by H. McKeating. Oxford: Oxford Univ. Press., 1964.

Simonsohn, Shlomo. *The Apostolic See and the Jews: History*. Toronto: Pontifical Institute of Mediaeval Studies, 1991.

Smalley, Beryl. *The Study of the Bible in the Middle Ages*. 2d ed. Oxford: Basil Blackwell, 1952.

Southern, R. W. *The Making of the Middle Ages*. New Haven: Yale Univ. Press, 1953.

Stacey, Robert C. *Politics, Policy and Finance under Henry III, 1216–45*. New York: Oxford Univ. Press, 1987.

Steinsaltz, Adin. *The Essential Talmud*. New York: Basic Books, 1976.

Stow, Kenneth R. *Alienated Minority: The Jews of Medieval Latin Europe*. Cambridge, Mass.: Harvard Univ. Press, 1992.

————. "The Church and the Jews: From Saint Paul to Paul IV." In *Bibliographical Essays in Medieval Jewish Studies*, 109–65. New York: Anti-Defamation League of B'nai B'rith, 1976.

————. *The "1007 Anonymous" and Papal Sovereignty: Jewish Perceptions of the Papacy and Papal Policy in the High Middle Ages*. Cincinnati: Hebrew Union College, 1984.

Straus, Raphael. *Regensburg and Augsburg*. Philadelphia: Jewish Publication Society, 1939.

Strayer, Joseph. "France: The Holy Land, the Chosen People, and the Most Christian King." In *Action and Conviction in Early Modern Europe*, edited by Theodore K. Rabb and Jerrold E. Seigel, 3–16. Princeton: Princeton Univ. Press, 1969.

————. *The Reign of Philip the Fair*. Princeton: Princeton Univ. Press, 1980.

Synan, Edward A. *The Popes and the Jews in the Middle Ages*. New York: Macmillan, 1965.

Talmage, Frank E., ed. *Disputation and Dialogue: Readings in the Jewish-Christian Encounter*. New York: Ktav, 1975.

Ta-Shma, Israel M. "Tosafot." In *Encyclopaedia Judaica*, vol. 15, 1278–83. Jerusalem: Keter, 1971.

Tellenbach, Gerd. *Church, State and Christian Society at the Time of the Investiture Contest*. Oxford: Basil Blackwell, 1940.

Tierney, Brian, and Sidney Painter. *Western Europe in the Middle Ages, 300–1475*. 4th ed. New York: Knopf, 1982.

Trachtenberg, Joshua. *The Devil and the Jews*. New Haven: Yale Univ. Press, 1943.

Wakefield, Walter L. *Heresy, Crusade, and Inquisition in Southern France, 1100–1250*. Berkeley: Univ. of California Press, 1974.

Wakefield, Walter L., and Austin Evans. *Heresies of the High Middle Ages*. New York: Columbia Univ. Press, 1969.

Wallace-Hadrill, J. M. *The Barbarian West: The Early Middle Ages* A.D. *400–1000*. 2d ed. London: Hutchinson, 1962.

————. *The Frankish Church*. Oxford: Clarendon, 1983.

Warner, Marina. *Alone of All Her Sex: The Myth and the Cult of the Virgin Mary*. New York: Knopf, 1976.

Watson, Francis. *Paul, Judaism, and the Gentiles: A Sociological Approach*. Cambridge: Cambridge Univ. Press, 1986.

Weill, Georges. "Armleder." In *Encyclopaedia Judaica,* vol. 3, 483–84. Jerusalem: Keter, 1971.

Weinreich, Max. *History of the Yiddish Language.* Translated by S. Noble and J. A. Fishman. Chicago: Univ. of Chicago Press, 1980.

Weinryb, Bernard. *The Jews of Poland.* Philadelphia: Jewish Publication Society, 1973.

Wilken, Robert L. *John Chrysostom and the Jews: Rhetoric and Reality in the Late Fourth Century.* Berkeley: Univ. of California Press, 1983.

Williams, Arthur Lukyn. *Adversus Judaeos: A Bird's-Eye View of Christian Apologiae until the Renaissance.* Cambridge: Cambridge Univ. Press, 1935.

Yerushalmi, Yosef Hayim. "The Inquisition and the Jews of France in the Time of Bernard Gui." *Harvard Theological Review* 63 (1970): 317–76.

———. Introduction to *Bibliographical Essays in Medieval Jewish Studies.* New York: Anti-Defamation League of B'nai B'rith, 1976.

Ziegler, Philip. *The Black Death.* New York: John Day, 1969.

Zuckerman, Arthur J. *A Jewish Princedom in Feudal France, 768–900.* New York: Columbia Univ. Press, 1972.

———. "The Political Uses of Theology: The Conflict of Bishop Agobard and the Jews of Lyons." In vol. 3 of *Studies in Medieval Culture,* edited by John R. Sommerfeldt, 23–51. Kalamazoo: Medieval Institute, Western Michigan University, 1970.

INDEX